STRIPPING GYPSY

NORALEE FRANKEL

STRIPPING GYPSY
The Life of Gypsy Rose Lee

OXFORD
UNIVERSITY PRESS
2009

OXFORD
UNIVERSITY PRESS

Oxford University Press, Inc., publishes works that further
Oxford University's objective of excellence
in research, scholarship, and education.

Oxford New York
Auckland   Cape Town   Dar es Salaam   Hong Kong   Karachi
Kuala Lumpur   Madrid   Melbourne   Mexico City   Nairobi
New Delhi   Shanghai   Taipei   Toronto

With offices in
Argentina   Austria   Brazil   Chile   Czech Republic   France   Greece
Guatemala   Hungary   Italy   Japan   Poland   Portugal   Singapore
South Korea   Switzerland   Thailand   Turkey   Ukraine   Vietnam

Copyright © 2009 by Noralee Frankel

Published by Oxford University Press, Inc.
198 Madison Avenue, New York, NY 10016

www.oup.com

Oxford is a registered trademark of Oxford University Press

Library of Congress Cataloging-in-Publication Data
Frankel, Noralee, 1950–
Stripping Gypsy : the life of Gypsy Rose Lee / Noralee Frankel.
p.   cm.
Includes bibliographical references and index.
Summary: "In this new biography of Gypsy Rose Lee, Noralee Frankel draws on
archival sources to strip bare the myths created by Gypsy herself and to tell the real story.
Although Lee published an autobiography that has sold steadily, this will be the first biography of
her. Frankel combines politics with twentieth-century popular culture."—Provided by publisher.
ISBN 978-0-19-536803-1
1. Lee, Gypsy Rose, 1914–1970.   2. Stripteasers—United States—Biography.   I. Title.
PN2287.L29F73 2009
792.702'8092—dc22
[B]
2008037532

Throughout text, material is quoted from *Gypsy: Memoirs of America's Most Celebrated Stripper*
by Gypsy Rose Lee, published by Frog, Ltd./North Atlantic Books, copyright © 1985 by Erik Lee
Preminger. Reprinted by permission of publisher.

1   3   5   7   9   8   6   4   2
Printed in the United States of America
on acid-free paper

To my husband, Bill Kost, who for all the wrong reasons
encouraged me to write this book, and to my parents,
Malvina and Herbert Frankel, whose politics
made it possible.

Contents

Preface: Stripping Gypsy

Dressed as a Victorian lady, auburn-haired Gypsy Rose Lee strode onstage in a tight-fitting satin dress with three layers of dark fringe on a skirt that flared at the bottom. Holding a parasol, she looked demurely at her audience. After strolling across the stage, she lifted up her elegant dress, showing off her gorgeous, slim legs. Removing the dress by taking out strategically placed straight pins, she stood for a moment, holding it close to her crotch, then let it fall on the floor. Underneath she wore a flag-inspired outfit with stars on the low-cut bodice and vertical stripes running down the short skirt. The GIs on home leave in her audience must have loved the moment. As she stretched her arms out, she separated the curtains. Stripping off the stars and stripes, she coyly held the garment against herself. Finally, backing offstage, she quickly wrapped herself in the curtain and dropped the outfit.

All through the show, Gypsy recited her lines: "At the age of nine I sang in the choir / And did transcriptions for the lyre. / I studied in Europe four years in Milan. / I could hit high C with my clothes all on." She continued: "It was all too discouraging trying to sing. / The Messrs. Minsky took me under their wing." After more witty patter about the problem of stripping to classical music, she ended her act with only her face peering out from the curtain. "Oh boys, if I take *that* off I'll catch cold," she cooed, in what was her most famous line.[1]

Men who saw Gypsy's striptease often described it as more "tease than strip." The phrase works as a metaphor for her public life. Onstage and off she created and recreated "Gypsy Rose Lee," stylistically, intellectually, and politically. In the process, she kept herself well hidden while seeming to reveal herself.

"Allergic to the truth," declared Arthur Laurents about her as he struggled to learn about her life while composing his musical *Gypsy*. Finally, he gave up and wrote his own story. According to Laurents, Gypsy gave him freedom "to explore, expand, and invent a character who, despite the title, was not really Gypsy Rose Lee." Gypsy had created herself; why not let someone else do his own version?[2]

Most people think they know Gypsy from Laurents's character, a Gypsy he based very loosely on her autobiography. Laurents made the musical *Gypsy* into "Rose's Turn," centering the story on Gypsy's fascinating and complex mother, Rose, rather than on an ordinary girl turned stripper. The Rose that Laurents fabricated in the musical, particularly as played by Ethel Merman and Rosalind Russell, was an awesome stage mother fanatically devoted to her daughters' success but basically caring. This Rose emerges as a pre-feminist mother who rebels against her daughters being "like other girls; cook and clean and sit, and die!" At the end of the musical, the older daughter—who had metamorphosed into Gypsy Rose Lee—reconciles with her mother by appreciating her sacrifice. She tells Rose, "You'd really have been something, Mother, if you had had someone to push you like I had." After embracing, they leave the stage together as a loving pair. Touching—and false.[3]

Rose's mental illness, emotional brutality, and overt bisexuality were not the stuff of a 1950s musical. Gone is Rose's attempt to foist her older, "no-talent" daughter off on other relatives; so is her pretty younger daughter's emotional collapse from overwork. Gypsy's success made Rose hungry for a part of it, particularly the money. One incident in the musical is true; the Minskys barred Rose from backstage at the burlesque theater on the grounds that "her river did not run to the sea." As the recent television series *Showbiz Moms & Dads* has shown, stage mothers still fascinate audiences. But Rose's story is not her daughter's, despite Laurents's brilliant musical.[4]

The musical *Gypsy* portrays its protagonist as a passive ugly duckling effortlessly transformed into a swan, never disclosing how hard she paddled below the surface. Gypsy remained a swan all her life through hard work, intelligence, and relentless self-promotion. Creating herself as a unique individual, she never fit the stereotype of a star, whether in burlesque, in the movies, on Broadway, or on television. Historical events and personal tragedies molded the circumstances of her life, but Gypsy was always an agent in her own destiny. She deserves full credit for her lasting fame.

I came to research Gypsy Rose Lee because many years ago I mentioned to my husband, Bill, that Gypsy lived within a writers' colony with the author Carson McCullers. Fascinated, Bill suggested to me that I write a biography of Gypsy Rose Lee. Busy with other projects, I demurred. I finally embarked on the research that led to this book when my husband discovered that in the 1950s the American Legion and right-wingers suspected striptease artist Gypsy Rose Lee of Communist leanings. And so *Stripping Gypsy* is not a conventional entertainment biography, even though different forms of entertainment make their appearance. Always personally ambitious and upwardly mobile, Gypsy possessed an unusual knack for keeping abreast of emerging trends in popular culture. She went to Hollywood shortly after "talkies" made movies more popular. She moved to radio and then to television as soon as she had the opportunity. Both times, politics interfered with her career.

This book connects family, work, and politics. The intermingling of the personal and the public weaves together the threads of Gypsy's story. Historical events such as the Great Depression, World War II, and the Cold War influenced her life and art as she created and recreated her own identity to fit changing times. This work grapples seriously with a person who often bobbed and weaved like a prizefighter so intent on staving off blows that she could not be pinned down. Gypsy hid the truth or lied so often that the fabrication of illusion is central to her life story.

Alongside the musical *Gypsy*, a second story needs to be told about Gypsy's rise to celebrity and then to legendary status. The musical's premise that the only moving force in Gypsy's rise to fame was her mother is an illusion that needs to be stripped. People not familiar with Gypsy Rose Lee may believe that Madonna's shrewd self-invention or Hollywood's leftist crusading has no precedent. Beyond prurient interest in a fascinating icon, Gypsy's story resonates across the decades. Through three failed marriages, she raised a son who never knew his father's identity. Gypsy managed her own multimedia entertainment career and rewrote her personal history as censorship and government intrusion pressed upon her. From her rise in burlesque in the 1930s until her death in 1970, Gypsy was one of the most interviewed and photographed women of her time. Few personalities hold the public's attention for such a long period of time.

Throughout my ten years of research for this biography, I have been stripping Gypsy to try to separate her invention from the ever-elusive truth. Fortunately, I selected a subject who always fascinates. Over the decade, she came to interest me more and I came to like her less. Her self-absorption and lack of empathy began to wear on me, even though I saw those characteristics as legacies of her mother. In the process of scrutinizing Gypsy's life, I discovered her genius, her humor, and her amazing tenacity. I reveled in her writing, her art (one of her paintings hangs on the wall of my office), and her leftist politics. I also uncovered her emotionally crippled mother (Rose's letters to her daughter made me physically sick) and Gypsy's own duplicity toward her son regarding the identity of his father. Others have told pieces of the story, but no one put them together.

Gypsy's tricks with truth as she invented her own reality seem to embody the postmodernist dream that we create our world through language. "I never know with mother, what's fact and what's fiction," Gypsy's son commented.[5] For Gypsy, truth was a moving target. Her close friend the writer and editor George Davis once reminded Gypsy of a sketch called "Illusion" in which she had performed. According to Davis, "Illusion" was an apt metaphor for Gypsy. He spoke of her as wearing a "mask" that would someday be stripped away. Her constant shifting of her truth kept her from being held accountable for her actions and staved off any perception of failure.[6]

Gypsy recreated herself many times, but she significantly defined herself twice: first in her transformation from working-class Rose Louise to the sophisticated stripper Gypsy Rose Lee, and later in her recreation of herself in her autobiography, *Gypsy*. Gypsy started her reinvention with her name. As with many things about which she told multiple tales, Gypsy herself forgot how this stage persona originated. "I've told it so many different ways there isn't any official version left," Gypsy confessed. In the musical, other strippers help her invent a new name. In her autobiography, she wrote that she ordered a workman to put a different name on the marquee because she feared that her grandfather would discover her stripping. In this version of the story, she told him the name was not the correct one: "Make it—Gypsy Rose Lee." Asserting her new power, she declared, "I happen to be the star of this show, and you'll put up my name the way I want it put up!"[7]

Even her age is a matter for speculation. Just as articles about her written during her life veered from the truth, recent efforts to uncover her biography have reproduced illusions that she and others created. Recent presentations have stripped Gypsy of her intellect and her early politics. In the last few years, a biography on the Arts and Entertainment network ignored her denunciation of fascism in Spain, her vice presidency of a labor union, and her blacklisting.

Given the mass of misinformation and disinformation I had to sort through, I found it helpful to anchor Gypsy in specific places—Seattle, New York, and California—as I navigated her story. Seattle, where Gypsy was born, was shaped by the rough-and-tumble frontier culture that prevailed in the Pacific Northwest. The booming port city allowed more flexibility in women's roles than did more stable, long-settled communities "back east." The women in Gypsy's family demonstrated a certain pioneering spirit; autonomy and freedom of action were more satisfying to them than the restrictive security of domesticity.

New York City, where Gypsy started her serious career as a stripper at Minsky's, had completed its transformation into the cultural center of the world by the time she arrived in 1931. New York reigned as the live entertainment capital of the nation. Gypsy aspired to Broadway, but a variety of theaters flourished elsewhere in the city, giving novices a myriad of gateways into show business. Nightclub performers charmed audiences large and small. Popular charity benefits gave visibility to aspiring talent. During the Depression, New Yorkers as well as tourists wanted to be entertained, and New York City entertained them. Gypsy thrived in this cosmopolitan environment. She expanded her interests from the stage to music, art, and literature, exploring the entire range of popular, avant-garde, and highbrow culture. She socialized with intellectuals and artists. Thanks to her many friends, including recent immigrants escaping the rise of fascism in Europe, Gypsy learned to love opera, antiques, and serious literature. A consumer's paradise, New York furnished her lavish but tasteful lifestyle.

Gypsy spent the last nine years of her life in California. By the 1960s, California had replaced New York City as the nation's entertainment center; only live theater remained concentrated in New York. Television offered Gypsy new professional opportunities. She even starred in a made-for-TV movie. In the 1950s, when many television productions were filmed in New York City, Gypsy had been denied access to the new medium because of her leftist political views. By the end of her life, Gypsy found a home on television as a talk show host.

Out of respect for her, I refer to her as Gypsy throughout this book, except for the opening chapter, in which I call her Louise or Rose Louise. Even what she was called during her childhood remains unclear from the surviving records. To Gypsy, if you could name it, you could become it. At some point she simply became Gypsy. When her mother inquired about her new stage name, Gypsy Rose Lee, she recalled, "I didn't answer her, but I knew that everyone was going to hear about us. What was the point of being a star if people didn't know you were one?" To Gypsy, the name signaled the celebrity status she claimed and hoped to convince others she had already attained.

The "Gypsy" in the new name probably derived from her fondness for fortune-telling, tea-leaf reading, and tarot cards, as well as her sense of always being on the move. Gypsies in Europe were famed as wandering performers associated with music and dance, as well as the circus. At the same time, they were profoundly distrusted for their supposed thievery of valuable property ranging from chickens to jewelry and their notorious talent for deceptive dealing, especially in horse trading. Imagined Gypsies in America were not simply itinerant musicians and dancers but exotics surrounded by an aura of mystery, sexuality, and danger.

The other element of Gypsy's moniker derived from her childhood name. The family considered Rose her given first name, although they called her by her middle name, Louise. Significantly, in making Rose into her middle name, she kept this tie to her mother despite her intense ambivalence. Lee, which became her surname, was condensed from Louise.[8]

Writing about Gypsy made me humble about the notion of historical truth. I was trying to track down a woman who told contradictory stories about her first strip, her childhood experiences, and her lovers and husbands. So I gave up searching for grand, indisputable truths and aimed for accuracy and insights. Since for Gypsy fact and fiction often blurred, I searched for documentary evidence in a variety of potential sources, disregarded dead ends, and carefully scrutinized the bits and pieces that remained in order not to be misled.

This book begins with Gypsy's amazing grandmother, Anna, and her impossible mother, Rose. Their legacy to Gypsy was a daring lifestyle filled with travel and a habit of making marriages secondary to their work and their monetary desires. From these women, Gypsy learned strength as well as ruthlessness. From them, too, Gypsy inherited cleverness with a needle and thread, a willingness to travel constantly to pursue fame and fortune, and a desire for a man who would not interfere with her career.

The book ends with Gypsy's views on fishing, which she loved. She felt frustrated when she failed to get a bite or the fish eluded her, and she gloated gleefully when she caught the "big one." Gypsy's attitude toward fishing is an apt metaphor for the way in which she faced professional and personal challenges. By the end of the book, if you follow the analogy, you will gain insight into this woman's fascinating life. Be prepared for surprises throughout: anyone who fishes frequently knows that the best spots have not yet been discovered.

STRIPPING GYPSY

1

Getting Started

ouise's mother wanted desperately to save her piano. While Rose Hovick was in labor to deliver Louise, the midwife tried to protect her from rain pouring in through a leaky roof by placing a canvas sheet over her. Rose saw her piano getting wet. "Hurry up and cover the piano," she yelled. "Don't mind us. You can always get more babies!" Even as the twelve-pound Louise struggled to escape her mother's womb, she was given her first lesson in life. Her mother, Rose, believed passionately that material objects were more important than people. She even made her daughters into objects to achieve her desire for fame and wealth. First she would shift her aspirations to her younger daughter, June, and then reluctantly to her elder daughter, Louise. "We are the living flowers of mother's thwarted hopes," Louise once explained. Louise ultimately shared her mother's goal.[1]

Entertaining fully engaged Gypsy Rose Lee, who was named Rose Louise after her mother and called Louise during her childhood but became known to the world as Gypsy Rose Lee. She learned to use her performances as a way of bringing order to a chaotic life. Onstage, she controlled her own act so that she concealed more than she revealed. A popular author, artist, and movie star and a successful talk show host, first and forever she became the cleverest, most famous stripper who ever lived. Well into her forties, Gypsy captivated live audiences by talking as she shed her clothes. Such a gimmick was audacious and risky. Louise, a.k.a. Gypsy, came from a long line of pioneering, ruthless women. She turned her relationship with her mother into the stuff of theatrical lore, memorialized in the stage and movie musical *Gypsy*.

Her maternal grandmother, Anna Thompson, and her mother passed on to Louise their tenacity, unbounded adoration for possessions, and insatiable ambition. These women's temperaments and talents benefited as well as cursed Louise. Valuing independence and resourcefulness, they bestowed on Louise the drive to achieve, an odd combination of materialism and parsimony, and tremendous charm. Like her mother and grandmother, Louise believed that women needed to be strong, in charge, and in control of their emotions. Louise fit the mold, except that she was smarter.

In Seattle, Anna Thompson created the unconventional pattern carried forward first by Rose and later by Louise. Anna felt stifled in her marriage and passed her bitterness on to her daughter. Anna and Rose both lived on the borders of respectable society. Nicknamed "Big Lady" by her granddaughters, Anna towered over most women and some men. She never shied away from sharing her opinion.

In 1885, barely in her mid-teens, Anna married Charles J. Thompson. A Catholic priest presided over their nuptials. The couple settled in Seattle, and Anna and Charles quickly had four children, one son (who drowned before reaching manhood) and three daughters: Belle, Rose Evangeline (sometimes referred to as Ronnie, but usually called Rose), and Mina. But Anna did not really want to be married, her granddaughter June observed. She found raising children and performing domestic labor for her family unfulfilling. Few married women with children worked for pay outside their homes unless their husbands were ill, unemployed, away at sea, off working in mining or lumber camps—or had deserted them. Defying social convention, Anna left the confines of the family home and became a traveling saleswoman.[2]

A superb seamstress, Anna sold her decorated hats and fancy intimate apparel to women in the booming city of San Francisco and throughout the mountain West. Fearlessly, she traveled throughout the region. According to Louise, her grandmother once "packed a trunk with corsets, some of them embroidered with real gold threads, and others trimmed with beads and lace, and went to Goldstream, Nevada."[3]

In the West, enterprising women freely crossed the boundaries between legitimate business and illicit vice. However others viewed them, they saw themselves as working women, even entrepreneurs. In the mining and logging camps where Anna plied her trade, many of the patrons for her flashy undergarments were undoubtedly whores.

Although most people did not consider the women who wore such clothes respectable, Anna accepted her clientele. Similarly, Louise denied that women in burlesque should be labeled as anything other than working women.

When her children were small, Anna only worked occasionally and grew frustrated by the myriad of chores involved in raising children. As soon as she perceived her daughters as old enough to care for themselves and their father, Charles, she traveled more frequently. In 1913, the *Seattle City Directory* listed her oldest daughter, Belle, as "the woman of the house."

When Rose was fourteen, Anna sent her to a convent school, perhaps to free herself for longer journeys as a saleswoman. Rose's father consented to her boarding there. Charles Thompson hoped that the nuns would instill in his daughter a more conventional view of a woman's role than that held by his traveling wife. The nuns failed him badly. At the convent school, Rose fell in love with acting. "How she got the theatre bug into her head is a problem for a biologist to solve," Louise once remarked. Rose's motivation stemmed from her wish to transform herself into someone else more glamorous and famous. Whenever a roving troupe of actors arrived in the vicinity, Rose ran away from school. According to Louise, she developed a regular pattern. She lied to the nuns, telling them she was going to visit her sick father. When she failed to return in a few weeks, the sisters checked with traveling small theater companies playing in the vicinity. They usually discovered Rose onstage in the front row of the chorus.[4]

To escape the convent school permanently, Rose detoured into an early marriage, just as her mother had done. At the age of fifteen, Rose married a man in his twenties. Olaf Hovick, born in Minnesota to Norwegian immigrant parents, had adopted the American name John and was nicknamed Jack. Hovick worked as a newspaperman and advertising salesman for the *Seattle Times*. When baby Louise arrived, Jack toiled as a cub reporter on the *Seattle Post-Intelligencer*, making a paltry eight dollars a week.

Rose's restless desire to be more than a housewife and mother created turbulence in her marriage right from the start. By the time Rose and Jack conceived their second daughter, Rose disliked her rocky marriage sufficiently to try various homemade abortifacients, but the tenacious fetus survived. June, whose given name was Ellen Evangeline Hovick, was born in Canada approximately two years after Louise.

Gypsy usually used January 9, 1914, as her birth date, and June usually used November 8, 1916. But they were incorrect. In 1949,

June wrote her sister that she had learned about a birth certificate in Vancouver that gave her date of birth as January 8, 1913; and another birth certificate in Seattle, which she assumed belonged to Gypsy, bore the name Ellen and was dated January 8, 1911. The birth certificate is still on file in Seattle. Their mother may have used "Ellen" as a place-holder until she decided on names for her daughters, not an unknown practice. In 1951, Gypsy raised doubts about the authenticity of these certificates. Throughout her life, she continued to celebrate her birth-day on January 9. To add to the confusion, Rose registered Gypsy for school in 1916 using the name Rose Louise and a birth date of January 9, 1911. Such evidence strongly suggests Gypsy was born in 1911.[5]

Ultimately, Rose wanted more for herself and her daughters than a working-class existence in Seattle. The fame she had missed for herself, she envisioned for her daughters. The ambitious mother submitted one-year-old Louise's picture to a "Healthy Baby" contest; she won. A few years later, Rose was determined that her firstborn daughter begin training in ballet and music. June accompanied Rose to one of Louise's lessons.

As soon as June heard the record playing, she started to move rhythmically. Having been frustrated by Louise's attempts, the danc-ing instructor "told Mrs. Hovick that June was a 'natural ballerina,'" but to avoid lifelong injury, the child must not be permitted to dance on her toes, Louise recalled. Rose immediately went out and bought the toddler ballet shoes. This often-repeated anecdote helped create Louise's image as the "no-talent" daughter in the family.[6]

Rose and Jack separated and reunited numerous times, and they fought constantly. According to June, her parents wrangled over dance lessons for her. Once June owned ballet shoes, Rose intended to launch her tiny daughter's dancing career. Her husband dissented, arguing that the family could not afford private lessons. Then Rose cruelly reminded Jack of her mother's opposition to her marrying at the tender age of fifteen. "She tried to save me from throwing my life away," Rose wailed. After this fight, Rose moved the girls to her father's house. Finally Louise and June's parents divorced.[7]

Throughout all the comings and goings of his wife, his daughter, and his granddaughters, Charlie Thompson provided family stabil-ity. Indeed, he was the only male who gave Rose loving constancy. Prematurely white-haired and with light blue eyes, Charlie stayed in Seattle and glued the far-flung family together. The women burst in on him whenever they were weary or broke. After a respite, they rein-vigorated themselves and returned to the road. While he puttered in his garden, they trekked around the country. Working faithfully for the Great Northern Railway for more than twenty-five years, he supported his family financially. Charlie permitted Rose and her two children to move in with him after her marriage to Jack Hovick failed. After the divorce, Rose tried marriage a few more times, but she preferred the meddling role of a stage mother to the duties of a housewife. Besides, she always returned to her father for solace and support.

After years of enduring his wife's absence and neglect, Charlie divorced Anna to wed a neighbor—a much calmer woman. Anna claimed that Charlie had never explained the divorce papers to her and that she signed them unaware of what they contained. Soon afterward, when Charlie and his fiancée were driving home from a picnic, they were hit by a train and killed. Anna rather than the neighbor received Charlie's railroad pension. Without a pension or savings of her own, she was rightly concerned about old age. Anna stayed in a small one-story wood house at 4816 Rutan Street, in West Seattle.

According to Rose, her father possessed a dark side. She suggested that he emotionally abused his wife. However, Rose is not a credible source. The women in the Hovick family were a troublesome group. Grandfather Charlie dealt with them far longer than any other male who unluckily entered their lives. Charlie loved his daughter and granddaughters even as he gave up trying to control them.[8]

And he had a soft side: Charlie paid fifty cents each for June's ballet lessons. Unwittingly, Charlie introduced Rose and her daughters to the entertainment business. He helped arrange his granddaughters' first show and played the piano for it. June and Louise opened at the Knights of Pythias Hall in *Just Kids*. June starred, and Louise sang "I'm a Hard-boiled Rose." A high-ranking Mason, Charlie used his abundant contacts with fraternal associations, and the girls were asked to perform for other men's organizations in the area.

Soon Rose traveled to other cities with June to find work for her young daughter. Although Rose sought to promote her daughter to stardom, she always commanded center stage in June's career. When a movie studio offered June free acting lessons for a year, Rose declined because the studio required that June cease performing while studying. Rose feared the loss of income, and she refused to cede control of her young daughter to others. June never forgave her mother for exploiting her talents while denying her professional training. Rose savored the money more than her child's education or well-being.

Immersed in June's career, Rose had little time or use for her "no-talent" elder daughter, who neither sang nor danced. Rose relinquished

Louise to various relatives and intermittently sent her to live with her father, Jack, and his second wife, Elizabeth. After his divorce from Rose, Hovick had moved to Los Angeles, where he worked for a newspaper and as a publicist for movie director D. W. Griffith. For a while, he edited a Masonic magazine; he also started an automobile magazine.

Occasionally Louise joined her sister and mother on the road and accumulated some entertainment experience. During her childhood, she worked with June as an extra in a few two-reel comedies. In a professional Christmas stage production of *Blue Bird*, June played a good fairy, Rose was fittingly cast as a witch, and Louise portrayed a frog. Given such roles, Louise resisted performing.

After Louise had been on several such forays on the road, Jack and Elizabeth gave her back to Rose. Their motives remain unclear. Louise's departure from their household may have been tied to the birth of their second child. Years later Elizabeth wrote to Louise, "It is a sad thing when boys and girls have to be deprived of their dads, and I am sure the dads also feel the loss deeply." Jack had missed his daughters and longed for another daughter from his second marriage.[9]

By the time Louise rejoined her mother, her younger sister was starring as Baby June. In 1920, Baby June and Her Pals traveled with the Pantages Circuit, which sought to dominate small theaters in the West. In 1924, June toured on the well-known Keith-Orpheum vaudeville circuit, which owned theaters as well as a booking office that actors were required to use. She also appeared in some two-reel movies for producer Hal Roach, working with comedian Harold Lloyd in such films as *Hey There* and with other silent film comics. The money from her movies helped finance her vaudeville stage production numbers. A three-year contract in vaudeville paid the seven-year-old star more than $1,500 a week.

Rose was not enthusiastic about Louise tagging along with her and June. While June worked, Louise attended a boarding school in New Canaan, Connecticut, her last formal schooling. Louise loved to read and missed school after she left. When with her sister and mother, she kept her distance from her sister's vaudeville performances. At first Louise was indifferent to entertainment as a career. She resisted attempting anything that her mother could convert into a moneymaking activity. So why should Rose bother with her elder daughter?

Louise's childhood was marked by traumatic experiences in which her mother attempted to give her away. After Louise came back from Jack and Elizabeth's, Rose tried to convince Jack's sister and her husband, Fred Braid, to adopt her. An advertising executive for the *Seattle*

Times, Braid had achieved financial security. Their own little girl had died, and her aunt and uncle were eager to add another child to their household. Louise pleaded with her mother to keep her. When she promised to work harder in the act, Rose relented and allowed Louise to stay. One of June's acts was called Dainty June and Her Newsboy Songsters. Billed as a comedian, Louise played one of the newsboys. In her early adolescence, she stood 5 feet 9½ inches tall and weighed more than 150 pounds, allowing her to be cast as a boy. Stagehands occasionally referred to her as Dainty June's kid brother. Louise also played the rear end of a horse.

Rose kept careful watch over June's act. Relying on her considerable dramatic talents to further June's career, Rose rewrote the girls' birth certificates and routinely lied about her daughters' ages to circumvent the child labor laws that would have limited the amount of time such young children acted for pay.[10] Her mother was ambitious and, "in a feminine way, ruthless...in her own words, a jungle mother," Louise later explained. Rose's competitiveness was boundless and amoral. She prevented the girls from befriending other children in vaudeville. She stole material from other children's acts and flushed young competitors' material down the toilet. She pilfered costumes, towels, blankets, silverware, and anything else portable. Her daughters followed her lead as first-rate shoplifters. Later Gypsy explained, "Once, when I thought Rose had been too insulting to a very kindly courteous theatrical agent, I chided her, 'Mother, don't you trust anyone?' She snapped, 'Trust in God but get it in writing.' "[11] While Rose took credit for her younger daughter's career, June worked very long hours to support the entire entourage. Without a second thought, Rose exploited her. At ten, June suffered a nervous breakdown. "I wanted to die—just for the vacation," she joked bitterly.[12]

Rose's obsession with June's top billing and the income this recognition yielded overrode concerns for June as a child. Rose denied June any formal education. When threatened by the authorities for the girls' chronic truancy, Rose hired a tutor. In March 1924, when the girls played in Minnesota, she enrolled them in a theater school near Minneapolis. These educational experiences lasted long enough to ensure that the press received pictures of her girls being taught. Louise complained that she and her sister were deprived of any knowledge of social amenities including etiquette, grammar, and caring for one's clothing and possessions.

"I can't tell you how I regret having had the sort of childhood I did, not being brought up in a regular family, and going to school or being taken to the dentist regularly," Louise reflected sadly. She spent much of her adulthood compensating for her unconventional childhood. Rose skimped on regular medical and dental attention for her daughters. Her sympathies for Christian Science may have deepened her suspicions of doctors. But stinginess more than theological concern explained Rose's neglect of her children's health care.

"When my sister June Havoc and I were kids and mother took us trouping all over the nation in our vaudeville act," Louise recalled, "we used to carry a cretonne bedspread, a trunk cover, a coffee pot and a [boudoir] lamp shade with us." As soon as they checked into the hotel, "we started fixing our room to make it look homey." Always working or traveling, the girls never knew a real home. Both daughters yearned for a more stable life than the one their mother provided them.[13]

Throughout their difficult childhood, Louise and June took comfort in animals. Indeed, animals became the girls' only consistent friends. Louise had a monkey, and June adored dogs. Animals gave the girls unconditional love and helped assuage their loneliness. Rose also loved animals, and she often lavished more affection on her dogs than on her daughters. In adulthood, the sisters never lost their passion for animals.

Rose did not neglect one aspect of the girls' education: She tried to instill in her daughters a deep-seated fear of sex and men. Rose's mother, Anna, had inculcated the same message in Rose. Big Lady expressed her philosophy with a one-sentence warning: "Men are just no damn good." Rose insisted that because men were physically different from the opposite sex, they were incapable of love and exploited women sexually. She explained that "God cursed them by adding an ornament here. Every time they so much as think of a woman, it grows." Rose concluded by explaining that pregnancy always followed kissing. That was the sum total of the girls' sex education.[14]

Rose denounced her former husbands, whom she married and divorced in rapid succession after Jack Hovick, because they had promised to maintain platonic marriages but always betrayed her. She only briefly interrupted touring to marry. Rose may have resisted sex within marriage because she did not want any more children, while her husbands had expressed an interest. Rose also suffered minor injuries to her reproductive organs that she left untreated for years, making sex with a man less pleasurable. Moreover, Rose was bisexual. Her sexual orientation seems to have changed over time, however; she was heterosexual when she was younger and became exclusively lesbian during her thirties.

While on the road with June and Louise, Rose flirted with men who could help her. Tough but nevertheless quite charming, she manipulated men's sympathy by claiming to be a woman alone caring for her daughters. Although she wore no makeup and kept her nails cut blunt, Rose had a devastating effect on men. They wanted to protect her. As long as they remained useful, particularly monetarily, Rose allowed them to help her and her daughters. June and Louise received an abundance of mixed messages from their mother about sex. Rose stressed sexual abstinence to frighten the girls. Although Rose often had a man on her arm (though it is unclear how often in her bed), while traveling, she wanted to protect her young daughters from unwanted pregnancies and emotional attachments to other people.

Sometimes Rose's male companions sexually abused June. June never informed her mother about the men that Rose "had liked temporarily who had put my hand inside their trousers, who cuddled alongside me in bed, rubbing a huge penis against me." June managed to minimize the experience by noting there had been "no rape or forcing. I had dismissed it as the male behavior Mother spoke of so often." Such experiences and silences probably underlay June's precocious sexual behavior, and her romantic activity with boys started young. She felt necking matured her. Increasingly, she wanted to be treated as a young woman, not "Baby June."[15]

While June learned about men, Louise cultivated her skills on the stage. Entirely unexpectedly, a new star was in the process of being born. Although her mother regarded her older daughter as lacking in talent of any kind, others recognized Louise's gifts for entertainment. While playing a minor part, Louise met vaudeville legend Fanny Brice, who helped Louise see herself as feminine and create an enticing stage presence. For one sketch, Brice requested an adolescent girl to say five lines. The manager suggested Louise. For Brice's sketch, Louise discarded the drab boy's clothes she wore for her usual role as a newsboy, and Brice loaned her an orange chiffon dress. Fake jewels covered the narrow shoulder straps, and a row of orange ostrich feathers decorated the full skirt.

Louise "looked scared to death," Brice recalled. She complained about her costume: "I can't wear this in front of an audience. It isn't modest." Brice wisely informed her, "Look, kid. You can't be too modest in this business." The future stripper took this advice to heart. Brice's shoes were far too small for Louise, so she wore her heavy oxfords from the newsboy act. Louise's footwear made the act unexpectedly humorous.

Louise performed only once in the splendid chiffon dress because the act was cut from Brice's routine. For the first time in her vaudeville career, Louise felt disappointed about not performing. Brice's interest in Louise piqued Rose's possessive interest in her elder daughter. After years of ignoring Louise, Rose acknowledged that she had some potential. At the same time, driven by jealousy, Rose attempted to squelch Louise's adoration for Brice. Rose told Louise that Brice canceled the skit because she felt upstaged: "Why, from the moment you walked on stage, not a person in that audience looked at her. I was out front and heard the comments. They were raves." Over and over, Rose taught her daughters that they could trust no one except their mother.[16]

Fanny Brice remembered the same incident differently. "The management of the Orpheum Theatre in San Francisco wanted me to put on a dramatic skit that I did occasionally, a tear jerker in which I gave motherly advice to a teen-age girl who was staying out all night and getting in trouble with police." Brice contradicted Rose's account of why the act with the future Gypsy Rose Lee playing the adolescent girl did not continue with a practical explanation: "The show was running too long, and the manager cut our skit." At the time Louise met Fanny Brice, vaudeville audiences worshipped her. Rose's argument that Brice felt upstaged by an inexperienced girl lacks credibility.[17]

Rose transferred her mistrust of everyone to her daughters. They even treated each other warily. As June and Louise reached adolescence, they became more competitive and jealous of each other's talents and successes. The sisters rarely communicated or even acknowledged each other. As Louise grew taller, she became overweight and appeared unattractive. Then, as Louise slimmed down, June envied her beauty. She always longed for the formal education that Louise had received, even though Louise lamented its limitations.

As an adolescent, June finally rebelled against her mother. She knew that her act as Dainty June grew ludicrous as she matured. She fought her mother's attempts to fake a childlike appearance for her. Both teenage daughters began to dream about a future without their mother. Louise wanted to be very wealthy and independent. June fantasized about a career as a real actress, not an untrained child star.

In December 1928, while performing with Dainty June and Her Newsboy Songsters in Topeka, Kansas, June escaped her mother by eloping with a twenty-one-year-old dancer named Bobby. June's marriage suggests emotional strength as well as desperation. After a childhood deeply marked by her mother's domination, June began her own search for autonomy through a youthful marriage. Describing her family's history, June perceptively observed that their early marriages allowed the women in her family—her grandmother and her mother as well as herself—to pursue freedom even if they failed to find personal happiness. After Rose discovered that June and Bobby had run off together, she called the police. June and Bobby were married by the time a policeman found the young couple and brought them to the station to reconcile with Rose. Bobby's advent enraged Rose. He had taken away her only livelihood, as well as her dream of stardom for her daughter. More infuriating, he gave June emotional independence from her mother. June recalled that when Bobby attempted to shake hands with Rose, "Mother produced a small automatic. Ten inches away from Bobby's chest, she pulled the trigger—once…twice." Fortunately, Rose "didn't know a thing about her gun, or any other gun. The safety catch locked the action." Bobby and June quickly exited and moved in with Bobby's more sympathetic parents. Soon June and Bobby left to tour movie houses as a dance team performing as an opening act before the film.[18]

Rose Hovick's attempt to shoot her son-in-law exemplified her dangerous mental instability. Throughout her life, Rose at times displayed symptoms of severe manic depression and paranoia, and at some point before 1940 she was briefly committed to the psychiatric ward of New York City's Bellevue Hospital. The women in Rose's family all showed signs of mental disturbance. Rose's sister Belle was an alcoholic as a young woman, and her sister Mina died of a drug overdose. The women "had a common strain of ambition and strength and bitter independence; they married early, divorced quickly and in the end succumbed to alcohol or drugs or madness," recalled June. Rose learned to survive. In part because of her mental illness, Rose concentrated exclusively on how to exploit other people to fulfill her own needs. Her illness also destroyed any pangs of conscience about the morality of such manipulation.[19]

After losing her meal ticket, Rose turned to her "no-talent" daughter Louise. By March 1929, eighteen-year-old Louise was starring with several other girls in an act called Madame Rose's Dancing Daughters. At first Louise was a poor substitute for her sister. A six-week tour of the Southwest included bookings at a cooking school and an auto camp. After an opening in Saugerties, New York, as Madame Rose's Debutantes, the disgusted theater manager attempted to cancel the act.

At a critical moment, Louise seized control over the show from her mother. With a sure instinct for what appealed to audiences, she transformed the group into a trendier and more distinctive act. The challenge to her authority must have offended Rose, but she wanted the income. Louise dyed the other girls' hair and changed their name to Rose Louise and the Hollywood Blondes. The Blondes performed a short musical comedy with a hula dance and a doll number. One review described the show as a "pleasant act."[20]

In January 1930 in Kansas City, Missouri, according to legend, Louise and the Blondes were shocked to discover they were appearing at a burlesque theater. Vaudeville was dying, hurt by the Depression and the movies. Only burlesque theater owners wanted to hire the Blondes. They needed "clean" acts to fend off the police. The Hollywood Blondes felt demeaned in burlesque. As this story of Louise Hovick's debut in burlesque goes, one of the burlesque stars fell ill and the theater owner was desperate. Impressed by Louise's beauty and poise onstage, he suggested that she replace the stripper in the comedic skits. At first Rose resisted, but she finally relented since the money was better than in vaudeville. As Louise walked around in unaccustomed high-heeled shoes, a stripper called Tessie commented, "You oughtta see how much better ya look. For a kid, you got a lot of sex in your walk." Tessie added, "A sexy walk is a pretty good thing to have in this business. Burlesque stars are made on how they walk."[21]

Louise adjusted to her new role onstage. Just as she expressed her unease to Fanny Brice about the orange chiffon dress, at first she was not quite comfortable in revealing outfits. Earlier, while rehearsing as a chorus girl in Cleveland, she had refused the director's suggestion that she wear a very skimpy outfit. Gypsy recalled, "I got huffy and said, 'Sir!' and quit on the spot."[22] After she had been playing in Kansas City for a month, the police raided the theater, and it closed. Louise was disappointed. She enjoyed her comedic parts, and she loved the appreciative applause. Louise lost her shyness about appearing onstage scantily dressed. She gained self-confidence and exquisite timing. She had never stripped, but that soon followed.

Louise Hovick was poised to embark on her stunningly successful career as a stripteaser. In order to win bookings that paid more money, she decided to develop a new and distinctive act. Strangely, her gimmick turned out to be her intelligence, coupled with her gift for comedy. She leaped from being a "talking woman" in vaudeville sketches to being a talking stripper. First she needed to learn how to undress seductively in front of an audience.

2

The Burlesque Stage

According to Gypsy's autobiography, the band at the Gaiety Theater in Toledo played "Little Gypsy Sweetheart." Slowly and sensuously removing black-headed dressmaker's straight pins from her lavender dress, Gypsy dropped the pins into the tuba in the orchestra pit below. They pinged as they hit the brass bell. Just as the music halted, she removed her shoulder straps and her filmy net dress fell on the floor. "Wrapping the curtain around me I disappeared into the wings," explained Gypsy, describing her first striptease.

For another act, she dressed as a bird. She started at the top of the stairs and slowly descended. The applause grew. Gypsy flapped her wings and exposed parts of her lovely body. "It was the least I could do, I thought, to show my appreciation," she explained. From the beginning, she acted like a star. "As the curtain began to close in I stepped forward and took the folds and brought them slowly together, smiling out at the audience until the two sides met." Playfulness with the curtain remained a part of her act throughout her career. Gypsy was probably nineteen.

During the second part of the show in Toledo, Gypsy performed "Powder My Back," an act she copied from an entertainer she had seen in Kansas City. Gypsy half sang, half talked the suggestive lyrics. "Oh, won't you powder my back every morning? 'Cause, Honey, there's no one can do it like you." After convincing a balding man in the audience to powder her back with a powder puff, she rewarded him by tying a red ribbon around a small strand of his hair. She coaxed the man to stand. When she kissed him, he squirmed with embarrassment. Gypsy's premiere—if this story about it is true—revealed her amazing aplomb and stage presence.[1]

As a stripteaser, Louise Hovick seized control of her life and never let go. Her transformation into a stripper began when the lead stripper of Ed Ryan's burlesque company landed in jail. When Ryan asked Rose if Louise stripped, Rose lied and answered in the affirmative. Originally performing only in comedic sketches in the show, Gypsy soon rose to starring stripper. With money as the incentive, Rose urged her adolescent daughter to strip. At seventy-five dollars a week, strippers earned far more than the clothed and poverty-stricken Rose Louise and the Hollywood Blondes did. Stripteasing, Rose argued, would lead to more respectable work such as acting on Broadway. An unconventional childhood with no real roots and few attachments prepared Gypsy emotionally for a career in burlesque. Gypsy desperately desired audience approval, perhaps to compensate for her mother's failure to be supportive and for her own fragile self-esteem. At the onset of the Great Depression, stripping offered one of the few stage careers open to untrained performers, and, with its emphasis on comedy and nudity, burlesque flourished as one of the most popular forms of theater for men. Since her mother accepted her stripping, Gypsy relaxed onstage. But she rebelled against her mother's authority by controlling her own act. Her striptease performance represented the one place where she gained independence from her mother.

To promote herself, Gypsy tinkered with her résumé in her early years in burlesque. Billed as a beauty contest winner from Seattle, she ordered the press to refer to her as "Miss Seattle." Soon after, she added a movie career to her publicity profile. Both stories had grains of truth buried within them, but Gypsy neglected to mention she won the beauty contest as a baby, and the two-reel films made before she was ten constituted her movie appearances. Hardworking and talented, Gypsy steadily moved up in burlesque, getting higher billing and working at better theaters. In January 1931, at the Rialto in Chicago, she achieved a milestone by acquiring her own dressing room and being designated a burlesque star. Soon after, Gypsy received a job offer from Billy Minsky, the most celebrated name in burlesque.

So, less than two years after her first strip, twenty-year-old Gypsy and her mother headed for Minsky's Republic Theater on 42nd Street in New York. The patriarch of the family, A. B. Minsky, opened the National Winter Garden in 1912. By 1920, the Minsky family, including sons Billy, Herbert, Abe, and Morton, ran twelve theaters. Possessing a genius for burlesque, Billy modernized the mode of entertainment. At the turn of the century, women onstage in the chorus were chosen for their ample curves, often weighing close to two hundred pounds. In the 1920s, in keeping with the flapper image, Minsky hired alluring young women like Gypsy.

Always the master, Minsky ruled even over the opinionated Rose. Gypsy affectionately portrayed Minsky as the theater owner H. I. Moss in her first novel, *The G-String Murders*. She described his attitude toward entertainment: "He was convinced that [burlesque] stood for the very best Broadway could offer." Gypsy quoted the fictitious Moss: "Girls! That's what the public wants!" And Moss encouraged the fictitious stripper in the book, named Gypsy, to think of herself as a headliner.[2]

Minsky advertised aggressively. Before Gypsy arrived, he sent a man on stilts up and down Broadway to announce her coming appearances. He even hired a plane to pull a banner with her name. To ensure that his audiences contained upper-class as well as working-class men, Minsky gave free tickets to members of the Harvard and Racquet clubs. The Minskys designed their theaters to match the clientele. Billy Minsky's Republic Theater, located near Times Square, impressed Gypsy with its elegance. A doorman with a mustache and a red-lined cape greeted patrons. Velvet curtains framed the stage. The female ushers wore French-inspired maid's costumes with short skirts and black silk stockings. Seating an enthusiastic audience of more than a thousand, the Republic produced two shows a day except on Sundays, when blue laws forced the theater to close. Minsky's elegant new Broadway theater provided the perfect backdrop for the upscale act that Gypsy perfected there.

At Minsky's, Gypsy refined elements of her routines such as teasing bald men. Over the next twenty-five years, she modified the details but kept their most significant elements. Part of Gypsy's genius lay in her ability to see herself through the lens of her male spectators. She had not internalized social conventions while growing up, so she was able to see herself outside of herself. She figured out what excited men and left them hungry for another show. She calculated the audience's attention span when watching comedic sketches and other strip routines and applied her knowledge to her own stage appearances. Some nine thousand men a week cheered Gypsy's acts. Minsky billed Gypsy above the comic, one of the first strippers so honored.[3]

Burlesque theater owners specialized in displaying the female body with variety and flair. The Minsky brothers' National Winter Garden theater staged "a special event each night": Monday, Chorus Girls' Shimmy Contest; Tuesday, Perfect Form Contest; Wednesday, Chorus Girls' Black Bottom Contest; Thursday, Oriental Dance Contest; and Friday, Living Picture Contest. Racial stereotypes of African Americans and Asians were considered exotic and sexually provocative. On Saturday, when their audiences peaked, the theater owners staged a "popularity contest for the entire company in which members of the audience participated," reminisced Morton Minsky. Saturday night featured a lavish midnight show.[4]

At burlesque theaters, comedians and strippers reigned. At Minsky's Republic Theater, Gypsy worked with comedians Bud Abbott and Lou Costello. She also shared star billing with Nudina, an exotic dancer who performed with fans, balloons, and birds, including doves and cockatoos. Nudina often costarred with a six-foot snake, which when offstage slept peacefully in a sink in the strippers' dressing room; she enjoyed working with the long reptiles and always mourned their passing.

The first time June saw her sister perform at Minsky's, she was amazed. When the curtain opened, Gypsy was standing in the center of the stage lighted by a huge spotlight. She wore a large red velvet hat with a matching dress, and "her beauty stunned the audience for fully thirty seconds before the wild ovation began." As she strolled across the stage, she slowly took off her gloves and flung them into the orchestra pit, and the audience roared. The climax exhibited Gypsy's unique creativity. Against the curtain, Gypsy "sang-talked in her elegant voice, 'And suddenly...I take the last...thing...off!' With one gesture, she flipped her entire gown into the air. A woman in the audience screamed. That was part of the act, of course." Gypsy shared in the audience's laughter. Gypsy had arrived. Her act was described as "Seven Minutes of Sheer Art."[5]

To stay popular, Gypsy conceived an individual style with distinctive elements in her specialty numbers. Her costumes were carefully designed. Creating her own burlesque outfits, she used straight pins to keep her clothing in place. She found zippers "cheap and vulgar." Besides, a sticking zipper could ruin an act or, even more seriously, damage her skin. The lucky redeemer of a pin won free admission to the next day's performance. Glue held up her stockings, and dental floss kept the G-string in place.[6]

Gypsy designed and crafted costumes that projected refinement. She preferred beautiful dresses for shedding. Onstage, she wore long skirts with organdy ruffles, lots of petticoats, and picture hats and carried a parasol. Audiences thought of Gypsy as a sexy southern belle or a nice but naughty Victorian woman; they could view her shedding of such garments as a rebellion against restrictive clothing and repressive social mores. As her income soared, her costume expenses increased. Upon hearing that Gypsy disrobed from one costume that cost $2,500, humorist H. Allen Smith exclaimed that taking off such an expensive outfit "was like buying a diamond-encrusted baseball bat to kill a cockroach." Gypsy responded, "I operate like that."[7]

In keeping with her tasteful outer frocks, Gypsy refrained from bumps and grinds done in rapid succession. Such blatantly sexual stripping was described as "hot." Instead, Gypsy worked "sweet." "Gypsy set New Yorkers on their ears with her completely unorthodox strip-tease routine," the composer and impresario Billy Rose proclaimed. "She glided on stage like a lady—a lady dressed from the Ascot Races in the Gay Nineties. In her perfect diction she recited an erudite patter while she slowly removed her white kid gloves finger by finger." Like many others, Billy Rose was as impressed with Gypsy's style as with her body. As he attested, "Gypsy was the essence of elegance, from her first breathtaking entrance until her last sophisticated shrug before she covered her beautiful bareness with her beautiful black picture hat."[8] Gypsy certainly knew how to build suspense. Her act drew audiences who perennially hoped that she would expose more at the next performance.

"Bare flesh bores men. Black silk stockings are more seductive than bare legs and black lace panties are more exciting than a rose-petal belt," Gypsy believed. "It's not how much I take off that matters," she knew. "It's the way I take things off that gives the effect." At Minsky's, Gypsy refined the art of "more tease than strip," taking off much less than most strippers. She promised and appeared to give far more in the way of sex and nudity than she delivered. "You don't have to be naked to look naked," she explained; "you just have to think naked." She perfected the illusion.[9]

Onstage Gypsy appeared completely confident, never embarrassed. She controlled all elements of her performance, including her exit. Although Gypsy made her performance look natural, she knew precisely where to unfasten her outfit. She insisted, "If a strip teaser ever fumbles with her clothes or doesn't time everything exactly with the music, she might just as well leave her clothes on." Gypsy looked directly at her audience to hold their attention. The noted trial lawyer Louis Nizer remembered Gypsy's act well. Walking "down the bejeweled circular stairs...the risk was tripping. She dared not look down to ensure a safe journey because it would break eye contact."[10] Since Gypsy pasted most of her last layer on her front and left her back uncovered, she permitted no one to be behind her during a performance. According to her son, "Mother was actually a very modest woman." In one cartoon about Gypsy, stagehands averted their eyes as she backed off the stage. Of course the cartoon exploited Gypsy's body by showing her completely nude from the back.[11]

Fans often envisioned her performance as more than just fantasized sex. One paperback pamphlet, *Sketches of Naughty Ladies and Secrets*, put the point rather pretentiously, but accurately emphasized the aesthetic aspect of her appeal: "There are many who insist that so perfect was Gypsy Rose in her disrobing act that she deserved to be classed as an 'artiste.'" Men regarded her as so beautiful that some insisted "their eyes never left her face all during her act."[12]

Gypsy's intelligence combined with her beauty and sensational legs compensated for her small breasts. She successfully maximized her physical assets and minimized other parts of her body. To lessen attention to her size 10½ feet, she wore simple shoes. Much of her length was made up of her beautiful legs that seemed to go on forever. She wore extra-long stockings and never used a razor, only a depilatory. Before beginning in burlesque, Gypsy auditioned for Earl Carroll, who produced and directed numerous musicals, including *Earl Carroll's Vanities*. Carroll criticized her figure as fat, and he nastily asked Rose how she had allowed her pretty daughter to gain so much weight. Gypsy never forgot. She maintained her weight at 130 pounds.[13]

Stripping avenged Gypsy, a heavyset adolescent constantly demeaned by her mother. Burlesque offered her glamour and fame. When she performed, the audience focused its entire attention on her. Sexual empowerment, however fleeting, was part of the art's appeal to her. On the burlesque stage, as in other forms of acting, the ability to play a role allowed Gypsy to both move outside of herself and dominate the scene. The audience's passivity contrasted with the entertainer's assertiveness. Gypsy manipulated the audience to produce the response she desired.

At Minsky's, writer L. Sprague de Camp confessed, "the only trouble with the performances was that, when time came to go, standing up presented a problem." He remembered seeing a man who "talked to his penis" during the show. Gypsy was aware of homosexual men who came to burlesque theaters to watch other men masturbate in the sexually charged atmosphere. She realized such male behavior brought her a larger audience.[14]

Gypsy feigned ignorance about the source of her own popularity. "I don't know myself what it is," she sometimes commented quizzically. Placing her hands on her small breasts, she said to Morton Minsky: "I don't feel any spark of genius *here*. Most of the girls have better figures than mine. I can't sing. I don't dance." She neglected to mention how often she refined her act. She constantly tried out new material and worked hard to perfect her timing. In public, she always underestimated her own talents. Rose's constant references to Louise as the "no-talent" daughter influenced Gypsy's public attitude about herself. Often on the defensive, she insulted herself as if to prevent anyone else from attacking her.[15]

The press quickly noticed this newcomer to burlesque. The *Washington Post* described her as a "swell looker." Her clipping file contained articles calling her act "one of the biggest attractions in burlesque" and "a sensational hit." "Miss Lee is a most attractive brunette with beauty and charm," said one. Photos of her in a filmy organdy dress with the skirt flared out adorned several newspapers.[16]

Always, she sold herself. Gypsy's obsession with her body grew from the reality that her body provided her livelihood. Her career exacerbated her narcissism, and burlesque trained Gypsy to think of her own body as a commodity. "Hell, I won't even take off my gloves unless I know what the money is," she once asserted. An astute businesswoman, Gypsy deducted as business expenses everything that pertained to her image. All adornment for her body was tied to her professional activity. Even after she left burlesque, her journals rarely reflected intimate thoughts. Instead, they were ledgers in which she detailed how she spent her money. She kept accounts for every trip to the hairdresser, as well as the cost of pedicures, manicures, wigs, dresses, and hats.[17]

Gypsy stripped with more finesse and style than almost anyone else, but she found the performance demeaning. When asked if stripping embarrassed her, Gypsy responded: "Only at the beginning, but that didn't last long. Only the first hundred stares are the hardest." Never easy or natural, her clever routines required a great deal of physical and emotional energy. She confessed that the act with the bald men made her nervous: "They would always be so embarrassed. And I was always so panicky, so very panicky."[18]

Privately Gypsy rebelled against her glamorous, sexy image. Away from the prying eyes of fans and reporters, she wore saggy long johns. Sometimes she slept in her old makeup and refused to brush her hair or fix her nails for days. Away from the stage, she deliberately assumed an unglamorous stance. Men who expected a sensual and willing woman were disappointed. Gypsy always considered stripping to be work, not leisure, and she never confused the two.

Her ambivalence about stripping showed in her alcohol consumption. Gypsy's drinking was not merely social. Early in her career, she kept liquor in her dressing room and drank liberally to keep from thinking about taking off her clothes in public. Her discomfort with stripping spurred her constant efforts to leave burlesque. She willingly accepted pay cuts to take jobs that furthered her hopes for a career on Broadway and in the legitimate theater.

The gangster Waxy Gordon, one of her earliest guardian angels, unexpectedly assisted her first climb out of burlesque. Like her mother, Gypsy periodically relied on men to advance her career. She knew how to use her beauty and brains, and part of her gift was recognizing those who might be helpful, although her judgment in men, such as Gordon, was hardly unerring.

One night while mingling with entertainers at a speakeasy, Gordon spotted Gypsy. Inez Worth, a burlesque singer, introduced Gypsy and her mother to him. Clearly smitten, Waxy sent champagne to the women's table. Gypsy noticed his bodyguards. Gordon ordered the waiters: "Give my friends here anything they want." To Gypsy and Inez, he said, "Eat hearty. You can't tell when you'll run into me again." Soon after this initial encounter, Gordon invited Gypsy to perform at Comstock Prison in upstate New York in a show he financed. "You'd think in his business he'd stay as far from prisons as he could," Rose mused. The cast traveled by train, eating a lobster dinner to music from the orchestra. When they arrived at the prison, the prison officials refused to allow Gypsy to perform because the guards feared she would corrupt the prisoners' morals.[19]

The free-spending gangster known as Waxy Gordon was born Irving Wexler sometime in the late 1880s to a family of Polish Jews living on the Lower East Side, New York City's densest immigrant neighborhood. His sticky fingers earned him the nickname Waxy; he had an uncanny ability to lift valuables from other people's pockets without being detected. He was sent to juvenile facilities, including Elmira Reformatory, but he never reformed. Waxy branched out as a bookmaker and ran the cocaine trade in several New York City neighborhoods.[20]

Once national Prohibition began in 1919, Gordon was among those who realized there were fortunes to be made in the illegal importation and sale of alcohol. With the aid of a partner, Max "Big Maxey"

Greenberg, he expanded his business into bootlegging, setting up thirteen illegal breweries. Some of these properties became available when the owners died suddenly even though they had enjoyed the best of health. Paying no taxes on his illegal profits, Gordon enjoyed the lifestyle of a multimillionaire.

Like other big-time gangsters, Gordon backed Broadway plays and subsidized favored women performers. Producers, actors, and chorus girls accepted these criminals and their fat bankrolls. Mobsters mingled easily with entertainers and producers, attending the same clubs and inviting them to parties. Burlesque theater owners did business with gangsters because they offered protection of their property against competitors (whether theatrical or criminal) and served as a deterrent to vice squads.

Both bootlegging and the entertainment business, which were closely allied during the Roaring Twenties, offered valuable opportunities to enterprising immigrants. American-born citizens of Western European descent controlled many occupations, industries, and institutions. Facing exclusion and discrimination, immigrants sought places where they could rise economically. Popular culture, with its expanding markets and rapidly changing fads, seemed wide open. American-born children of Eastern European Jews starred as comedians and dancers, attained fame as composers and directors, and accumulated wealth as producers and financiers in all forms of entertainment, ranging from highbrow theater through Broadway and the movies to lowbrow vaudeville and burlesque. Recognizing the potential profits that lay in providing illegal pleasures as well, Jews and Italians both formed powerful criminal gangs. In fact, because the children of immigrants often lived in ethnic neighborhoods near or next to other groups, some formed alliances across ethnic lines. Waxy Gordon worked with the Italian Moretti brothers, Salvatore and William, in northern New Jersey. By creating an ethnically diverse network of criminals, gangsters demonstrated their Americanization.

Like Gypsy, Waxy craved respectability. He dressed elegantly, with a wardrobe that included silk shirts made by Al Capone's tailor. He possessed more than two hundred suits and dinner jackets and wore silk underwear and French ties. Waxy, like Gypsy, regarded books and education as a source of prestige. Aspiring to the manners of an upper-class gentleman, he enjoyed opera and classical music. He sent his children to reputable private schools. Filling his library with leather-bound copies of books by Dickens, Cooper, and Twain, he gave biographies of Jefferson and Lincoln to politicians, some of whom he bribed.

Gordon presented Gypsy with unusual gifts. One evening, he gave her a magnificent Mission-style oak dining room set consisting of thirty chairs and a massive long table for her new house in Rego (from "real good") Park, a development in suburban Queens built on former farmland. Soon afterward, she could not afford to make the payments and lost the new house to foreclosure.[21]

Waxy also sent her to a dentist to fix her long-neglected teeth. Gypsy's mother had promised to have her teeth straightened, and her grandfather had saved money to pay for the procedure, but Rose had spent the funds, probably on June's act. Years later, at Gordon's request, a dentist filed Gypsy's teeth to make them appear straight. The treatment was not a lasting success. The filing damaged nerves and contributed to the abscesses and other dental problems that continued to afflict her.[22]

Gordon protected Gypsy by providing her with henchmen to guard her against fans' unwelcome advances or thugs who might try to steal her expensive jewelry. Gypsy used Gordon to further her career, but she also found him exciting. Their shared working-class background enhanced their friendship. His dangerous occupation fascinated her. Given her own struggle for respectability, Gypsy accepted Gordon on his own terms. She did not worry about his reputation.

Gypsy denied having any sexual relationship with Waxy Gordon. Many of their mutual acquaintances, including Morton Minsky, did not believe her protestations. Although Gordon was married, he slept with prostitutes, and men of his ilk who backed actresses on Broadway usually expected sexual favors in return. Besides, Waxy was Gypsy's type; she often preferred shorter men who possessed a distinctive sensuality.

Gordon left Gypsy's life quite dramatically. With the impending repeal of Prohibition, Gordon persuaded those of his partners who had no criminal records to obtain liquor licenses so they would be in position to control the supply for the unleashed demand. Meanwhile, Dutch Schultz, a rival bootlegger, decided on a "hostile takeover" of Gordon's business. Schultz attempted to have Gordon shot, but his men managed only to kill Gordon's partner, Max Greenberg. The FBI labeled Gordon "Public Enemy Number One." Gordon may have welcomed being arrested by the police, calculating that, with Schultz on the loose, prison was safer than freedom. In late 1933, Chief Assistant U.S. Attorney for the Southern District of New York Thomas E. Dewey prosecuted Waxy for tax evasion. Dewey wanted to win a big, splashy case against a gangster to advance his political ambitions, and his victories in this and later cases against the mob made his reputation; in 1942, New York voters would elect him governor. The jury convicted Waxy

Gordon after only fifty-one minutes of deliberation, and the judge sentenced him to ten years' incarceration and fifty thousand dollars in fines. Out of jail after seven years, he reestablished himself in the drug trade. Rearrested in 1951, Gordon died in prison the following year.

Before his arrest, Gordon contributed to Gypsy's quest to leave burlesque by asking Lew Brown, a songwriter for Florenz Ziegfeld: "How about using Gypsy in your show? She's as good looking as some of the other dames you got." He added, "Besides, she's a friend of mine," recalled Gypsy. People in the entertainment business knew to pay attention to Gordon's friends, both because Gordon backed Broadway productions financially and because upsetting Gordon could be harmful to one's health. The very next day after Gordon spoke to Brown, Gypsy arrived, with a bathing suit, at Ziegfeld's theater on the corner of Sixth Avenue and Fifty-fourth Street. Once Ziegfeld saw her luscious legs, he hired her as a chorus girl. Ziegfeld preferred long legs to big breasts, so the women in his productions often measured larger around the hips than around the bust. Alluding to the famous hybrid rose, Ziegfeld referred to his chorus girls as "long-stemmed American beauties." Outfitted in silk stockings, their firm legs glistened as they danced.[23]

Gypsy's desire to leave burlesque induced her to relinquish the thousand dollars she earned each week at Minsky's and take sixty a week in a Ziegfeld production. She signed on in January 1932, less than one year after she arrived in New York, for a show initially called *Laid in Mexico*, later renamed *Hot Cha!* Dutch Schultz and Waxy Gordon were rumored to have provided financial backing. Comedian Bert Lahr (later famous as the Cowardly Lion in *The Wizard of Oz*) had star billing. Gypsy played a minor part as the Girl in the Compartment. Embarrassed over her career in burlesque, she appeared under the name Rose Louise. But she could not escape entirely: Her rating as a "chorus girl" by Actors' Equity meant she was excluded from the finale. Gypsy was devastated by her inability to appear.[24]

"I traveled in and out of burlesques, leaving for the prestige of musicals, and returning for the money of burlesque," Gypsy explained. During the early 1930s, she periodically left strip theaters for other stage productions, but they never paid well or lasted long. Although the newspapers reported the sensation of a burlesque performer being signed by the more respectable Flo Ziegfeld, reporters took no notice of her role in *Hot Cha!* When the show closed, Gypsy appeared briefly at Earl Carroll's theater, which ran racy revues similar to Ziegfeld's. In 1933, she took a tiny part in George White's romantic musical comedy *Melody*. The reviews never mentioned her.[25]

The next year, Billy Rose's nightclub, Casino de Paree, provided another slightly more respectable venue, but Gypsy found that it differed from burlesque only by paying a lower salary. Her brief career at the popular club ended abruptly. In one version, Gypsy got so frazzled when she saw his wife, Fanny Brice, that she muffed her lines, so Rose fired her. Rose's sister told another version, which is probably closer to the truth. Gypsy worked as a showgirl at Billy's nightclub. To increase his audience, he decided to have the women in his chorus appear semi-nude. Gypsy responded, "If I'm going to strip down to Mother Nature, I'm not going to do it for the $60 a week you're paying me. Not when I can get $500 a week stripping for the Brothers Minsky." Billy Rose replied, "So your modesty is monetary." Gypsy confirmed his conclusion by leaving and asking the Minskys to take her back.[26]

Gypsy acknowledged that "burlesque has always been my financial paradise." Stripping brought her both fame and fortune. At Minsky's, she received star billing.[27] Throughout the Depression, Gypsy's career as a burlesque queen soared. When she first returned in 1934, the Minskys offered her a paltry ninety dollars, knowing that was more than she had been paid by Ziegfeld and Billy Rose. A desperate Gypsy took the money, confident that her salary would rise. Wooing large audiences, she quickly worked her way back to a munificent income, especially by Depression standards. Minsky profited, too. Gypsy may have started in burlesque because she had no viable alternative, but she stayed because of the fame and fortune she earned.

In these early years of her career, Gypsy looked for people to help her. Soon after she arrived at Minsky's, she discovered a backer who filled a void in her life. Gypsy spoke teasingly about how she had sacrificed a personal life for her career as a stripper. Few men wanted to wait for a woman who performed onstage until midnight or toured for months. She confessed that "the strain of stripping makes me so nervous and upset that no man would want to see me more than once a week anyway." Of course, men often paid to see her more than once a week. Yet she raised a serious issue that plagued her life. Most single, marriageable men preferred their women to stay home and lead a more conventional life. Ever the comedian, Gypsy swore that she was "going to make up for this abstinence when I am thirty." She planned either to marry five husbands in a row or to give birth to five children at once like "Mrs. Dionne," the Canadian mother of quintuplets. Actually, Gypsy's personal life entered a new phase. She did not have to wait until thirty for sex, but her lover was married.[28]

3

Sophisticated Stripper

Back at Minsky's, Gypsy recreated herself as a sophisticated stripper. "She quickly got the idea from the ritzier people that attended the show that if a stripper could speak even two lines of French, it would be considered a miracle," noted Morton Minsky. She learned that if she quoted from a book she had read, "she would be considered an intellectual genius, so she went about cultivating these talents." Gypsy's married lover, whom she identified only as Eddy, supplied the money for her to cultivate an urbane and chic lifestyle that merged with her new image onstage. Gypsy loved books as a child, and she used a uniquely bookish approach to her act. Unwillingly forced out of schooling, Gypsy must have been pleased to rely on her intellect onstage, unlike any other stripper.[1]

Talking as she stripped, Gypsy conveyed humor and intelligence as well as sexuality to her audience. Witty patter worked for Gypsy. It emphasized her brains and her gift for comedy. Since Gypsy talked all the time, why not onstage? Her dialogue covered up any insecurity about her own talent. Gypsy appeared to relish performing. Presenting sex as mutually pleasurable and nonthreatening to anyone involved, she stripped it of guilt. Ordinary strippers seemed bored or sad and left their audiences feeling sordid. Gypsy left her audiences happy. "Did you ever hold a piece of candy or a toy in front of a baby—just out of his reach?" she queried, and went on to say that if you do, the baby will laugh. Her audience reacted the same way. She was the only stripper "who can make nudity witty," columnist Ashton Stevens once wrote.[2]

Gypsy had watched the strippers in burlesque houses and entertained her mother by parodying them. They both thought audiences would enjoy seeing a woman who took stripteasing less seriously. When Gypsy suggested these humorous imitations to her bosses, they resisted her attempts to poke fun at their stars. Later, as she gained confidence, she converted her own act into a burlesque of burlesque. Along with her audiences, her bosses learned to love it. The new act catapulted her into stardom.

Gypsy divided stripteasers of the 1930s into four types. The "coy" type, typified by Ann Corio, wore ruffled outfits and carried parasols. The "slinky" type paraded in tight gowns and memorable G-strings. The "exotics" worked with snakes or added fancy ballet routines to their strips. Harem settings where women served the pleasure of men were popular. Gypsy did not mention them, but exotics included women of color. Since they were never considered respectable by white society, they gained attention as more sensuous and sexually daring than white strippers. Although Josephine Baker did not strip, her scantily clothed routine exemplified a use of ethnic and racial exotica popular at the time.

Finally, Gypsy considered herself and Georgia Sothern, her closest friend in burlesque, "comediennes." Gypsy brought laughter to burlesque by relying on sexually provocative satire. Her routine made fun of other types of strippers. "Why, my strip tease act all started because I thought some of the acts at Minsky's were so ridiculous," she would later say. In the 1940s, Gypsy confided to a gossip columnist: "Few of these girls have any real talent and it's surprising how much money they make without knowing anything about acting."[3]

Gypsy added naughty poetry to her act, particularly bawdy songs written by the witty, slightly naughty author Dwight Fiske. She stripped to Fiske's risqué "Ida, the Wayward Sturgeon," reciting: "Ida was a little wayward sturgeon who said, 'There must be more to this sex life than just swimming back and forth over each other's eggs.'" Before long, Fiske's publishers insisted she stop performing his material without compensation, but Fiske personally asked her to continue.[4]

Not everyone adored Gypsy's performances. Men who enjoyed bumps, grinds, and daring nudity were disappointed. "Is this all of it?" one stagehand protested after watching Gypsy's act. "There isn't enough here to hang in the men's room," he sneered. And a man in her audience complained, "She makes a joke of the thing. You can't be funny about anything as serious as that."[5]

In 1935, at age twenty-five, Gypsy performed at the Irving Palace, a burlesque theater on Forty-second Street that played a full fifty-two-week season. The owners paid her approximately one thousand dollars per week, matching her Minsky's salary before she left for Ziegfield, an amazing amount for a working woman during the Depression. She worked the more provocative midnight show as well as earlier in the evening. At the Irving Palace, Gypsy encouraged limited audience participation. She wore pink bows glued strategically and sang-talked suggestively: "I'm a lonesome little Eve looking for an Adam." Without much coaxing, she convinced men in her audience to take bites of her apple, which clearly symbolized female breasts and genitals. One night she threw away the bitten apple and a man leaned too far in an attempt to catch it. Falling into the orchestra pit, he emerged with the trophy: the core. Gypsy encouraged such staged antics and cajoled the audience to laugh at appropriate times.[6]

Publicly, Gypsy expressed ambivalence about whether she viewed her act as art. She often justified her work in those terms. "I have always thought of it as an art, and I do not mean that as a gentle jest, not in high-browish form. I merely contend that anything one might do, and do well, must be trade marked as an art." She explained, "There is an art in the timing which is very important, in the costuming and in the selection of songs. From that point of view it probably is as much as art as any other act." At the same time, Gypsy kept her image lighthearted and unpretentious, commenting, "I certainly don't take it seriously enough to go high-brow about it and pretend it's something it isn't."[7] Privately, Gypsy thought that stripteasing as a whole did not come close to approximating an art form. She considered her own act an exception. In court after her three arrests for obscenity in the early part of her career, Gypsy openly defended her act as a creative enterprise. She always convinced the judges that "her art was art."[8]

While Gypsy developed her witty routines, Eddy gave his mistress the lifestyle that crowned her image as a stylish stripper. Eddy and Gypsy created a new personality for her: clever, always quotable, and glamorously sexy. With his money and coaching, she gained a reputation as an upper-class stripper. Eddy's generosity enabled her to rent a luxury apartment. He paid for a maid to assist her at the burlesque theater and at home, and for diamonds and a mink coat. He provided her with entrée into a new social milieu.[9]

Gypsy never disclosed his true identity in her autobiography or in interviews, but she did not create a fictitious character in

Eddy—although she was a skilled enough writer to do so had she wished. One article referred to him as Freddie. Another reporter, who disclosed his correct first name, pressed Gypsy about him. "He's so darned handsome," Gypsy said coyly, "I have to keep him undercover so no one else will go for him." She wisely left out the fact that his wife already had him.[10]

The handsome and wealthy Eddy was Edwin Bruns. From a rich family, by 1931 he worked as a broker in his father's Wall Street firm. He lived in an apartment on Park Avenue, while his wife maintained the family home in New Jersey. With his wife safely tucked away elsewhere, he could freely indulge in sexual liaisons with lower-class women in the city. Yet Eddy wanted his mistress to be more than a stripper.

Eddy met Gypsy when she was only in her early twenties and he was in his early thirties. By the time Gypsy left *Hot Cha!* Eddy had become a fixture in her life. Unlike her mother, who ignored her for so many years, Eddy gave her "someone special to be," Gypsy told June. Like the Beast in Disney's 1991 version of the fairy tale *Beauty and the Beast*, who wins Belle by opening his library to her, Eddy gave Gypsy books. He helped Gypsy's public transformation, and he cared enough about her to educate her. Gypsy learned philosophy as well as French. She craved knowledge almost as much as money.

In return for enhancing Gypsy's public image, Eddy acquired a ravishingly beautiful young mistress. He became a Pygmalion without the frustration of cold marble. From the 1930s until his death, Eddy remained in Gypsy's life, although after the late 1930s they met more sporadically. June considered him Gypsy's best friend. After Gypsy married, she maintained at least a friendship with Eddy, and the liaison resumed after Gypsy and her husband separated.

Eddy came with a stiff price: He was unwilling to get a divorce. A respectable stockbroker, Eddy resisted embarrassing himself or his family by publicly acknowledging his affair with a stripper. Gypsy welcomed the independence that an affair with a married man brought. Her liaison with Eddy kept her from a conventional marriage in which she might have become subordinate. With Eddy, she remained unencumbered, keeping her own schedule and social life. Gypsy certainly did not desire to burden him or herself with a child, and she noted to her pregnant sister that Eddy would have quickly lost interest in her if she had gained weight. She understood Eddy's underlying attraction to her. Besides, given her profession, Gypsy could not afford to sag.[11]

Eddy set the pattern for Gypsy's male lovers. Men gave sex and money rather than security. The men's own married status allowed Gypsy to keep her independence without being bothered domestically. They encouraged and even contributed to her career as a stripteaser, an occupation that would have had less appeal to most husbands. With the exception of her third and last husband, Gypsy always kept romance and marriage separate, with devastating results. Gypsy desired unattainable men.

Eddy helped Gypsy feel comfortable with a new set of people. On the road with her mother, she had never mixed with the upper class, and she had a lot to learn. Quickly grasping the difference between old and new money, she figured out how to classify people: Either they were in the *Social Register* or they weren't. "It was surprising who was in the book," she would recall. "Eddy, for instance, with all his money wasn't, but that nice couple who looked so shabby and took me swimming at the River Club were." Eddy's ethnic background kept him from gaining a place in the *Social Register*, but his wealth gave him entrée to those with old money. Gypsy's family background was unmentionable, but her visible talents won appreciation. As Eddy's companion, Gypsy began to socialize with people she had only dreamed of while in vaudeville.[12]

Diligent and tenacious, Gypsy constructed every aspect of her public life. She worked on every detail of her appearance and her social skills. One night June and her mother visited Gypsy right before one of her parties. On that occasion, Gypsy was teaching herself to drink quantities of alcohol without suffering an upset stomach. Becoming a sophisticate required holding one's liquor. After swigging brandy, she threw up, drank again, and tried to talk to keep from regurgitating. She needed to impress the social elite whose company she now enjoyed. She had to learn to consume alcohol in a style fitting her conception of the rich.[13]

Being a sophisticated stripper required luxurious, even lush personal settings. When Gypsy returned to Minsky's, she moved to a beautiful apartment with a Moorish motif facing Manhattan's Gramercy Park. The mink toilet seat covers impressed visiting reporters when they photographed her bubble baths. Gypsy sewed them from Eddy's first gift to her, a mink coat. Later Gypsy lived on the top floor of an apartment building off Park Avenue near Eddy's.

As Gypsy evolved into the thinking man's sex symbol, Eddy helped her appeal to an upscale crowd. "A now dead breed called Cafe Society, in a bored search of thrills, heard about her and went slumming on

Times Square just to sit with the bald, T-shirted guys and applaud her," a reporter explained. Gypsy realized that the men who attended burlesque shows came for a sexual experience strategically clothed with the trappings of fun. She provided naughtiness without risk for both upper-class and working-class men.[14]

As Gypsy and Eddy developed her image, they sought expert help to market it. Gypsy's first major exposure to publicity began with Bernard Sobel, the press agent for Ziegfeld's *Hot Cha!* In 1932, Sobel decided to promote first Gypsy's beauty and then her brains. When the musical opened in Washington, D.C., Sobel flooded the newspapers with pictures of the stunning young woman. The papers willingly ran the photographs. Sobel found Gypsy easy to work with, since she was ready to participate in any escapade that he created.[15] To aid his friends who owned a nightclub, Sobel arranged a bogus contest to replace Gypsy in burlesque as she departed for *Hot Cha!* Gypsy helped a male judge as the women stripped. The evening boosted the nightclub's business and Gypsy's reputation. In New York, when Sobel escorted Gypsy to a dinner party for publishers, he was amazed at her ease in talking about books. During a party given by Broadway columnist Ward Morehouse, Gypsy conversed about Pearl Buck's recently published book, *The Good Earth*. "Rose Louise is the most animated conversationalist in *Hot Cha!* Her wit is swift and terse, her knowledge wide," a columnist proclaimed.[16]

Upon her return to Minsky's, Gypsy hired her own publicist. Articles about Gypsy appeared in men's magazines as well as other venues. Even the young men from the *Princeton Tiger* decided to interview her. Gypsy easily outmatched them. She complained that the *Harvard Lampoon* boys "came into my dressing room in droves and you can't tell me they were all connected with that paper. I never saw such a rowdy crowd in all my life. Yale boys are tough too but Princeton men are nice and mild." When the Princeton novices inquired whether Gypsy would allow her hypothetical daughter to come to a Princeton house party, she retorted, "Hell no, I'd go myself. Just give me an invitation to Princeton and I'm good as there." The Princeton men returned the compliment. In November 1935, the *Princeton Tiger* ran photographs of the university's important athletes and their positions: "Hedblom: Back; Gaffney: Guard." Under "Captain Kelly: End," came "Gypsy Rose: Right End."[17]

Gypsy knew that a sophisticated stripper could fill a news void and sell papers. So she used them to advance her career, just as they used her to compete with their rivals. Tabloids such as the new *Graphic* touted anything to do with sex. Popular syndicated gossip columnists reigned. "A whole lot of credit for my small degree of success goes to the writing fraternity," Gypsy acknowledged. "The Winchells, the Sullivans and the boys who are not even by-lined on their sheets." Gypsy successfully courted these men.

Once when Gypsy saw the popular syndicated gossip columnist Walter Winchell in her audience, she asked him to return the next night. She created a special number based on his current column. Charmed, Winchell always wrote favorable copy. Sexy, funny, and clever, Gypsy provided the perfect subject.[18]

When dealing with the press, Gypsy developed her own style. She only "permits a glimpse of her well-developed mind," one interviewer mused. Like her act, her conversations were more "tease than strip." Although she chattered, she kept verbal and intellectual control of interviews. She told reporters only what she wanted; she rarely, if ever, allowed an unguarded moment.[19]

Thanks to Eddy, Gypsy epitomized glamour and elegance on public occasions. In 1935, she went to the Broadway opening of the smash hit about a circus elephant, *Jumbo*. Wrapped in a full-length ermine coat over a simple, form-fitting white gown, she wore one ring—with a twenty-five-karat diamond Eddy had given her. On another occasion, Eddy persuaded Gypsy to wear a full-length cape made of orchids to the Metropolitan Opera. The press noticed her presence on both occasions.

Gypsy never wavered from her goal. For her, any notice equaled fame, but it required deliberate action. No one understood Gypsy's incredible tenacity and the effort she put into achieving fame. "Mother says I'm the most beautiful naked ass—well, I'm not. I'm the smartest," she remarked to June. Her ambition drove her and kept her in the public eye. When her sister asked about her goal, Gypsy responded that she wanted "to be a legend." Her image and her commercial success were intertwined. Publicity, she said, was "essential for me to gauge what I must do to keep ahead of the procession, because that is just what Gypsy Rose intends doing."[20]

Gypsy even converted an unfortunate event involving the jewelry Eddy had given her into publicity about her glamorous lifestyle. Her affiliation with Waxy Gordon had made gangsters and thugs familiar with her and her taste in expensive accessories. With Waxy safely in prison, other criminals targeted her. In November 1936, thugs mugged her and stole all the jewelry she was wearing. Gypsy lost two diamond and sapphire bracelets, a seven-karat diamond ring, another diamond and sapphire ring, and a pin with pearls, diamonds, and a ruby. She tried to swallow a ring, but the thieves managed to get hold of it and break some of her teeth as well.

"Gypsy Rose Lee Stripped by Burglars," the *New York Post* proclaimed. The rival *New York World* declared, "Six Strip Gypsy Rose Lee and They're Not Teasing." Both articles described how, shortly before midnight, Gypsy entered a Greenwich Village nightclub with two men. A woman known to police as Madame Ladyfinger noticed Gypsy's diamonds and unobtrusively left the club. Around two o'clock, when Gypsy arrived home, six gun-toting thugs greeted her. Her dramatic description of the robbery delighted reporters, and they quoted her suggestive statements, such as "Without my jewels I feel practically naked."[21]

"Gypsy Rose Lee Tangles with the Murder Mob," announced the magazine *Complete Detective Cases*. On the cover, a glamorous Gypsy, wearing a black dress, black satin gloves, and a fur coat, looks distressed. A swarthy man with a mustache is holding her up. The article portrayed Gypsy as a victim of the "murderous Broadway jewel mob." Although Gypsy failed to recognize any of her attackers, Rose was convinced that her daughter knew the gangsters; the thugs who stole her jewelry may at one time have been connected to Waxy Gordon. Gypsy may have felt that not identifying them was safer for her. In any case, the incident provided Gypsy a great deal of publicity.[22]

A few years later, on January 13, 1941, Eddy died of a heart attack at his New York City apartment in the middle of the night. He was forty. When Eddy stayed in the city, he lived the fast life, with heavy drinking and little sleep. Gypsy was performing in Chicago when she received the telegram telling her of Eddy's death. She regretted not being in New York at the time. "Now I'm really alone," Gypsy moaned. "I never felt that way before....I always knew he was there behind me." During sleepless nights, she worried about Eddy's wife finding her letters, some of which were several years old.[23]

Though Gypsy loved Eddy, Eddy's feelings about Gypsy remain less clear. He cared about her a great deal, but he refused to leave his wife and children for her. He found her exciting, and the challenge of transforming her appealed to him. Eddy died before he carried out his promise to provide for Gypsy with a trust fund. His lasting legacy to Gypsy was her image as a glamorous, smart woman and stripper—along with his material gifts, which were worth an occasional insult from Rose about the "flashy jewelry Eddy tosses your way."[24]

By the time of Eddy's death, Gypsy was no longer playing in burlesque houses. She moved along with burlesque as it shed its name and carried its performance style into what was regarded as legitimate entertainment. During the late thirties and early forties, burlesque shifted to more respectable theaters and ultimately to Broadway, drawing middle- and upper-class audiences who paid much higher ticket prices. Burlesque houses had flourished in part because of the popularity of striptease during the Depression. Burlesque as a form of entertainment for lower-class men and mixed audiences died in New York City. Mayor Fiorello H. La Guardia and the coalition that supported him regarded burlesque as corrupt and a danger to public morals, so they endeavored to kill it.[25]

From the early 1930s on, burlesque was subject to constant criticism by censors and periodic attempts at repression by city officials. Gypsy's popular act was among their most visible targets. In April 1931, the police raided Minsky's Republic Theater on the grounds that the show was "thoroughly indecent." The censors objected to Gypsy's sketches set in the exotic tropics, especially when she went "into a clinch with a man in a blackout scene." Salaciously emphasizing the seminude women and this embrace shrouded in suggestive darkness, the newspapers delighted in reporting the police invasion of the burlesque show. Gypsy's witty quips turned this conflict into good publicity. "I wasn't naked. I was completely covered by a blue spotlight," she coyly informed reporters.[26]

Gypsy relished telling the story of the policeman who arrested her and worried about her fleeing. She forced him to stand on the fire escape outside her dressing room while she changed for jail, but "he kept peeking in the window. And he hadn't even bought a ticket for the show." More than one hundred telegrams expressed sympathy and concern for Gypsy after her detention. NEVER MIND, GYPSY, one telegram boasted, YOU'RE A LILY AMONG WEEDS. Another offered MY SERVICES FOR FRIENDLY OR FINANCIAL AID STOP YOU'RE ADORABLE. One cautioned, YOU NEED A PROTECTOR. An "admirer" plaintively wished that he could help because she did not deserve the "cheap publicity." The judge freed her because at no time had she appeared totally nude onstage.[27]

Reform-minded New Yorkers demanded tougher standards. Civic groups and religious organizations exerted constant pressure on the city to shut down the burlesque houses. In fact, Minsky's insistence on owning theaters on Broadway rather than remaining in working-class neighborhoods precipitated the final crisis. All across the country, big cities confined burlesque theaters, sleazy nightclubs, houses of prostitution, gambling dens, and other illicit forms of adult entertainment to specific districts through zoning codes and selective policing. City officials and the police often ignored activities defined as "vice" and allowed these enterprises to operate in certain areas, sometimes in exchange for bribes. Thanks to the Depression, Minsky bought bankrupt theaters on Broadway, and by 1937 the Minsky dynasty had converted seven legitimate theaters to burlesque houses. As burlesque invaded such respectable places, public-spirited groups worried that stripteasing would cheapen all entertainment in the city.

Elected to end corruption and raise civic morals in New York, Fiorello La Guardia felt obligated to take action against burlesque. A former alcoholic who resolved to stay sober, he felt passionately about what he considered vice. As a congressman, he had fought corruption. Reform groups, an interesting mixture of old money, ethnic voters, and labor, supported the Republican La Guardia for three terms from 1934 to 1945. By removing burlesque theaters and forcing stripping into nightclubs, the city attacked physical spaces without really affecting people's morals. The dramatic battle for the virtue of Forty-second Street ran for more than fifty years.

In 1937, however, the New York City government began to close burlesque theaters, permanently ending the fun for audiences of working-class men. Paul Moss, New York City's commissioner of licenses under La Guardia, rejected the Minsky brothers' application for a license. Theaters granted new licenses could not use the terms "burlesque," "striptease," or "Minsky" in their name, on their marquee, or in their advertising.

La Guardia defended Moss against complaints brought by organizations committed to defending freedom of speech and expression. An official of the National Council on Freedom from Censorship criticized the mayor's decision, calling it "the climax of a series of increasingly high-handed acts of totalitarian censorship." Civil liberties activists believed that this monitoring would have a deadening effect on creativity and feared that theater would be scrutinized for any allusion to sexuality and other subjects targeted by the Production Code that determined what could and could not be shown on movie screens. Opposing censorship, southern writer W. J. Cash wrote an editorial for the *Charlotte News* entitled "Phase of Obscenity: The Censor's Lewd Eye Scans Gypsy Rose Lee." Banning burlesque in New York City, he argued, "invariably results in dozens of essentially poisonous and corrupting plays getting off scot free while some sound piece of work, with the breath of life and thought and sound and true morality in it, gets the axe" because it "shocks the notions of convention." The courts, however, agreed with the mayor, and in 1942 New York Supreme Court Justice Aaron J. Levy pronounced burlesque "inartistic filth" and upheld the denial of the license for burlesque theaters.[28]

Gypsy, like W. J. Cash, disagreed with the courts. She pronounced closing burlesque theaters "silly and rather provincial. If anyone's morals could possibly be jeopardized by burlesque, he's pretty far gone anyway." Refusing to accept the notion that her profession was dishonorable and made her unworthy of respect, Gypsy never spoke of stripping as a moral issue. She ignored the conventional double standard that considered strippers to be loose women while the men who enjoyed watching them maintained their social status as respectable gentlemen. Gypsy avenged burlesque's reputation by giving the burlesque theater owner in her first novel Moss's surname.[29]

Gypsy always disputed the idea that burlesque was obscene compared to other popular forms of entertainment. Minsky's offered the finest in burlesque; their shows were extravaganzas. Ziegfeld's *Follies* presented lavish musical productions featuring naked women. Their respectable audiences accepted female nudity as "artistic" and refined. City officials and much of the public considered Minsky productions vulgar and obscene, while audiences viewed Broadway shows such as George White's high-class girly show *Scandals* as legitimate entertainment.

In Gypsy's view, the major differences between burlesque and Broadway were in ticket prices and therefore audiences. The *Follies* charged much more than Minsky's. The most expensive seat at the *Follies* was $3.85, while Minsky rarely went higher than $1.00. Higher admission prices screened out working-class audiences and enhanced the reputation of the entertainment. The *Follies* drew middle- and upper-class male and female patrons. Audiences at the *Follies* behaved in a more acceptable manner than at Minsky's, too. Well-dressed men watching the *Follies* in mixed company did not masturbate in the theater.

For the performers, burlesque theaters proved superior to the nightclubs that replaced them. Theaters built runways that removed performers from the rowdy audience. At nightclub floor shows, men in the audience groped the female performers and expected the strippers and chorus girls to sit with them after the show for more pawing. Nor did burlesque theaters ever serve alcohol. Alcohol ruined the audience, Gypsy thought. "People who are a wonderful audience in a theatre take four drinks in a night club and become absolutely cretins," she complained. "You never know when someone is going to act up on the dance floor" or someone's husband "will have to be carried out."[30]

Without romanticizing the experience, Gypsy appreciated and defended the positive aspects of burlesque. "Old time burlesque was really an institution—you could make a life in it. There was a great deal of esprit de corps." The burlesque theater circuit, unlike nightclubs, fostered a regular ensemble. The women and comics worked together for months, and lasting friendships were formed.[31]

Onstage, Gypsy tried to elevate burlesque even as she planned to leave it. She felt that the character of stripping depended on the performer's attitude. "It's all mental," she explained. "If you think it's vulgar and this and that and the other thing, the audience will think it's vulgar too. But if you approach your work with a clean, aesthetic viewpoint, the audience senses your attitude." Arguing that sheer visual pleasure attracted audiences to stripteasing, Gypsy believed that men attended a "strip-act because they have a keen sense of appreciation for beauty, and more specifically beauty in the raw." Taking jabs at respectable entertainment, she remarked, "the majority of things I've seen that I considered off-color were done by the people who wore clothes, not those who were scantily dressed."[32]

Ironically, Gypsy's new persona made her more uncomfortable with her profession. Always vowing to get of out of burlesque, Gypsy finally left to star in the 1936–37 *Follies*, formerly under the management of Florenz Ziegfeld, who had died in 1932. Even though she felt that public condemnations of burlesque were unfair, Gypsy recognized when she joined the *Follies* that the audience would see her as an immoral burlesque queen rather than as an elegant *Follies* star. Her mother overheard women talking as they left the *Follies* theater: One asked, "Do you really suppose she's as bad as all that?" Disheartened, Gypsy commented to a reporter, "So you see how it is—I have to live down something every time I go out on stage." Gypsy had to prove she was worthy of being in the legitimate theater. According to the *Hot Cha!* press agent, the *Follies* showgirls were opposed to hiring Gypsy, since they would have to "share our dressing rooms and associate with a burlesque queen."[33]

Gypsy realized that stripping, even in the *Follies*, offered her well-paying employment but excluded her from other potential venues. She pronounced her stint in burlesque "a painstakingly planned accomplishment," but she understood that "burlesque is, for an actress, the End of Everything." Gypsy knew the paradoxes inherent in burlesque for a performer with more serious aspirations. "The experience was a selling point for me, professionally, which was good. But it led people to expect me to start tearing my clothes off the minute I entered a drawing room, which was bad." Given her reputation, Gypsy always had to work doubly hard as a performer to be taken seriously. In every venture, she had to prove herself again. The insecurity of her position strengthened her determination to attain perfection "in everything I have and do. *Everything.*"[34]

4

Follies with Girlfriends

During the *Follies* run in Chicago in early 1937, Gypsy appeared eleven times in the show, not because of her extraordinary ability, Gypsy maintained, but because fewer performers were cheaper. Gypsy performed in five comedic sketches with Bobby Clark. In his sketches, Clark played the lecher, with oversized glasses that he drew on his face. In a satire on the New Deal, Gypsy acted as Clark's secretary at the Federal Spending Administration. She also played a sexy nurse and an older woman in a skit in a satire on a popular show, *Major Bowes' Amateur Hour*. In a Baby Snooks scene, Gypsy acted as Fanny Brice's mother. Before the first act's finale, Gypsy performed a striptease. Those "appearances, along with both finales, kept me moving," Gypsy complained wearily.[1]

While starring in the *Follies*, Gypsy cemented two deep friendships, with Fanny Brice, an older star, and June Havoc, her younger sister. Gypsy cherished her close women friends. She rebelled against her mother, who discouraged her daughter's friendships and even set up a virulent competition between Louise and June. With women, Gypsy relaxed offstage. She did not have to remain her onstage self in the way that men expected from her. Gypsy and Fanny Brice performed together in the *Follies*. Demanding almost nothing in return, Brice was the perfect mentor because she knew far more than Gypsy did and was completely noncompetitive. Brice understood Gypsy's act and served as a mirror so Gypsy could see herself in front of audiences.

And Brice possessed something Gypsy had rarely encountered: a big heart. Further enhancing Gypsy's reputation as a sophisticate, Brice taught her invaluable lessons in achieving a sense of style in her dress, furnishings, and artistic expression. She also influenced her political interests. Female friendships and the *Follies* broadened Gypsy in unexpected ways.

Gypsy was the first major stripper to star in the *Follies*. Her reputation for sophistication appealed to the *Follies'* producers. A more prosaic stripper would not have projected the right image, but Gypsy had developed the kind of elegance tailored to the *Follies'* audiences. In contrast to the first time she left burlesque for Ziegfeld's *Hot Cha!* Gypsy already possessed a national reputation. This time, Gypsy bade farewell to burlesque in order to headline in the *Follies*, not to perform in the chorus. Her training in comedy scenes served her well in the *Follies*, whose humor ranged from clever topical satire to the broad physical comedy popular in burlesque.

Gypsy's devotion to cultivating her chic presence on and off the stage brought her public attention. Reviewers responded intensely to her new act. Commenting pretentiously on her routine by using fashionable buzzwords, one wrote that she sublimated "nudity into an esthetic abstraction by singing detachedly of frustration, psychoanalysis, philosophy and vitality." One fan pronounced her "the Voltaire of the twentieth century." Gypsy took her act less seriously, stating forthrightly: "Men don't like me for my mind but for what I don't mind." Lorenzo Hart later parodied her in the musical *Pal Joey* in a song called "Zip." While performing her act, the stripper sadly announced, "Walter Lippmann wasn't brilliant today" and queried, "Will Saroyan ever write a great play?"[2]

The 1936–37 *Follies* sparkled with talent from various fields of entertainment. The ballet choreographer George Balanchine helped with the dance numbers. Composer George Gershwin supplied some of the music. Bob Hope officiated as master of ceremonies. Comedian Bobby Clark, like Gypsy, had begun on the burlesque circuit and moved to the *Follies*. For years "Funny Girl" Fanny Brice had given consistently creative performances in the Ziegfeld *Follies*, and the new producers, the Shuberts, asked her to return. Josephine Baker and actress Eve Arden were also in the cast, performing earlier on the bill than Gypsy.

Like the Minsky brothers and Ziegfeld, the Shuberts creatively presented the supple and youthful female body. Eastern European Jewish immigrants, the Shubert brothers, Lee and J. J. (Jacob), opened theaters across the country starting in the early 1900s. Former rivals of

Ziegfeld, the Shuberts acquired the *Follies* from the Ziegfeld estate. Florenz Ziegfeld lost more than a million dollars in the 1929 stock market crash, and two years later he managed his last *Follies*. When Ziegfeld died in 1932, he left his widow, Billie Burke, with significant debt. But his major legacy, the Ziegfeld name, was a saleable commodity. The Shuberts paid Burke to use the name and staged the new *Follies*.

Gypsy equivocated about joining the *Follies*. Other performers gave working conditions there mixed reviews. In Gypsy's partially autobiographical first novel, she expressed her own ambivalence through her characters. One stripper mused that in the *Follies*, one performed only once a night and did not work on Sundays—"boy, what a racket." Another stripper corrected her: "Racket is right! You rehearse four weeks, spend four more weeks on the road, then come into New York and run four days. . . . Nope, I'll stay in burlesque."[3]

Gypsy's dialogue reflected conversations she had with her closest friend in burlesque, Georgia Sothern. Born Hazel Anderson in Atlanta, Sothern fashioned her stage name after her state and region. She started stripping at Minsky's at fourteen. At first she was jealous of Gypsy, but she soon came to respect her. The redheaded Georgia worked "hot," rapidly gyrating her hips in bumps and grinds to the driving beat of very loud music. As she explained the contrast between her act and Gypsy's: "Our styles were completely apart, like at both ends of the earth, the slow, sedately stalking strip she did and the frenetic hurry-hurry effect of my act." The two strippers became allies rather than competitors. At Minksy's Gypsy created and sewed costumes for Georgia, and they socialized after shows. Gypsy brought Georgia into the world that Eddy had helped open to her. For Georgia, "Gypsy reflected a world that I had never known." Gypsy "enjoyed going to all the better places and I found myself attracted to her and many of the people she knew and our friendship grew more solid every day." Describing how Gypsy was offered a starring role in the *Follies*, Sothern commented, "I remember trying to talk Gypsy out of that one. To this day I am glad that Gypsy was sensible enough never to take my advice. From Ziegfeld the ladder led all the way up for Gyp and never could it have happened to anyone nicer."[4]

Other entertainers loved the *Follies*. Singer and actor Eddie Cantor recalled the show affectionately. He adored acting before society's upper crust. Cantor laughed, "Everybody from the Mayor down, or from the Mayor up, was there. The *Follies'* performers were the elite among entertainers." He added, "We stayed in the finest hotels, we were invited to the finest homes, people considered it a privilege if we talked to them."[5]

Although most *Follies* performers shared Cantor's attitude toward the high-class character of their show, the unpretentious Fanny Brice was unimpressed with *Follies* entertainers. Instead, Brice praised performers she recalled from other, less prestigious venues. "The funny part about burlesque is, the people were so nice. They were always paying off some little house in Long Island. Circus people were the same way, also vaudeville people." Women in burlesque had higher moral standards, she thought, than did the women in the *Follies* chorus. "I noticed the difference when I got into the *Follies*. My season in burlesque, there were twenty chorus girls, and eighteen were virgins. There were hardly any virgins in the *Follies*. If there was one around, I didn't know about it."[6]

Born Fania Borach on the Lower East Side, Brice never hid her working-class immigrant background. Her mother and father owned several bars in New Jersey, and Fanny sang to their customers. Stardom came with Brice's performance in the *Follies* of 1910, where her gift for comedy was among her stellar attractions. People gravitated to Brice's warmth and wit—including lyricist and showman Billy Rose, who married her. Billy Rose remembered the first time he spotted Brice, when she came into his nightclub as part of a large party. Rose proudly enlightened the interviewer: "Did you ever see her walk into a joint? She made the waters part, sonny, and don't you ever forget it."

Brice shared herself with Gypsy. She was intimately acquainted with leftist politics, gangsters, antiques, and painting. Like Brice, Gypsy found room for all these interests. Brice engaged in the easy and mutually beneficial interactions between Jewish performers and Jewish gangsters that occurred so naturally in New York City. Billy Rose declared that Brice had a high "standing...with the hoodlums in this town. In this town and all over the country, they had a big respect for Fanny."[7] Brice's extensive relationships with gangsters surpassed Gypsy's. Her brother Lew, a gambler, mingled with enough suspected criminals for the FBI to keep a close watch on him. The FBI labeled Lew one of its small-time thugs. He was known to be "a swindler, gambler, and friend of Benjamin 'Bugsy' Siegel," a bootlegger during Prohibition. Having divorced her first husband, Frank White, after a brief marriage, Brice lived with, adored, and married Nicky Arnstein, a charming con man. Their troubled relationship was made famous in the musical *Funny Girl*. In 1920, Arnstein stole five million dollars' worth of bonds in New York City. In 1924, a judge sentenced Arnstein to Leavenworth Penitentiary. In 1929, Brice married Billy Rose.[8]

Gypsy and Fanny wrote about each other, describing the sources of their close friendship. Gypsy roomed with Brice during the road version of the 1936–37 *Follies*, which ran for twelve weeks in Chicago. Fanny and Gypsy stayed at the exquisite Sherman House near the theater. They shared a suite and put their maids in another bedroom. When Gypsy had worked in Chicago before, both as a child and as a new performer, she had resided in cheap hotels. Now she stayed in much finer accommodations.

"What Fanny Brice did, I would do," recalled Gypsy. Brice, like Gypsy's mother, was frugal to the point of being tightfisted in some respects while remaining extravagant in others. She expected quality in what she bought. Never a lavish tipper, she teased Gypsy about leaving comparatively generous tips as they left restaurants and hotels; she often yelled, "Tipping like a whore again, eh?" Gypsy recalled Brice telling her, "They respect you more when they know you aren't a sucker." Brice, like Gypsy, carried her own provisions and accounted for their cost. During the train ride to Chicago, Brice carried two beers in her purse and, after giving one to Gypsy, charged her twenty-five cents.

Brice taught Gypsy to focus on the social meanings of consumption. "Spend your money where it shows," Brice advised her. Gypsy followed this edict throughout life, in her public appearances and in the furnishings in her house. "Better still, don't spend it at all," Brice added. "An actor's best friend is money, kid. They can talk all they want about scrapbooks, but it's the bankbooks that count." Brice taught Gypsy the art of frugality, a skill that Gypsy much admired. Entertainers whose earnings and even employment depended on something as ephemeral as popularity had to be concerned about financial security. But Brice, unlike Gypsy's mother, gave very generously to people who worked for her and to charities. She purchased a bicycle for a paperboy at the theater in New York, bought a layette for her doorman's granddaughter, and paid hospital expenses for a wardrobe woman.

As an entertainer, Brice provided a role model for Gypsy. Brice also remained unpretentious, a trait Gypsy publicly espoused and consistently practiced. With Brice, Gypsy wandered through art galleries, antique shops, and museums, excursions that were followed by trips to the racetrack. "I learned a lot from Fanny that season. Not just about show business, but about furniture and friendship, and paintings, and pearls—and how to be a lady, even when I was taking my clothes off," Gypsy recalled with admiration. Gypsy later quipped that Brice and her third husband, Billy Rose, taught her "the difference between Rubens, the painter, and Reuben's, the delicatessen." Brice found art relaxing and enjoyable and was something of a painter herself. She once painted Gypsy as a nude in the style of Degas. Gypsy treasured the portrait. Gypsy, too, soon discovered that painting offered her a way to express herself artistically. To return the compliment of her own portrait, she painted Brice.[9]

Brice may also have influenced Gypsy politically as they discussed their views of current events. Gypsy had been exposed to Communists in New York City, stopping to listen to left-wing speakers in Union Square on her way to work at the burlesque theaters.[10] According to the FBI, the same year Brice and Gypsy starred in the *Follies*, Brice had joined the Los Angeles Communist Party.[11]

Brice's alleged membership in the Communist Party, which attracted thousands of progressives, did not mean she was un-American or supported the violent overthrow of the government. At that time, the party tripled its membership through broadening its appeal and extending its outreach. In 1935, Earl Browder, head of the American Communist Party, promoted the popular front, a coalition that encouraged party activists to ally with labor unions, which were organizing mass production industries such as coal, steel, and automobiles, during the late 1930s. The party maintained a vehemently antifascist viewpoint, appealing to liberal Jews like Brice who believed in civil liberties. The alliance with the popular front gave Communism a wider appeal.

For many thinking people in New York City and across the country, Communist and socialist ideas made sense in the 1930s. To caring liberals, the Great Depression proved that unrestricted capitalism did not work. In his first term, Franklin Roosevelt and his administration followed many of former president Herbert Hoover's policies and offered no radical solutions to improve the economy. Activists on the left discussed issues of social welfare and civil rights for minority groups. The major parties shied away from such topics, as did the mainstream press. In order to pass New Deal legislation, Roosevelt needed the backing of white southern Democratic congressmen. To obtain their support, the president refused to promote civil rights legislation, even antilynching laws that would protect African Americans from racist mobs intent on defending white supremacy. When Joseph Stalin signed a nonaggression pact with Adolf Hitler in 1939, many members of the Communist Party were disillusioned, but after Hitler invaded Russia they rallied around the United States' new ally. American Communists ignored Stalin's brutality to millions of his people, but so, too, did the United States government when it suited its purpose.

In addition to shaping Gypsy's political views, Brice helped further her urbane image. Brice offered to sell Gypsy her Rolls-Royce town car since she never drove it but had to pay to keep it in a garage. Brice explained to Gypsy: "It cost me fourteen thousand new, but I'll sell it cheap. I feel like a damned fool riding around in it, but it would be a swell publicity gimmick for you." The car had fewer than six thousand miles on it and featured a chauffeur's seat out in the open. Brice ultimately gave Gypsy the car, but to avoid embarrassing her, Gypsy recalled, Brice said, "Tell you what, you give me fifty bucks for the car and I'll throw in the fur lap robe."[12] Brice had correctly assessed the car's impact, if not its value. Riding in a Rolls garnered Gypsy more publicity. With a maid at the theater helping her prepare for her act, her chauffeur and Rolls, Gypsy enhanced her upper-class image. According to Gypsy, "The customers loved it." She added triumphantly, "The gag worked." Gypsy's fame spiraled.[13]

During the *Follies* run, Brice helped Gypsy negotiate the transition from burlesque to more "respectable" theater, and later she remembered Gypsy's insecurity. At first, the Shuberts were not quite sure how to use Gypsy other than to show off her body. They "warned her that she was playing for a high-class audience—and would have to be more subtle," even though Gypsy had successfully performed before upper-class males in her audiences for years. "You mean that I can't throw my garter belt into the orchestra pit and say 'gone with the wind'?" she fretted. That was "exactly what they meant," she learned, even though referencing current best-selling literature such as *Gone with the Wind* in her act was a trademark of hers.

Brice knew show business and mankind far better than the *Follies* producers did. When she found Gypsy terrified and crying on opening night, Brice offered her the best advice: "Listen, kid, I played burlesque before you were born, and I played Broadway a long time. Believe me the four-dollar chumps [high-class ticket buyers] on Broadway go for the same stuff they love on Fourteenth Street. Just go out and do your stuff."[14] Gypsy won over the Shuberts and kept her act much the same as it had been in burlesque. Actually wearing less than she had at Minsky's, at one point Gypsy stripped down to a bow glued on each breast and a very small piece of satin below the waist.[15]

Even with her growing fame in the *Follies*, Gypsy's fear that she had "no talent" continued to plague her. Her anxiety increased as she grew more successful. After developing a serious ulcer, she was hospitalized in 1934 and again during the 1936 *Follies*. Brice wisely explained, "It's having your name in lights that's done it. You've got a billing ulcer, kid. Getting to be a star is easy; nobody gets ulcers on the way up. It's staying there that's hard."[16] But Brice underestimated the factors contributing to Gypsy's recurring ulcers. Heredity made her prone to ulcers—her father suffered periodically from the same affliction—but Gypsy's own habits made her ulcers worse. Although ulcers are caused by bacteria, they are easily exacerbated by drinking and smoking, as well as by stress. In all these, Gypsy remained a champion. Drinking had become an integral part of her identity and image. She drank to calm her nerves at the theater and at home, as well as in social settings. Gypsy's alcohol intake slowed after her first hospitalization for ulcers, but she continued smoking cigarettes. In the final analysis, Gypsy suffered from the stresses of creating and sustaining her identity as Gypsy Rose Lee, not just the anxieties that followed her success onstage.

As her relationship with Brice developed, Gypsy also began a lasting friendship with her sister. Their bond endured, with highs and lows, until Gypsy's death. June set the same high standards for her sister's career and personal life that she established for herself. Professional and personal interests sometimes brought them into conflict, but as adults they did not allow such issues to divide them for long.

June, like Gypsy, performed constantly in the late 1920s and early 1930s, but she received much less compensation than her sister. After divorcing her husband, June supported herself as an accomplished marathon dancer. Her career started when she was hired as a tap dancer for five dollars during one of the marathon breaks. She realized that marathon participants could earn more than tap dancers, especially if they were among the last dancers left standing. June's good health and tenacity underlay her extraordinary endurance. Her slender, even frail appearance enhanced her appeal to spectators. The rules for a marathon required that dancers stay on their feet, moving around the dance floor, for forty-five minutes out of each hour. Participants slept while dancing, as their partners kept them moving. Judges disqualified those couples whose feet did not move every three seconds. During the Depression, audiences were drawn to this extreme form of cheap live entertainment that prized endurance over all else.

Horrified, Rose bemoaned June's failure to fulfill her aspirations for her talented younger daughter. "A marathon dancer! Dancing in a marathon after all I sacrificed for her!" Rose wailed to Gypsy. "She could have been a big star. If only she'd listened to me. If only she'd waited. I could have done for her what I've done for you." Few mothers celebrated their daughters' careers in striptease as Rose did, much less took credit for their success in an occupation conventionally regarded as disreputable. To Rose, public acclaim and financial success were everything. Rose lost interest in her younger daughter as soon as she lost the status and income of a star.[17]

While June danced on the marathon circuit, she was courted by a married man, fell in love with him, and became pregnant. He offered to divorce his wife and marry June, but she refused. Like the rest of the women in her family, she valued her independence. She also wanted to act, and, like her sister, she willingly sacrificed to achieve her goal. So June gave up marathon dancing as too stressful and came to New York City, where she hoped to be able to support herself and, all too soon, her child. She lived with Rose and worked as a model and, like many women during the Depression, at any other casual job she could obtain.

Appalled by June's pregnancy, Gypsy and her mother were both convinced the baby would interfere with June's acting and ultimately ruin her career. Gypsy suggested that June release custody of the baby to their mother. She vehemently refused.

Rose had recently converted her apartment into a salon for lesbians, who rarely felt comfortable in nightclubs. Rose charged the women for spaghetti dinners and watered-down drinks. According to June, her mother's homosexuality during the 1930s stemmed from her belief that all men were untrustworthy. "She turned toward her own sex," June explained. Occasionally Gypsy dominated the party, drinking and telling stories. She also paid June's rent to Rose, only to learn that June also gave Rose money for room and board.[18]

In April 1935, June gave birth to her daughter, April, and just a year later, she starred in the musical *Forbidden Melody*, receiving excellent reviews.[19] As June grew more successful and self-confident, her relationship with her older sister matured. As Gypsy recalled, "When June first came to New York we had met almost like strangers." In the fall of 1936, Gypsy and June met weekly for dinner at a Chinese restaurant. According to Gypsy, they stayed "until the waiters began piling the chairs on the tables. There was so much, it seemed, to talk about: her marriage, divorce, and April, the baby. My Eddy, his wife and, of course, Mother." Their problems with Rose cemented their relationship. Rose had shown little sympathy for her out-of-work, unmarried, pregnant younger daughter. Rose focused all her energy on Gypsy. As Gypsy's fame grew, Rose's interference increasingly grated on her.

Gypsy attempted to put some physical distance between herself and Rose. During the burlesque years, they had moved to New York City together, and at first they lived together in inexpensive accommodations. When Gypsy moved to an apartment on Gramercy

Park, she decided not to let her mother live with her any longer. By that time, Eddy and Gypsy were engaged in an intimate relationship and she was recreating herself as an upper-class woman. Living with her mother detracted from her new image as an urbane striptease artist and limited her freedom of movement. So Gypsy gave Rose money to rent her own apartment in New York and kept Fridays for her mother. Their once-a-week chats ended a few years later, never to resume.[20]

In New York City, the sisters finally developed an alliance to protect themselves from their mother. On many levels, Rose never accepted Gypsy and June casting her off once they succeeded as adults. Rose had lived through both of them professionally, emotionally, and financially. At the same time, she could never replace her daughters. They gave her excitement, status, and a mission. Throughout her life, amid her own tumultuous relationships with other people, Rose remained maniacally preoccupied with June and Gypsy.

Along with commiserating with each other over their problems with their mother, June and Gypsy talked about their ambitions. "June had definite ideas about where she was going," since she knew she wanted to act, Gypsy later recalled. The sisters confided in each other about all aspects of their lives, and they were more honest with each other than with anyone else.[21] One of the few people who could be completely honest with Gypsy, June was her biggest fan and harshest critic—after Gypsy herself. June disapproved of Gypsy's profession. June expected more from Gypsy than stripping, even if Gypsy stripped on Broadway at the famous *Follies*. Emphatically, June told her, "You can't go on doing this same act all your life, Gypsy. You have to have an aim, something real to shoot for." While publicly self-confident, Gypsy vacillated about her goals when she spoke privately with her sister. Deeply insecure about her own talent, haunted by an anxiety her mother had instilled and cultivated in her, she answered, "I'm a Hard-boiled Rose? That's the only success I can remember. From Hard-boiled Rose to Gypsy Rose—the story of my life." On that occasion June suggested that Gypsy consider writing, a respectable and more intellectual career.[22]

During this period, Fanny Brice suggested that Gypsy raise money for various political and social causes. Gypsy focused on benefit performances for social welfare charities and labor unions. In 1936, her numerous charity appearances included the Beaux-Arts Ball, where famous architects dressed up as their buildings, staged that year for the relief of unemployed architects. Gypsy also participated in the Grand Street Boys Benefit for economically deprived youth. In February 1937, while performing in Chicago, Gypsy took part in a charity ball sponsored by the Department of Sociology at Northwestern University to raise money for its settlement house program serving impoverished immigrant neighborhoods. The same month, Brice, Gypsy, and Bobby Clark performed for a Stage Hands Ball, an event that supported the International Alliance of Theatrical Stage Employees, a union representing stagehands and movie theater projectionists.[23]

As Gypsy had hoped, starring in the *Follies* led to appearances in more respectable entertainment venues. On November 23, 1936, an early issue of *Life* magazine ran a photograph of Gypsy taken by Alfred Eisenstaedt at the NBC studios. While sitting in front of a mirror, Gypsy fixed her makeup. Seemingly oblivious to the camera, she looked luscious in a low-cut evening gown. *Life* frequently provided tasteful sexual titillation for its readers. Her picture carried the caption: "She has not retired. From being an obscure strip artist, her success in the *Follies* has made her shape familiar to thousands. A recent guest on Rudy Vallee's hour, her voice was heard by millions." The beautiful and photogenic Gypsy offered a perfect combination of naughty and nice for magazines and newspapers. *Life* courted Gypsy, starting a love affair that lasted throughout her life. In December 1936, the respectable *Collier's* magazine ran a feature on Gypsy that included a picture showing a glimpse of her breast wrapped in fur. The article stressed her upper-class following.[24]

Her new fame next elicited interest from Hollywood. In the fall of 1936, Gypsy took a screen test for Twentieth Century–Fox, performing some of her regular routines in front of the camera. She asked radio newscaster Lowell Thomas to watch, since she wanted a live audience. Thomas recalled that "it was beguiling." The studio managers lusted after Gypsy to such an extent that they bought out Gypsy's *Follies* contract with the Shuberts for $20,000. She signed with Twentieth Century–Fox in January 1937.[25]

Just before she left for Hollywood, Gypsy had to appear at the Municipal Court in New York to respond to a suit brought by her booking agents at William Morris. They argued that they possessed exclusive rights to represent her, and that she had to pay them the usual commission for her Hollywood contract even though their agency had not negotiated it. While working with the William Morris firm, Gypsy hired two other booking agents, including her personal manager, Irving Sherman. The judge suggested that Gypsy not be penalized because her lawyers and the Actors' Equity Association had erroneously advised her that the Morris contract was void. The parties should, he said, try to reach an agreement before he issued a judgment.

Out of court, Gypsy and the three agencies decided that Gypsy would pay each of them one-third of the 10 percent commission.

Gypsy defended her actions by declaring on the witness stand, "Of course I'm only the guy that's gonna do all the work." Reacting to William Morris's demand for a full 10 percent of her Hollywood earnings, she declared, "I won't kick in with another slim dime." Finally, she noted if they did not "hurry up and agree, I'll miss my train to Hollywood and we'll all have another broken contract to worry us."[26]

This incident was only the first of many legal problems Gypsy faced in her career. A shrewd businesswoman, she wanted full control professionally; she always felt that her agents never worked hard enough for her, and she routinely disputed their fees. In the press, Gypsy expressed her anger over the court case. "When I was in burlesque not one [agent] wanted a piece of me," she raged. "When I got the Hollywood contract—and I do mean when *I* got it—they all sued." The hypocrisy infuriated her. "The four years they've handled me they haven't gotten me so much as an Elks smoker! NOT ONE DATE!" Responsible in large part for her own success, she hated others taking any credit—or, even more important, money.[27]

When Gypsy left burlesque for the *Follies*, the move represented the possibility of escaping a career about which she was ambivalent. She went to Hollywood for the same reason: to finish with stripping once and for all. After achieving the status of a Hollywood actress, she remained unsympathetic with women with less drive. During an interview in the Twentieth Century–Fox cafeteria, Gypsy asked why the stock women, often used as extras in movies, did not attempt to look more glamorous while eating lunch there. Someone might discover them while they ate, she argued.

Her companions informed her that the stock women knew they would never break into the movies and had fallen into a rut. "People like that make me furious," she responded. "There isn't any such thing as a rut." Gypsy continued vehemently, "There isn't a spot in the world that can't be used as a stepping stone." She compared the stock women with the strippers at Minsky's. They were "hopeless. They had just as much chance as I had but I'm the only one who ever got out of the rut they thought they were in." Invoking memories of traveling with her mother, Gypsy recounted being stranded in Miami. She had learned that "you may be out of a job and not have a dime, but what of it. You can pitch a tent in the park and put on a show." Now she had finally managed through her own efforts to leave burlesque. "Once you get out, something happens to you inside. Nothing can stop you."[28]

5

The Rise and Fall of Louise Hovick

The Hollywood that Gypsy entered in April 1937 had recently undergone profound changes. The full-length talkies, shown first in October 1927, were now entrenched. To help audiences forget about the Depression for a few hours, movie studios produced comedies such as *It Happened One Night* with Clark Gable and Claudette Colbert and musicals such as *The Wizard of Oz*. Women formed an increasing proportion of movie audiences, and studios sought to appeal to their interests. Studio heads looked to the stage for talent and signed performers from vaudeville and *Follies* acts. The Depression bankrupted some studios and strengthened the survivors, resulting in a major consolidation of the industry. Movies became big business. Studios grew cautious, resisting unionization, trying constantly to lower costs, and counting on the star system to make money. Although popular stars were paid well, actors had no influence on the roles they played and the movies they made. If actors refused to perform in a movie they felt was substandard, their contracts allowed the studio to suspend them without pay and prohibit them from working anywhere else. Through binding seven-year contracts, the studios dictated all facets of their stars' lives, not least their images.[1]

In the early 1920s, the mysterious murder of director William Desmond Taylor and the drug-related death of actor Wallace Reid tarnished the industry's reputation. Mary Pickford's divorce in Reno, in 1920, scandalized the American public. Pickford's remarriage less than one month later to Douglas Fairbanks strongly hinted at adultery, sullying her status as "America's Sweetheart." The arrest of popular actor Fatty Arbuckle following the death of a young actress after a wild party in 1921 triggered a scandal involving sex and violence as well as alcohol. Although Arbuckle was ultimately acquitted of manslaughter, police originally accused him of raping the young woman and killing her through overzealous sex. Even more lurid versions of her demise circulated in the media. This shocking story helped sink Hollywood's reputation even further.

Given these scandalous events, in 1922, the heads of the movie production companies, including Sam Goldwyn and Lewis J. Selznick, invited Will Harrison Hays to head the newly created Motion Picture Producers and Distributors of America, Inc. (MPPDA). Appointed U.S. postmaster general by President Warren G. Harding in 1922, Hays had been responsible for prosecuting the shipment of "obscene" material, including birth control information, through the U.S. mail. Known as the "movie czar," he reviewed movies before their release. By 1937, movie companies anxiously sanitized their movies to avoid censorship by the Hays Office. While the Hays Office did not have governmental authority, it was effective in getting studios to conform to the Production Code standards.

Hays himself repudiated the word "censorship," deeming it "contrary to everything our nation fought for at Valley Forge and Bunker Hill.... Besides, it doesn't work." For the MPPDA, Hays preferred the term "self-regulation." Although an elder in the Presbyterian Church, he formed an alliance with the powerful Catholic Church to scrutinize movies. Church officials, also interested in upholding moral standards, often agreed with Hays's decisions about movies and would mount campaigns to mobilize the church's extensive membership to support Hays's pronouncements. Since the movie industry feared boycotts after a movie opened in theaters, film companies cooperated with Hays before they released a movie.

On March 31, 1930, the MPPDA established the Production Code to ensure that movies upheld a high moral tone. "Hence the sympathy of the audience shall never be thrown to the side of crime, wrong-doing, evil or sin," declared the Production Code. The largest section of the code concentrated on sex. Movies had to uphold the sanctity of marriage and the home. Adultery was never to be "presented attractively." The code prohibited such topics as "sex perversion" (homosexuality), "white slavery" (prostitution), sex across the color line, "sex hygiene" (information about sex and reproduction), and "venereal diseases" (STDs, mostly syphilis and gonorrhea).[2]

Hays became Gypsy's nemesis in Hollywood. Darryl F. Zanuck of Twentieth Century–Fox ran into resistance as soon as he signed Gypsy to a contract. The Legion of Decency, an organization established in 1933 by Catholic bishops, usually protested only the content of a film rather than a particular actor. For Gypsy, the organization made an exception. The Legion encouraged church groups and mothers' clubs to oppose Gypsy's movie career because of her previous success as a striptease artist. Zanuck received four thousand letters. The well-organized letter-writing campaign contended that Gypsy would contaminate Hollywood and threatened a boycott of her films. With such headlines as "Is Sex Coming Back to Hollywood?" editorials in trade papers raised the specter of a return to movies before "self-regulation." Allowing Gypsy to act in films, they said, threatened to throw movies back to their sordid past, with their blatant sexuality and occasional exposed breast.[3]

To defend its hiring of Gypsy, Twentieth Century–Fox countered with a form letter, saying, "We are not seeking to exploit her through sensationalism." The studio assured the naysayers that Gypsy's parts would not offend the audiences and asked "that you judge her worthiness as a screen artist solely in the light of her future appearances." Keeping these promises and protecting its revenues required Twentieth Century–Fox to control Gypsy's image carefully.[4]

Will Hays offered a compromise in which the studio would not bill Gypsy as Gypsy Rose Lee but would use Louise Hovick, a variation of her birth name. The name change, accepted by Zanuck, signaled an attempt to shed Gypsy's reputation as a stripper. The Hays Office also planned to review every movie in which Gypsy appeared to make sure it was acceptable. Publicly, Gypsy responded to the Hays Office nonchalantly: "People will forget the name and recognize the body, so what's the difference?" Gypsy correctly guessed the newspapers' reaction. The press announced, "Gypsy Rose Lee Stripped—But Only of Name." Many reporters simply put the name Gypsy Rose Lee in parentheses after her movie name.[5]

Typically, Gypsy tried to defuse the tense situation with humor. On her arrival in Hollywood, she wore a heavy coat with a luxurious fur collar. A reporter pointed out that the warm Hollywood weather made a coat unnecessary, but Gypsy refused to remove it and quipped, "It might be misinterpreted."[6] The reporters, she explained, would be disappointed because she was not going to shed anything in their presence. She also acknowledged that Gypsy Rose Lee was not a good moniker for a serious actress.

Gypsy swore, however, that she was "GOING to be an actress, anyway." She ended more lightly, "At least, I'm going to try very hard, and if I'm cute in this picture, then I'll do another one right away."[7]

To distance herself from her former occupation, Gypsy increased her fastidiousness regarding how she appeared in photographs. The studio submitted countless publicity pictures of its own to the Hays Office. Hays approved very few. Such cautiousness frustrated photographers. Frequently, newspapers ran publicity photographs of her from the Follies—which displayed large portions of her legs and shoulders—rather than her demure Hollywood shots.

In New York, she sustained wonderful relationships with photographers, but in Hollywood those associations soured. One man with a camera hid in her dressing room shower hoping to shoot some candid pictures surreptitiously. Gypsy drenched him by turning on the water. When he complained that his camera had rusted, she responded unsympathetically that the present condition of his camera was fine with her.[8]

The press did not intend to let Gypsy forget her professional roots. On Gypsy's arrival, the *Los Angeles Daily News* announced, "Welcome Wasted—Gypsy Dressed." Columnists always mentioned some aspect of burlesque when reviewing her movie performances, even when they complimented her. After one of her movies, the *New York Herald* proclaimed, "Louise Hovick—better remembered as Gypsy Rose Lee— has given up stripping to play a sultry siren and demonstrates that she has talents for more then undressing." The press did not acknowledge that Gypsy displayed her acting ability when she stripped. During Gypsy's stay in Hollywood, one comedian observed, "She runs the gamut of emotions from A to G-String." Zanuck disliked the publicity because it reinforced her image as a stripteaser, which the Hays Office found offensive.[9]

Gypsy, too, complained about the reporters. "Whenever any bum takes off her clothes in public, the paper talks about her doing a Gypsy Rose Lee. You would think I was a sort of international nudist," she objected. She preferred that the press see her career in Hollywood as a "triumph for dear old 14th Street." She proved that strippers possessed other talents, and the press frustrated her by rarely getting the point.[10]

On her arrival in Hollywood, Gypsy confessed to the press that she was "nervous" because she was camera shy. She knew little about moviemaking and lacked experience acting for film. She even admitted that she had not seen a movie since *Mutiny on the Bounty* was released more than a year earlier. Gypsy acknowledged she had signed the contract before she had read the script for her first film. She said simply, "I like working in pictures, I hope pictures like me."[11]

Intimidated by the official censor and the aroused public, Zanuck toned down Gypsy's humor and sexuality. The degree of control studios exercised over actors astounded Gypsy. Her naïveté about Hollywood left her totally unprepared to deal with her situation. The studio paid Gypsy two thousand dollars a week for her two years in Hollywood, so Zanuck wanted to get his money's worth. He demanded that she act in a demure manner and took the slink out of her walk. The changes annoyed Gypsy, although she attempted to fit his image of respectability.[12]

Gypsy acceded to the studio to a limited extent. For a short time, she gave up her name and her identity. Even while she struggled as a legitimate actress, she rebelled. In spite of the protests against her appearance in movies, Gypsy never fully repudiated her previous career while in Hollywood. As she had always maintained, she stripped for the money and had always expected other work. "Of course, I would rather play straight dramatic roles than continue with burlesque work, who wouldn't?" she protested. But she added dangerously, "I know that my strip tease act helped me a great deal. It gave me more poise and grace." A confession that burlesque was immoral might have helped her with Hays and the Catholic Church.[13]

The movies in which Gypsy starred mixed screwball comedy with musicals. Most often these movies revolved around a poor, virtuous girl who won the wealthy guy through luck, pluck, and hard work. Marriage was the final reward in this gendered twist on the Horatio Alger story. In film after film, Gypsy played the cruel, calculating, rich woman who lost the guy. Her behavior signaled a predatory, unnatural woman. Providing escapist fare well suited to the Depression, the films played on the hope that anyone could become rich.[14]

In 1937, the studio released *You Can't Have Everything*, Gypsy's first movie. In its plot about turning an unsuccessful play into a musical, an alcoholic director, George McCrae (played by Don Ameche), falls in love with a starving playwright, Judith Poe Wells (Alice Faye). Wells's determination to establish herself as a serious writer and the director's marriage to Lulu Riley (Gypsy) thwarts their relationship. Nevertheless, in the process the author reforms the director. As the spoiled hussy Lulu, Gypsy provided a perfect foil for Alice Faye's noble character, who sings several numbers and stars in the musical.

Gypsy's appearance in *You Can't Have Everything* received mixed reviews. *Variety* raved, "Sensational is the screen debut of Gypsy Rose Lee," pronouncing Gypsy "a potentially excellent actress, dominating every scene in which she gets a chance." The positive reviews took her lack of experience in film and her prior stage career into account. Favorable reviews often added such caveats as "She handles herself with poise, and except for a bit of bad luck on a couple of tough lines of dialogue, there is no indication that she is an inexperienced actress." Other reviewers believed she possessed a good comic sense. In an optimistic assessment, one writer felt that with a "little more experience in shading her lines" she "should make an altogether competent actress" and closed by stating, "I would be last to throw the first stone."

Other reviewers willingly hurled boulders. The movie "will go down in history and we are careful not to say how far down as the first time a strip tease artist has appeared before her public without revealing anything, not even her ability," complained columnist Frank Nugent. One reviewer added, "With its customary perverse generosity, Hollywood gave Gypsy the two things she needed least: another name and several complete changes of clothing." She looked stunning in the clothes she wore, and, in fairness, her acting proved adequate for the part she played. Had it not been for her previous fame as a stripper, the critics might have been kinder to her.[15]

The same year, *Follies* performer Eddie Cantor starred in *Ali Baba Goes to Town*, with Gypsy playing a prominent role. After falling off a train, a hobo lands in a film set for a movie about the Near East. Given the backdrop, the tramp dreams he is Ali Baba's son and the new prime minister. In a gentle spoof of the New Deal, he establishes projects similar to Roosevelt's Works Progress Administration to help end unemployment, and he introduces both democracy and jazz to the population. Gypsy plays a scheming sultan's wife. Once again, Zanuck dressed Gypsy fully.

After her second movie, Gypsy began to chafe at the restrictions Zanuck imposed on her acting in order to pacify Hays. The studio's removal of a scene in which she made love to Cantor annoyed her. While her reviews mentioned how lovely she looked, none of them reported favorably on her acting. She commented in the press that she would prove to those movie moguls that she could do comedy parts and indicated that she preferred to return to the stage.[16]

The next year, however, Gypsy starred in *Sally, Irene,* and *Mary*. This musical comedy centered on three manicurists who desired to sing professionally. Singer Tommy Reynolds (played by Tony Martin, then Alice Faye's husband) is caught between Joyce Taylor (Gypsy), a gold digger, and Sally Day (Alice Faye), while a rich, potbellied Eastern European baron has fallen for Sally. Trying to buy Tommy's love, Joyce invests in a musical for him. But he refuses to be bought. Down to their last penny, the four singers (Sally, Irene, Mary, and Tommy) have their pride intact but no work until Mary inherits a leaky boat. Their agent secretly persuades Joyce and the baron to invest in turning the tub into a showboat. Of course, the showboat achieves huge success and provides an excuse for more musical numbers by the stars. On opening night, Gypsy and the baron meet and are captivated by each other in a typical Hollywood happy ending. One review described Gypsy as "adequate." As with *Ali Baba*, most of the press commented favorably on her appearance but ignored her acting.[17]

In 1938, Twentieth Century–Fox gave Gypsy an insultingly small part in *My Lucky Star*, a vehicle for skater Sonja Henie. The studio cast Gypsy as the evil wife of lecherous George Cabot Jr. (Cesar Romero), who falls for the saintly Kristina Nelson (Henie). Although Gypsy appeared in only a few scenes, she always looked enchanting. But her performance was hampered by stiffness in her acting. For the fourth time, the studio had cast her as the unfunny bad girl in a weak comedy. By this point, Gypsy knew that her Hollywood career had failed.

Only once did Zanuck allow Gypsy a comedic role. In *Battle of Broadway*, released in 1938, Gypsy finally broke her typecasting, but the film could not salvage her screen career. The plot revolves around two American Legion members who leave their Pennsylvania steel town and go to a convention in New York to break up an alleged affair between their boss's smitten son and a showgirl, Linda Lee, portrayed by Gypsy. The two yokels become infatuated with the woman. Soon after, their boss meets her, begins an affair with her, and then marries her.

Gypsy finally received the role and reviews she wanted. As performer Linda Lee, Gypsy sang two songs in the film. The part allowed her to rely on her humor and sexiness, and Gypsy liked her part better than any of the other movie roles in the 1930s. One reviewer, who confessed that she had not liked Gypsy in previous films, admitted she had "real charm" and gained "in screen confidence all the time." A columnist commented, "For the first time on the screen she looks beautiful, sings and has definite charm." Handling "the feminine lead with just the necessary sex appeal," she was impressive "with her natural manner and talent for light comedy." Many recognized that her acting had improved.[18]

Battle of Broadway came too late, however, to save Gypsy's Hollywood career. The studio had vacillated about whether to use Gypsy in *My Lucky Star*. After the film was completed, Gypsy asked to be released from her contract early, and the studio eagerly complied. Speaking about Hollywood, Gypsy declared, "I was very dissatisfied with my work there."

Hays telephoned Gypsy before she left Hollywood and threatened that if she reestablished herself as Gypsy Rose Lee she would never work in the movie business again. When Gypsy told the press about the call, she humorously recounted the irony of the conversation: Hays, who had insisted that the studio change her name, called her "Miss Lee" rather than "Miss Hovick" throughout. Even he never fully accepted her movie name or identity.[19]

For Gypsy, the best part of her movie career entailed not shedding her clothes before an audience. She adored wearing beautiful clothes and keeping them on in the movies. As she tried to determine what had gone wrong in Hollywood, Gypsy recognized her lack of preparation. Her experience onstage was not helpful for the movies. Onstage, Gypsy could remain the center of everyone's focus. In the movies, she learned that if "you time a scene carefully, saving the right expression to climax a certain situation," you will be disappointed. "When you see the scene in the cutting room you find that your carefully saved right expression never appears. At the psychological moment when you were giving your facial all, the camera was focused on the butler bringing in the drinks." Onstage, Gypsy's act flowed logically from her dramatic entrance to a stunning climax. But movie directors did not shoot scenes in sequence, and she found skipping around confusing. She had mistakenly believed that directors filmed movies from the first scene sequentially.[20]

Gypsy understood that she should have insisted on better roles. She had an excellent sense of what characters were well suited to her. She accepted her limitations. "I know I could never play *Camille*, and I wouldn't try. I'll leave that to Garbo, my favorite actress." In her best imitation of her mother, she contended, "I know I can't dance or sing, but I can play sophisticated comedy."[21]

Gypsy correctly identified all her problems: "I was not a tremendous success. It was mainly my fault that I did not click on the Coast. I do know that my make-up was all wrong. I was a trifle overweight, and the casting left something to be desired." Gypsy chose not to fit the Hollywood body image. Rejecting dieting, she ate only one large meal a day but devoured whatever she craved. Drinking a vegetable essence throughout the rest of the day sustained her.[22]

Gypsy's food choices reflected her philosophy toward her career. In one of her first encounters with Hollywood reporters, they ate at a cafeteria. She ignored the soup and fruit cocktail. "I'm a meat and potatoes girl," she explained. "I hate the preliminaries and like to get down to fundamentals right away."[23] Gypsy also adored Hollywood's fancy ice-cream parlors. Several columnists, particularly women, commented on Gypsy's eating habits. They exclaimed that no starlet ate with Gypsy's abandon. Bravely, Gypsy refused to change her menu for Hollywood. "I could have lost weight easily. I could have stopped eating pork chops, and potatoes and gravy, and pie, much as I love them, but I just didn't," Gypsy said. She went on to defend her appetite: "I weighed then, just what I do now; that's 130 pounds. It's really not too much for my height. But the cameras made me look heavier."[24]

Everyone seemed aware of Gypsy's failure in Hollywood. On one occasion, desperately trying to reach June, Gypsy told the operator that she was trying to make an emergency call. When the operator asked if it was prompted by a medical crisis, Gypsy replied in the negative. Explaining that she wanted to help her sister decide on a movie part, she heard the operator reply condescendingly, "Well, I don't see what good your advice would do. You didn't do so well out there yourself, you know."[25] People remembered Gypsy's disasters. When she returned to Hollywood during the war, she applied for a gas ration book. After she explained that she planned to live in California for at least a year but her contract might be extended, the dour gas clerk asked her why she displayed such optimism since she had done so poorly the first time.[26]

A few reporters defended Gypsy against all the negative reviews. One writer concluded, "Let it be said to her credit that Miss Hovick looked positively radiant and displayed dominant, dramatic determination that could have been developed into stellar possibilities." The article fingered the villain in the demise of Gypsy's Hollywood career: "It is presumed, the Hays office was not at all assured that the public could be made to forget the former specialty of abundant appeal, and Miss Louise Hovick became, once more, Gypsy Rose Lee upon leaving the movies."[27]

Gypsy's problems escalated while she was in Hollywood. She never adapted to the star system. She rejected a glamorous lifestyle off the set. Right from the start, she lived more simply than she had in New

York with Eddy as her companion. Refusing a wealthy façade, she lived in a five-room bungalow. She sent money to her mother and bought annuities to be prepared for her future. Demure in public, she often skipped the popular spots, believing in "the simple life for me."[28]

Gypsy never fawned over Hollywood stars, which aspiring actresses were expected to do. She rarely socialized or mixed with what she labeled the "Norma Shearer–Clark Gable axis." Actress Norma Shearer was married to producer Irving G. Thalberg, and together they wielded considerable power in Hollywood; Gable, "the King of Hollywood," appeared with her in three films. In contrast, Gypsy enjoyed the people she knew in burlesque, particularly Fanny Brice and Rags Ragland, a comic. Worse, from Zanuck's viewpoint, her working-class roots surfaced in Hollywood, as she entertained the grips and electricians from the studio. Gypsy complained that the studio "wanted me to play down my background and act sedate"—surely an impossible assignment.[29]

Nasty about women who criticized her as less respectable than themselves, she always responded with a quotable quip. When Mae West called her "Lady Peel," she retorted that West was "the weakest link in the Vassar Daisy Chain." When actress Carol Landis referred to Gypsy's "leg art," Gypsy berated Landis's hypocrisy: "Leg art requires no protection from Miss Landis. I am sure no one will mind if she does Salome in long underwear and a fire helmet." After male Yale students voted luscious actress Ann Sheridan first in a popularity contest and Gypsy second, Gypsy replied to a question about Sheridan, "I think he was a swell general." Gypsy never gave up her own style sufficiently to fit the Hollywood mode.[30]

In the summer of 1937, describing herself as "a girl officially censored and naturally chastened," Gypsy wrote Walter Winchell, who often wrote about her, a funny but cynical open letter about Hollywood. While New Yorkers condescendingly thought of Hollywood actors as people who lacked the talent to make it in real theater, to the denizens of Hollywood, she said, "a Broadwayite is someone who hasn't the carfare to California." Chastised by the studio, she was deflated by executives' criticism about her imperfect body, her need for a facial makeover, and her poor taste in fashion. Daily she left the movie set "pooped out and with the conviction that maybe you're not so hot after all."[31]

Gypsy was fed up with Hollywood, and her venture ended in failure. In New York, she had created Gypsy Rose Lee out of Rose Louise Hovick and outlasted the politicians who shut down burlesque. The movie studio, even more frightened of threats of possible censorship than Broadway producers had been, decided to recreate Gypsy as Louise Hovick. Throughout her performing career, Gypsy relied on her best asset: her own personality. Hollywood repressed much of her comedic wit, sparkle, and intelligence and kept her fully clothed, even when playing a sultana, a sultan's wife, in a harem.[32] Gypsy's experience in Hollywood reinforced her old insecurities about her lack of talent, but during her years at Minsky's and Ziegfeld's she had also discovered her strengths. She believed that Twentieth Century–Fox squandered her abilities out of fear.

Once in Hollywood, Gypsy had desired more than work, money, and fame. "It's never hard to get a job or hold one. But that isn't enough—if that's all there is to life, then what's the point of living?" she said to an interviewer in 1937. In Hollywood, she believed for a time that her stripping days had ended and that she could enjoy a fulfilling personal relationship with a man while pursuing her career. For a short time those hopes seemed to bear fruit.[33]

6

Failure as a Dutiful Wife

One day Morton Minsky's aunt Mae Cohen, whom Minsky described as "one of the most proper and distinguished women in our family," came to call on him. "Morton," Aunt Mae began, "I have a problem you may be able to help me with. One of my good friends is a Mrs. Mizzy." Mrs. Mizzy was concerned because her son was dating one of Minsky's employees, "a certain Miss Gypsy Rose Lee." Mrs. Cohen pointedly queried her nephew about Gypsy. She wanted him to tell her everything he knew. Discreet in his answer, Minsky stressed Gypsy's intelligence and left out her alliance with gangsters. For Mrs. Mizzy, the problem of Gypsy was not solved when her son married a Hollywood actress, rather than carrying on with a burlesque stripper; it ended only when her son and Gypsy divorced. She waited a very short time.[1]

Bob Mizzy's background differed significantly from Gypsy's. Bob's Jewish parents had immigrated to the United States from Russia. In 1912, his father, Albert Mizzy, bought a dental supply production company that he renamed Mizzy, Inc., and the business prospered. Bob's mother defensively assured Gypsy that Bob had always attended excellent schools and summer camps. Actually, Bob attended a string of different schools. He was very smart, but he quickly became bored and got into trouble. On more than one occasion, school officials asked him to leave. Bob was far more independent and unconventional than his parents found acceptable.[2]

Gypsy and Bob shared multiple interests including reading and the theater. Both had liberal political views. They were both gifted raconteurs and enjoyed photography. As a child, Gypsy took pictures with her little Brownie camera. In 1936, she teased a reporter that her hobbies were "amateur photography and pork chops." Acting as Gypsy's unofficial photographer in Hollywood, Bob took pictures of her at the openings of her movies—once he even stood on a marquee trying for a creative shot—and on the set while she was working. Such a wide range of common interests can form the basis for a good marriage, but in this case they did not ensure it.[3]

Bob and Gypsy dated in New York City. They may have met at one of the Minsky theaters or at a political meeting. When Gypsy departed for Hollywood, at first Bob stayed behind. He joined her in California after gossip columns linked Gypsy's name to other men. Violinist David Rubinoff, who played in Gypsy's first picture, *You Can't Have Everything*, escorted her to nightclubs. When Gypsy asked him how she looked, a smitten Rubinoff gushed, "Marvelous. Your gown looks like it was sprinkled on your body." Observers also spotted Gypsy with other male companions. If she missed Mizzy, she did not display her sorrow publicly.[4]

Once Bob arrived in Hollywood, the leadership at Twentieth Century–Fox insisted that she marry him rather than engage in a relationship outside of marriage. Given his headaches with the censors, Darryl Zanuck worried about any appearance of nonmarital sexual activity. Studio interference in actors' personal lives was normal operating procedure. Every so often studios decided to clean up the messy affairs of employees under long-term contracts. Zanuck ordered his actors to marry to satisfy the public's concern about visible immorality and Hays's demand for decorum and propriety. Gypsy acquiesced because she and Bob loved each other and preferred wedlock to separation.[5]

Since Gypsy viewed embarking on marriage in terms of public relations, she planned a unique wedding ceremony that was sure to get publicity. On August 13, 1937, Captain James Williams married Bob and Gypsy on a chartered water taxi twenty miles off the coast of Long Beach, California. Some cynics, probably reporters, called it "a stunt, done for the greatest glory of Zanuck." Gypsy denied it: "It was done to preserve a Hovick tradition. The Hovicks are all Norsemen and since time immemorial they have been Hovicking around just under the fringe of the North Pole. Even my name is a contraction of the phrase 'Ho Viking!' Anyway, all Hovicks are married at sea." The claim that this ceremony represented a family tradition rather than a publicity stunt was not convincing. But sea captains were empowered to act as justices of the peace and to marry couples without advance notice or a marriage license.[6]

While conceding to Zanuck's demand that she marry, Gypsy had rebelled against a conventional wedding. But she did arrange a second wedding ceremony to please the studio. Zanuck refused to accept the first ceremony as legally valid, claiming that their sea wedding did not meet the three-day-notice requirement of California law. The lawyer Gypsy consulted also encouraged a second, more conventional wedding. Between the first and second ceremonies, the studio chaperoned the twenty-seven-year-old Gypsy and twenty-five-year-old Bob. Gypsy and Bob were married on land in Santa Ana.[7]

Gypsy received numerous suggestions for her wedding and honeymoon. One telegram promised a "colorful wedding" including cowboys and Indians at the altar at the Phoenix airport. As the couple traveled on their honeymoon, other venues used them for publicity. Bob and Gypsy happily agreed to participate in such events. At the Pan American Exposition in Dallas, officials arranged dinner for them and dedicated the first bullfight to Gypsy.[8]

Foreshadowing their stormy marriage, Bob and Gypsy argued almost immediately after the first wedding. They screamed insults at each other, Gypsy recounted, "and we were both resourceful, especially me, with a diploma as a master cusser from all the burlesque wheels I've toured." She predicted the demise of the marriage and would not have gone through with the second ceremony. But during the fight, her dachshund began to give birth. They did not have time to get her to a veterinarian. Knowledgeable and caring about animals, Bob served as a fine midwife for the dog. Gypsy teased that a woman with as many pets as she possessed should hold on to such a handy husband. Bob shared Gypsy's love of animals and was a resourceful spouse, but his useful skills, like his other good qualities, did not solidify the marriage for long.[9]

The second honeymoon proved even more stressful than the first because Gypsy's mother joined them. When Gypsy first arrived in Hollywood and was faced with the Hays Office's opposition to her movie career, she felt alone, and she turned in desperation to her mother. Gypsy invited Rose to join her, making a mistake that complicated her life. When Gypsy went to work, Rose felt ignored by her daughter and she cultivated an attention-getting act. She complained to the studio behind Gypsy's back that her daughter made her live in poverty.

Rose dressed up in old clothes and went to see Mr. Zanuck about her daughter's neglect. Gypsy described Rose as resembling a cleaning woman, "an old skyscraper nightlark without her bucket and mop." Familiar with stage mothers' performances, Zanuck politely but firmly ushered her from his office.[10]

Rose did not stay with Gypsy her entire time in Hollywood—for part of the two years, she lived in Witchwood Manor, Gypsy's country house near rural Nyack, about thirty miles outside of New York City—but she returned to Hollywood immediately after Gypsy's second wedding to Bob. Bob and Rose were antagonistic toward each other. Furious when Bob married Gypsy, Rose chased him around a room with a gun; neither Bob nor Gypsy knew the gun was not loaded. Gypsy joked about this incident later, but Bob, who usually enjoyed a good story, understandably missed the humor.

After their marriage, Bob and Gypsy hitched a trailer to the back of their car and drove across the country to New York, taking Rose along. The trio must have made an uncomfortable ensemble. Bob, Gypsy, and Rose ended their journey at Witchwood Manor.

On their honeymoon there, Gypsy cooked for Bob and even baked biscuits. "A gal has to know something besides wearing a jewel studded G-string if she's going to hold her husband," she commented, bowing to convention. Bob worked in the family business and commuted to his New York City office; like the rest of the local wives, Gypsy drove her husband to the station every morning. A perfectionist in everything, Gypsy bragged about becoming "very wifely. Isn't that marvelous? And I love it!" Still, Gypsy could never find happiness as a housewife chauffeuring her commuting husband, even though she occasionally enjoyed playacting the role. After returning to Hollywood from her honeymoon, she discovered she lacked the energy for two demanding jobs, as actress and housewife.[11]

Early in the 1930s, during her relationship with her married lover Eddy, Gypsy explained her strong distaste for a marriage in which the wife subordinated herself. Even though she refused to admit it to Mizzy, Gypsy craved financial independence. She longed to control her own destiny, both personal and professional, without interference from another person or trying to fit another adult into her life. Gypsy could conceive of marriage only as a subordination of her will. She warned her sister that in marriage, women performed uncompensated domestic labor such as cooking and gardening and everything, even their children, belonged to the husband. Gypsy's mother taught her this conceptualization of wedded bliss. Unmarried women could possess both love and freedom. Of course Gypsy needed to be center stage, personally and professionally.[12]

After that stressful cross-country honeymoon trip, Bob and Gypsy returned to Hollywood by themselves, but returning did not bring a happy marriage.[13] Gypsy and Bob had conflicting expectations about living in Hollywood. Bob was delighted with Gypsy's movie career. Although he acted as her manager on occasion because he had business experience, for Bob, Hollywood represented play. For Gypsy, Hollywood meant work. This difference had existed from the very start of their relationship. The public social life they led was part of his entertainment and her career. In New York City, Bob often escorted Gypsy to nightclubs. Needing little sleep, Bob expected plenty of evenings like these. In Hollywood, he enjoyed socializing more than Gypsy did. She hated what she called "artificiality," but Bob thrived on it. He became friendly with the actors Tony Martin and Alice Faye, while Faye and Gypsy at first maintained a cool working relationship. Gypsy preferred evenings spent reading her favorite author, Somerset Maugham; Bob, who loved jazz, was eager to explore Hollywood's nightlife. Bob had married a sexy stripper, and he must have been disappointed when she turned out to be a homebody.[14]

Mizzy possessed "the most intriguing frown when he growls," Gypsy once commented affectionately. Bob growled frequently. Besides the typical problems of a young couple in their twenties, such as Gypsy's lack of domestic skills and inadequate communication between partners, Gypsy and Bob had to overcome more serious obstacles. Gypsy poured ten thousand dollars into her country estate, which she had bought in the mid-1930s before she married. Though she rented apartments in Manhattan, the beautiful farm represented Gypsy's first permanent home. She probably named the place after the 1927 novel by John Buchan *Witch Wood*, which dealt with witchcraft and devil worship. Gypsy may have thought it was amusing to see herself as a witch. Remodeling the seventy-year-old, fourteen-room farmhouse, Gypsy painted much of it herself. She worked hard to make her house a home. In this, as in all her pursuits, she found intense activity relaxing. Her hobbies included gardening and canning. In one season, she canned eighty-five quarts of fruits and vegetables. She raised poultry and sheep and kept numerous dogs and cats.[15]

Decorating the place with care and pride, Gypsy ensured that each room reflected her taste and her desire to show refinement. Having inherited her grandmother's gift with a needle, Gypsy stitched gray and rose needlepoint cushions for her antique dining room chairs. Her library displayed many first editions. In the playroom resided a piano autographed by celebrities such as Billy Rose and producer Heywood Broun. Signed photographs covered the walls. Above the piano, Gypsy hung pictures of burlesque stars. Gypsy even had a stage installed with complete backstage equipment where she practiced and experimented with new specialty routines. Having been raised in the city, Bob hated country life and wanted to move into the city if they returned from Hollywood. The couple's debt level concerned Mizzy, but he rarely talked to Gypsy about it.

Between Gypsy's doldrums in Hollywood and her failure as a legitimate actress, living with her grew difficult. As she obsessed over her professional mistakes, she compared her Hollywood career to her former successes. In burlesque and the *Follies*, people had fawned on her. She lavished them with delicacies and entertainment while they fed her ego. She craved the adoration that neither the movie studio nor Bob gave her. Never having seen her parents work through disagreements, Gypsy held in her petty complaints against Bob and then, after a bout of drinking, would lose her temper. In addition to her occasional alcohol abuse, she suffered from premenstrual syndrome that plunged her into depression. At night she thought compulsively about the horrors that had occurred throughout her life. Suffering from fitful sleep during her period, all she saw was darkness and despair.[16]

Only in his mid-twenties, Mizzy lacked any skills that would have helped him to cope with Gypsy's emotional state. Occasionally moody and sulky himself, he usually retreated rather than deal directly with his wife's problems. He responded to her mood swings with stony silence. Gypsy accused him of selfishness and occasional mean-spiritedness, and she felt unappreciated. Sometimes she did not understand why he was upset. The matters over which they fought seemed trivial but spiraled downward. A skating expedition for Bob's younger sister, Eleanor, turned into a contest of wills. Since she did not ice-skate, Gypsy went only to please Eleanor. Bob did not want to join them; he consented sulkily and rode with them in silence. When they finally arrived at the lake, it had not frozen solid enough for skating. Bob's face, though, was a glacier; he refused to laugh over the situation. On issues large and small, the two remained inflexible. Even though she agreed with his politics, she chafed at the endless meetings for social and political causes that he wanted her to attend. She was particularly galled that he expected her to attend them alone because he found them boring. Similarly, she resented attending benefit performances at the theater with people she detested.

Though they loved each other, Gypsy and Bob had different motivations for marriage. Bob appreciated Gypsy's art as a stripteaser and her potential acting career, but his background and main occupation removed him from the entertainment business. He was all that she was not. Raised in a stable, two-parent household, he was provided with a fine education. Everything that he took for granted from his childhood bored or antagonized him, but Gypsy had never possessed such things, and she coveted them.

While they lived in Hollywood, Gypsy liberated Bob from his family, particularly his mother, and the family dental business. Marriage to a stripper and movie actress represented an act of rebellion against his upbringing and his family's career plans for him. Throughout his life, Bob maintained cool and distant relations with both his parents.

Barely five feet tall and 105 pounds, Bob's mother, Ruth Mizzy, bristled with determination. A member of the Communist Party, she donated thousands of dollars to causes such as the Joint Anti-Fascist Refugee Committee. She served on the executive board of the left-leaning New York League of Women Shoppers. The Mizzys' landlord described her as a person who cared about the people who suffered discrimination. When an African American woman visited her, Ruth Mizzy insisted that the doorman and elevator operator treat the woman with respect.[17]

Ruth Mizzy's correspondence demonstrates her impressive ability to manipulate others. When she complimented Gypsy, she simultaneously managed to make it a criticism. Pleased that Bob had remembered her on Mother's Day, she credited Gypsy with his thoughtfulness. Simultaneously, she was miffed that Gypsy had not thanked her promptly for cups for a fruit bowl. Although she supported the antifascist forces in the Spanish Civil War, she chided Gypsy for stripping to raise money for the cause and demanded that she refrain from stripping for any charity. Gypsy had failed to demonstrate behavior proper for her son's wife. Mrs. Mizzy encouraged Gypsy to return to New York City and pursue a career as a dramatic actress.

In a letter dated just a short time after she assumed the title of mother-in-law, Ruth Mizzy pleaded her case since she desperately wanted her son to leave Hollywood and return to his predetermined life in the dental products supply business. She attempted to show her understanding of the young couple. Although she believed that a man should be the main breadwinner in the family, she understood that Gypsy desired a "career," but a career as a stripteaser was unacceptable.[18]

No doubt Gypsy resented her opinionated mother-in-law. Ruth made her disapproval of her daughter-in-law clear. Even so, Gypsy respected Ruth Mizzy, perhaps because she was a strong woman who knew her own mind. In spite of Ruth's attempts at control, Gypsy told June she would miss her in-laws once she and Bob finalized their divorce, five months shy of their fourth wedding anniversary.[19]

Bob Mizzy's mother must have been equally disappointed in his subsequent choices of female companions. Within six months after the divorce, Bob was dating Myra Stephens, a showgirl, whom he eventually married. His next wife was Jean Dorsey, Tommy Dorsey's young and attractive widow. Later he married Jeanne LaMarche, a theatrical press agent. Mizzy never lost his interest in show business, even as he climbed up the ladder at Mizzy, Inc.

On March 17, 1941, in a court in Cook County, Illinois, a judge granted Gypsy her divorce on the grounds that Arnold R. Mizzy had been "guilty of extreme and repeated cruelty toward the complainant, Rose L. Mizzy, in Chicago, Illinois, on November 6, 1938, and November 13, 1938." According to newspaper reports, Mizzy had knocked her down on those two occasions. Since these events supposedly happened in Chicago, Gypsy could file in Illinois. Gypsy and Bob may well have agreed that she would bring false charges so the divorce would go through uncontested. Even a cursory investigation of Gypsy's allegations turned up fabrications. For Gypsy, lying came easily. In her chronology of "Highlights" for 1938 in her scrapbook, Gypsy noted that she performed in Chicago on November 11 but on November 13 was in Columbus, Ohio. The scrapbook contains no listing for November 6, but on November 5 she was performing in Kansas City, Missouri. Newspapers covering the story attached glamorous pictures of Gypsy from her movies to such headlines as "She Moves to Shed a Husband." Articles referred to her "trying to strip herself of a husband." Emphasizing Mizzy's alleged "obscene and abusive language" to his wife, they neglected to divulge Gypsy's fine-tuned skills in the same vein. After the divorce, Gypsy's lawyer told the press that she "would remain single a while to please her public."[20]

While speaking with reporters, Gypsy never so much as hinted that she had been physically abused or even expressed feelings of bitterness. According to Gypsy, she and Bob had an enjoyable time in Hollywood and later in New York after their separation. They met for "midnight lunches" and, although they planned to divorce, would "always be good friends." She did not plan to remarry "unless I marry him again." The tone of her statements does not suggest that she was lying to protect his reputation, although she certainly concealed from the public her distaste for domesticity. Gypsy seems to have genuinely appreciated her husband's good qualities. Later, she referred to him as "a nice guy."[21] Hiding any pain over her failed marriage, Gypsy converted Bob into one more funny line. She quipped that she divorced a husband for eating "gefilte fish in bed." When asked about her pet peeve against men, she complained: "Flooding out the bathroom seems to be one masculine habit that annoys me. My first husband was like a walrus in the bathtub."[22]

Gypsy conceived of her first marriage as part of a public relations campaign in Hollywood and approached wedlock as if she were acting in a new role.[23] Neither Gypsy nor Bob had realistic expectations of marriage. They both believed it would bring them happiness, but instead they inflicted emotional pain on each other. Seeking to escape their controlling mothers and to enhance their self-image by acquiring an attractive spouse was not enough to hold them together. The conventions of 1930s middle-class domesticity were particularly ill-suited to their personalities, interests, and aspirations. Gypsy knew nothing about the domestic chores a wife was expected to do. Before she married, she rarely cooked, although she was learning; she had never shopped for groceries or washed and ironed. She had never done domestic work on a continual basis and found it a chore. Gypsy confessed to Bob that she had never run a household and had made mistakes.[24]

In California, Gypsy's personal life deteriorated along with her career. She married, but the relationship worked no better than her movies did. By the time she left two years later, the marriage had disintegrated. Simultaneously with the end of her movie career, Gypsy, with great emotional pain, broke from her husband and her mother.

7

Death, Dies, and Mother

When Gypsy and Bob bade Rose adieu after their honey-moon, they could not have realized that Rose would soon gain her own publicity. Two months after Rose returned to Witchwood Manor, she testified before a grand jury about the death of a twenty-nine-year-old New York City art teacher, Genevieve Augustin. On June 2, 1937, the coroner was summoned to Witchwood Manor and found Augustin on a bedroom floor with a rifle by her side. The coroner determined that Augustin had shot herself in the temple during a house party for some of Gypsy's friends, although Gypsy was not there and Rose acted as hostess. In November, a grand jury convened to investigate the supposed suicide at the request of Augustin's mother, who had raised concerns. The grand jury ultimately agreed with the coroner.

The incident greatly disturbed June. June's baby daughter, April, had been staying with Rose while June worked in summer stock theater, but June removed her permanently after this incident. Fussing over a pot on the stove while she described the circumstances of Augustin's death to June, Rose seemed more concerned about her recipe for jam than the late young woman. Rose explained that Augustin wanted to live with her but Rose rejected her. Rose stood near her with a gun and suggested that if the woman was so distressed, she ought to end her life. The woman grabbed the rifle and placed it in her mouth and shot herself. Afterward, Rose burned the woman's diary, which she claimed was full of lies and might hurt Gypsy's reputation in Hollywood. Recently, when Gypsy's son recounted the story, instead of describing it as a suicide he stated that his grandmother shot the woman. According to Gypsy's son, "the girl was Rose's lover and she made a pass at my mother."

All these accounts have inconsistencies. The official coroner's version is suspect given the difficulty of shooting oneself in the temple with a rifle. Rose's story about where Genevieve placed the gun is inconsistent with the woman being shot in the temple. Eric's version ignores the fact that Gypsy was not present that weekend; she was probably in Hollywood. Whether Rose actually shot her or goaded her, the story demonstrates Rose's callousness.[1]

A few months after the episode with Augustin, Rose moved out of Witchwood Manor and bought a small house nearby. In the spring of 1938, the caretaker at Witchwood Manor wrote to Gypsy in a panic. He was concerned that she might fire him because Rose had removed items from the house. Even though Rose had reassured him that she had received Gypsy's permission, he was aghast when Rose hauled off furniture, including the dining room set, antiques, books, and, even more infuriating to Gypsy, some of Gypsy's dogs. He sent Gypsy a long list of everything that Rose had stolen. Gypsy assured him that Rose would be returning everything.

Gypsy's reaction to the theft was informed by her deeply held craving for roots and property. All her homes represented stability and financial security. Anyone stealing from her house threatened her sense of order. Gypsy recognized that Rose's thefts stemmed from her mother's inability to view her daughter as an autonomous adult. Rose took credit for everything that Gypsy had accomplished, so she assumed that everything Gypsy owned belonged to Rose. Rose's actions infuriated Gypsy, even though she understood that "material things always fascinate[d] her mother." In an interview much later, Gypsy applied the same statement to herself. Rose and Gypsy shared the sense that possessions defined the self; they struggled over objects that represented Gypsy's independent identity.

When Gypsy stood up to her mother and refused to allow Rose to retain the items she had stolen, Rose immediately began fawning adoringly over her daughter. In these affectionate letters Rose pleaded to see Gypsy, talk in person, and straighten out their tangled relationship. Should Gypsy spurn her, the martyred Rose would wait patiently until God intervened and softened Gypsy's heart. She urged Gypsy to conjure up pleasant memories of times when her mother had helped her. Rose reasoned that such visions would inspire kindness, sweetness, and understanding. Suffering from asthma, dizziness, and other physical symptoms, Rose asked for very little, she said, but she depended on her daughters because of her poor health. In Rose's calmer letters she blamed menopause for her nasty attacks on Gypsy. She ended these letters with love to both Gypsy and Bob.

A few days after the sweet conciliatory letters, the tone would change to vicious denunciation. In her nastier letters, Rose claimed that Gypsy victimized her: Gypsy had promised her a house to live in and now had reneged on the agreement. She accused Gypsy of poisoning her relationships with June and with the girls' father, both of whom had distanced themselves from her. Amazingly, even after she chased Bob with the gun, she could not understand why Bob detested her, so Rose blamed Gypsy. Rose complained that Gypsy had exploited her for years as a personal housekeeper and maid. While living lavishly in Hollywood, she said, Gypsy had given her only two thousand dollars a year—a sum that was more than most families' income during the Depression.

Ranting in one letter, she claimed that Gypsy introduced everything despicable into Rose's life, including alcohol, pornographic movies, and "fags" (the old slang for cigarettes or the then-current slang for gay men). She vowed that Gypsy and Bob would be punished someday for treating her so unfairly and making her suffer. She intended to be avenged.[2]

Rose's protestations proved her incapable of taking responsibility or admitting she ever erred. Her complaints also underscored her profound loneliness. At one point, she expressed her wish to die because those she cared about did not love her. Unwanted, she had no purpose in life.

Gypsy's written responses to both the vicious and the pathetic letters took the same tone. They showed cold fury toward her mother. Gypsy focused on the thefts as the sole cause of the fights between them. Gypsy punished Rose by refusing to give her any more money until Rose returned the furnishings and animals. She also threatened to inform the police. Tired of coping with her mother's theatrics, and convinced that her mother was more of a distraction than help to her work, Gypsy finally told Rose she did not want to see her again. After playing such a central role in her daughter's early career, Rose must have been hurt very deeply by this dismissal.[3]

Rose's emotional state had worsened as Gypsy grew into adulthood. Her mental illness went untreated, except for one hospitalization. Her psychological problems led to bizarre behavior, including armed assaults on both of her sons-in-law. In her angry possessiveness toward her daughters, she ceased to distinguish right from wrong. Rose's emotional abuse of family members knew no limits. She exploited people through a potent, deadly combination of charm and stubbornness until she finally wore them down.

Well aware of Rose's emotional volatility and manipulation, Gypsy counseled her sister to find a resourceful attorney as she had done. During this period, Gypsy had contrived a system to deal with her mother by not seeing her, sending her money, and keeping a careful record of her payments.[4] June's lawyer worked out a settlement with Rose: She would receive fifty dollars a month, but the agreement barred her from contacting June by telephone, letter, or any other means. Though June hated to give money to her mother that rightfully belonged to her daughter, April, she felt squeezed. Always thinking ahead, Rose attempted to keep Gypsy from discovering June's contribution. She was afraid that if Gypsy knew about it, she might consider decreasing her own payments.

Rose periodically tried to extort even more money from her daughters. June learned from Gypsy that their mother had plotted against her. When June refused to increase her contribution to Rose's income in the manner she expected, Rose threatened to blackmail June about her married lover during her marathon days, her subsequent pregnancy by him, and April's illegitimacy. Rose's scheme involved revealing letters written by June's former lover that she had found and planned to sell back to her daughter. When Gypsy informed her mother that this scheme was illegal, Rose switched targets. She suggested offering them to the man. Gypsy pointed out that he had died. Undaunted, Rose wondered aloud if his family would pay to protect his memory. Only Gypsy's insistence to her mother that she would be prosecuted for extortion kept Rose from carrying out her plan.[5]

In addition to all the problems that she caused directly, Rose involved Gypsy in other family difficulties. Emotional conflicts and arguments over money were always intertwined in the maternal Hovick-Thompson clan. Over time, Gypsy understood the financial burden imposed on her by both her extended family and her home. She once remarked that "I go where the dough is" because of her mortgage and the fact that she had "about half the people of the United States to support."[6]

At the same time that Gypsy was fighting with her mother, she learned that Big Lady, her seventy-year-old grandmother, needed an operation. In August 1938, Gypsy paid the first set of medical expenses. Gypsy's aunt Belle had previously suffered from alcoholism but had given up drinking and moved in with her mother, but she could not support Big Lady. Because of a childhood knee injury and her recent operation to remove a kidney, Belle was unemployable. In November, a letter from the Seattle Welfare Department informed Gypsy that the women were destitute. Belle and Big Lady required $36.75 a month to keep them off the dole. Such situations were common during the Depression, and welfare authorities routinely demanded that relatives support their poverty-stricken kin. Gypsy sent money to Big Lady and Aunt Belle. According to Belle, they had no money to pay for necessities, taxes, or doctor bills other than Gypsy's contributions. She never mentioned whether her mother received her husband's railroad pension.[7]

Occasionally Big Lady sent Gypsy cheery letters thanking her for notes and checks. Usually she mentioned Rose only to complain that she had not heard from her daughter, or that Rose sounded unhappy but that Big Lady was too impoverished to help her financially. Meanwhile, Big Lady, hedging her bets, was sympathetic to Rose about her problems with Gypsy. Because Rose did not explain the fight over the thefts to her mother, Big Lady did not comprehend why Gypsy acted so nastily to Rose. Big Lady suggested that Rose leave Bob and Gypsy alone for a while, reasoning that someday Gypsy would regret her actions toward her mother. In a tone reminiscent of Rose's, Big Lady vehemently declared that a mother is the only friend that a woman possesses. Big Lady also pointed out the practical side to Gypsy's fury. Gypsy's desire to remove Rose from her life meant paying Rose to exit. Big Lady urged Rose to come home to her mother, on whom she could depend, and soon afterward Rose did indeed visit her. Rose spent Big Lady's limited money, probably provided by Gypsy, quite freely while in Seattle, ignoring her mother's poverty and her meager resources. During one of her mood swings, Rose physically threatened Big Lady with her fists; two neighbors removed her from the house. In Gypsy's mother's family, tangled and sometimes twisted relationships between mothers and daughters were passed down the generations.[8]

So the pattern of hypocrisy and emotional abuse continued. Over the years that followed, first Big Lady, and then Belle, complained about Rose to Gypsy, bewailing her inattentiveness and failure to send money. Big Lady grumbled that she did not understand her daughter or her scams to get money from her family, including her own mother. Simultaneously, even after her disastrous visit, Big Lady and Belle wrote to Rose grumbling that Gypsy's support payments were occasionally late and that she never bothered to see them. They pleaded with Rose not to share their grievances with Gypsy. Rose may not have held their confidences, because she enjoyed fostering ill will between other family members. Gypsy gave money to her mother, grandmother, and aunt, especially in times of crises, but they never gave her emotional support or unconditional love. Gypsy knew they used her, so she kept away from them and never gave of herself.

"Columns and critics, even box office [receipts] mean nothing to us," Gypsy noted cynically about her and June's success. "We know how we're doing by the number of letters we get from needy relatives." When Rose refused to pay her own bills, collection agencies and medical personnel hounded Gypsy. To avoid unfavorable press, Gypsy regularly paid off her mother's creditors. Meanwhile, Belle frequently requested funds to start her own businesses, which always failed after Gypsy gave her the money. No one in Gypsy's family seemed to realize that Gypsy worked hard for her living. They also never comprehended that their own unpleasantness and mendacity caused the neglect they deplored.[9]

Conflicts with her mother added to Gypsy's Hollywood woes. Both Twentieth Century–Fox and her mother demanded obedience. Gypsy's mother wanted her to behave like a docile daughter without needs or desires of her own. For Gypsy to maintain her own personal and professional identity, she needed to break with her mother. Gypsy's short-lived marriage helped make a separation from her mother possible. The Hollywood years reinforced her determination to rely on her own instincts for survival.

Right after leaving Hollywood in the fall of 1938, Gypsy created a successful road show called the *Merry Whirl Review*. She resumed the stage name Gypsy Rose Lee and traveled throughout the United States. Although the income was lower than what she had received in Hollywood, Gypsy enjoyed the work more. She preferred the stage, where she controlled her own character and elicited an immediate response from the audience. In sharp contrast to her movies, the tour garnered sensational reviews. In *Merry Whirl*, she parodied a character named Mr. Censor. Gypsy had begun her revenge on the Hays Office.

Gypsy's political activism brought her more troubles. While in Hollywood, she joined the fight against fascism by supporting the

Spanish Republic against the right-wing rebellion led by General Francisco Franco, Her dedication to the cause led to her first skirmish with the U.S. Congress. During the 1936–39 Spanish Civil War, Britain, France, and the United States maintained an arms embargo, while fascist Italy and Germany supplied Franco with soldiers and military hardware. Only the Soviet Union provided armaments to the Loyalist military forces. Liberal Americans were outraged both by Franco's attempt to seize control of the government and by the United States' official neutrality. Some progressive young men and women from Western democracies, including the United States, formed International Brigades and fought alongside the people of Spain. With a stunning lack of parity in weapons and defenseless against Franco's aerial bombing, Madrid fell in 1939. The dictatorship that Franco established would control Spain for almost forty years.

Gypsy joined the Women's Committee of the Motion Picture Artists Committee to Aid Republican Spain (MPAC), which opposed the fascist takeover. The membership included writers, composers, and actors; Gypsy's friend Fanny Brice was among them. MPAC sponsored various fund-raising events such as carnivals at celebrities' houses. Its efforts funded a ship of relief supplies such as clothing and powdered milk for suffering and orphaned children in Loyalist Spain.

Gypsy chaired the clothing division of the relief committee. In Gypsy, sexuality and politics met, and she exploited the one to help the other. The committee exhibited Gypsy's lovely, partially stripped body in its advertisements, declaring: "Clothes? Any New Clothes, Old Clothes?" Gypsy Rose Lee "Appeals for Clothing for Spanish Refugees...and she is not teasing!" The ad proclaimed, "This artist who has given her ALL on stage, now asks you to give." Occasionally Gypsy gave speeches against the United States' policy toward Spain. "I've come here not to lift my skirt but to help lift the embargo," she began.[10]

Gypsy's political activity for Loyalist Spain caught the attention of the House Un-American Activities Committee (HUAC). Since the Texan Democrat Martin Dies Jr. chaired the committee at the time, contemporaries referred to it as the Dies Committee. Its mission was to investigate so-called subversive activity against the United States. Both Democrats and Republicans who were hostile to the New Deal served on the Dies Committee, and these conservatives pursued alleged Communist influence in labor unions and in Roosevelt's programs, such as the Federal Theater Project and the Works Progress

Administration. The committee may have been aware that out of the fifteen thousand members in the MPAC a few hundred had joined the Communist Party; Communists supported antifascist efforts in Spain, so their interests intersected with the mission of MPAC.

In November 1938, Representative Harold G. Mosier, a Democrat from Ohio and a member of the Dies Committee, telephoned Gypsy, who had stopped off in Ohio on her cross-county tour from Hollywood to New York City. He asked her to appear before a subcommittee in Cleveland to discuss her fund-raising for Spain. (The full committee never officially subpoenaed her.) In the midst of performing four shows, Gypsy coyly explained to Mosier that she had no time to testify. She offered to give a deposition, but the subcommittee refused.

One headline explained the purpose of the committee's invitation by declaring, "Red Prober Gets Publicity by Phoning Gypsy Rose Lee." If Dies Committee members expected more press coverage by questioning Gypsy, they seriously miscalculated. Gypsy proved more than a match for them, retaliating against the implication that she was disloyal to her country through her political activities. With humor, she made fun of the committee at the same time that she made serious points about her political activities. By 1938, Gypsy certainly knew how to gain favorable publicity, so she took the offensive. She impugned the committee members' motivation in seeking her testimony, charging that they wanted the publicity to raise money for further investigations. Gypsy suggested that instead they enter the Movie Quiz contest to raise additional funds.[11]

Referring to the committee's request that she appear in Cleveland, she quipped, "I'll bare everything if they will come to Columbus." Planting her tongue firmly in her cheek, she offered the committee her dressing room for the hearings. Gypsy pointed out the lunacy of the committee's actions by reminding the public of their criticism of a beloved child star: "My goodness, first they pick on little Shirley Temple and then on me. Are they crazy?" A committee staff researcher, J. B. Matthews, had alleged that Communists had duped Temple into supporting the party but the public ignored the unfounded charge that Temple was a Communist sympathizer. Gypsy crowed that the committee had given her the first joint billing she'd ever had with Shirley Temple, and she thought it was marvelous.

Denying any Communist Party affiliation, she explained in an innocent tone, "Why, I couldn't be, I voted the Democratic ticket." When the quilted robe she wore during one of the interviews with reporters about the Dies Committee slipped off her knee, one photographer yelled, "Hold it," so he could snap a shot. "Better not," she laughed as she covered her beautiful legs; "They might even call that un-American." Later she joked that between her act and Dies's attempts for publicity they could bring back vaudeville.[12]

With comedic wit and feigned naïveté, she attacked the committee. She demanded to know who would investigate Dies. "Why," she wondered, "doesn't Dies stop running down the 70,000 Reds and go after the 700,000 Nazi Bund members?" The government was investigating Americans who supported fascism, but those activities drew less attention than Congress's campaign against the left.[13]

Gypsy defended her actions as pro-American rather than pro-Communist, a theme she would repeat when the American Legion branded her a Communist sympathizer in the 1950s. Regarding the Dies investigation, she agreed that in Hollywood entertainers did give parties to raise money for poor women and children in Spain, but she argued such activity was the antithesis of un-American behavior. Aiding the unprivileged was a core American value. Gypsy compared her charity abroad with her contributions at home such as visiting American orphans. She entertained at numerous shows at hospitals and other venues to benefit poor children. Justifying her activities with a class-based argument, Gypsy insisted, "When you have a name, you should do things for charity no matter where it's needed. After all it's these same people who gave you that name." Wealthy patrons had not contributed to her rise to fame, she argued. Neither, of course, did the children of Loyalist Spain, but Gypsy understood that verbal assaults on the rich played well during the Depression.[14]

After she refused to appear, the Dies Committee did not pursue Gypsy's testimony. Smarting under the negative publicity, it decided not to risk a live performance. During the controversy, a cartoon appeared in the *Washington Herald* in which a huge theater marquee declared, "Dies Un-American Activities Investigation: Next Headliner Gypsy Rose Lee." On a ladder in front of the theater, a man identified as Dies asked, "Who said this show is getting dull?" The caption read, "Burlesque Isn't Dead After All."

Gypsy's exchange in the press with the Dies Committee encouraged other people to ridicule the committee's work. It did nothing to stop that work, however. In its twenty-year history, the committee's investigations never produced any significant findings involving the entertainment industry's supposed threat to national security. But it did serious damage to the careers of many progressives, including writers, actors, and directors in Hollywood and New York.[15]

In spite of her brief run-in with the Dies Committee, Gypsy reestablished her image as a sophisticated stripper on the tour. When she returned to New York, she changed the direction of her life by establishing herself as a successful writer and a true "intellectual stripper." Writing boosted her self-esteem by proving she was more than a failed movie actress with a lovely body. It also let her vent her frustration about Hollywood and about her mother, whom she portrayed in an unflattering light.

8

Finding the Body

F inding dead bodies scattered all over a burlesque theater isn't the sort of thing you're likely to forget. Not quickly, anyway," begins *The G-String Murders*. "It's the little things, incidents that don't seem important when they happen, that slip your mind. With me, for instance. As long as I live, I'll remember seeing that bloated bluish face, the twisted, naked body, and the glitter of a G-string, hanging like an earring from the swollen neck."[1]

After returning to New York City in 1939, Gypsy decided to write a mystery novel, *The G-String Murders*. "People think that just because you're a stripper you don't have much else except a body. They don't credit you with intelligence," she later complained. "Maybe that's why I write." Gypsy worked as hard on her writing as her stripping, and *The G-String Murders* became a best seller.[2]

Gypsy contended in interviews that Walter Winchell got her started in writing. He urged Gypsy to write his "Walter Winchell on Broadway" column while he vacationed, and she reluctantly accepted. Winchell gave her paper and carbons for making copies on the manual typewriter she borrowed. She enjoyed the experience and especially relished pounding away in her dressing room between her striptease acts. Gypsy knew little about the mechanics of the typewriter. She composed without capital letters. "It was months before somebody told me about the shift," she explained.[3] In her guest column published in August 1940, Gypsy recounted her career. Beginning with the teasing headline "The Men I Love," she detailed her innocent childhood crushes. Readers looking for scandal came away disappointed.[4]

In spite of the stories that credited Winchell for making Gypsy an author, it was George Davis who most significantly influenced Gypsy's writing. Truman Capote's biographer described Davis as "a fat, lazy, but always brilliant, editor." From 1936 to 1940, he worked as a fiction editor at *Harper's Bazaar*. In 1927, while working in Detroit as a teenager, Gypsy took refuge from her mother's fights with her current boyfriend by visiting the Seven Arts Bookstore. The avant-garde of the working-class city met there and analyzed the hottest authors, F. Scott Fitzgerald and James Joyce. George Davis, who managed the bookstore, befriended Gypsy. The youthful and gentle Davis sympathized with the pretty young girl and was attentive to her. He suggested she read classics such as Shakespeare's sonnets. After hearing it mentioned in discussions, she bought Karl Marx's *Das Kapital*. Her eclectic taste in reading started under Davis's tutelage.

Davis renewed their acquaintance while working in New York City as an editor at *Vanity Fair*. In 1936, he wrote about her for the magazine. They developed a close friendship and corresponded when Gypsy moved to Hollywood. Consumed with the desire to write the Great American Novel, Davis wanted to live the bohemian life of a writer. He opened a writers' colony at 7 Middagh Street in Brooklyn Heights, borrowing money for the down payment from Lincoln Kirsten, who believed in the cultural richness of New York City and did what he could to facilitate its flowering. Among other things, with Russian-trained choreographer George Balanchine, whom he persuaded to come to the United States from London, Kirsten created the New York City Ballet. Kirsten decided that Davis's plan for writers fit into his overall vision for the city. The writers' colony flourished briefly.[5]

Located on a tree-lined block not far from the Brooklyn Bridge, the brownstone was home to writers such as poet W. H. Auden and novelist Carson McCullers. Davis allowed writers and artists to rent rooms inexpensively, an arrangement that helped him pay the mortgage. In the middle of 1940, Gypsy decided to move in to write her mystery. She brought her cook Eva with her and lent Davis two hundred dollars to fix the furnace and finish renovating the parlor. Often on the road, Gypsy moved out in December, but she frequently returned to attend parties. She met other writers, composers such as Benjamin Britten, and artists such as figurative painter Pavel Tchelitchew—both of whom, like Auden and Davis, were homosexual. Interviewed by the *New Yorker*, Davis called 7 Middagh a "boarding house," but the reporter thought he said "bawdy house"—a more accurate description of the goings-on there, particularly in the evenings.[6]

One tenant of 7 Middagh Street described Gypsy as "a whirlwind of laughter and sex." As always, Gypsy chatted incessantly, and the other residents appreciated her witty conversation. In the early evening, residents and guests started drinking, and their activities proceeded far into the night. While intoxicated, Gypsy, Davis, Britten, and others played parlor games such as charades. They also staged impromptu ballets.[7]

At Middagh Street, Gypsy's provocative clothing and scintillating presence made artists and writers feel more avant-garde. They flaunted convention, or so they thought, by socializing with a stripper. Davis occasionally shed part or all of his attire while talking with friends. Gypsy exposed parts of her beautiful body. Bisexuality and homosexuality were common orientations among the people who frequented Middagh Street, and Gypsy, who, like her mother, may have been bisexual, readily accepted the unconventional sexuality that pervaded the place.

Some evenings, Gypsy, McCullers, Davis, and Auden frequented bars on Sands Street, across from the Brooklyn Navy Yard, that attracted sailors and prostitutes. Often given to intense crushes on both women and men, McCullers reveled in Gypsy's company. Having studied at Columbia and New York University, McCullers later returned again to the city from her native South with her husband, Reeves. After her novel *The Heart Is a Lonely Hunter* was published in June 1940 and well received, she separated from her husband, and later that year she moved to 7 Middagh Street.

McCullers treated Gypsy as a fellow author, not just a friend, and shared plot ideas with her. Gypsy was flattered that a successful writer took her seriously as a budding author. McCullers, after recounting to Gypsy the story she was then composing, was inspired to change the plot of one of her best-known works, *Member of the Wedding*. After struggling with the plotline, she suddenly decided that her protagonist, a young girl preparing for her brother's wedding, was in love with both the bride and groom. McCullers remained Gypsy's friend, occasionally sending roses and other gifts when Gypsy was on tour.[8]

Gypsy spent much of her time at the brownstone in the company of George Davis. He edited her work and occasionally typed while she dictated. As they shared their writing, their relationship intensified. George sent Gypsy a valentine thanking her for his Christmas stocking and ended with a line from a sonnet, "Let me not to the marriage of true minds admit impediments." He signed it "All my Love, George."[9] For a while, Gypsy and Davis told people they were engaged. Since Davis was homosexually inclined, the engagement may have been a temporary lark, or even a cover for them both. Davis's sexuality did not preclude him from later marrying the singer Lotte Lenya, widow of Kurt Weill and best known for her role in Bertolt Brecht and Weill's *Threepenny Opera*. Some of Gypsy and George's friends took the engagement seriously. One of the editors of *Harper's Bazaar* sent flowers to Gypsy to thank her for making George so happy.[10]

Davis and Gypsy confided their deepest fears to each other. Gypsy rarely trusted people sufficiently to open up, as she did with Davis. She let him see her weaknesses as well as her strengths. Now in her late twenties, she confessed her worries about her late thirties and early forties, when youth and beauty would desert her. Since he knew Gypsy believed in him, Davis finally told Gypsy about his inability to write. Pleading with Davis to leave the madness of the Brooklyn house, Gypsy urged him to seek solitude in the country. She felt that 7 Middagh Street did not create an environment hospitable to writing. Davis himself did not blame the house for his writer's block. Defending his desire to reside in New York City, he countered that Gypsy expressed herself in her country house, Witchwood Manor, through its furnishings and decor. The house provided a refuge and security for Gypsy since she planned to retire there after she gave up stripping. Similarly, the house at Middagh Street provided an outlet for Davis's personality and expressed his identity.[11]

Candidly cataloging Gypsy's faults in a letter, Davis rightfully criticized her weakness for material things. To Davis, Gypsy radiated enormous beauty when showing off her "improvements" to her property. While Davis did not understand this nesting impulse, he admired her drive to create and control her physical environment. At the same time, he hated her obsession with acquisitions. He also disliked her manipulation of people and her insincerity toward them. People metamorphosed into objects to be used. Over time, her ability to capitalize on her beauty and youth to obtain what she desired from people would lessen, he warned.[12]

Despite his criticism of her materialism, Davis shared Gypsy's passion for Victorian antiques. He advised her about what she should buy and how much she should pay for it. They both preferred Victorian styles but purchased whatever interested them at the moment.

In 1944, their mutual love for antiques caused a rift that created distance between them, although it did not destroy their friendship.

Any romantic attachment, if one ever existed, had ended earlier. Davis loaned some furnishings to Gypsy, including an antique fireplace mantel and some chairs. Originally they decided that she should take them to her country house to prevent their being destroyed amid the wild antics at Middagh Street. Later, when George requested their return, Gypsy refused. Davis reacted angrily, and Gypsy responded with equal fury.[13] The fight echoed the earlier one she had with her mother, although in that case her mother had taken the property, and the episode reinforced to Davis his view of Gypsy as a material girl.

Before the fight over the furnishings, Davis had carefully read and edited early drafts of Gypsy's novel, *The G-String Murders*. He told her he liked the manuscript's quick pace and realistic dialogue, which buoyed her confidence. More important, he offered suggestions and helped her work on revisions. Such an experienced editor proved invaluable to Gypsy's first major writing project. He also spoke on her behalf to editors at Simon & Schuster, who had already heard about the manuscript from Janet Flanner, who met Gypsy at Middagh Street.

Flanner wrote for the *New Yorker* as a foreign correspondent; she recorded the rise of Hitler and spent time with American expatriates such as Gertrude Stein. Gypsy and Flanner became friends, or perhaps, as the writer Alexander Woollcott suggested, more than friends. Woollcott once announced to Gypsy that her "boy-friend," referring to Flanner, was coming to visit and he hoped Gypsy would join them. When the publishing house accepted the manuscript, Davis tried to accelerate the process of publication. Meanwhile, he cautioned Gypsy against her growing impatience to see her work in print.[14]

Gypsy wrote herself into her novel. *The G-String Murders* briefly describes Gypsy's entrance into burlesque and her move to New York City. Her boyfriend, Biff Brannigan, works as a comic, and her closest girlfriend, Gee Gee, also strips. Someone strangles a stripper, La Verne, with her G-string. The police turn up an abundance of suspects, including Louie, La Verne's gangster boyfriend. After someone tries to frame Biff by placing the lethal G-string in his pocket, he aids the police in solving the crime. Biff is concerned that the police suspect Gypsy, and he wants to clear her by finding the actual murderer. Deducing the identity of the murderer, Biff proves his theory by suggesting that Gypsy act as bait and remain in the theater alone to tempt the murderer to strike again. At the end of the novel, with the case solved, Biff proposes and Gypsy accepts. Their honeymoon set the stage for Gypsy's second and last mystery novel, *Mother Finds a Body*.

The editors at Simon & Schuster liked the setting in a burlesque theater and appreciated Gypsy's natural style, with its unpretentious and casual tone. Her knowledge of burlesque enabled her to intrigue readers who were as interested in the theater as in the mystery. Providing vivid local color, the novel describes comedic sketches, strip routines, costumes, and what happens backstage. In a typical scene in the book, Gypsy muses about her strip act: "The theater had been full of men, slouched down in their seats. Their cigarettes glowed in the dark and a spotlight pierced through the smoke, following me as I walked back and forth." Describing her band with precision, she wrote, "Musicians in their shirt sleeves, with racing forms in their pockets, played *Sophisticated Lady* while I flicked my pins in the tuba and dropped my garter belt into the pit."[15]

Gypsy's novel describes the strippers' dressing room with a complete lack of sentimentality. Burlesque comics pool their meager resources to buy the strippers a new toilet because the theater owner was indifferent to the disgusting condition of the old one. Fighting over a man, strippers scratch, gouge, and pull hair. Women also sympathize with each other over man problems. The novel stresses the camaraderie among the women. Sharing a dressing room, they throw parties with everyone contributing to buy drinks and food. The women joke, drink together, and confide in each other.

Gypsy based Biff, the burlesque comic in her novel, on Rags Ragland, who was reputed to be her lover at Minsky's. Ragland may have been Gypsy's first significant love interest. He moved to Hollywood to film a role he had played on Broadway and had a brief but successful acting career. Reputed among his coworkers to be well endowed, Ragland slept with many strippers. Throughout the novel, Biff uses Ragland's pet name for Gypsy, Punkin.[16]

Gypsy based Gee Gee, her best friend in the novel, on the stripper Georgia Sothern, who was her closest friend in burlesque. The novel also describes a vicious gangster, Louie Grindero, who was indicted for selling dope and imprisoned for coercing young women into prostitution. Described as short, full-chested, and thick-necked, Louie was accused of forgery and grand larceny. Worse, he beat his stripper girlfriend. Louie's body type and the crimes he was charged with matched Waxy Gordon's. Gypsy's experiences influenced other parts of *The G-String Murders* as well. Even the food Gypsy orders in the novel reflected her own taste for Chinese cuisine.

For the cover, the publishers capitalized on sexy pictures in the pulp style then popular. Simon & Schuster placed women in various stages of undress on different versions of the book. One revealed a woman in sexy underwear similar to a two-piece bathing suit. On another, a cigarette-smoking brunette wore a halter top off one shoulder. Likewise, Simon & Schuster emphasized Gypsy's sex appeal as part of its marketing campaign. "From January through July," ran the promotional blurb, "Gypsy toured the country, writing the first draft of her book in crowded dressing rooms, in planes, in the tub." Photographers had taken enough pictures of Gypsy in a bubble-filled bathtub to enable readers to imagine the scene. Gypsy verified the claim by complaining that she had dropped the manuscript into the bath water.[17]

Gypsy peddled the book in the same clever ways that she publicized herself. In a prepublication letter to her publishers, she offered to "do my specialty in Macy's window to sell a book. If you prefer something a little more dignified, I'll make it Wanamaker's window."[18] In an interview, she joked that if people did not know her in bookstores, she would remove an earring and ask, "Now, do you recognize me?"[19]

Critical response was mixed. Gypsy's writing meandered, and the convoluted and unconvincing plot offered many red herrings. Discussing clues, she confided to author Robert Service: "I sprinkle them around in the early chapters and then go nuts trying to tie them all together at the end. Usually I say to hell with 'em and let it go at that. But I know that's not good." In a generally favorable review, John Mason Brown wrote in the *New York World Telegram*, "It would have been better for everyone concerned if Miss Lee had just tossed the plot aside as if it were a garment." An El Paso, Texas, newspaper was headlined "Gypsy's Murder Mystery Has a Bare Plot but It's Authentic if It Ain't Literary." Gypsy lamely countered, "Maybe it doesn't have much plot. But neither do a lot of mystery stories."[20]

Nevertheless, the book secured a great deal of favorable coverage. "To her name (if not notoriety) as Queen of all Burlesque Queens, Miss Lee adds another notch, as a marvelous story teller," one newspaper wrote. The Richmond, Virginia, *Times-Dispatch* ran the headline "It's Good Entertainment, G String or No." Will Cuppy wrote in the *New York Herald Tribune*, "It's a pleasure to report that *The G-String Murders*—any way you look at it—and there are several—is a high spot of the season, a book to read and to reread when life seems dull and drab."[21]

Simon & Schuster had a hit. In a *Saturday Evening Post* cartoon, a man complained to a bookstore employee, "This book by Gypsy Rose Lee—the cover keeps coming off"—a hint of the book's broad appeal. A piece in *Life* magazine featured photographs of Gypsy and colleagues such as Georgia Sothern acting out scenes from the book. *Life* pronounced the book "third rate" as a murder mystery but enthusiastically endorsed its vivid presentation of burlesque.[22]

United Artists bought the movie rights to *The G-String Murders*, although Gypsy retained the stage rights. The independent producer, Hunt Stromberg, cast former vaudeville comic Michael O'Shea as Biff and the lovely and appropriately hard-edged Barbara Stanwyck as Gypsy. "I think I had Barbara Stanwyck in mind when I wrote *G-String*," Gypsy told reporters. She was very pleased with the casting.[23] Stromberg's expertise and reputation enabled him to produce and promote the film, which was titled *Lady of Burlesque*, successfully. With gross box office receipts of $1.85 million, the movie was as much of a hit as the book.

Stromberg's ads for *Lady of Burlesque* featured his personal testimony. "The first few pages of Gypsy Rose Lee's *The G-String Murders* convinced me that here was something new in screen material. The farther I read, the more excited I became. The story had pace, excitement, and a robust humor. Above all," he explained, "it had colorful characters that were made to live on the screen. The burlesque background was different, intriguing, and lustily alive."[24]

The censors, however, did not share Stromberg's enthusiasm. The movie created a sensation reminiscent of Gypsy's own ordeal in Hollywood. The Legion of Decency of the Catholic Church threatened to condemn the film. In an attempt to meet the powerful organization's demands, Stromberg made cuts. The Legion rejected the changes as inadequate. Stromberg altered the film again, but the Legion still found it lewd. When the studio released it in several cities, the Legion condemned it, declaring, "The film contains double meaning lines, salacious dances and situations and indecent costumes, presented against the background of a sensuous form of entertainment." Such language provided sensational publicity for the movie.[25]

The furor over the movie's condemnation increased its gross revenue by as much as 40 percent. For a third time, Stromberg cut the film. In this version, the strippers received a new sink instead of a toilet, and shots of the audience's reaction to Stanwyck's strip replaced views of Stanwyck onstage. Such indirection actually enhanced the provocative nature of Stanwyck's strip. Reviews complimented both Stanwyck and O'Shea. Gypsy criticized the movie, but she commented philosophically, "No one ever does like the movie made of one's own books."[26]

Given its scandalous content, Hollywood wisely did not attempt to make a movie based on Gypsy's second novel, a sequel with the same leading characters. *Mother Finds a Body*, published in 1942, begins with Biff and Gypsy on their honeymoon in a trailer with Gypsy's mother. Two strippers and two comics accompany the trio. Assorted animals also chaperone the newlyweds. In the novel, Gypsy has left burlesque to star in movies, and Biff is starring on Broadway. After Biff drives into a trailer park in Ysleta, a town on the Texas/Mexico border, one of the dogs discovers a body in the bathtub. To protect Gypsy from scandal, Gypsy's mother buries the body near the trailer park and sets fire to the site. Biff discovers that his former girlfriend Joyce works as a stripper in a bar owned by her unsavory boyfriend, a Mexican American gangster. A good-old-boy police chief hunts the killer relentlessly. Meanwhile, another murder is committed and the police uncover an illegal drug trade. As in the first novel, Biff manages to untangle all the evidence and solve the crime with the help of the sheriff. A crucial twist occurs when the sheriff becomes enamored of Gypsy's mother. She rejects him because the character of Gypsy's mother, like the real McCoy, could never have lived in Ysleta.[27]

The plot of the second novel is even more convoluted than the first. *Mother Finds a Body* offers Gypsy's characteristic mix of humor and gritty realism. She depicts the border town as hot and grimy and portrays the women, including herself, as sweating, unwashed, and for the most part unattractive. As in *The G-String Murders*, the police suspect the gangster bar owner who physically abuses his girlfriend. The gangster, a slimy character who puts his hand on Gypsy's knee under a table, lives by a certain code. Although all the evidence points to him, he ends up not guilty. Gypsy reminded readers that she knew gangsters intimately: "I made a quick guess about his underwear. I had an idea it would be wild, with his name spelled out on the chest in a contrasting color." Given Gypsy's relationship with Waxy Gordon, she had reason to know about a gangster's undershirt and briefs.[28]

The stock character of the sheriff provided an easy target for old burlesque comic routines. After the sheriff tosses back a drink, the bartender asks him if he wants a chaser. Biff quickly replies, "Chaser, hell....Nothing can catch that last one." Both in the bar and in the trailer, the protagonists' drinking is essential to the story. Strippers ply the customers with drinks and the owners pay them a kickback.

Gypsy shared her insights into acting as it pertained to the world of stripping. When a beautician asks the girls if they become embarrassed onstage, Dimples responds defensively, "Where do you get that embarrassed business? Why should I get embarrassed? I got a dark-blue spot on me all the time, ain't I?" Then, when asked what strippers think about while performing, she replies, "I ain't thinking anything, I got a job to do." Voicing Gypsy's insight, she adds, "I let the jerks do the thinking. That's what they paid their dough for. I'd look cute out there, thinking. Boy, that's rich! Me, with a rhinestone in my navel, thinking!"[29]

Bars like the one Gypsy created in the novel had replaced burlesque theaters. "If I had ever wondered what happened to burlesque when the license commissioner banned it, one look at The Happy Hour would have given me my answer," Gypsy wrote. She explained, "All the place needed was a couple of comics and a runway. I'm glad the orchestra didn't play *Gypsy Sweetheart*, or I would have gone into my number out of sheer habit." Acutely aware that bars were greatly inferior to theaters, Gypsy described the restricted physical space. One stripper complained, "The stage is so small, and instead of it going long ways, it goes up and down. I'll feel so silly doing my number up and down. And having the audience so close to me."[30] In bars, as in sleazy nightclubs, customers tried to paw the dancers.

Gypsy relied on her brief marriage to Bob Mizzy for the honeymoon scenes. In the novel, Biff enjoys Gypsy's new domesticity: "Punkin, the Personality Girl of the Old Opera, making breakfast! I bet if I told the boys they'd never believe it." The book gave Gypsy the liberty to write about what mattered to her in ways she never revealed in interviews. She described her reasons for marrying: "Now I would never have married Biff if I hadn't had a feeling of affection for him. I had known him for years and we always had fun together. I laughed at most of his jokes because they amused me." Most important, Biff makes Gypsy feel special and safe: "I liked the way his eyes twinkled when he looked at me. Being married to him gave me a sense of security I had never known before."[31]

In *Mother Finds a Body*, Gypsy's mother, called Evangeline, is a main character, and the novel allowed Gypsy to put into print some of her nastier thoughts about Rose. She characterizes her not simply as a ruthless woman but also as a possible murderer and emphasizes her misdeeds as a stage mother. Evangeline reads other performers' personal correspondence. She is "very quick about it and I noticed that she hadn't lost the knack of placing the things back just as they were before. Mother prided herself on that."[32] Gypsy exposes the woman's lack of maternal instinct in a chilling description of how Evangeline told bedtime stories to a child in another trailer. "Mother's stories are enough to give little Johnny permanent indigestion," she wrote. "I wondered if she told him the one about the woman throwing her eleven children to the wolves, or the one about the man cutting off his wife's head with a meat ax. They were Mother's favorites."[33]

At the same time, Gypsy shows her affection for her mother. Late in the novel, she explains Evangeline's threatening disposition as the result of her inadvertent use of illegal drugs. Biff wants to take his mother-in-law on their honeymoon in spite of her asthma and her hostility toward him. He brags about Evangeline's moving the dead man into the forest and burying the body: "It was kinda cute of her at that. They don't make women like that today."[34]

Privately to June, Gypsy explained how she tried to turn Rose from a threat into an asset. A mentally unstable and oppressive mother would not have fit Gypsy's own lighthearted presentation of herself as a witty stripteaser or her mother as an idiosyncratic stage mom. Gypsy did not fancy the public viewing her as a pathetic victim of a sick mother. She coached June to take a similar approach when describing Rose. She advised her that in public she should make their mom humorous: "Nobody buys a subplot like ours. Make 'em laugh or you lose the audience."[35]

Right before the release of *Mother Finds a Body*, Gypsy publicized Rose's antics while being interviewed for a newspaper article entitled "Gypsy and June—Mother's Girls: Hovick Sisters, in Chips Now, Can Grin at Frantic Youth." Consciously Gypsy reinvented her mother as a quirky eccentric. Her presentation matched the tone of her novel. She wanted to present her mother to the public rather than allow Rose to define herself and Gypsy publicly. "All the remarkable and insane things that happen to the Hovicks stem from Mother," Gypsy laughed. Her coupling of the word "insane" with her mother was telling and effective, as well as subtle. Given people's romanticized visions of motherhood during the war years, Gypsy kept her remarks lighthearted against a very deadly domestic enemy. Her approach worked in her writings and with the press.[36]

Any book about Gypsy's mother, even a fictional one, induced anxiety in publishers. Rose constantly threatened litigation against her daughters. In the novel, Gypsy's casual remark that her mother commonly steamed open people's mail made Simon & Schuster editors nervous. The publisher asked Gypsy to convince her mother to promise in writing that she would not sue for libel. Rose acted perplexed. She saw no reason to sue, so Gypsy explained that she had "steamed open envelopes and that's a criminal act." Rose retorted that it could not be illegal—"why, I've been doing it all my life." Most likely, Gypsy paid Rose for her acquiescence. Just to be safe, Gypsy's lawyer, who was quite familiar with Rose's tactics, insisted that Rose sign an agreement releasing any claims on the book. Gypsy was not interested in sharing her royalties with Rose.[37]

A few reviewers liked the second novel better than the first. The characterizations were stronger, and it had a better detective story. One review noted: "Written with the assurance and authority of a successful writer, one who has found her field and demonstrated her fitness. Make no mistake about that Gal. She can write." Despite favorable reviews, the sales figures were disappointing, far lower than for *The G-String Murders*.[38]

After completing these two novels, Gypsy expressed her excitement about the process of writing. "I'd no more think of saying that was a swell performance when I come off the stage," she confessed, "but when I finish a piece of writing, I read it over and I say to myself 'say, that's a hell of a hunk of writing!'" Gypsy compared herself to serious authors who felt compelled to write. "Mystery storywriters are like Proust—they have to write: they get a murder going on inside of them...and it has to come out." She viewed her literary career as a way to escape from burlesque, and she learned to take her craft seriously. "I used to come home at night full of inspiration, and sit up with a bottle of Scotch. As I wrote, the words seemed wonderful, just too wonderful to be coming from me," she confessed. "Next morning I always found they were terrible and I could never use anything I wrote." Other writers taught her to create a sensible routine. She started writing in the morning at about ten o'clock and wrote steadily for four or five hours. Using that system, she composed approximately a dozen pages a day.[39]

With the success of her two mysteries, Gypsy became a sought-after author. Trying a different genre, she wrote in an openly autobiographical style. During the early 1940s she published stories in magazines such as *Harper's Bazaar* and *Mademoiselle*. "Mother and the Knights of Pythias," published in the *New Yorker*, described humorous scenes from her childhood. Writing for the *New Yorker* and *American Mercury* proved troublesome because they demanded rewrites. Other authors had warned Gypsy that writing for the *New Yorker* could be ulcer forming. Gypsy "thought it was a gag, I felt fine when I started. Now, sure enough my stomach has gone to hell." The editor at *Mercury* rewrote Gypsy's first page. "He told me he had had difficulty with amateur writers before. An amateur," she fumed; considering that she had written two books and several articles, she wanted to kill the pretentious editor in cold blood. Gypsy retaliated by teasing about the magazines' paltry pay scale: "Of course the articles haven't paid enough to put me in the high income tax brackets....Their abacus only goes up to fifty bucks." Given the prestige of the *New Yorker* and *American Mercury*, she was actually thrilled to be published in those magazines.[40] Moreover, the novels led to occasional star appearance on the radio show *The Adventures of Ellery Queen*.

After her two novels, Gypsy liked to inform people that she had brought in more income from her writing than from her stage work. In the cause of gaining respectability, Gypsy donated her original manuscript of *The G-String Murders* to Princeton University. Her writings were even enclosed in the Rockefeller Center's time capsule then being constructed in midtown New York. Wondering aloud whether stripping was acceptable for a woman over thirty, she hoped that her career as an author would substitute for stripping.[41]

Gypsy aspired to the respect given a serious author. Even though she succeeded commercially as a writer, reporters and others condescended to her. When asked, "Who would you like to be?" Gypsy responded, "Elsie Dinsmore or Pearl Buck. Any literary female...who is not a butt for jokes like, 'I hope to be invited to one of Gypsy's literary tease' or 'She has another G-String added to her bow.'"[42]

Gypsy's literary career had its share of more serious problems. Other people took or were given credit for her writing. Suspected ghostwriters included George Davis and the female mystery author Craig Rice. A former newspaper reporter, feature writer, and theatrical press agent, as well as a short story writer, Rice worked for a time as Gypsy's publicist. Rice was hired to draft the screenplay for *Lady of Burlesque*, the movie based on *The G-String Murders*. That role helped spark the persistent rumors that she really wrote Gypsy's books.

Rice's affectionate letters to Gypsy suggest that Rice did not write either mystery. In one letter Rice gushed compliments. *The G-String Murders* left her "breathless." In the next line, Rice asked, "How do you do it?" She referred to Gypsy as a "smart girl."[43] Rice also complimented Gypsy on the second mystery. In January 1946, *Time* magazine ran a feature article about Rice that credited her for *Mother Finds a Body*. Outraged, Rice wrote to Gypsy that although she wished she had written it, she had already sent the magazine a letter telling *Time* it had erred. She hoped Gypsy would also refute the charge.[44] Gypsy constantly had to defend herself as an author. When one newspaper reporter rudely asked who wrote for her, she retorted, "Who have you had reading it to you?"[45]

After *The G-String Murders* became a best seller, a young mystery writer who was George Davis's assistant at *Harper's Bazaar* considered suing Gypsy. At Davis's suggestion, the assistant had drafted chapters for Gypsy, but Gypsy immediately rewrote them. The writer never received any compensation for her contribution. Although Gypsy admitted they had planned to write the book together, she denied that they had actually collaborated. Gypsy's lawyers quickly settled the claim. Her lawyer bragged about how well prepared his argument had been, describing his preparation as being as serious as a lawyer's in a homicide case.[46]

Like many talented authors, Gypsy admitted to receiving help with every book. Still, when asked if she wrote her books, she answered affirmatively: "I'm not very good at punctuation, you know, but the words and the arrangement of them are all mine. Why I wouldn't have it otherwise." Gypsy also spelled atrociously. She turned the publisher's changes into a joke. After an editor made modifications in *The G-String Murders*, she recounted: "In one place they had one of my burlesque characters saying, 'Whom in the Hell.'" She complained that she tried to telegraph them "Whom in the hell says whom?" but Western Union refused to send the message because of the obscenity. "I got that whom out by air mail," she explained.[47]

Gypsy's publisher stepped in to stop the gossip that Gypsy did not write *The G-String Murders*.[48] Lee Wright, who worked for Inner Sanctum, the mystery book division of Simon & Schuster, published a booklet of Gypsy's letters. The literary nature of her own letter writing demonstrated that Gypsy crafted and wrote her own books, particularly the settings and dialogue. The witty letters showed the growing warmth between author and editor as Gypsy struggled with her text. The last chapter was a "bitcheroo. I've really gotten to the point that I don't give a damn who killed 'm," wrote a frustrated Gypsy. Sending her publisher the first draft, she promised to continue to work on the motive. She had originally wanted to blame an insane man, but her publishers refused to let her use madness as the root cause for the murders. Playing with the arrangement of sections, she did not remember how material ended up in one section rather than another. She excused it teasingly, "Must have been drunk."[49]

Incontrovertible proof of Gypsy's authorship never stopped the rumors about her books. Gypsy knew she wrote the books and remained proud of them. Her writing career soon snagged on the bad reviews of her play, but she never gave up writing entirely. Ultimately, her autobiography enshrined her legend.

Gypsy's career as a writer finally earned her the title "Intellectual Stripper," a soubriquet suggested by an article about her in *American Mercury* magazine entitled "Striptease Intellectual." The two words were always used together, and she never lost the stripper part of the equation. She told a reporter, "I wish I could be remembered by the jackets on my books rather than those I take off." Her published works helped her gain entrée into New York's artistic and intellectual circles. In 1943, she even made it into the *World Telegram* crossword puzzle. With a lovely headshot of her in the middle of the puzzle, the clue read: "Pictured writer of mystery stories."[50]

9

Cultured Stripper

ypsy socialized with the intelligentsia of the Big Apple. By the middle of the twentieth century, New York City had become the cultural and intellectual mecca of the nation. Many European authors and artists fleeing fascism and those who emigrated earlier during the World War I era mingled with their American counterparts and fostered the spread of modernist currents throughout the arts. The fusion of cosmopolitan, avant-garde aesthetics with the popular, distinctly American (and African American–influenced) styles of live performance was a heady mix. Just as European intellectuals showed a special appreciation of jazz, so they were amused by an intellectual stripper. The reaction of critic and writer Jean Cocteau was typical; after he saw Gypsy perform, he chirped, "How vital." Gypsy often repeated the remark.[1]

During the early 1940s, Gypsy rented a fourth-floor walk-up apartment at 206 East Fifty-seventh Street from Anna Della Winslow. An interior decorator based in New York, Winslow knew actresses and opera singers throughout the world. She was starstruck by Gypsy's beauty and fame, while Gypsy soaked up culture from her new friend. In a relationship similar to that in *My Fair Lady*, Winslow improved Gypsy's diction and her manners while sharing her love of classical music. Gypsy adored Anna and wrote to her when she toured.

Located under the elevated train tracks and over a bar that housed an all-night skeet ball game, the apartment cost Gypsy only twenty-eight dollars a month, equivalent to approximately $450 in current dollars. Thanks to George Davis and her own carefully cultivated taste, Gypsy decorated her apartment exquisitely. Given the yellow walls, Gypsy chose pink for accessories. She bought Victorian antiques from junk dealers on Second and Third avenues, sometimes with Davis's advice. She had pieces restored and upholstered to match her color scheme. Occasionally she stitched needlepoint chair seats, as she had done for her country house. With her apartment as backdrop, she loved to entertain. In the garden in back of her apartment, Gypsy held Sunday brunches.[2]

Frequent guests at her parties included literary historian Carl Van Doren and his wife, Jean; music critic Deems Taylor, with whom Gypsy debated modern orchestral music; Marcel Vertes and Pavel Tchelitchew, artists whom she met at Middagh Street; and John P. John and Fred Fredericks of John-Fredericks milliners. John and Fredericks created hats for an exclusive clientele including Gypsy, and Tchelitchew designed striptease outfits for her. Her good friend and sister stripper Georgia Sothern was also a regular guest at her parties. Sothern described one of Gypsy's soirees as "something else. It was a blast. A swell party with great conversation and good drink and food." Grasping the reason for Gypsy's success as a hostess, Sothern explained that Gypsy had "a knack for making everyone feel important, of bringing out the best in them." Although she did not fawn over her guests, Gypsy showed her admiration for them.

The guests reciprocated by entertaining Gypsy, because they enjoyed her company and she added zest to their gatherings. The letters of congratulation on the publication of *The G-String Murders* from her former publicist Bernard Sobel, Deems Taylor, and others showed her friends' genuine affection. One of Jean Van Doren's postcards began, "The trouble with life is that you ain't enough in mine." Appreciating her wit, her friends also admired her ability to tell a good story and her wide knowledge on a variety of topics.[3]

Gypsy treasured her relationship with Anna Della Winslow, the Van Dorens, and other knowledgeable people because she sorely regretted her lack of formal education. She was grateful that they taught her to appreciate art, literature, and music. Although she exaggerated the extent of her intellectual dependency, Gypsy never stood awestruck in the presence of writers and artists. She never encountered a conversation in which she neglected to participate, and she frequently dominated the exchange. She talked incessantly, and her friends provided a willing audience. Adding a different perspective to social events, Gypsy fascinated them with her clever stories. Her experiences as a stripper were entirely beyond their purview, and they found her exoticism as intriguing as her conversation was engaging.[4]

Defensive about her intellect and education, she resented it when people thought she read or attended the opera only for the publicity. "Why should it be unusual for a girl to do this, even if her mode of earning a living [was] somewhat [of] a contrast?" she asked. "The appreciation of a wider intellect is not restricted to any particular calling, nor class." When she asked the writer Philip Wylie, known for the searing social criticism in *Generation of Vipers*, as well as *Opus 21* and *Finnley Wren*, for a copy of his latest book, he responded that she probably could not finish the text. Gypsy retorted, "I don't know. I read *Europa* all the way through and you can hardly call that scintillating!"[5]

The press always noticed Gypsy when she joined the New York literati. Everyone recognized her, while other artists and writers were often ignored. By reporting on her presence, columnists spiced up their descriptions of cultural events. One newspaper noted that on her return from Hollywood, she joined the elite at an exhibition of sculpture by the African American artist Richmond Barthes, who had created a bust of her. Reporters also commented on Gypsy's attendance at the New York opening of Tennessee Williams's *A Streetcar Named Desire*. On another occasion, a newspaper informed the public that Gypsy "stripped the book shops" buying works on art. For Gypsy, such publicity was double edged. She enjoyed the notice from reporters, but she hated their constant harping on her primary occupation.[6]

Besides searching for art, antiques, and books, Gypsy also browsed secondhand shops for phonograph records. She commented, "Music... belongs to everyone in the world. If you let it go by you're missing something. I wouldn't want to do that, and I haven't." Many impoverished European immigrants sold their record collections when they came to the United States, and Gypsy snapped them up hungrily. Her musical taste reflected her eclectic approach to all art forms. She appreciated jazz but was bothered by the pretentious fuss made about it in certain literary circles. Although she liked and collected both Armstrong and Ellington, "after a few Armstrongs I'm just about dead. These 'listening sessions' that go on for hours really bore me—too much of one thing to be good."

During her marriage to Robert Mizzy, Gypsy had cataloged his extensive record collection. Mizzy played the piano and was a serious student of jazz. He and Gypsy even celebrated their wedding night at the Open Door Club in Hollywood. Louis Prima's band played a jazzed-up version of the "Wedding March" in Gypsy's honor. Gypsy's wifely gesture of organizing the records gave her a wide knowledge of jazz that allowed her to discuss it intelligently: "Each album contained 12 records and there must have been at least 100 albums. By the time I got through with that job I knew about Bix Beiderbecke, Louis Armstrong, Bing Crosby (when he was with The Rhythm Boys), Jimmie Lunceford, Duke Ellington, Benny Goodman, Gene Krupa, and a whole lot of bands whose name I can't even remember." Such knowledge gave her confidence when she wanted to impress people.

Over time, Gypsy's taste in classical musical grew more sophisticated. At first she appreciated only music that painted a picture or told a story, but she came to value more complex compositions. She outgrew Ferde Grofé's *Grand Canyon Suite* but retained her adoration of Prokofiev's *Lieutenant Kijé* and *Peter and the Wolf*. Gypsy enjoyed works by contemporary Russian composers, including Shostakovich and Borodin. A Debussy fan, she preferred the melodic *Nuages* and *La Mer* to the more experimental *Études*. She loved Chopin but found Bach too difficult to comprehend and "never got farther than his Toccata and Fugue in D Minor." Although she disliked Brahms for the "abruptness of his crescendos," she savored Beethoven because "the listener is better prepared for the climaxes." Beethoven's Fifth Symphony was a favorite.[7]

In addition to attending concerts and visiting museums, Gypsy collected art, antiques, and an unusually wide variety of decorative objects. She gained publicity for her collectibles, so prettily displayed in her New York City apartment and at Witchwood Manor. "Ever since I was three I trouped the country, living in hotel rooms and theatrical trunks. We had no real possessions except props for the act," she explained, so as soon as she grew more successful, she started buying small collectibles. "When I bought my home I really started. You can probably call it making up for lost time." Her collecting sprang from her insecurity about what constituted home. Her material possessions belonged to her, and no one could take them away.

Just as an interviewer for a jazz magazine found her musical taste sufficiently fascinating to warrant an article, *Hobbies* described her collections to make the magazine's subject matter more erotic. It published one of the sexiest articles ever written about Gypsy. While the writer focused on her collectibles, the piece started and finished with suggestive remarks about her profession. The author even intimated that after posing for the discreet photographs published with the article, Gypsy modeled nude or seminude for the photographer. A photograph of Gypsy admiring a piece of glassware showed a great deal of her long, slender legs. Such an approach sold magazines—and Gypsy. The *Hobbies* author wrote, "Stroking the silky texture of her figure, my hand was following the exquisite curve lines. I was entranced with admiration of her, I was thrilled by the most perfect thing in the world—the divine female form." He finished, "It was a Satin glass vase with a repoussé figure of Venus. It was not Gypsy Rose Lee at all."

The author did, of course, write about her collections. Eager to talk about her belongings rather than discuss stripping or burlesque, Gypsy proudly showed him her possessions. She owned a few treasured pieces of expensive Meissen porcelain. Her glass collection consisted of Mary Gregory—at least she believed it did. Discovering her first piece of Gregory glass in a secondhand store, Gypsy paid twenty-five cents for it. Since Mary Gregory is very rare, Gypsy's pieces may have been good fakes, but they were beautiful nonetheless. She loved the characteristic blues of Royal Copenhagen china. She collected and restored frames, matchboxes, and even a small house made from shells. She also bought numerous objects adorned with cherubs, including lamps and vases. With their chubby bodies, cherubs appeared both innocent and sensual.

Remarking that as a child she had few dolls and little time to play, Gypsy described her paper doll collection wistfully. She liked to decorate objects such as tables and trays with paper dolls she purchased. Gypsy even confessed that she enjoyed dressing and undressing the dolls. She preferred "children, but I do have some lovely ladies. Some are partially dressed as actresses... ballet dancers, I should imagine. Their legs and arms are flexible and they have real hair. Needless to say, they are my favorites."

Gypsy acquired drawings by the tattoo artists Charles Wagner and John Bonzles, an early practitioner, proudly displaying them on velvet matting in a gold shadow box. The writer for *Hobbies* wittily observed that while Gypsy was "probably the only one in the country who prefers to see tattoos on paper, she can also appreciate a well-painted arm or chest."[8]

The Berkshire Museum located in Pittsfield, Massachusetts, and the Museum of the City of New York displayed Gypsy's plate collection in special exhibitions. She owned rare plates painted by Charles Dana Gibson, who originated the "Gibson Girl" in pen-and-ink drawings of the epitome of the modern independent white woman at the turn of the twentieth century. From one set of twenty-one plates, Gypsy lacked only three. The series was called *Life and Friends of a*

Widow, and each plate represented a scene from a youthfully attractive widow's life. The story line, depicting a slightly unconventional lady whom society criticizes but loyal friends understand, must have pleased Gypsy. She also had a set of plates depicting the Gibson Girls: buxom and wide-hipped but always properly attired. Like Gypsy onstage at the beginning of her act, they wore big, plumed hats and long, flowing skirts. With a provocative mixture of femininity, independence, upper-class poise, and a hint of mischievousness, they were the respectable pin-ups of their generation, and the public adored them.[9]

During the Gibson exhibition at the Museum of the City of New York to which she lent her plates, Gypsy quarreled with the artist's widow. Mrs. Gibson, who had modeled for her husband, commented that modern girls lacked the same appeal as Gibson Girls because they wore fewer clothes and concealed less. Rarely one for romanticizing women's status in the past, Gypsy grew irate. Never shy about sharing her opinion, she countered sarcastically, "Those Gibson girls concealed more, they certainly did. They concealed stays and bonded corsets and all kinds of padding." She fumed, "Men in those days just didn't know where they stood, so to speak, so far as a woman's figure was concerned." As she later argued, being natural was superior to artificiality: "Those girls have an illusion of beauty. Today the beauty is more genuine."[10]

During the early 1940s, Gypsy began serious art collecting. She enjoyed showing others her paintings and drawings by Marc Chagall and Georgia O'Keeffe. Gypsy also kept many portraits of herself. One of her favorites was by Marcel Vertes, who was known for his depictions of Parisian street scenes and cabarets, prostitutes and performers during the 1920s. Vertes rendered Gypsy as the burlesque queen turned writer: sitting at a typewriter in her dressing room with her legs exposed. Gypsy appreciated the image sufficiently to print it on her stationery. It also graced the inside cover of the British hardback edition of *Mother Finds a Body*, and she suggested that her publisher reproduce it in a new version of *G-String Murders*. Vertes was pleased, according to Gypsy. She gushed that she loved foreigners who had come to New York City: "Aside from the hand kissing they really make like gents."[11]

Her collection gave Gypsy a reputation as a serious art connoisseur. The Albright Art Gallery in Buffalo, New York, organized an exhibit of artwork collected by people in the entertainment industry. The curators of Dramatic Choice: The Theater Collects requested a contribution from Gypsy. From her extensive collection, she loaned the museum five pieces, including works by Edgar Degas and Joan Miró. Gypsy commented that these paintings "don't really present my tastes because the paintings I want most I could never afford. In Holland, when I looked at Rembrandt originals I saw beauty that I could not believe."[12]

Although Gypsy was rarely depicted in the nude, she did pose for quite a number of artists—some seventeen busts and thirty portraits. When posing for Carl Hallsthammar's sculpture of a female centaur, Gypsy wore strategically placed leaves. Artists, including photographers, appreciated Gypsy's beauty and body. When Gypsy commissioned Arnold Newman to photograph her, he posed her beneath her art collection. She reclined in her drawing room on a divan in a long black dress. People viewing the picture saw it as a parody of a stripper looking like an elegant upper-class woman of leisure. He knew she prided herself on her intellect, her possessions, and her array of well-educated friends. The picture represented both a lark and the truth. "This was almost a send-up and she loved it," Newman commented proudly.[13]

Gypsy purchased several works by Max Ernst and often visited Ernst and his wife, Peggy Guggenheim, at their home. Guggenheim's biographer referred to Gypsy as "one of Ernst's few paying collectors." After fleeing Paris during the Second World War, the European Dadaist painter and his well-connected American-born wife rented a New York town house named for the Revolutionary War hero Nathan Hale, where Guggenheim threw enormous cocktail parties with an eclectic guest list. Her wealthy relatives and friends mingled with artists, musicians, and other celebrities. Her uncle Solomon had endowed the Guggenheim museum of modern art in New York City, designed by Frank Lloyd Wright, and Peggy donated the modern art she had collected in Paris before World War II to that museum. Guggenheim and Ernst attracted those on the cutting edge of aesthetic innovation. Artists Marcel Duchamp and Piet Mondrian and composers Virgil Thompson and John Cage frequently attended. The hostess offered only small snacks, such as potato chips. To compensate for the lack of food, she always supplied an abundance of cheap alcohol so that the guests liberated themselves from the few inhibitions they may have possessed.[14]

At Hale House, as at 7 Middagh Street, people either came less than fully clothed or soon got that way. Recalling one Guggenheim party, painter Theodoros Stamos noted that "in the forties the art world also involved theater people—there was lots of sex going on—that sort of sex." He then made a "seesaw of his hand" as he commented, "actors, actresses,...also the *Partisan Review* crowd." Known for its spirited defense of literary modernism, the *Review* published many up-and-coming American writers. In the late 1930s, the editors were closely connected with the Communist Party and published radical social criticism. After breaking with Stalinism in the early forties, the *Review* developed into an independent left-wing magazine popular among New York intellectuals. Gypsy's lawyer served on the board. At Guggenheim's parties, the guests' radical politics and avant-garde inclinations, coupled with their sexual unconventionality—Guggenheim prided herself on her numerous affairs—meant that no one complained of boredom.[15]

In October 1942, Peggy Guggenheim opened a gallery at 30 West Fifty-seventh Street called Art of This Century, which showcased the abstract expressionists Jackson Pollock and Mark Rothko. Designed by the artist and theater designer Frederick Kiesler, the gallery boasted experimental lighting, sound effects, and movable walls. Gypsy displayed her own art in shows of women artists that Guggenheim organized. One of the first all-women shows at any gallery, the *Exhibition by 31 Women*, opened in January 1943. Gypsy contributed a collage of self-portraits in a shadow box. She created a funny but disturbing picture of her own body in a revealing costume with the head of a dog and another of her head on a Victorian bathing suit. In the foreground, she placed seashells. The work showed her ambivalence toward putting her body on display. Gypsy's work appeared again in *Collage*, a spring 1943 show at Guggenheim's gallery, and in the summer of 1945, in Guggenheim's second all-women show, *The Women*.

Gypsy made her collages from greeting cards, photos, and advertisements. Her pieces appeared among works by such distinguished artists as Pollock and Alexander Calder. In contrast to avant-garde artists who articulated elaborate aesthetic, philosophical, and political views under such terms as Dadaism and Cubism, Gypsy did not explain her artwork. She once advised, "Don't talk about a painting, just look at it and let it talk to you." She said of her collages, "I'd rather each person make up his own interpretation."[16]

Before Peggy Guggenheim's gallery closed in 1947, artists criticized Guggenheim for her frivolousness in displaying work by her own family members and by close friends, including Gypsy. Artists such as Marc Rothko and Robert Motherwell, whose careers Guggenheim had helped launch, left the gallery. The art community began to lose faith in Guggenheim's commitment to serious art. The surrealist artist

William Baziotes noted, "The gallery became a plaything. The artists were uneasy." Serious artists felt that showing with Gypsy cheapened their work. After all, she was only a stripper. Although Gypsy's work probably brought more people into Guggenheim's gallery, the artists failed to appreciate her as an artist.[17]

No doubt Gypsy resented other artists' objections to having their work exhibited with hers. Such snobbishness angered and hurt her. Gypsy enjoyed her interaction with artists and writers, but it also reminded her of her lack of formal education and made her feel more insecure. Gypsy exploited her career as a burlesque queen to promote her books and collages. The constant references to stripping in relationship to her writing or artwork frustrated her, but she refused to recognize her own complicity in this way of building her reputation. Her writing, creative work, and collections brought her the respectability she craved. Authorship allowed her to mingle as an equal with writers and artists at parties and literary teas. In settings she created for herself, Gypsy shone. Gypsy tried to prove herself intellectually by reading, viewing, collecting, and practicing art and learning about jazz and classical music. Collecting possessions helped block out the deprivations of her childhood.

10

World's Fair Stripper

In early 1939, after her unsuccessful attempt at movies, Gypsy returned to New York City. New York saved Gypsy from Hollywood, furnishing different options for work, friends, and intellectual stimulation.

A reporter asked Gypsy if, back in New York, she was finished with stripping. "I don't say yes to that," she cautioned. Having left burlesque before, she knew that she had returned. She held no illusions about burlesque's appeal, but Gypsy was aware how difficult it was for her to gain employment in legitimate theater.[1] Upon leaving Hollywood, after her contract ended early, Gypsy repeated her favorite goal: to play "a straight drama, the one thing I've wanted to do all my life."

Once in New York City, she was given her chance. In July 1939, she replaced the lead actress in *I Must Love Someone* at the Vanderbilt.[2] The fictional musical was based on the backstage lives of the real Florodora Girls, who had sung "Tell Me Pretty Maiden" in hundreds of performances of the 1899 British musical *Florodora*. In *I Must Love Someone*, the girls' main interests revolved around money and love. Gypsy received good reviews, but the press refused to accept her new career without mentioning her old. Even after her Hollywood movies, Gypsy could not shed her former profession. One headline announcing her role declared, "Gypsy Rose Lee Will Play Role with Clothes On." Such publicity infuriated Gypsy.[3]

After *I Must Love Someone* came a week's tour in August 1939 of *Burlesque*, a story about the stress professional success placed on the relationship between a comedian and his leading lady. Gypsy played Bonnie, the main romantic interest. Although the dramatic role in *Burlesque* pleased her, the theater productions paid far less than either Minsky's or Twentieth Century–Fox. Maintaining her lifestyle proved burdensome. The mortgage on Witchwood Manor and the cost of furnishing her apartment in New York City—not to mention supporting her mother, grandmother, and aunt—required large amounts of money. Crucial to any future employment, her glamorous image needed to be sustained. Visiting the beauty parlor, buying expensive clothes, being seen at the right restaurants—all took cash. She grew frantic for well-paying work.

Once again the tension surfaced between lucrative employment in stripping and lower-paid work in acting. And again, stripping emerged victorious. Gypsy found excellent pay and more when Michael Todd, producer and entertainment genius, resolved to find a classy stripper for the New York World's Fair. In 1935, during the Depression, leaders of the business committee of the City of New York decided to hold a World's Fair in 1939–40 to help bring money into the city. Grover Whalen of Schenley Distilleries helped design the fair and choose the theme "The World of Tomorrow." The fair was located at Flushing Meadows, Queens, in the eastern part of the city. A bond issue supplied the money. Some of the planned entertainment required special structures, and the workers started building the fair in late June 1936.

During its first year, twenty-six million people visited the fair. Crowds flocked to Billy Rose's Aquacade in the amusement area to look at lovely women in bathing suits. At the Music Hall on the fairgrounds, Todd staged the musical *Hot Mikado*, based loosely on the Gilbert and Sullivan operetta. But for the second year of the fair, he decided to produce a vehicle with more sex appeal, something that could compete with Billy Rose and surpass the Aquacade at the box office.

Though Rose's Aquacade touted plenty of bare flesh, audiences at the 1939 fair were deprived of a big-name stripteaser. Great fairs in the past had invented adult entertainment for the masses. The 1893 Chicago World's Columbian Exposition showcased Little Egypt and her hoochie-koochie dance. At the 1933 Chicago World's Fair, Sally Rand made a dramatic entrance as Lady Godiva and shocked and thrilled audiences with her fan dance on the Midway. Todd's plans for a burlesque act conformed to the new tone set for the fair during its second year when its leadership switched from the suave Grover Whalen to Harvey D. Gibson. Gibson, chairman of the Manufacturers

Trust Company, emphasized a carnival or state fair atmosphere to keep the fair from losing money. The chairman found his man in Todd.[4]

Providentially, Gypsy's sister, June, met with Todd soon after Gypsy returned to New York City. June was performing with a left-wing theater group, the Theatre Arts Committee. The committee was hopeful of financial support from Todd, but he showed no interest. During their conversation, however, Todd shared his dream of a new act for his Music Hall at the World's Fair. June suggested Gypsy and even offered to contact her. Todd responded enthusiastically to June's brainstorm, knowing that Gypsy would bring in the crowds. He told June, "[I'd] give my right ball to get her into a show of mine." After June relayed Todd's witticism to her sister, Gypsy replied, "Great, that's worth a nickel of anybody's money." Gypsy and Todd formed the perfect team.[5]

Like Gypsy, Todd came from a working-class background, but he never let his family's economic status define him. "Being poor," he once said, "is a state of mind. Being broke is a temporary situation." Born in Minneapolis around 1909 to Polish Jews, he was named Avrom Hirsch Goldbogen. To supplement the family income, Avrom labored at odd jobs. By age six, he was selling fruit and newspapers. At twelve, he became a roustabout at a carnival, where he learned how to rig the games of chance. By the eighth grade, he was skilled at cheating with dice. He helped the local pharmacist sell illegal alcohol during Prohibition. When he saw that bricklayers made fifteen dollars an hour, he learned that trade. Still in his teens, he opened a construction company, which soon failed. By the age of twenty, he had learned about commerce, hustling, and bankruptcy. Throughout the Depression, he displayed tenacity and resourcefulness.[6]

Goldbogen married at seventeen. Two years later, he and his wife, Bertha Freshman, had their first and only child, Michael. Given the pervasive anti-Semitism in the United States, he believed that minimizing his Jewish identity would help him and his new son succeed. Goldbogen decided he needed to change his name. Adopting his son's first name, he became Mike Todd.

For Chicago's Century of Progress exposition in 1933, Todd invented the Flame Dance, in which a woman dressed as a moth danced around a huge gas-driven candle. When she approached the gas lighting, the flame intensified and her wings caught fire, stripping the costume. "I burned up four girls before I got it right," he commented sarcastically. Much to his wife's displeasure, he began a long affair with one of the flame dancers. She joined a long list of his infidelities.[7]

For the second year of the New York fair, Todd replaced *Hot Mikado* with the Broadway show *Streets of Paris*, a variety show that featured well-endowed seminaked women. He starred Gypsy and comedians Bud Abbott and Lou Costello. Todd cleverly promoted *Streets of Paris*. He created a poster of Gypsy "even bigger than Stalin's," she recalled, quite a brag given the Russian leader's penchant for huge images of himself. No longer a failed movie actress, Gypsy received star billing. When rain descended for sixteen straight days, Todd had loudspeakers blaring, "Here it is, folks! Step right up! The only dry show on the midway! The only show indoors!" An enraged Billy Rose complained to the fair management. Both the rain and the hawking stopped.[8]

In *Streets of Paris*, as Gypsy slinked down the runway, a young Richard Blackwell, future fashion critic, watched carefully. "Every slight smile, curved hip, raised arm and seductive thrust created a frenzy among the wide-eyed, open-mouthed men," he recalled in his autobiography, *From Rags to Bitches*. Gypsy knew how to give the impression of enjoyment. Blackwell purred: "She loved her audiences, as animalistic as they were, and as she slowly peeled away her layers of carefully applied clothing—although never completely—the phrase 'stopping the show' became the understatement of the decade." Rehashing a burlesque technique, producer Mike Todd hired a prudish-looking woman to scream as Gypsy started to strip the last article of clothing. Gypsy added a waiter who dropped a tray after the women yelled. Todd referred to the gag as "honest larceny."[9]

Gypsy played various parts in acts reminiscent of Minsky's and the *Follies* for mixed audiences of men and women. She performed in wacky sketches such as "Rest Cure," in which she played the nurse and in which Abbott and Costello received little respite from gangsters fighting each other. *Streets of Paris*, like the *Follies*, dripped with style and class as well as little plot. Gypsy wore a dress designed by Schiaparelli given to her by fashion editor Diana Vreeland. A padded train shaped like a fishtail trailed after the black sheath.

For the fair, Gypsy performed "A Stripteaser's Education." It was a routine she had done at the *Follies*, but it was at the fair that she received acclaim for the performance. "Have you the faintest idea about the private thoughts of a stripteaser?" she asked her audience while she was still fully dressed in a frilly blouse and long skirt. "Well, the things that go on in a stripteaser's mind would give you no end of surprise. And if you're psychologically inclined, there's more to see than meets the eye." She continued: "And though my thighs I have revealed and just a bit of me remains concealed, I'm thinking of the life of Duse, or the third chapter of the *Rise and Fall of the Roman Empire*." In this highly intelligent act, Gypsy created a comedy of sex onstage.[10]

"A Stripteaser's Education" ended: "I stand here shyly, with nothing on at all—well, practically nothing—clutching an old satin drop and looking demurely at every man. Do you believe for one moment that I'm thinking of sex?...Well, I certainly am." By asking her audience that final rhetorical question, Gypsy created a subtle form of reverse psychology. Throughout the act, she reminded her audience that she was not contemplating sex. Instead, she was cogitating on higher subjects. While unbuttoning her blouse, she pondered, "I am wondering how much I should contribute to charity." As she removed her garter belt and stockings, she mused, "Art is my favorite subject. I like reading Shakespeare, too." Sometimes she stood there at the conclusion with her blouse open and holding her skirt in front of her. Before or after having sex, a woman might stand in front of a lover with the same slightly coy and seductive stance. She managed to create intimacy while simultaneously remaining distant from the audience.[11]

Gypsy lied when she ended the act by confessing to her obsession about sex during the performance. She actually concentrated on her movements and her timing. With her climactic affirmative answer, Gypsy pretended, as all great strippers do, that stripping for men's pleasure sexually aroused the stripper herself. The male audience, amused by her protestations during her routine that she was not thinking about sex, knew the "truth," so the act made them part of a private joke. At the end, Gypsy reassured them of her availability and interest and affirmed the men's projection of their own lust onto her. The idea stayed fresh and clever even when the audience failed to grasp the subtlety. Onstage while stripping, she was inaccessible to her male audience and at the same time seemed totally available to them. By discussing her inner thoughts, Gypsy seemed to strip her own mind before the audience. Psychology had entered the popular imagination, and Gypsy played with the unconscious and the body.

With women, the private joke was exactly the opposite of the joke with men. The fair gave Gypsy a chance to perform in front of mixed audiences of women and men, which she especially enjoyed. Other women identified with Gypsy's being looked at as an object of desire and knew that, in certain instances, that situation provoked humor. In front of women her act was even funnier, a parody of sexual submission that actually was empowering. Subversively, the woman stripteaser controlled the situation. Women understood that sometimes they acted sexy just to manipulate men. After all, men were really boys at heart and easily flummoxed. Women far more than men knew it was all an act—but a very fine one. "A Stripteaser's Education," later called "Psychology of a Strip-Tease Dancer," served her well throughout her career. She modified the act for various venues, including Broadway. Periodically she updated her routine by replacing older book titles with current best sellers.

In another number, Gypsy stripped off an ensemble conceived by the Russian immigrant artist Pavel Tchelitchew, her friend from 7 Middagh Street. In New York, he was prominent among the Neo-Romanticists and designed costumes for the Metropolitan Opera. For Gypsy's appearance at the fair, Tchelitchew created an Edwardian dress under which a top and pants covered a skimpy nightshirt. Tchelitchew envisioned that after stripping down to the last layer Gypsy would leave the stage in the nightshirt, return with a candle, and begin to strip off the nightshirt. Just as she reached a strategic place, she would blow out the candle and leave the audience in darkness as she exited. The act encouraged the audience to imagine her nudity.

The printed program for *Streets of Paris* revealed more than the "girlie" magazines of the 1940s. The program notes rewrote Gypsy's professional history. "She returns to New York at the call of Michael Todd, who feels that the Fair is in need of the 'feminine touch that makes a Fair a hit.'" Gypsy intended to prove that the "'tease' is still an important American art form."[12]

Gypsy garnered great publicity from her performance. In the *New York Times*, Brooks Atkinson wrote, "She is contributing the idea of strip-teasing without the sin." Gypsy created a style of stripping that satisfied the censors. She stripped from the inside out. First, she discreetly took off the underneath parts of her ensemble while she remained dressed. After that, she slowly removed part of the top layer. As Atkinson put it, she perfected her tradition of regarding "the whole thing with a sanitizing sense of humor." By the end of July, Gypsy's draw surpassed *Hot Mikado*'s record audience for the summer by four thousand. Such a feat gratified Gypsy, even though the acclaim came through stripping.[13]

In 1940, as in the 1930s, Gypsy won admiration from highbrow culture writers and artists as well as fans of the lowbrow popular culture of burlesque. Writing about burlesque, the cultural critic H. L. Mencken coined the word "ecdysiast" for Gypsy's art from the Greek for the act of molting—a fancy way of saying she shed her clothing. Gypsy fumed that Mencken was "an intellectual slob. We don't wear feathers and molt them off." She declared that Mencken did not "know anything about stripping." Uttering less a threat than a promise, she proclaimed: "I hope he comes out to the Fair this summer to see me toss 'em off and that he lets me know he's in the audience. I'll make his hair stand on end!" Although Gypsy parodied stripping, she resented that Mencken made fun of it. She later remarked condescendingly, "I figure he needs the publicity more than I do." Gypsy agreed with Mencken that the word "striptease" was vulgar. Rather than "ecdysiast," she suggested a variation of the French word for disrobing, *déshabiller*. Gypsy's use of French poked fun at Mencken's pretentiousness while making her sound both knowledgeable and slightly risqué.[14]

Nineteen million people attended the World's Fair in 1940. Gypsy received as much as four thousand dollars a week. One day, thousands of people watched her strip to "I Want a Girl Just Like the Girl That Married Dear Old Dad." In one of the sillier stunts during the 1940 presidential race, the fair installed an applause meter to measure Gypsy's popularity against President Roosevelt and his opponent, Wendell Willkie. She received a longer round of applause than either one of them.[15]

During the fair and her separation from Bob Mizzy, Gypsy renewed her social life. Occasionally, she saw her former lover Rags Ragland. She gained a new escort, the freelance photographer Eliot Elisofon, who worked for *Life* magazine. Elisofon shot *Life*'s depiction of *G-String Murders* and other photographs of Gypsy. His public statements stressed Gypsy's intellectual gifts. "The thing I most admire about Miss Lee is her art criticism," he said with a certain irony. Gypsy and Elisofon shared an appreciation of good food. After the war, Elisofon wrote a cookbook for which Gypsy wrote the foreword. Elisofon "cooks because he likes to eat," she wrote. "I'm a pretty fast kid with a knife and fork myself, but Eliot's the only guy I know who can make sparks come from his." Work interfered with their short time together, as Elisofon traveled to shoot on location and Gypsy stayed in New York City to perform, but they remained friends.[16]

The fair revitalized Gypsy's career. In October, when it ended, Gypsy replaced Ethel Merman at the Royale in *Du Barry Was a Lady*, a play in which a washroom attendant at a nightclub falls asleep and dreams he is Louis XV of France. In the play, Gypsy portrayed two characters, May Daly, a singer, and La Contesse Du Barry. The caption for a promotional photograph showing Gypsy in costume read, "Stripped of all her 18th century glamour, this will turn out to be Gypsy Rose Lee." One article review gushed, "When it comes to romance and comedy, Miss Lee takes over with assurance and finesse."

Once again, Gypsy hoped her success on Broadway would mean that she would never have to return to stripping. Meanwhile, Todd plotted Gypsy's future in undressing.[17]

"Man has forged ahead since 1940. New and better things have sprung from his industry and genius," boasted the General Motors Futurama exhibit at the fair. The Futurama motto fit Mike Todd. Gypsy recalled that after the fair ended, Todd kept all the costumes and scenery to reuse them. After Gypsy's appearance in *Du Barry*, Todd sent for her to appear in his next great experiment.[18]

On Christmas Day 1940, Michael Todd opened what was billed as the biggest nightclub in the world, Michael Todd's Theater Café in Chicago. He envisioned an audience of both working- and middle-class people. "There are plenty of swell joints for the rich but there ain't enough of the rich to interest me," he joked.[19] The club sold champagne cocktails for a quarter and dinner for a very reasonable seventy-five cents. Sunday, when other entertainment establishments were closed, proved one of the café's best nights. The evening's early shows catered to families. Todd hired acrobats and a clown. He installed a huge dance floor and brought in a variety of bands. In the late evening, the club exhibited racier entertainment. The floor show recreated another of Todd's productions for the World's Fair, *Gay New Orleans*. Gypsy starred. Once again, Todd promoted the business himself. "All of this and Gypsy Rose Lee too," the ads touted. "Smash business. Fifty-five thousand dollars a week. Unheard of in those days," Gypsy explained. Everyone loved it. One newspaper hailed the opening, "Todd does it well and wholesale." The press credited Gypsy for the nightclub's success, calling it "chiefly Gypsy Rose Lee's show."[20]

The demise of Michael Todd's Theater Café was a vintage Chicago story. Todd's partner had borrowed the original funding from gangsters, one of whom was Al Capone's former associate Frank Nitti. When he learned about Nitti, Todd told his partner that he had not suspected who his backers were and that he refused to work for them. The mob tried to persuade him to cooperate by carjacking the limousine that Todd provided Gypsy. Todd had sent the car to pick up his sixty-seven-year-old mother and his sister. The thugs who hijacked the car drove off without realizing they had kidnapped Todd's family rather than Gypsy. The incident made Todd disillusioned about the entire venture.

While working in New York, Todd discovered that his partner, Joe Miller, at the insistence of the backers, had instituted a minimum cover charge, higher prices for drinks, lower wages for the employees, and crooked gaming tables. Todd was appalled. He demanded that his name be removed and gave up any further profits for a lump sum. The police later moved in and closed the club after fining it for serving alcohol to minors.

During the summer of 1941, Gypsy went on the road with an act borrowed from Todd's *Gay New Orleans*. She performed three shows a day, six days a week. She backed the productions financially and shared the profits with Todd. To the editor of *The G-String Murders*, Gypsy described the joys of working as a stripper outside of burlesque theaters. These incidents, which were common on the road, resemble scenes in her second book, *Mother Finds a Body*. In Milwaukee, two policemen stood in the wings; "they really thought the second they left I would peel off a few layers of skin." In San Francisco, she worked on a stage six feet long and two feet wide, "which is dandy for a coffin, but not so dandy for me." Given the space needed for the orchestra, "Mother Lee," she wrote sarcastically, "has to crawl around through the tables while she does the act that sky-rocketed her to fame." The sleazy manager barged into her dressing room to leer at her and to coax her to mingle with the male customers.

In San Francisco she fell off a trolley and accidentally smashed the bottle of rum she was carrying. "With no pants on," Gypsy sprawled out on the street. She added ruefully, "If we don't do any business tonight I'll know the reason. You can't give it away and expect to get paid for it too." During August, she played a fair in cold and rainy Syracuse, New York. The so-called orchestra, an American Legion band with two tubas, added an accordion for Gypsy's number. The roustabouts used Gypsy's dressing room to groom the horses. "If I smell a little gamy when I get home, blame it on the trotters," Gypsy warned her editor. She swore never to perform at a fair again, a promise she would eventually break.[21]

Although pleased when her audiences laughed at her act, Gypsy was not convinced that they actually understood her witty dialogue. "There must be something amusing about a naked woman talking," she speculated. "Most of the fan, muff, and bubble dancers keep their mouths shut—then I came along with dialogue and they laugh at anything." She received two thousand dollars a week with tips.[22]

In 1942, bringing their dreams to fruition, Todd and Gypsy reached Broadway—but with Gypsy still stripping. Given their successes at the World's Fair, in the Chicago nightclub, and on tour, Todd and Gypsy planned to bring burlesque to Broadway but cleverly avoid the wrath of Mayor La Guardia and the censors. Todd's new show, *Star and Garter*, emphasized what he called "tall dames and low comedy."[23]

Gypsy wrote of this baby photo, "A few months after this was taken I grew so fat they had to saw the bracelet off my wrist." *The New York Public Library for the Performing Arts, The Billy Rose Theatre Collection.*

Gypsy with June in 1928. This photo was probably taken right before June left the vaudeville act. *The New York Public Library for the Performing Arts, The Billy Rose Theatre Collection.*

A provocatively clad Gypsy holds her perennial cigarette in a 1936–37 advertisement for Lektrolite lighters. *Author's collection.*

LOUISE HOVICK - - - 20th CENTURY-FOX PLAYER

Gypsy was forced by Darryl F. Zanuck, the head of Twentieth Century-Fox, to use her birth name, Louise Hovick, while in Hollywood in the 1930s. *Author's collection.*

Ali Baba Goes to Town with Eddie Cantor was released in 1937. Gypsy played an overdressed Sultana. *Author's collection.*

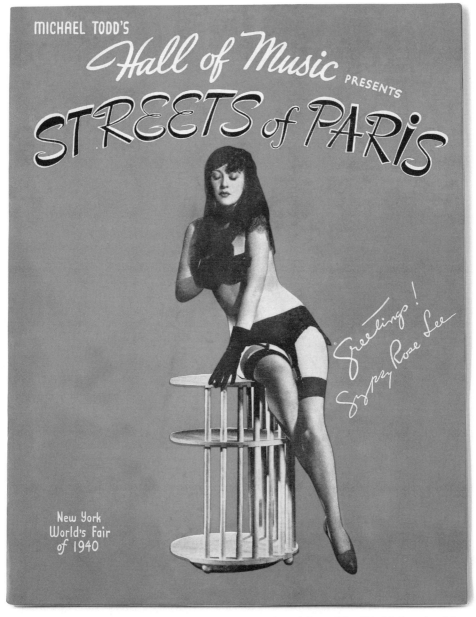

Gypsy starred in *Streets of Paris*, a show produced by Mike Todd for the New York World's Fair in 1940. The printed program for *Streets of Paris* revealed quite a good deal of what made the show popular: barely clothed women. *Charles Mosberger collection.*

Flanked by their mothers, Gypsy and actor Alexander Bill Kirkland cut their wedding cake in 1942. *The New York Public Library for the Performing Arts, The Billy Rose Theatre Collection.*

Gypsy gives a Christmas Eve performance for sailors in 1943. By the end of the war, ten regiments selected her as their "sweetheart." *Official U.S. Navy Photograph; author's collection.*

Gypsy does a mock striptease in the film version of *Stage Door Canteen*, released in 1943. Dancer and actor Ray Bolger introduced Gypsy as an "eminent authoress, a lady of letters, a young lady who went from without rags to riches." *Author's collection.*

Wearing extremely tight dresses with special corsets, Gypsy played temperamental entertainer Belle De Valle in the title role of *Belle of the Yukon* (1944), opposite Randolph Scott. *Author's collection.*

Gypsy and her son, Erik, on the Lancaster and Chester Railroad train, also known as The Springmaid Line, in 1958. As a publicity stunt, Elliot White Springs, the railroad's owner, named Gypsy the company's "Vice-President in Charge of Unveiling." *Courtesy of the White Homestead Archives, Fort Mill, SC.*

"I couldn't give a top performance,"

says Gypsy Rose Lee, famous author, actress, and ecdysiast,

"For fear a wriggle would turn into a wrinkle

A tousled torso is a serious liability in my profession. But see my new dress made of D A Z Z L E, the astounding wrinkle-resistant Springmaid fabric that is sweeping the country. Now I can confidently put my liabilities on skids and my assets on D A Z Z L E."

Gypsy and her troupe appeared in an advertisement for Springmaid Fabrics in the 1950s. They wore these costumes during a carnival tour across the country and into Canada. *Courtesy of Springs Industries, Inc.*

Mrs. Julio de Diego, **charming collector of modern art, and one of the ten best dressed women in New York, entertains the Debutante Committee for the coming Colonial Ball at Madison Square Garden to raise funds for the restoration of George Washington's Distillery.**

Joan Smith will represent Massachusetts, *Georgia Washington* will represent Virginia, *Jeannette Lafitte,* Louisiana, and *Andrea Jackson,* South Carolina, in the tableau depicting their ancestors.

Herself a relative of the Colonial hero who gave his name to Fort Lee, *Mrs. de Diego* is a playwright and author of distinction, whose works have been translated into many languages and dialects, including the Southern, and she has traveled widely.

Mrs. de Diego says, "I always carry my own linens with me, and on my last world tour I took only Springmaids. They are everywhere considered the best example of American superiority.

In Calicut a Nabob forced his way into my bedroom and I was terribly frightened until I found he only wanted to unravel a sheet to see how the smooth yarns were spun. In Yokohama a pillowcase was stolen off my bed by a Japanese spy so they could try to copy the lustre of the finish.

"The *Bey of Algiers* is now wearing a fitted sheet as a dinner coat, and the *Sultana of Sarawak* has made quite a riotous romper out of a purple percale pillowcase.

"In Monte Carlo they used one of my green sheets to cover a casino table, which inspired the *Duchess von Bourbon* who is an ex-chambermaid, to double her bets and break the bank."

Another advertisement for Springmaid Fabrics in which Gypsy appeared mocked women's charitable activities in the 1950s. *Courtesy of Springs Industries, Inc.*

Gypsy Rose Lee indulges in one of her favorite sports: fishing. She endorsed the sport for the Wisconsin Conservation Commission and was *Fishing* magazine's 1957 "Fisherman of the Year." *Courtesy of the Wisconsin Historical Society.*

Gypsy at her typewriter in 1956. She yearned to be taken seriously as a writer. *Fred Palumbo, courtesy Library of Congress.*

Gypsy Rose Lee played a good-gal saloonkeeper in *The Over the Hill Gang* (1969), which also starred Pat O'Brien. *Author's collection.*

Gypsy Rose Lee as Mrs. Mabel Dowling Phipps, teacher of interpretive dance, with Mother Superior Rosalind Russell in *The Trouble with Angels* (1966). Four years earlier Russell had played Gypsy's mother in the film *Gypsy*. *Author's collection.*

Gypsy suggested the comedian Bobby Clark, who had worked in burlesque as well as the *Follies*, as her costar. With his penned-on glasses, the cane with which he playfully hit chorus girls on the fanny, and his perpetual leer, he was instantly recognizable and always funny. Stripper Georgia Sothern adored working with Clark because he "was so methodical. Everything with him went line for line and his timing was beautiful," she said. Todd hired the talented Carrie Finnell, then ample and middle-aged, who amazed audiences with her ability to swing her pendulous breasts in different directions, independent of each other.

Gypsy touted Sothern, her closest friend in burlesque, for a part. One night Gypsy visited Georgia backstage. She explained about the plans for the burlesque-inspired Broadway show and said Todd had come to watch Sothern's number. Given her complete confidence in Sothern's capacity to impress him, Gypsy told a nervous Sothern, "So do it, honey. Like I know you can." After her act Sothern met Todd and Gypsy at Luchow's, a German restaurant frequented by celebrities. Right away, Todd complimented her and asked her to be in his show. Thrilled, Sothern agreed.

Todd offered Sothern a lower salary than she was accustomed to earning in burlesque. Although Sothern found Todd mesmerizing, she argued with him until he agreed on more money. Suspicious of Sothern's haggling with him, Todd asked if she and Gypsy had discussed the salary behind his back, and Sothern confirmed that they had. Meanwhile, Gypsy and Todd wagered on how much Sothern would demand. Gypsy won the side bet, and she kept her friend from being exploited.[24]

Todd's concern over Sothern's salary foreshadowed his financial problems. They became acute throughout rehearsals, and Todd canceled several previews. "When am I supposed to work the kinks out of the show?" asked the director. "Don't put any in," Todd responded. "We can't afford 'em." When a few of the backers threatened to pull out, Gypsy decided to invest in the show. Todd needed twenty-five thousand dollars, and he was convinced that Gypsy could not raise it. She proved him wrong by only taking an hour to deliver the money. The show grossed approximately two million dollars. Under her agreement, Gypsy had her take removed from the gross profits, not the net. This arrangement circumvented the myriad accounting techniques that were utilized to prove a Broadway production was in the red even when it made money. Todd referred to it as "salting your sugar for a rainy day." Gypsy willingly invested in herself when she believed she could salt her sugar for the future.[25]

While negotiating the agreement, Gypsy told Todd's lawyers, "I don't know anything about percentages. What I'd like you to do is make me a pie. Yes, just make a big round circle like this and put a mark like that and say, 'That belongs to Mike Todd.' Put another mark over there. Then that belongs to the other backers. And whatever is left is mine." Todd intervened, "Will somebody please make the dame a pie? She doesn't know from arithmetic." A visual learner and savvy bargainer rather than the dumb broad she was too often mistaken for, Gypsy asked that her portion be shaded and insisted they both sign their initials. Gypsy accepted the pie as her contract.[26]

Gypsy's arrangement with Todd made her one of the few women in the entertainment industry who received part of the profits. From then on, Gypsy rarely worked for only straight salary. She always insisted on obtaining some percentage, whether she invested or not. Gaining from the receipts kept her from feeling sexually exploited. In this way, she participated in her own commodification and profited from it. She was well aware of this dynamic, but she did not mind as long as she retained control. On June 24, 1942, *Star and Garter* opened at the Music Box. The show drew a Broadway clientele even though many elements of burlesque enlivened the entire show. Todd sold seats for $4.40. When a colleague told him that no one would pay such outrageous prices for "old" burlesque acts, Todd replied, "You see, that's where you're wrong. They're not old to a $4.40 audience, they're only old to a 40 cents audience." Featuring burlesque routines about sexy nurses, leering judges, and pickles, the skits included a xylophone player with a stripper behind him drawing the actual applause. In one number, a chorus line sang suggestive lyrics such as "Who'll buy my bunny?" In this company, Gypsy's strip appeared clever and refined.[27]

Gypsy's act, "I Can't Strip to Brahms," covered the essentials. The witty song explained how she tried to dignify burlesque by stripping to classical music. At twelve, she decided to be an opera singer, but those aspirations were dashed when she developed a problem with her chest tone—"too much chest, not enough tone." Although she tried to mix her classical training with burlesque, she learned at Minsky's that she "can't do the bumps to Puccini." Stripping to Wagner, she tried dropping her spear and then slowly, sensuously taking off the helmet. Her parody of stripping culminated in a succession of rhymes so forced they were funny: to the music of Rimsky-Korsakov, she had never been asked to take her "corset off"; to the music of Tchaikovsky, "they have never yelled take it offsky"; and she "can't roll a sock to Bach."[28]

Gypsy began the number in her customary frilly blouse with a bow, long skirt, picture hat, and black net stockings with garter belt. Most of the critics adored the new number, but reviewer Gilbert Seldes felt that Gypsy displayed "a snobbish superiority to her material." He liked the raunchier material, and the show contained plenty.[29] In another scene, Gypsy stripped to "The Girl on the *Police Gazette*." Gypsy admired the *Gazette*, a racy magazine that took a lighthearted view of human behavior in the guise of reporting on vice and other risky pleasures. "Everything about it appeals to me. I liked the name. I liked the pink cover. I liked the meat and potatoes Americana it prints." For that routine, she wore a netted outfit with fringe and a gargantuan feathered picture hat. Together Gypsy and Bobby Clark performed "That Merry Wife of Windsor," listed in the program as "stolen from William Shakespeare."[30] After intermission, Clark as a lecherous judge questioned Gypsy, the defendant. When accused of slaying a man, Gypsy protested that she "bumped" him off. Periodically, the judge slipped down to an opening in his bench to get a better view of Gypsy's exposed legs.

In bringing burlesque to Broadway, Todd barely escaped La Guardia's prohibition against the form. The mayor faced new pressure from civic and religious groups. Archbishop Francis J. Spellman of New York, an activist clergyman who occasionally attacked movies he felt were immoral, decided to clean up the city's theaters. With his encouragement, the Catholic Theater Movement listed five New York productions as "wholly objectionable." The five included *Native Son*, a play produced by Orson Welles based on Richard Wright's novel about an African American man's murder of a white woman, and *Wine, Women, and Song*, based on material from burlesque sketches. Mayor La Guardia ordered Paul Moss, New York City commissioner of licenses, to revoke the theater license of *Wine, Women, and Song*. When a New York court sentenced the producer of the Broadway show to six months in the penitentiary, Todd took notice.[31]

Public denunciations of *Star and Garter* brought it notoriety. A cartoon showed a hotel concierge explaining to a clergyman, "I think you would enjoy *Star and Garter*, sir. Excellent material for a sermon." Even Gypsy tried to be conciliatory to the mayor. Through gritted teeth, she told reporters she favored self-censorship as it was done through the Hays Office in Hollywood. At Commissioner Moss's insistence, Todd removed one suggestive song and fired Carrie Finnell, who outraged Moss's sense of propriety. While Moss allowed *Star and Garter* to stay open, he leaned toward not renewing the theater's license. Preemptively, Todd closed the show and put it on the road.[32]

Star and Garter garnered publicity in mainstream magazines that occasionally ran "naughty" pictures. *Life* displayed several photographs of the show, including one with a stripper having seltzer sprayed on her backside; the magazine noted approvingly that Gypsy "performs a striptease like a duchess at a garden party."[33] The musical gave newspapers and magazines a legitimate excuse to use Gypsy's seminude body to sell copies. Even *Mechanix Illustrated* ran an article about the show. On the first page of an article titled "The Mechanix of Gypsy Rose Lee," Gypsy wore an elaborate open cape, a headpiece, long gloves, and very little else. The piece began with an anecdote about a four-hundred-pound staircase that barely missed Gypsy when it collapsed onstage. The rest of the article discussed how sets and props were made and moved around for the show.[34]

Mechanix Illustrated could well have run an article about the construction of the costumes. Broadway designers Irene Sharaff and Karinska worked on Sothern's and Gypsy's outfits and found them a challenge. As a stripper who worked "hot," Sothern needed clothes that would practically jump off her body. In *Star and Garter* she wore a ball gown with invisible breakaway construction. When the song "Hold That Tiger" began, parts of her costume flew off as she gyrated her pelvis. Sothern's costume included a curtain-like panel of material that hung down because it was weighted with lead. She endured five fittings to ensure the outfit worked correctly.

Since Gypsy worked "sweet," her ensemble created different challenges. Her usual full skirt, starched petticoats, crisp white blouse, and large picture hat formed the outer layer. The innermost layer consisted of a small G-string and tiny decorative patches for each breast. For *Star and Garter*, both were crocheted in pastel-colored wool to form flowers. When she touched the blossoms on her breasts, the stems unwound. Gypsy created this effect herself, and it yielded a stunning finale. Karinska, who designed costumes presenting Gypsy as a nineteenth-century woman, understood her style of performance.

Together Gypsy and Todd created a classy burlesque show on Broadway. Gypsy commented on the perfect timing of the show. "It was wartime, and it was the first girlie show that had been done on Broadway in a long time—beautiful girls, scanty costumes, low comics." The show ran for 609 performances and paid her three thousand a week.

Star and Garter made Gypsy feel more successful than ever. The extravagant show embodied many of her dreams, even though she stripped. Audiences responded as Gypsy hoped they would. She overheard a woman breathlessly telling her friend after seeing the show, "Mabel, I have just seen without a doubt the dirtiest, filthiest show I've ever seen in all my life. Don't miss it." In the newspaper *PM*, Louis Kronenberger described *Star and Garter* as "a leg and laugh show with plenty of good filthy fun." One reviewer tied its success to the state of the nation: "for those wartime jitters there's nothing quite so restful as a good leg show." Soldiers and sailors on leave in New York City helped fill the theater.

Columnist Louis Sobel reported that Eleanor Roosevelt's secretary called Todd's office for tickets for the first lady and her visitor from Japanese-occupied China, Madame Chiang Kai-shek. Educated in the United States, Madame Chiang knew English fluently. When the assistant responded dubiously, "You know that's the one in which Gypsy Rose does—well, Gypsy Rose is in it and . . . , " the caller replied yes, Madame Chiang "was particularly eager to see that one."[35]

In publicity for the show, Todd revised Gypsy's mother's characterization of her. He hired Gypsy's dog, Popsy, and billed them both as "the two greatest no-talent queens in show business." During the show, trained dogs performed clever stunts. Afterward Popsy ran across the stage, to the delight of the fans. By just being herself she won the audience's hearts. The dog performed by instinct; Gypsy cultivated her act. The comparison between Gypsy's supposed lack of any stage skills and Popsy's disinterest in doing tricks shrewdly promoted the show, but it also played on Gypsy's insecurities as an entertainer. She confessed to a friend, the writer Elizabeth Wilson, "June has all the talent in our family." Gypsy's fear that she had "no talent" created another, more subtle myth. Gypsy's genius involved pretending that her act took no effort. Gypsy made everyone believe she played herself onstage. But Gypsy had consciously created the "self" that she portrayed while stripping. The "real" Gypsy was far more complicated and vulnerable than the glib stripper onstage.[36]

Gypsy triumphed in New York City. With Mike Todd, she received fabulous publicity and attained financial independence. She lacked an emotional attachment to a man, but that condition soon changed when Gypsy fell in love with Todd. Despite her usual drive for control, Gypsy gave herself totally to a man who had already proved to his wife and his lovers that he could not be trusted. Together Todd and Gypsy made money and made love. As her lover and as the manager of her career, Todd replaced Eddy, Gypsy's married lover while she was at Minsky's. As June saw it, "Mike picked up the myth machine where Eddy left it. They were both born promoters. Both loved the game." She also noted that both were married but Todd, unlike Eddy, acted as if he were a free man.[37]

11

The Naked Genius

At the New York World's Fair in 1940, Mike Todd, the impresario of Gypsy's show *Streets of Paris*, posted a large sign proclaiming NO COOKING BACKSTAGE. Gypsy ignored it. When Todd confronted her, she explained that she loved to cook and it was more frugal than constantly eating in restaurants. Todd countered that the food smells wafted through the entire theater. Todd demanded to know what Gypsy was cooking. When Gypsy replied that she was frying knockwurst, Todd insisted, "It better be good. I'm a maven." Before eating, so as not to be a hypocrite, he tore down the sign. Their romance began over their shared passion for sausage.[1]

During the most intense part of their relationship, Gypsy would have willingly given up her independence. Their successful business achievements and the excitement Todd brought to a relationship enthralled her. She admired Todd for being beyond any person's control. He loved risk and adored gambling. "Nothing frightened Mike, not even fear," his third wife stated. Such recklessness extended to the way he treated the people around him.[2]

Gypsy and Todd's affair started while they were working on *Star and Garter*, or perhaps even earlier. While quite free sexually, he never divorced his wife to wed his lovers. He and his wife fought over his liaisons, including his relationship with Gypsy. Todd endeavored to keep both his intimacy and his business arrangement with Gypsy relatively quiet. In spite of these attempts at discretion, Walter Winchell reported, "Gypsy Rose Lee...and Mike Todd are on fire."[3]

A macho man, Todd hated it when reports informed the public of his financial dependence on Gypsy or any woman. When the gossip columnist Earl Wilson wrote a piece on Gypsy's financial backing of *Star and Garter*, Todd, according to Wilson, purchased hundreds of copies of the magazine it appeared in from newsstands in Times Square. He wanted to prevent his wife or son from seeing the article since they would be displeased and he would be embarrassed.

In his private correspondence with Gypsy, Todd exuded sexual eagerness and fun. He confessed his love for her. Hinting at the pleasure of spending the night with her, he gushed that she was beautiful. He expressed his desire that she work only for him and declared that he would try to make her very happy. He courted her like a smitten teenager but with more style and zest. In one telegram, he added that he would see her on Wednesday and urged, "Be good—but only until Wednesday." But he apologized for his inability to share the depth of his feelings in writing. Accepting this flaw, Gypsy once described him as "no pen and ink boy."[4]

Todd thrived on his relationships with beautiful but insecure women. He focused all his attention on them. His courting resembled a hunter startling deer with high-beam headlights—with the same paralyzing, near-fatal results for his prey. He made women feel unique and worthy of adoration. Todd's women after Gypsy included such enticing actresses as Marilyn Monroe and Elizabeth Taylor. He exuded charm when he went after a woman. Wisely, he constantly complimented them on their physical beauty while reminding these talented but uncertain women that they deserved their success.[5]

"He is attractive to women in a rough way, like Humphrey Bogart or Marlon Brando," Gypsy explained. "You don't like him for his ties or syntax." Gypsy knew Todd affected some of his bad grammar. People underestimated him. His unschooled language put people who dealt with him in business off their guard and gave him the advantage. But privately, Todd read history, literature, and philosophy. His drive for self-education impressed Gypsy.[6]

Unlike Gypsy's other men, who committed time and/or money to political causes, Todd seemed oblivious to politics, and his FBI file showed him to be apolitical. However, his friend the writer, film director, and producer Art Cohn, who wrote a book about him, argued that Todd fought anti-Semitism for the FBI. Cohn wrote that when an opportunity arose, Mike Todd infiltrated the Union Party, a right-wing organization led by Gerald L. K. Smith, for three months while arranging to rent the Masonic Hall in Chicago for Smith. At that time, Cohn contended, Todd informed on Smith's activities to both Walter Winchell and J. Edgar Hoover. According to an FBI agent, however, Todd and Smith's FBI file contained no evidence to support the assertion that Todd had leaked information about Smith. An agent also checked references to Todd and Smith in other FBI files and found no connection, so Todd and Cohn may have exaggerated or even fabricated the entire episode.[7] Regardless of his political affiliation, Gypsy was in love with him.

As Gypsy became more frustrated with the status of her relationship with Todd, she plotted to entice him into marriage. Meanwhile, Carl Van Doren introduced the actor William Alexander Kirkland, called Bill, to Gypsy. A smitten Bill and Gypsy began dating. Before starting his career onstage and in film, Kirkland attended the University of Virginia for two years. In 1925, he starred in his first play on Broadway, *The Devil to Pay*. During the 1930s, Kirkland also acted in film; in the 1940s, he returned to the stage to act and direct.

Gypsy's and Bill's interests overlapped. He worked with Theatre of Action, a theater company that performed politically liberal plays sympathetic to the concerns of the working class. Like Gypsy, he possessed a passion for antiques. Her dazzling range of friends and acquaintances impressed Kirkland, just as they had Bob Mizzy, Gypsy's first husband. With Gypsy at his side, this relatively unknown actor became more visible. Gypsy's interests in Kirkland were somewhat underhanded. She presented Mike Todd with an ultimatum: She would marry Kirkland if Todd did not propose. Six months after she met Kirkland, she announced their engagement. Kirkland was on the rebound from a relationship with Phyllis Adams, a young socialite. Two months before his marriage to Gypsy, rumors spread that he had proposed to Adams and she had accepted, but her parents vetoed the match. Kept apart from the people they most desired, Gypsy and Kirkland settled for second best.

Gypsy's marriage to Kirkland surprised everyone, even Gypsy herself. She planned the nuptials for midnight on a Sunday night in August 1942. If Gypsy believed Todd would rescue her, she seriously misjudged his interest in marriage. The event was staged to emphasize maternal love. Rose showed up at the wedding and quite happily posed for affectionate mother-daughter photographs; in one, Rose fussed with Gypsy's veil. A reporter pointed out that Rose spent most of the wedding getting the best camera angles. Her presence symbolized the general sham of the proceedings. The wedding ballooned into a media event, including reporters and photographers from *Life* and

Spot magazines. As with many of Gypsy's parties, an odd mix of people showed up for the celebration. Stripper Georgia Sothern corralled guests into the library of Witchwood Manor for the wedding ceremony by hamming it up and announcing in her best southern drawl, "There's a minister marryin' heah tonight." Max Ernst and Peggy Guggenheim attended, and so did Herman and Henrietta, chimpanzees from *Star and Garter*. After drinking beer, one of the apes urinated on Kirkland.

Gypsy's feelings about the wedding bordered on the sardonic. She wore an exquisite black silk dress. Artist Pavel Tchelitchew designed an impressive headpiece containing real purple and green grapes. At the wedding, Gypsy announced that she felt like "an Aztec virgin being prepared for the sacrifice." Nervous during the ceremony, Gypsy cried when it concluded. At that point, Georgia Sothern declared, "My Gawd, what a performance!"

According to *Spot* magazine, "The couple honeymooned 'until their gas ran out,' [and] were back at their respective theaters within 24 hours." The marriage ran out of gas almost as quickly; the couple separated barely four months later. Contracted under false pretenses, the union was doomed from the start. In October 1944, they divorced officially in Carson City, Nevada. Gypsy had stayed for six weeks at a dude ranch to establish Nevada residency. She hated the place. "I am up to my Ass in boots and saddles in a Dude ranch I have renamed Purgatory Pines," she wrote to her friend Anna Winslow.[8]

After she separated, Mike Todd wired her that he missed her and instructed her not to wed "any actors not even a butcher." But no marriage proposal was forthcoming. Even by the time Gypsy married, unbeknownst to her, Todd's roving eye had found another target: actress Joan Blondell, whose early fame originated from playing dizzy blondes and gold diggers for Warner Brothers. A beautiful, buxom actress, Blondell seemed a more malleable woman than Gypsy.[9]

Publicly, Gypsy mourned the demise of her marriage to Kirkland. For an article in *Personal Romances*, a women's magazine, Gypsy rewrote her marital history. Leaving out her affair with Mike Todd, she managed to make the end of the marriage Bill Kirkland's decision. As she had done with Bob Mizzy, Gypsy blamed her commitment to her career: "With Bill, possibly the career woman I am, is responsible for the wife I am not. Some career women soft-pedal their careers. I don't. I am strident." She elaborated, "Whatever I was doing," whether performing or writing, "it was an all-consuming, all-out effort." In an earlier interview she emphatically stated, "My hobby is work. I get up, do housework, sit down and write all day long, then go to the theater."[10]

During the breakup of her marriage, Gypsy performed in *Star and Garter*, wrote a play, and entertained soldiers. June urged her to go on vacation and rest. No one was hounding Gypsy for money, she pointed out. In her usual wry fashion, June teased her that when Gypsy dropped dead from overwork, Rose would happily spend all her money. Gypsy ignored all her sister's good advice.[11]

After publishing her two successful mystery novels, Gypsy now ventured into playwriting. *The Ghost in the Woodpile*, like her second novel, turned on the tension between respectability and stripping. She laced the manuscript with true stories about not being taken seriously as an author or an actress. The protagonists of *The Ghost in the Woodpile* are Gypsy and her manager, Tracy. A fast-talking salesman when he meets Gypsy and her mother, Tracy simply changes products, marketing Gypsy as another commodity. Tracy convinces Gypsy to allow a ghostwritten autobiography, *I'll Bare All*, to be published, arguing that the book will bring her fame. Not only does the ploy of a book fail to bring Gypsy respectability, the ghostwriter blackmails her.

Tracy proposes. Gypsy declines, convinced that doom awaits them because their astrological signs are incompatible. Her pretentious publisher, Charles Goodwin, enters, unaware that she has lied about actually writing her memoirs rather than using a ghostwriter. Charles also proposes to Gypsy. In contrast to Tracy, he promises to act as her protector and provide her the security that only a man can give her, rescuing her from the debasement of burlesque. Although Gypsy argues that their backgrounds and interests diverge, she decides to marry Charles because she is tired and scared about her future.

Arriving just in time, Tracy stops the wedding, declaring that he has found Gypsy's real birth certificate and that their signs are compatible. Out of desperation, he threatens to disclose that her book was ghost-written. To preempt him, Gypsy announces to all the wedding guests that she didn't write her own book. Charles informs her that several months earlier he had already discovered the truth. With the book a best seller, he did not wish to jeopardize his investment, so he concealed his knowledge from Gypsy. Enraged by his deceit, Gypsy refuses to marry him and declares that burlesque was where she belonged.

The play reflected Gypsy's heartfelt ambivalence about her pro-fessional life as a stripper. She openly expresses her cynicism about a stripper's body as a commodity. At the same time, class consider-ations keep her from condemning burlesque. In one scene, when her publisher criticizes her theater audiences as "derelicts" and tells her that, as an author, she does not have to degrade herself by stripping for "leering truck drivers," Gypsy insists that her act has never lessened her. Her audience is no more depraved, she argues, than the "morons" who attended her lecture about writing.[12]

Although sprinkled with sophisticated repartee, *The Ghost in the Woodpile* had a rambling, disorganized plotline. The material was better suited to a novel, with more fully developed characters with clearer motivations, not just disconnected humorous anecdotes. Under no circumstances was staging it a smart idea. But for both personal and professional reasons, Mike Todd decided to produce *A Ghost in the Woodpile* during the run of *Star and Garter*. Throughout his career, Todd fluctuated between musicals and more serious plays. As he was skilled at adaptations, perhaps he thought that the idea could be turned into a madcap send-up of Broadway, a surefire hit to help his bank account. Todd suggested the play be renamed *Naked Genius*, a pen name Gypsy used when she signed letters to her editor. Gypsy confided to June, "I wrote *Naked Genius* for myself, but Mike doesn't think I can play it, so we have Joan Blondell." Gypsy failed to discern that Todd wanted Blondell in New York to start his conquest of her while he continued his affair with Gypsy. To reporters, Todd insinuated that Gypsy thought of casting Blondell as the lead, rather than playing the role herself. He told the press, "She's found she can make money without taking her clothes off and it's a new kind of thrill for her." Rather, when Todd had insisted on an actress other than Gypsy, she had suggested the uninhibited and seasoned Tallulah Bankhead.[13]

Todd convinced the Pulitzer Prize–winning author and director George Kaufman to direct the play. During the staging of *Naked Genius*, Gypsy felt both grateful to and intimidated by Kaufman, and she attempted to accommodate him by incorporating his recommendations into the play even when she disagreed. Familiar with what audiences enjoyed, Kaufman replaced Gypsy's subtle wit with broad comedy. As a result, *Naked Genius* had more colloquial dialogue than *Ghost in the Woodpile*, and Charles's mother, a bit player in *Ghost*, became a controlling viper. In later rewrites, the play included more bawdy references to burlesque. Gypsy was opposed to inserting "jokes about honeymoons and ladies toilets" because they were "in very bad taste," but she succumbed.[14] Kaufman's staging could not improve the play; it was beyond saving. In keeping with its new sillier tone, the protagonist, no longer called Gypsy, was named Honey Bee Carroll.

In *Naked Genius*, Honey Bee refuses to marry Tracy because of his alleged affair with another stripper. Charles insists on marriage to counteract his intense fixation on his mother. Honey Bee's mother, a former stripper, fences stolen merchandise in cahoots with a friend. The ghostwriter arrives to blackmail Honey Bee by revealing the authorship of her autobiography, but the police stop the wedding to arrest him for theft. During her farcical wedding, Honey Bee realizes the silliness of her pretensions and returns to Tracy, who still loves her.[15]

Both versions of the play, even without their intrinsic defects as drama, veered over the edge of what could be presented as humorous subjects in 1943. They mocked a sacred ritual: the wedding. During wartime, Americans held marriage in particularly high esteem, as soldiers either postponed marriage or rushed into matrimony before being shipped abroad. Women waiting at home were romanticized as the reason why men fought. *Naked Genius* portrayed a wedding as both an extravagant commodity and an epitome of bad taste. It also took aim at another highly valued institution: motherhood. *Naked Genius* portrays Gypsy's mother as more vicious and less likeable than in Gypsy's earlier writings. One reviewer remarked that her mother and her thieving friend were "not figures of fun...as they are meant to be, [but] figures of evil."[16]

Naked Genius premiered in Boston at the Wilbur and also played in Baltimore and Pittsburgh, cities known for their love of burlesque. To keep the play afloat, Gypsy advanced ten thousand dollars in addition to the money she had already loaned the production. After it bombed in Boston, the play underwent multiple rewrites. Onstage the characters seemed one-dimensional and the humor went limp. Predictably devastating reviews followed. The play "was something of a private joke, but when brought out for the public to inspect, the humor did not come across because human oddities and wise cracks alone do not make a play," stated film and movie critic Elinor Hughes.[17]

Reporters in Pittsburgh implied that Gypsy blamed the play's problems on the cast, especially Joan Blondell. Denying to Kaufman that she had spoken negatively to the press, she refuted the charge that she tried to "sabotage" the play. Gypsy swore that she had expressed her doubts about Blondell only to Kaufman, Todd, and her lawyer. Although she realized the play's flaws, she believed that it would make a good movie. Angrier with and more candid to Todd, she told him that while publicly she blamed her own script for the terrible reviews, privately she did not believe it. She blamed Todd for keeping her from rehearsals and dismissing her views regarding the cast, sets, and costumes. Todd's effort to fix the play with "razzle-dazzle" had failed. Gypsy did not mention the other cause of her pain: that Todd had willingly demeaned her artistic efforts in order to court Blondell and to make money from a movie deal based on the play. Todd's intellectual and artistic betrayal hurt her almost as much as his infidelity with Blondell.[18]

The personal and professional dramas collided during the play's opening on the road in Boston. One night in a restaurant, Todd finally admitted to Gypsy that he loved Blondell. He presented Gypsy with her consolation prize, an expensive cigarette case (or in her son's version of the story, a makeup compact). Refusing to create a scene, she simply left the present on the table. Todd returned it to the store. Buying Gypsy a huge, expensive painting of a nude entitled *La Toilette*, Todd wrote on the accompanying note, "You ain't going to leave that in no restaurant."[19]

In spite of the negative reviews, Todd brought the play to Broadway. For the movie rights, Todd was to receive $187,000, along with 10 percent in a complicated deal. But the studio demanded that the play run at least thirty-five performances on Broadway for Todd to get his share as producer.[20]

Kaufman and Gypsy pleaded with Todd not to take the play to New York. In desperation, Gypsy asked that the play's author be listed as Louise Hovick. Kaufman suggested sarcastically that his credit be changed to "Directed by Jed Harris"—a screenwriter and producer whom he detested. Todd utilized their negative feelings about the play as a publicity ploy. A few days before the play opened, he announced that Gypsy and Kaufman had pleaded with him not to open it. In his review, John Chapman mentioned Todd's public confession and said he "figured it was another of Michael's smart gags. Now I report same out of fairness to the director and author."[21] Todd could not afford to close the show; he needed *Naked Genius* to run long enough to secure the movie contract. On October 21, 1943, the play opened at the Plymouth in New York City. Kaufman stayed at his home in rural Pennsylvania. Gypsy attended an auction. They missed nothing.[22]

The reviews savagely attacked the author. In spite of Gypsy's successful publication of two novels and several articles, the reviewers all insinuated that she lacked the skill and intelligence to write and that her talent lay solely in stripping. One review snapped, "Playwright Lee has snubbed her recollections, which might have been gay...to indulge her imagination, which is chaotic, and display her wit, which is calamitous." Gypsy creates a world that she "never makes funny and somehow manages to make sexless." "In a poor theatrical season, the *Naked Genius* is a very poor play," *Life* magazine snarled. The article characterized *G-String Murders*, which the magazine had originally reviewed favorably, as "inept." The reviewer for the *New Yorker* wrote, "Only the monkey seemed to have much confidence in the script."[23]

Furious with Todd both for betraying her and for ruining her work, she vowed vengeance by withholding any further financial backing. But publicly, she turned the making of *Naked Genius* into a joke. She placed an announcement in the entertainment newspaper *Variety*: "For the sake of the legitimate theater, I have just tossed my typewriter out the window." The play's failure distressed Todd, too, of course. In addition to his intense dislike of losing money, he hated to look stupid in front of Blondell. The day after the play bombed on Broadway, Todd, who was usually only a social drinker, got smashed. Later he noted philosophically, "In show business you invite criticism. If you can't accept it, you should find another line of work."[24]

Todd pursued his financial interest by keeping the show open on Broadway. A master of public relations, he ran ads placing the uncomplimentary reviews in tiny type with the words "DON'T STRAIN YOUR EYES—THEY DIDN'T LIKE IT ANYHOW." Promotions proclaimed: "Guaranteed not to win the Pulitzer Prize. It ain't Shakespeare, but it's laffs!" The publicity worked. Reviewer Robert Garland's analysis in the *New York Journal American* proved prophetic: He expected the drama critics to hate it but believed the customers would like it. In the cheaper seats, he reported, "the laughter was long, loud, and spontaneous. I, too, enjoyed it." Garland's prediction was correct; the show boasted full houses for several performances. At one point, Todd informed Kaufman that the theater sold out and fourteen people had to stand. "Send me the statement verified," Kaufman responded, "and if what you say is true, then I'll quit show business."[25]

At Todd's insistence, the play ran thirty-six performances before he closed it on November 20. In 1946, Twentieth Century–Fox released the movie *Doll Face* based roughly on the play. When Blondell mentioned to Todd that she doubted that the Hays Office would approve the title *Naked Genius*, Todd joked that the censor could change the title to *The Half-Naked Genus*. Gypsy refused to have her name used, so the credits revived Louise Hovick—the actress who had bombed in Hollywood. According to Todd's son, Gypsy received $100,000 from the movie. One reviewer remarked, "With all due respect for Miss Hovick, her talents have been better demonstrated otherwise."[26]

Gypsy endured the jokes made at her expense while her personal life and her career as a writer disintegrated. Her tenuous persona as an author disappeared. Once again her mother's assessment of her "no-talent" first-born rang true. For the next decade, Gypsy wrote only magazine articles. More than a dozen years passed before Gypsy published her autobiography, which vindicated her reputation as an author.

But before long, Gypsy was personally avenged. Two months after Todd married Blondell, his creditors declared involuntary bankruptcy against him. Gambling on horses and cards exacerbated his financial problems. In 1950, three years after they married, Todd and Blondell divorced. Gypsy later confessed, "I was very much in love with Mike. He was wonderful fun to be with but he wouldn't make a good husband. We didn't have fights like he did with Joan. Maybe because we weren't married."[27]

One of Todd's legacies presented Gypsy with great headaches and enormous joy. While they were lovers, Todd convinced Gypsy to buy a house in New York City. The place was her most elegant setting—and her most extravagant expenditure.

In 1942, Gypsy bought a twenty-eight-room, Spanish Mediterranean–style white stucco two-story house at 158 East Sixty-third Street for $12,500, which was inexpensive for the neighborhood. According to one newspaperman, her neighborhood was "lousy with Social Register." The house contained special touches that Gypsy adored; eighteenth-century French design influenced the dolphin-shaped gold faucets in the bathroom.

The new house plagued Gypsy. The basement leaked, the furnace did not function well, and the house required a great many other repairs. Gypsy wrote that a huge piece of plaster fell on the real estate agent while he was showing Gypsy the place, "knocking him colder than a mackerel." In spite of all the problems, Gypsy loved the house and would live there for two decades. While she wrote *Naked Genius* and performed in *Star and Garter*, she hired workmen to restore the house. "Even the plumbers ask me why I ever got roped into a deal like this," admitted Gypsy. "Whenever a pipe needs fixing it crumbles into dust in their hands." When she could, Gypsy labored alongside the professionals. For three months, she claimed, she lived in overalls and painter's cap. She wondered why she had not appeared onstage in that getup and decided that "had they been easier to take off, I probably would have." Gypsy renovated the dining room to exhibit her china, coloring the dark north room a light blue and commissioning the painter Marcel Vertes to create a mural.

The renovations were designed to fit Gypsy's furniture and style. The drawing room featured an expensive Aubusson rug along with a four-dollar sofa bought at auction. The large formal dining room possessed an elegant marble floor, and Gypsy furnished it with Victorian furniture. The house boasted an elevator with gilt and mirrors and an atrium. Gypsy painted the fixtures in the guest bathroom a vivid blue with golden cherubs. She reported that one of the plumbers commented, "A bathtub painted blue?" His unimpressed colleagues grumbled, "It ain't normal, that's what it ain't." The rose-patterned wallpaper she chose made Gypsy's bedroom feminine. The room showcased her papier-mâché bed inlaid with mother-of-pearl, reputedly once owned by Sarah Bernhardt. In one of the guest bedrooms, she placed an antique bed that President Benjamin Harrison had slept in. On the fourth floor, a paneled study held two French Provincial tables, but the space, Gypsy confessed, "is just about as 'French Provincial' as the back line of a Minsky chorus."[28]

At a rough time in both of their lives, she invited her recently divorced sister to move in, and June lived with Gypsy for four years. During that time, June explained, "I've discovered Gypsy is quite a person, and she seems to like me as well." June described them as "two old dowager duchesses." While Gypsy and June lived together, Gypsy sewed clothes for her sister.[29]

Meanwhile, in 1943, the rest of Gypsy's family resembled sharks gathering around a potential meal. During the summer, Rose had asked Gypsy for two thousand dollars for a house. Rose had bought a pretty eight-room house in Nyack, New York. Having given her three thousand dollars at the beginning at the year for her living expenses, Gypsy ignored the demands for affection and money. To force Gypsy to pay the back taxes she owed on her old place and her new mortgage, Rose escalated her campaign. Wrapped in a mink coat and driven in an expensive car Gypsy bought, Rose sashayed into domestic court to begin nonsupport proceedings against her daughter. Again she attempted blackmail, seeking to embarrass her daughter through the press. Rose claimed that she was going to lose her new house to foreclosure.

Gypsy denied that she had stopped support, but she pointed out reasonably to the press, "Mother has me to take care of her but who have I?" She had "to worry about grandmother, Aunt Belle, and mother herself."[30] In the articles about Gypsy's alleged nonsupport, as well as other stories about Rose, Gypsy's excellent relationship with the press worked to her advantage. Rose never received the public sympathy she craved. Newspapers only quoted Gypsy and usually awarded her the punch line. Walter Winchell wrote that once, when Rose threatened to "give" her story about her daughter to the newspapers, Gypsy replied: "Look, Mom, don't be a fool. Don't give it to the papers. Sell it to them." All the articles painted Rose as mercenary, with her furs, jewels, and car all "paid for by Gypsy's art."[31]

Shortly after Rose brought suit against Gypsy, Aunt Belle wrote her that Big Lady's doctor wanted to operate on her colon. Gypsy sent Big Lady a wire promising the money and telling her to follow the doctor's orders, to be brave, and "remember I love you very much." One doctor wired Gypsy directly for compensation. Later she learned he had not even showed up to operate. Apparently he also never paid the nursing staff the money Gypsy sent for them. Big Lady fretted about the unpaid bills and nagged Gypsy about money. The next month, Gypsy sent more.[32] Gypsy wired her mother about her grandmother's operation. Soon after, she had to telegraph her grandmother to tell her that Rose had been in a car accident. Suddenly, Gypsy faced family crises on two coasts. Rose was admitted into a Baltimore hospital the same month *Naked Genius* opened.

Whenever members of her family became seriously ill, Gypsy displayed tenderness and caring. Gypsy reminded her mother of her Christian Science teaching: With the right thoughts about people being made in God's image, pain ceased to exist. She suggested that Rose repeat that belief over and over to ease the discomfort. In the same tone, Rose responded by telling Gypsy that her mother loved her very much. Gypsy charmed the doctor into letting Rose's dog visit her in the hospital. Even though civilian nurses were scarce during the war, Gypsy paid for nurses to care for her mother. Realizing that her relatives were not to blame for their physical ills, Gypsy acted with compassion and gave whatever help she could.[33] While she was in the hospital, Rose returned Gypsy's kindness by dropping her lawsuit.

Not surprisingly, in 1943, Gypsy's ulcer worsened substantially, and the doctors forced her to give up smoking and drinking. "It drives me crazy not to smoke," she complained; "I play with lace handkerchiefs." Not drinking was "a hardship too. I used to take a little nip because after the show has been running for a while, it gets goddawful dull." Gypsy finally quit heavy drinking but only temporarily abstained from smoking. Problems with ulcers recurred over the years.[34]

To outsiders, Gypsy covered her pain over the loss of Todd, the failure of her play, and her concern for the health of her family. A month after *Naked Genius* opened, she threw a housewarming party.

Gypsy had probably fantasized about entertaining in her New York house with Mike at her side to greet her guests. Although this dream was never fulfilled, another significant person attended with his wife: H. William Fitelson, an entertainment lawyer. Fitelson energetically represented Gypsy, June, singer Ethel Merman, and director Elia Kazan. He successfully got Kazan an unprecedented 20 percent of the profits to direct *A Streetcar Named Desire*, a negotiation that, Kazan recalled, "altered the position of the director on Broadway." Fitelson took no prisoners.[35]

While practicing law in the firm of Fitelson and Mayers, Fitelson advocated for many causes. He served as general counsel and managing director of radio and television programming for the Theatre Guild. With the sponsorship of the U.S. Steel Corporation, the group adapted plays by leading American playwrights such as Eugene O'Neill for radio. Fitelson believed that, although a business, radio could also produce art. "If more capable craftsmen would recognize this," he wrote, "and seriously devote themselves to this important medium they could introduce both greater artistry and higher quality that would be welcomed by listeners, and also by sponsors." In 1948, he joined the original board of directors of the Actors Studio, a radical ensemble known for acting coach Lee Strasberg's teaching of method acting.[36]

Fitelson served on the boards of various progressive organizations, including the *Partisan Review* and the American Civil Liberties Union, and helped found an organization to aid refugees from Nazi-occupied Europe. He supported the National Association for the Advancement of Colored People (NAACP), then a controversial organization because of its systematic campaign against legal segregation.

If Todd became Gypsy's villain, then Fitelson was her hero. More than any other man, Fitelson cared about Gypsy's happiness. Over the years, his law partners criticized him for undercharging her and for refusing to settle the many suits brought against her. Fitelson explained that if he allowed one person to extort money from Gypsy, others would follow. His tough position saved Gypsy thousands of dollars. He would remain with her through her darkest hour, when she was blacklisted by television and radio, and during her greatest triumph, with the production of the musical *Gypsy*. Few people have friends as loyal as Fitelson, and even fewer people have a lawyer like him.

Even though she had recently bought and remodeled her house, Gypsy decided to leave New York for Hollywood. With Todd gone, Gypsy willingly gave up her life in New York City to accept a movie part. But living a cultured life as an author and artist and as a successful performer did not totally fulfill Gypsy. She sought a deeper sense of purpose. Just as she had earlier transformed herself from "just a stripper" into a creative participant in New York's cosmopolitan culture, she turned her stripping into a way of supporting causes in which she believed. She displayed her support for unions and strutted her stuff for World War II soldiers.

12

Stripping for Labor and the War Effort

B ecause Gypsy was known as a Democrat, fans jokingly urged her to put herself forward as President Roosevelt's running mate in 1944. She quipped, "I'd like to but I haven't kissed a baby in years."[1] Publicly, Gypsy joked about her loyalty to liberal causes. She attended the Greenwich Village Fair, joining other writers to raise money for the Spanish Refugee Relief Campaign. Gypsy performed along with Al Jolson and Paul Robeson, the gifted African American singer, former athlete, and political activist. A newspaper photographer from the *Mirror* requested that Gypsy pose for a picture, and she consented. Cheekily, the photographer asked her to lift her skirt, and she complied. Then she informed the photographer she would remove her skirt only for the *Daily Worker*, the Communist Party newspaper. "She has very spontaneous comebacks for someone with so much leg power," an acquaintance wrote about the incident.[2]

Her exchange with the Dies Committee following her first stay in Hollywood had not frightened Gypsy away from publicly declaring her political beliefs, and her contributions to progressive causes continued to provoke controversy. For example, she consented to model for pictures for Ralph Ingersoll's radical publication, *PM*. Unlike other serious publications with a political message, *PM* wrapped its message in lighter clothing, featuring attractive, skimpily dressed women in such displays as "Bathing Girl of the Week."

When the first issue of *PM* appeared in 1940, a Brooklyn clergyman, Father Edward Curran, who headed the conservative International Catholic Truth Society, attacked the magazine as immoral. Photographs of Gypsy stripping at the New York World's Fair, with her blouse open, her breasts covered in material that matched her polka dot blouse, outraged him. Taken from a distance, the photographs showed very little, but Gypsy's mere presence in the magazine provoked criticism. For Curran, the pictures of Gypsy represented the moral degeneracy of the left. The magazine's radical political stance equally aggrieved the right.[3]

During the Second World War, Gypsy supported the rights of labor and other progressive causes. Boosting the morale of workers striking against the Helena Rubinstein Company and Hearns' Department Store, she explained how unions in the entertainment industry had been instrumental in improving working conditions. She exhorted department store employees, who were members of the Congress of Industrial Organizations (CIO), and factory workers to support their labor organizations and encouraged these workers to strike until their demands were met. In November 1942, she spoke before a meeting of the Newspaper Guild. A member of the audience complimented her on her remarks: "You were the only one who seemed to know it was a union you were talking to...the only one who talked union."[4]

Gypsy "talked union" because of her personal involvement. At Minsky's, comedians and strippers met in Gypsy's dressing room to discuss working conditions. The boss forbade these informal sessions, and they stopped. Then Gypsy joined the Burlesque Artists' Association. The union lasted only a short time, but Gypsy never wavered from her pro-union views. She expressed her strong belief in the importance of organized labor through a character in her first book. Jannine, one of the strippers in *The G-String Murders*, had recently been elected secretary to the president of the Burlesque Artists' Association. When the strippers received a new toilet, the candy seller suggested having a nonunion plumber install it to save money. She refused, forbidding any non-union-member to enter the women's dressing room. She snapped, "Plumbers got a union. We got a union. When we don't protect each other that's the end of the unions." She reminded the other strippers of conditions before they joined a union, when they performed close to a dozen shows without additional compensation, and the burlesque theater managers could fire them on the spot if they chose.

In the novel, Gypsy provided Jannine with another opportunity to talk about solidarity among burlesque performers and the unequal class structure in the United States. In a tirade against the police over their treatment of the strippers during the murder investigation, Jannine raged that the performers, both the strippers and comedians, might squabble but they were loyal and would not inform on each other. When a police sergeant tried to interrupt her, she retorted: "It's the social system of the upper classes that gives you guys the right to browbeat the workers!" Such class-consciousness contradicted Gypsy's own upper-class lifestyle, but she never forgot her working-class roots. She identified with the workers even though she lived far above their means. She felt she needed to pay working people back for her success.[5]

In addition to supporting labor unions, Gypsy turned her talents to stimulating patriotism during World War II. "If you only knew how difficult it is to strip one's heart clean," she confessed in an open letter to servicemen, "and to tell you boys how proud I am of you for the fine service you are giving to your country and to the strengthening of the arsenal of Democracy." Promising to send an autographed photograph to any soldier who requested one, she concluded, "You may paste it on your locker door, or if you want to carry it close to your heart, that's o.k. with me, too."[6]

In May 1942, Gypsy published a humorous article for *Mademoiselle* in support of the war effort. "They Need It for Bullets!" recounted strippers' problems obtaining materials for their costumes because of wartime shortages. Items such as beads and lacy stockings, even garter belts, were rationed or impossible to buy. The body paint that strippers applied contained a substance used in munitions. Materials used to make flame dancers' wings were reserved for bullet production. Rubber balloons presented a moral dilemma, since the army needed the rubber for tires and other equipment. "I can get them, of course, but I think it's unpatriotic," one balloon dancer explained to Gypsy.

Gypsy left the serious point of her article for the concluding paragraphs, where she encouraged women to take jobs usually held by men to help the war effort. "Girls…get a good, sturdy pair of dungarees and learn to dissect a motor. Learn how to fly a plane or drive a taxicab. Anything but the career of nude, or semi-nude, dancing. You can't get the merchandise." Well aware of the problems faced by employed women, she appeared at a benefit to raise money for the Child Study Association of America to help provide child care for working mothers.[7]

As part of the war effort, Gypsy advocated and raised money for various organizations. Helping to publicize the Japanese invasion of

China, she performed with comedians Abbott and Costello at a rally to promote a boycott of Japanese silk. Gypsy refused to wear Japanese silk stockings to protest Japan's aggression against China. "I've read that the American boycott of Japanese silk has cost the Japanese about 3 million dollars in trade," she told an interviewer. "The bombs that are being dropped on China cost about $10,000 each. Three million dollars will buy quite a few bombs."[8]

She made several personal appearances for the Red Cross. Like many other entertainers, she sold War Bonds and supported the USO. In the pouring rain, she performed in a benefit at Fort Monmouth, New Jersey, in July 1941, for twelve thousand soldiers. By donating an original script to be auctioned, she raised $100,000 in bonds for weapons. On March 20, 1945, the Treasury Department publicly thanked Gypsy for her participation as a speaker at War Bond rallies. The Treasury Department was "most grateful" to Gypsy for supporting its War Finance campaign.[9] Gypsy also volunteered in the same ways that ordinary citizens did, contributing to the British War Relief Fund and knitting for the soldiers. Her specialty was toe socks, which soldiers whose legs were in casts wore to keep their toes toasty. During the Christmas season of 1942, she sent her friends an ad for army duffel bags and explained that, instead of mailing out two hundred Christmas cards, she bought duffel bags stuffed with toiletries such as shaving cream at $3.30 apiece. She and her friends donated five hundred of these bags to the Merchant Marine Canteen.

As in her writing and her art, Gypsy utilized humor as well as sexuality to entertain the soldiers and raise money. At a Victory Book Committee rally, she and the distinguished and popular author Clifton Fadiman were both scheduled to give speeches. By mistake, or perhaps as a planned gag, Gypsy began reading Fadiman's speech. "All my life has been spent in the world of books," she intoned. The audience roared. Asked later if she had been nervous, she responded, "How would you like to stand up here before such a mob, with all your clothes on?"[10]

At one event that dramatized the importance of collecting aluminum for the war effort, she stripped pots and pans off her costume, then auctioned these household goods to raise money for the USO. Two strategically placed dippers went last. In September 1942, Gypsy performed for the Army Emergency Relief at Madison Square Garden. Before a crowd of twenty thousand, she led a male chorus in a striptease entitled "Heir to a G-String." Her fellow strippers included actors, singers, and comedians.

Critics questioned the tastefulness of Gypsy's acts of charity. The August 1942 issue of the girlie magazine *Sir!* ran a photo that showed society women placing gold stars on Gypsy's filmy net outfit. Men in the audience paid a dollar or more to remove one of the stars from her costume. Although this kind of audience participation was discouraged at Minsky's, it was encouraged for charity. The upper-class audience enjoyed themselves just as much as the crowd at Minsky's had.[11]

Life magazine described a similar event in a less flattering tone. The magazine discussed the 1940 Star Spangled Ball held to benefit William Allen White's Committee to Defend America by Aiding the Allies, an organization for which Gypsy often appeared. The *Life* article had headings such as "Society & Show People Make the Biggest Noise in Behalf of Britain." The article stated that many people who support aid "had begun to wonder if the cause of relief were not being harmed more than helped by the dilettantes who noisily appeared and reappeared at its big city shows." The article suggested that these lavish affairs consumed proceeds needed by the Allies. "War relief has become big business," *Life* stated, "but little by little it has assumed also the characteristics of show business, seeking support from those who care less for the quality of mercy than for self-indulgence and personal fame." *Life* concluded that recently many of the generous patrons were questioning whether these lush events were appropriate. The magazine decided good and bad examples of relief fund-raising. Gypsy's strip exemplified the bad.

Life's high moral tone did not prevent it from running a full-page picture of Gypsy with most of the gold stars removed from her net costume The scandalized mayor of Youngstown, Ohio, disagreed with *Life*'s decision to print the photograph and forbade the sale of *Life* at newsstands. A sixty-two-year-old man scoffed at the mayor's prudishness, suggesting that if the mayor "got a naughty thrill from looking at it, he should have quickly turned the page and said, 'get thee behind me, Satan.'"[12] Regardless of the criticism, over the years, *Life* reprinted the picture in several photographic retrospectives. Despite these detractors, Gypsy was not among those seeking personal fame by appearing for charitable causes. Her professional career had soared after she returned to New York City, so she did not need such events to foster her reputation. Gypsy loved public appearances and craved audience approval, but she dedicated herself to the war effort and to the soldiers more fully than to almost anything else. The soldiers mattered to Gypsy.

And though her family scolded her for never writing to them, Gypsy regularly corresponded with several soldiers she knew personally. Composing witty messages, she teased one friend that she would send him candy, books, or cigarettes—but not a blonde; she knew that, even in the military, he would find one himself. In spite of her casual tone, she expressed her concern about the dangers soldiers faced. As she wrote a neighbor, "These brave babies have really dug themselves in under my skin." For *Mademoiselle*, she wrote an affectionate and gentle article on "War-Wolves." Rather than portraying the usual stereotype of sex-starved servicemen, Gypsy described how soldiers begged her to autograph copies of her novels or meet their mothers.[13]

Gypsy enjoyed interacting with the troops. When entertaining the military during World War II, Gypsy appeared at her loveliest and most unselfish. In December 1943, she embarked on a trip across the United States that included a highly successful variety show tour of forty army and navy posts, mainly in the South. Even though many shows for the soldiers featured women in tight dresses and lots of double entendres, other performers considered themselves too respectable to perform with a stripper. In response, Gypsy toured more isolated camps, explaining, "I'm trying to hit small or out of the way places that ordinarily do not [have] any so-called celebrities."[14]

According to her records, Gypsy paid for the programs, costumes, music, and traveling expenses herself. When officials at Fort Bragg, North Carolina, asked about remuneration, she responded that she needed one double room for herself and her secretary, Jo Healy. She and Jo traveled in her trailer. One day they drove 380 miles in spite of gas rationing. "Trouble was the ration boys saw all land as level and seemed to figure I had a tail wind when they passed out the coupons," she complained. Flat tires also slowed their journey.[15]

In January 1944 at Fort Bragg, military doctors diagnosed a very sick Gypsy with pneumonia. The doctors insisted she stay for three weeks to recuperate. She teased that she contracted the disease from washing her hair or from changing out of her red flannel G-string too soon after she came south. At first she thought she had contracted a cold, and she joked that the doctors never examined her nose.

After her illness, she only briefly postponed her engagements. Although the doctors wanted her to fly to Florida to recuperate, she refused. The physicians insisted that she drive only a hundred miles a day and perform only one show in the evening instead of two. Sending the scripts as well as the scenery ahead, she planned for only one rehearsal in the afternoon. On arriving, she visited with the soldiers.

She always arranged a tour of hospitals and sometimes performed a special abbreviated show for the patients so she did not tire them. After sitting on the lap of one disabled soldier, she insisted fondly, "Mae West can have her tall, dark and handsome men. I'll take mine tired, lonely and strictly GI."[16]

While on tour, Gypsy complimented the Women's Army Corps (WACs), who performed noncombat tasks on base and even flew airplanes, as "one swell bunch of women." The WACs often helped Gypsy apply makeup to the male soldiers who performed in the show. Gypsy refused an honorary membership in the WACs out of respect, arguing that she lacked the essential qualifications and that the honor was suggested only as a publicity stunt. Gypsy complained that frequent public relations activities kept her from her true mission of visiting and performing for the soldiers. In all other venues, Gypsy never balked at promotional activities; her resistance signified her primary commitment to the servicemen.[17]

Gypsy encouraged soldiers' participation in the act, even though their contribution brought more rehearsals and a less polished show. One Friday night, Gypsy performed for Army Air Force pilots in training at Gunter Field, Alabama. Her number "Gimme a Little Kiss" depended on at least three volunteers. Another number, "I Don't Get It," included Gypsy and the Gunter Field Rockettes. With Gypsy supplying the costumes, soldiers dressed as strippers. The program indicated that "the use of enlisted men in the supporting cast tonight is the first attempt by this post to put on its own stage show of any type."[18]

The humor in skits Gypsy performed at the bases was based on role reversal. Gypsy acted as the sexual predator against a poor, helpless enlisted man. After taking a soldier out on a date and spending six dollars, including candy and flowers, Gypsy tried to convince the soldier to let her come into his home. The soldier demurred, remarking on the lateness of the hour. When Gypsy tried to kiss him, he exclaimed, "Certainly not! I'm not that kind of boy!" He insisted, "I'd hate myself in the morning." Gypsy responded that she loved him "like a sister." The soldier retorted, "My sister never looked at me like that." A military police officer misreading the situation assumed the soldier had been bothering Gypsy. He ordered the soldier to move along.[19] At Bergstrom Field in Austin, Texas, the male chorus line wore costumes with heart motifs and GI mops for wigs. Gypsy donated one of her outfits to a soldier who impersonated her amazingly well in a show entitled *This Is the Army*.

Gypsy was immensely popular with soldiers. Along with other celebrities, she performed on *Mail Call*, a radio program heard by the military. With a literary flourish, she and the dancer Roy Bolger performed the Henry Wadsworth Longfellow poem "The Courtship of Miles Standish." Armed Forces Radio Services aired Gypsy's appearances on the radio show *Command Performance*. On one of these broadcasts, she described the art of stripteasing. Familiar with her through her tours or the radio, soldiers named a stripped-down model of the Curtis P-40L Fighter A/C the *Gypsy Rose Lee*. By the end of the war, ten regiments had selected her as their "sweetheart."

While the troops loved her, army officers scoffed. To demonstrate their opposition to strippers, the chaplains often refused to greet her upon her arrival. Although Gypsy deplored the view that her act exemplified dangerous moral turpitude, she tried to sway the chaplain, who often sat right up front at her shows to watch for vulgarity. The soldiers would watch their chaplain, and if he chuckled, they relaxed and laughed as well. "So I played right at that chaplain for the first three minutes of my act," Gypsy bragged, "and I was in." In a gesture reminiscent of her burlesque days, she always tried to kiss at least one bald officer in the audience.

Such tactics did not win over all the officers. When one general told her that her kind of entertainment was not essential, she retorted, "You are just giving away your age." On another occasion, when an officer called her show "a bit too robust," Gypsy snapped, "Are you trying to tell me that this war is being fought by Boy Scouts?" One commander ordered a subordinate to cancel the show just before it was scheduled to begin. Gypsy suggested that the commander go onstage and announce that she would not be performing. She argued, "Thousands have seen me at my—ah—best—and thousands have made no objections." Gypsy performed at the post without any further delays or censorship. After she described her strip in detail for a special services officer at another camp, he demanded several changes. "OK Toots!" she responded. "You wear the rhinestone in YOUR navel."[20] Similarly, the post commander at Fort Benning, Georgia, wanted to sell a large number of bonds at a breakfast held for the soldiers on Easter morning, and one of the captains suggested that Gypsy attend the event. The plan was to cover her body with War Bonds and remove them as the bonds were bought. Gypsy agreed to come, and the soldiers greeted her impending arrival enthusiastically. But when the commander discovered whom the men had invited, he raged against having her attend an Easter breakfast and canceled her appearance. Occasions such as this, when she could not appear, were rare.[21]

Pleased by her encounters with soldiers and convinced of the importance of her work, Gypsy finished her tour of army camps and continued west. She drove to Hollywood for her second attempt at the movies. This time Gypsy returned to Hollywood on her own terms and with her own recognizable name. She was still anxious, of course. In her early thirties, she considered herself too old to be starting over as a movie star. As she reentered "La-La Land," her personal life took a strange turn.

13

Motherhood

Gypsy appeared in a cameo role in a movie based on the New York Stage Door Canteen, a center for the armed forces during World War II. Proceeds from the Hollywood film went to the USO, which ran these clubs for servicemen. During *Star and Garter*'s run, Gypsy actually appeared on Friday nights at the canteen in New York with other celebrities.

The movie, entitled *Stage Door Canteen*, was stitched together by a clichéd romantic plotline about three servicemen and three canteen hostesses. Released in 1943, it featured a stellar array of talent. In the film, as at the actual canteen, the acts ran the gamut from serious to humorous. Pulitzer Prize–winning novelist, film critic, and screenwriter James Agee described it as "a nice harmless picture for the whole family, and a gold mine for those who are willing to go to it in the wrong spirit." Gypsy provided that "wrong spirit."[1]

Dancer and actor Ray Bolger introduced her as an "eminent authoress, a lady of letters, a young lady who went from without rags to riches." Gypsy barely stripped, to a modified version of her best-known routine, "Psychology of a Strip-Tease Dancer." For the movie, she changed the word "stripper" to "exotic dancer," as if this euphemism made it more respectable. Gypsy wore a picture hat, a frilly blouse, and a very long skirt with a diamond motif, but she removed only her hat. She arranged her hair in long braids, which gave her a girlish appearance. After losing twelve pounds when she arrived in Hollywood, she noted that she was a "little gaunt for whoring but for pictures, good."[2]

In her act, she explained what a "fan dancer" thinks about during a performance. First she talked about her imagined childhood, mentioning her early training in ballet. Before making her professional debut, she studied psychology, zoology, biology, and anthropology at the all-women's Sweet Briar College. After this long monologue she finally exposed a tiny bit of shoulder. She explained she was uninterested in the audience's reaction to her shoulder but actually was contemplating a painting by Van Gogh or Cézanne or the pleasure she found in reading *Lady Windermere's Fan* (the 1892 play by Oscar Wilde). Without removing her blouse, she explained that she was not thinking about the "whiteness" of her shoulder but about "her country house or the jolly fun in shooting grouse." She slowly lifted up her skirt, explaining that when she raised its hem, she was mentally computing how much she would give to charity. As she rolled down her stockings, showing off her comely legs, she confessed that she was pondering "the third chapter of *All This and Heaven Too*." With an amazingly swift gesture, she managed to remove her garter belt and then the bow from her hat, which she placed on a soldier's head. Next, with an excruciatingly slow gesture, she took off her cummerbund and unbuttoned her blouse, displaying one arm.

Turning her back, she removed her slip without exposing a leg. She dumped her petticoat on a soldier's head in the front row, much to the delight of the audience. Taking off a glove, she said, "I take the last thing off and stand there demurely looking at every man. Do you really believe I am thinking about art?" When they shouted no, she laughingly assured them that she was contemplating painting. In this movie version, the word "art" replaced "sex," her usual ending. At the end of the number she stood fully dressed. When one soldier pleaded with her to perform as she had in *Star and Garter*, Gypsy protested by uttering her classic line, "Oh boys, I couldn't. I'll catch cold." From behind the stage, she threw out her garter belt, and the soldiers fought good-naturedly for it.

In *Stage Door Canteen*, Gypsy played Gypsy brilliantly. On-screen, she parodied her own act. She appeared to enjoy her routine, and her enthusiasm infected the audience. Gypsy's scene in *Stage Door Canteen* turned out to be her finest in any movie. The real Stage Door Canteen never allowed Gypsy to perform "Psychology of a Strip-Tease Dancer," but the movie audience relished it. Reviews of Gypsy's performance in *Stage Door Canteen* were flattering. The *New Republic* raved, "Gypsy

Rose Lee steals everything without removing anything but a garter belt." She exuded as much "gracious femininity by face, timing and voice as Katharine Hepburn." Of course, not everyone thought the strip appropriate. Columnist Ed Sullivan was outraged that Gypsy did a striptease in front of a row of Allied flags. Sullivan thought the scene particularly objectionable when one item of clothing fell "on the base of the American flag and the tag of the scene, with fine looking boys in uniform fighting over one of the flimsy discards."[3] The Legion of Decency disapproved of Gypsy's act for more fundamental reasons. Although she showed far less than an actress in a bathing suit, the concept of a woman stripping as entertainment indicated moral turpitude. The producer refused to take Gypsy's scene out of the film, and the Legion of Decency gave the movie only a B rating, rather than its top score.

In spite of the controversy, Hollywood called her back less than a year after *Stage Door Canteen* showed in theaters to star in *Belle of the Yukon*. As the female lead, Belle De Valle, Gypsy played opposite Randolph Scott, an actor who had appeared in numerous westerns. In contrast to her earlier sojourn in Hollywood when she confessed to knowing almost nothing about how films were produced, Gypsy learned about the producer's other films and reviewed the work of the cinematographer. When asked if she stripped in *Belle*, she retorted, "It's about time I start keeping 'em on, don't you think?"[4]

Part of Gypsy's confidence in returning to Hollywood lay in her ability to control the entire process. Her lawyer and protector, H. William Fitelson, crafted a very careful five-year movie contract, ensuring that she could approve the script. In a memo to her he reassured her that the contract was not exclusive. She could write or perform elsewhere, whatever would make her happy. Since other work might pay more and offer greater stability, Fitelson guaranteed that she had the right to pursue it. Her lawyer's determination and ability to work out such a favorable contract may have stemmed from other actors' discontent with inflexible studios. Around the time that *Belle of the Yukon* was being filmed, actress Olivia de Havilland, star of *Hold Back the Dawn* and supporting actress in *Gone with the Wind*, sued Warner Brothers over her restrictive contract.[5]

In *Belle of the Yukon*, as in *Stage Door Canteen*, Gypsy played a stage performer. Set in Malamute, Alaska, during the gold rush, *Belle of the Yukon* revolves around a rogue from the U.S. mainland, crooked but lovable John Calhoun, who adopts a new identity as an honorable man. To maintain the image, Calhoun refuses to allow a gambling concession in his dance hall, Honest John's Emporium. For entertainment, Calhoun hires a new act, Belle De Valle and Her Girls. When Calhoun first encounters De Valle, she immediately shatters a vase over his head. Back in the States, they had been intimate and Calhoun had then deserted her. But in Alaska, they reconcile. De Valle is pleased that Calhoun seems to have given up dishonest schemes, but she learns that he intends to rob the bank. She convinces Calhoun to drop the plan. Then, when crooks try to steal money from the bank, Calhoun heroically protects it.[6]

The role suited Gypsy, since she performed onstage as an entertainer as well as playing comedy. The critics greeted the film kindly. One concluded that if she received the right roles, she could achieve lasting stardom in movies. Comparing her to a young Mae West, another raved, "Miss Lee steps neatly through her role with the same contagious sense of enjoyment that she has on the stage."[7]

In a funny review of her own movie that Gypsy wrote as a guest columnist for the *Detroit Times*, she acknowledged the weak plot. "But in the picture I get my guy...and the audience gets their money's worth." She complained, however, that the film shared billing in theaters with *Tarzan and the Amazons*. Tarzan "plays the entire picture in nothing but a dirty make-up towel and I play mine bundled up to the ears," she protested. "That isn't my idea of justice but that's Hollywood, I guess."[8]

In the film, Gypsy wore tightly fitted gowns, and the wardrobe department struggled to create the right corset. The first one proved so tight that Gypsy fainted on the set. Commenting on the problems of nineteenth-century women, she grumbled, "No wonder girls were straitlaced in those days! They couldn't even bend the Golden Rule." Finally the studio hired an expert corsetiere who, Gypsy noted with relief, "gave me a corset in which I could work the day through, without rigor mortis setting in."[9]

While in Hollywood, Gypsy seized control of her personal life and never let go again. No man would ever be able to hurt her as Mike Todd had. Gypsy consciously decided to have a child. How she had managed to avoid pregnancy with Rags Ragland, Waxy Gordon, Eddy, Bob Mizzy, Mike Todd, and Bill Kirkland cannot be known for certain. In the early 1930s, Rags Ragland mentioned in a letter that Gypsy had uterine problems. Gypsy may have suffered from medical conditions that precluded pregnancy. Of course, she or her partners may well have used some form of birth control. With the right physician and pharmacist, condoms and diaphragms were available, especially to entertainers on the margins of respectable society. Celebrities' doctors expected such behavior from their patients.[10]

Gypsy's motivation for wanting a child revolved around both her achievements and her losses. Thirty-three years old in 1944, Gypsy had achieved astonishing success. She had performed at the World's Fair and on Broadway, and she had written two well-received novels. As she began her second Hollywood career, her professional future seemed promising, and she was prepared to support her child. At the same time, Gypsy had known devastating failure, including her divorce, her relationship with Todd, her early movie career, and her play.

Since the man she most desired had betrayed her, deciding to have a child promised compensation. Unfulfilled romantically, Gypsy expected her child to give her unconditional love. After Todd left, she explained years later to her son, "I felt so alone that I decided to have something no one would ever be able to take away from me." As her son explained, "She had a brief affair with Otto Preminger for the purpose of conceiving me."[11] The desire for complete independence in raising the child played a part in her selection of Otto Preminger as the father.

Born in Austria around 1905, Preminger had studied law. Meanwhile, he worked in amateur theatrics and directed his own company for a short time. In 1935, in response to the alarming rise of fascism in Europe, the Jewish actor left for the U.S. By 1941, Preminger was working for Twentieth Century–Fox. As a director, Preminger engaged in legendary fights with studio vice president and cofounder Darryl Zanuck as well as with the actors in his films. Preminger shared Gypsy's politically liberal views, and he stood up against the censors. Gypsy remarked that she respected his mind.

Having met Preminger at a party, Gypsy entertained him in the evenings. She even cooked intimate dinners for him over a hot plate in her rented bungalow in Santa Monica. Since the hour commute from Santa Monica to the studio tired her and used up her gasoline allotment, Gypsy moved into the studio while she worked on *Belle of the Yukon* in 1944. Her large dressing room consisted of a living room, bathroom, dining room, and kitchenette. Both the bungalow and the dressing room provided fine locations for an affair.

Preminger turned out to be the perfect choice as the father of her child. Cosmopolitan, charming, and experienced, Preminger suited Gypsy. After divorcing his wife, he slept with a number of young actresses on a very casual basis but stayed unmarried and uncommitted. According to one of Preminger's biographers, the women "all had to be slim, tall, long-legged and willing."[12]

Close to the time of her child's conception, Gypsy mentioned her new relationship to a friend: "I'm having my next ulcer by a real monster." She realized that her friends would disapprove but she planned to end the affair before anyone found out about it. Todd and Preminger were quite similar: charismatic, smart, daring, and users of women. Gypsy's experience with Todd prepared her for Preminger. She understood the type. For Gypsy, the difference lay in her ability to control her relationship with Preminger emotionally and practically. She left him before he could leave her, and the affair proved that she did not need Todd.[13]

After a few short months of sex with Preminger, Gypsy was pregnant. This fling resulted in no serious or lasting emotional ties for either party. A reporter once queried their son as to whether his birth father had really loved his mother. "I don't know," he responded honestly. "They did not discuss such aspects of the past, just accepted each other." In truth, neither of them searched for or even desired love from each other. In spring 1944, Gypsy left Hollywood without bothering to say good-bye to Preminger.[14]

At first Gypsy refused to mention her pregnancy publicly. When she was more than three months pregnant, she was asked to pose for publicity pictures for *Belle of the Yukon*. She demurred on the grounds that she was writing and possessed few clothes or wigs. Typing had taken its toll on her body. She claimed she had sunken eyes and sagging cheeks from the exhaustion of being an author. Gypsy begged the studio to recycle stills from the picture, since the movie showed her with false eyelashes and fake breasts. Back in New York, sounding like a pregnant woman who had just endured a few months of morning sickness, she added that the only product she could promote was Bromo Seltzer. She never mentioned her pregnancy in the letter.[15]

Gypsy's personal life always connected to her professional life, and she carefully calculated the timing of her child's conception. Only a small window of opportunity existed between when she met Preminger and when her divorce from Kirkland in October 1944 would be finalized. Gypsy was determined to create the fiction of legitimacy for her child. Gypsy no doubt worried about how a public revelation of her child's illegitimacy would affect her movie career. A certain amount of "bad girl" behavior might have been tolerated from Gypsy; the expectations and standards for Gypsy differed from those for the actress Ingrid Bergman, for example. Anyone looking at pictures in *Life* magazine of a deified Bergman in various nuns' habits could have predicted the huge reaction over her adultery and subsequent pregnancy. Gypsy maintained a more flexible reputation, but she desired a legitimate movie career, and if she openly had an illegitimate child, the censors might have targeted her again.

Her soon-to-be ex-husband Bill Kirkland rescued her. The personal disaster of their short marriage was not unmitigated. Three years after they wed, without bitterness and at some personal risk, her second husband willingly lied for Gypsy. Although the couple had separated long before the baby's conception and he was not the biological father, Kirkland pretended that he was. His motivation remains unclear, except that he wanted to help her and vaguely felt that he had failed her. If Kirkland suspected that Gypsy had used him as bait in her attempt to lure Todd into marriage, he never displayed any tendencies toward revenge. A month before the baby was due, he told Gypsy that he was trying to "look like a proud papa without talking like one."[16]

Gypsy's views of pregnancy defied convention. A jumper she tried on "was terrible in the first place, and besides it made me look positively pregnant," she complained. Since she loved haute couture, she hated maternity garments. She rejected commercial maternity clothes—shapeless dresses with little ducks and bunnies on them— that made women look simultaneously unattractive and juvenile. She commissioned designers such as Charles James to make clothes for her, but the beautiful outfits did not expand. Gypsy solved the problem by cutting holes in the front of the skirts and inserting drawstrings. Long, flowing jackets covered the holes.[17]

Gypsy fumed about her expanding girth. "The typewriter seems so damn far away from me, you know, reaching all the way over my stomach to get at it." She obsessed about staying in shape. "There's such a thing as going back to work again," she noted. "And it's so easy to let yourself go, you know." She particularly resented the mounting fatigue.[18]

During her pregnancy, Gypsy converted her child into one-liners, just as she had done with her mother. She told a reporter, "All I have for the baby is a cap and a pacifier—Egad I was arrested in Boston with more on than that." She shared her concern about the possibility of a C-section: "'Wouldn't I look great with a rhinestone-studded operation?" Once the child was born, she did not plan to follow the rigidly scheduled child-rearing practices popular in some circles. "Well, after all, my sister and I ate chili when we were infants, and it didn't affect our health."[19]

In the later stages of Gypsy's pregnancy, Shana Alexander interviewed her for *PM* magazine. Sent out on her first assignment as a cub reporter, Alexander, later a formidable journalist for *Life*, pronounced herself terrified. She interviewed Gypsy in the atrium, the coolest part of Gypsy's New York town house. Gypsy, her hair arranged in curls on top of her head, wore an elegant, colorful chiffon caftan. Alexander nervously peeked at the notes she had tucked into her glove and asked if Gypsy intended to resume her career after the birth of her child. Gypsy's flip response capped the interview: "Honey, I can't have everything going out and nothing coming in."[20]

June invited twenty women to a baby shower for her sister. "I felt like a damned fool," Gypsy remembered, "but the loot was impressive." She received a bassinet, blankets, and baby sweaters. "The cake and tea were good, but not worth the price of admission," she noted unsentimentally. "One or two of the presents are bankable, in case the baby is anything like his grandmother." Guiltily, Gypsy acknowledged that the "whole set-up reeks of blackmail, but June tells me it goes on all the time."[21]

"I think everybody pretends they want a boy for the first one at least," she responded after being queried as to whether she wished for a boy or girl.[22] On December 11, 1944, Gypsy gave birth to her son, Erik, at Women's Hospital on 109th Street in New York City. Gypsy later announced, "It's chic to have a baby these days." It became even more prevalent after the boys came home from the war, and Gypsy's son grew up with the baby boom generation.[23]

The press emphasized that on the same day Erik was born, Bill Kirkland married Phyllis Adams, a twenty-year-old debutante. On being informed about the birth of his son, Kirkland told the press, "No comment." After describing the ceremony, one reporter mean-spiritedly contrasted Kirkland's wedding with Erik's arrival, commenting, "Gypsy wore a night gown and bed jacket, but her ceremony was attended only by a medical staff."[24] Kirkland's behavior seemed callous to the reporters, who viewed him as the father of Gypsy's child.

One day, Preminger called the studio and learned that Gypsy had returned to New York City. He assumed that "perhaps I had done something."[25] In fact, Preminger was shocked to discover the consequence of their romantic fling. Visiting New York City in December, he learned that Gypsy was in the hospital. When he called, she told him that they had a son.

Gypsy never gave Preminger any option to be involved in a continuously meaningful way in Erik's life. Preminger relinquished his child with some reluctance. He offered a monetary arrangement to provide for Erik, but Gypsy turned him down. After some hesitation, Preminger promised not to interfere with the child's upbringing. He even agreed never to tell his child the identity of his father. Preminger's own analysis perceptively described Gypsy's motivation. "She just wanted the baby," Preminger said. "She was a very independent, sophisticated woman, way ahead of her time!" Gypsy invited Preminger to visit as a family friend when he occasionally came to New York City, but he felt uncomfortable, so he gave up seeing his son.[26]

Erik's arrival created a new family for Gypsy, but it also meant dealing with her extended one. Tired of watching Gypsy and June squeezed dry by their mother's demands, Fitelson suggested pointedly to Rose that she get a job after she came to him requesting more money from her daughters. Discovering, probably from a relative or magazine article, that Gypsy was pregnant, Rose decided to come to New York City, ostensibly for employment. In late fall, a hotel near Broadway hired Rose as a hospitality desk manager for thirty dollars a week. A month before Erik was born, she wrote to Gypsy to congratulate her on her pregnancy and to announce her move to New York. Pleased about her new job, although nervous at first, she eagerly looked forward to each day. Just two and a half weeks later, Rose complained to Gypsy in a letter about her poor physical health, rat-infested apartment, and general misery. In this letter full of recrimination, she accused Gypsy once again of lying in an article about her childhood. In her warped version, Rose had set her own chances for happiness aside to help the girls succeed. The girls were never overworked. Then, when they no longer needed her, they dropped her. Over the years, she pleaded for reconciliation, but her contemptible daughters refused to soften. While Rose struggled, both girls lived well. Rose threatened to expose her daughters by writing her own book. She reminded them that they could easily be ruined. Her life with her daughters had been "anything but a bed of roses," she proclaimed. Soon after the baby was born, Rose left the job.[27]

While sitting in a coffee shop, Rose discovered from a morning newspaper that Gypsy was in the hospital giving birth. The hospital staff informed her that Gypsy was not receiving visitors. Given Rose's unpredictable emotional state, Gypsy probably wanted to avoid a possible scene when she needed her rest immediately after giving birth. Rose pleaded for an opportunity to see the baby, and barely a week after Erik was born, Gypsy relented. Rose dropped in at the nursery to view Erik. She adored him at first sight, and she gushed to Gypsy about the alert and cooperative infant.

In less than a year, the relationship between Rose and Gypsy soured again. After years of threatening to write a book about her daughters' flaws, Rose had promised in writing not to expose her daughters' supposed cruelty to their mother or any other so-called secrets that she possessed. The legal document Rose had signed most likely came from Fitelson, who sought to protect his clients from their dear mother's constant threats of blackmail. In return, Gypsy and June agreed not to discuss their unfavorable view of their upbringing. Apparently the columnist Jack Lait violated Gypsy's part of the deal by quoting something Gypsy said, most likely humorous, about her mother. Rose's letters reiterated all her old allegations of Gypsy's cruelty and abuse. Five days later, after one of Rose's accusatory missiles, she wrote Gypsy asking for forgiveness. If Gypsy would visit her, she promised, she would hand over all the materials for her book. Rose asked for a picture of Erik, which Gypsy sent. As soon as she received the picture, Rose wanted to see Gypsy and Erik.[28]

In spite of the turmoil with her mother, Gypsy concentrated on the practical side of raising her son. She hired a nurse, known as Nana, for Erik. Gypsy hated her pretentiousness. "I should pay fifty a week and call her a stage name?" Gypsy complained. Nana developed a "standard dialogue." When visitors cooed, "What a nice body Erik has!" the nurse responded, "Look who bore him." Gypsy grumbled, "Sometimes when I don't toss her the cue she goes into the script anyway. Someday I'm going to look her straight in the eye and say, 'Look girlie, you'll get your dough. You don't have to con me out of it.'" Gypsy planned to release the nurse in a few weeks and take over full responsibility for her son. She explained, "I didn't traipse from class to class in the hospital learning how to take care of him for nothing."[29]

An adorable baby, Erik charmed performers and the press, and he delighted Gypsy. She told the press humorously, "In a way Erik disappoints me. He was four months old this week, and he hasn't said a cute thing yet. But you should see him eat a banana." Gypsy teased that Erik "was afraid that if he was photogenic I'd put him to work."[30] In fact, the baby provided photo opportunities for Gypsy. The February 19, 1945, issue of *Life* featured a full-page picture of adorable Erik looking thoughtfully into his mother's face as she pinned his diaper. Fully made up and wearing a lace top, she managed to look both sexy and domestic. She represented the perfect image for the postwar era, although not all *Life* readers took it so seriously. One letter from a sergeant in the army parodied Gypsy's picture with a gender reversal. In a picture he sent in to the magazine, the sergeant in a frilly apron diapered his baby under the watchful eye of his wife.[31]

Less than a month after Erik's birth, Gypsy resumed her charity work, an activity deemed proper for a young matron, participating in a benefit for the March of Dimes. For this occasion, she modeled an elegant suit. As a joke, she stripped off her gloves and stole as she walked down the runway and faked embarrassment when she suddenly remembered where she was.

Moving beyond mainstream charities to political activity, Gypsy joined the campaign against racism promoted by the Writers' War Board. Mystery writer Rex Stout, known for his popular detective, Nero Wolfe, led the group founded to support America's war effort. Stout believed that the myth of racial and ethnic inferiority lessened Americans' commitment to democracy. In keeping with the practice of staging theatrical extravaganzas for popular causes during the war, Stout organized *The Myth That Threatens America*, a show with an antiracism theme. In January 1945, he invited six hundred radio and movie scriptwriters as well as artists working in various media to attend the event. The show sought to heighten sensitivity to the diversity of the American people by influencing the image-makers in attendance. Appalled by the prevalence of racism and anti-Semitism in Nazi Germany, liberals such as Stout expected Americans to renounce such views.

The evening opened with a skit titled "Education Please," a parody of Clifton Fadiman's radio show *Information Please*. Without stridency, dramatist and director Moss Hart, writer Carl Van Doren, humorist, writer, and publisher Bennett Cerf, and Gypsy reinforced the need to respect minority groups. Although this campaign may in retrospect seem naive, at the time ethnic and racial stereotyping still dominated the media. Radio shows such as *Amos 'n' Andy* and *Abie's Irish Rose* and movies such as *Gone with the Wind* reinforced racist and anti-Semitic images. The media portrayed Jews as stingy and difficult and African Americans as dull-witted and lazy. The Writers' War Board's effort was aligned with the African American civil rights movement's "Double V" campaign for victory over fascism abroad and victory over racism at home.[32]

After a few months, Gypsy started working again for compensation. "His appetite and his expensive tastes are throwing his mother right back into Vaudeville where she started," she observed wryly. During Erik's first year, Gypsy would return to her home as soon as she was able after each show, but these intermittent visits failed to satisfy her. At first she tried working two weeks and staying home two weeks. She fantasized about retiring to a blissful life as a writer and homemaker. She hoped for a solid and secure foundation for Erik in contrast to her own upbringing. As opposed to Gypsy, Erik would always know a home. Gypsy tied her identity firmly to her work, and she never retired to devote herself exclusively to motherhood. Instead, she integrated her child into her working life as fully as possible. Having a baby barely slowed her.[33]

As a baby, when Erik traveled with his mother, he slept in trunks, bathtubs, and cupboards for holding props. Once Erik reached a year old, he often joined her on longer tours, accompanied by a nanny and housekeeper. Gypsy cooked for them in a trailer and washed their clothes in laundromats to save money. In Chicago, Gypsy strolled through the zoo with Erik, where he happily referred to every animal as "puppy," his newest word. Such wit delighted his mother. "Later, he traveled with kiddie car, tricycle, and schoolbooks—and a guinea pig in his pocket."[34]

"My couturiere says my figure is better than ever since Erik arrived," Gypsy proudly noted. Even after Erik's birth, she resisted the emphasis on large breasts, fashionable in the postwar era as a sign of sexiness. She willingly added a wire in her brassiere for support but resisted "a cyclone fence." When a saleswoman suggested she pad her bra for a more voluptuous look, Gypsy snorted that if women "stuff 'em any bigger they'll have to wear license plates." On her 1946–47 tours, Gypsy was convinced that more women than before came to see her because they were curious about how her body had been changed by childbearing.[35]

Gypsy must have felt insecure about regaining her figure after childbirth. Cleverly, she decided to distract the audience from concentrating solely on her body. Shifting the focus of the audience's attention partially away from herself, Gypsy added four luscious younger women to her troupe and created the reverse strip. Her female colleagues sashayed onto the stage wearing very little. Gypsy peeled off her clothes and dressed the other women with them. Describing the women who worked with her as beautiful, she defined beauty as "a combination of facial and physical features to which one must add that intangible, personality, and of course, intelligence." Her statement perfectly described herself as well.[36]

In the new act, Gypsy discussed unclothed women throughout history, starting with Eve. Popular songs such as "In Your Easter Bonnet" and

"Jeanie with the Light Brown Hair" described, according to Gypsy, women who wore very little. With the song "When You Wore a Tulip," Gypsy pointed out, "even I wear more than a tulip." She also teased: "There have been times in history when it took several million silk worms many many days to clothe the average young lady. There have been times when a baby silk worm knocked off the same assignment during its lunch hour." The reverse strip turned out splendidly, and audiences loved the new act.[37]

As always, Gypsy complained about conditions in nightclubs and dinner theaters. In Milwaukee, the stage proved dangerously small for Gypsy, the four other women, and four musicians. "We aren't four feet from the people sitting at the bar," Gypsy protested. "They tell me the Three Stooges have played there. If one of them falls off a stage, it would be funny. If one of us falls off—disaster." Nightclub audiences did not always comprehend her highbrow humor. "If the customers can read at all, they read the *Reader's Digest*," she noted disgustedly.[38]

The 1940s permanently transformed Gypsy. She built on the career forged by her alliance with Mike Todd but soon went beyond it. Gypsy avenged herself on Hollywood by making movies she wanted to make in which she played herself performing, and on Todd by manipulating an uncommitted romantic relationship to her own advantage. Life grew more complicated, busier, and more fulfilling. A thirty-four-year-old stripper with a baby, Gypsy developed two new acts: first as a sexy mother and second as part of a group with younger stripteasers onstage. Inventing her image of sexy motherhood, Gypsy used it to counteract the sexual and political innuendo that pervaded postwar culture. During the late 1940s, she lived very much on her own terms both professionally and personally.

Gypsy turned her attention to other interests than work—romantic ones. In March 1946, *Life* magazine ran a feature with the title "Julio De Diego: He Paints Weird War and Peace." A half-page photograph depicted a rugged-looking man with very dark hair. He wore a shirt with the sleeves rolled up and a lambskin vest over it. Five bracelets hung on his arms, and he held a cigarette between his lips. With one eye partly closed, he reeked of sensuality and exotica in the era of clean-cut men in gray flannel suits. The article complimented De Diego on his use of color and his technique. De Diego's technique also fascinated Gypsy.[39]

14

On the Carnival Circuit

Gypsy and the sexy, exotic painter seen in *Life* magazine, Julio De Diego, met at a friend's party. Julio brought his delicious homemade paella. Since much of the dish had been consumed by the time Gypsy expected to eat, she complained to him. He recalled meeting a "beautiful girl whose black petticoat edged with red ribbons swirled at the bottom of her dress." Such an outfit appealed to Julio because it showed Gypsy's sense of flair.[1]

Julio De Diego was born in Madrid in 1900. After his father opposed his desire to train as an artist and destroyed some of his early attempts, he left home at age fifteen to apprentice himself to an opera set designer. While still in his teens, he joined the military and served for three years in the Spanish cavalry. In North Africa an enemy wielding a saber wounded him (or so he told the press later, explaining his rejection from serving for the Allies during World War II). In 1924, De Diego immigrated to the United States, where he obtained citizenship in 1941. Soon after his arrival with twenty-five cents in his pocket, he spent ten cents for the elevator to the top of the Woolworth Building, the world's tallest, and threw the rest of his money off the roof. "I wanted to start from scratch," he explained. Experimenting with a new camera, Julio refused to read the instructions, saying, "I want to do it by instinct."[2] Julio's spontaneity charmed everyone, particularly women.

A successful commercial artist, he drew fashion illustrations. In 1926, he began to devote himself primarily to painting and began showing his work, surreal and abstract people and landscapes, across the United States. In 1931, he won two prestigious prizes for his art. He developed a fascination for Mexico and spent time with artists there such as the muralist Carlos Merida. While painting surrealistic scenes of this dynamic society and culture, he designed costumes and scenery for Mexican ballets. After his visit to Mexico, the Art Institute of Chicago hosted an exhibition of his work entitled *Mexican Journey*.

Moving to New York, De Diego presented his paintings on *War and Peace*, including canvases lamenting the tragic defeat of the Spanish Loyalists as well as works inspired by the struggle that raged across Europe. In 1946, the Museum of Modern Art opened a show of De Diego's silver jewelry. After the United States dropped the bomb on Japan and went on to develop a massive nuclear arsenal, De Diego did a striking series of paintings depicting the profound, proliferating evils of atomic weapons, which he said turned the deepest secrets of the earth into forces of destruction. Demonstrating respect for the artist despite his views, the State Department added one of his paintings to its art collection in 1948.

When asked that year how long it took him to paint a picture, he replied, "Forty-eight years," his age at the time. De Diego had been married twice before. He seemed a perfect match for Gypsy. Like Waxy Gordon and Michael Todd, he stood a few inches shorter. He shared Gypsy's dramatic flair, love of art, and teasing sense of humor. When asked what she liked in a man, Gypsy responded, "I just like nice ones, but most of the nice ones I've met are witty. I suppose wit is the one quality a man must have to attract me."[3]

He also shared Gypsy's compulsion to work and be self-supporting. "I am not in sympathy with the idea the world owes an artist a living," he stated emphatically. He used his aptitude for design to generate revenue. He saw no shame in designing a laundry bag—in fact he was proud of it "because it attracts attention and gets the laundry 20 percent more business." De Diego spent at least two months every year working as a commercial artist drawing advertisements, earning "all I want, $15,000." Though his paintings often commented on contemporary issues, the advertisements he designed conveyed more art than information. They left him free to devote himself to more creative work.[4]

Like Gypsy, De Diego supported progressive political causes. During the Spanish Civil War, he vehemently opposed Franco and fascism. He was also active in the radical American Artists' Congress, which at its height at the end of the 1930s had nine hundred members. In its statement of purpose, the organization, which advocated better working conditions for artists, painted a picture of what fascism had done to living standards, to civil liberties, to workers' organizations, to science and art and reminded American artists that the governments in Italy and Germany threatened world peace and safety. Artists should be concerned and should act. Along with hundreds of others, De Diego signed a call to all artists to recognize the Depression's devastating impact on them. The document opposed censorship and the suppression of civil rights along with advocating for equal participation of African American artists in federally funded public art programs.[5]

Saying she was "happier than I've ever been," Gypsy expressed great excitement over her engagement to Julio. Gypsy and Julio entered into marriage without any external pressures. Bowing to her Hollywood studio, Gypsy had married Bob Mizzy. Although they loved each other, they might not have wed if they had stayed in New York City. Mizzy never represented Gypsy's grand passion. Gypsy wed husband number two, Bill Kirkland, in an unsuccessful attempt to force Mike Todd to marry her. Although they cared for each other, she and Kirkland were both in love with other people during their short interlude. The freedom with which Gypsy and Julio approached marriage seemed to augur well for the longevity of their union.[6]

Gypsy planned to inaugurate a new image—"Gypsy the housewife," she called it—by keeping the occasion simple. The couple attempted to marry on St. Patrick's Day, a serious holiday in heavily Irish New York City. Unable to catch a cab, Gypsy and Julio rode the subway to the Municipal Building. But, having forgotten all the required documents, including her divorce papers, they left unmarried. Even so, they celebrated at a wedding reception that night.

The next day, they journeyed to the marriage license bureau in the Bronx rather than Manhattan. Gypsy recounted: "The ceremony was subdued, just as we'd hoped. But when we started to leave—whew!" Having spotted Gypsy, a crowd gathered to wish her well. Fans standing in the rain threw rice. From the steps of the courthouse, a blind violinist played Mendelssohn's "Wedding March." "It was noisy, but it sure was wonderful," Gypsy enthused. "All those lovely people in the rain—I guess it was the right way after all to make my bow as the new Gypsy." *Movietone News* and newspaper photographers, possibly tipped off by Gypsy herself, joined the crowd at the courthouse. Understating the case, Julio told the press, "I think she will be a great help to me in my work." Julio and Gypsy spent their honeymoon in a trailer once owned by bandleader Tommy Dorsey. They drove to Colorado, where Julio taught art at the University of Denver summer session and Gypsy painted.[7]

During their honeymoon trip, a thermos of coffee fell on the new light-colored carpet Gypsy had purchased to spruce up the trailer. The spill perturbed her, but Julio mollified her by declaring the stain a "nice design." After outlining it with a marker, he made it into a monster, then added a bright scarlet fish with Gypsy's lipstick. Gypsy was delighted by his whimsy and skill. All in all, with his joyous artistic temperament, Julio De Diego enthralled Gypsy and captivated Erik.[8]

As wife and mother, Gypsy positioned herself to garner a new type of publicity. A month before Gypsy gave birth to Erik, *Personal Romances* displayed a lovely headshot of Gypsy on the cover. The magazine titled the article inside "The Things I Want" under which it added: "A husband—a baby—a home—don't all women want them?" In an effort to adopt the views articulated by women's magazines from the mid-forties well into the sixties, Gypsy affirmed that "more than anything else in the world, I want the baby I'm going to have and the husband I may soon be divorcing." Gypsy did not mention, of course, that the father of the child was not her soon-to-be-former husband, Bill Kirkland. All "real" women preferred a husband and child to a career, and Gypsy fit the mold—at least for this article.[9]

Gypsy's marriage to Julio allowed her gradually to shift her public image. With him, she conformed at least superficially to the postwar image of women as mothers without losing her sex appeal. As often happens during and after a war, the United States became more conservative in regard to women's roles. The line between "good" and "bad" women increasingly rigidified in popular culture. Mothers epitomized "good" women, although sometimes they veered danger-ously into emasculating overpossessiveness, particularly of their sons. With skill and daring, Gypsy walked the tightrope between "naughty" and "nice" during the late 1940s.

Publicly, Gypsy reveled in her new domesticity. She was convinced that she and Julio would enjoy being married because they shared interests and were compatible. She added, "I won't say I'm the perfect housewife, but, after all, you do have some responsibilities. I even have to make out a laundry list, darn it." Pictures of the couple in Gypsy's Manhattan house showed them eating a gourmet meal with Gypsy looking glamorous in a low-cut dress. She stressed that they ate dinner together every night.[10]

Erik, who was three years old when his mother remarried for the last time, enhanced the family portrait. In one charming picture taken later for *Life* magazine, Julio sat contentedly with a pipe in his mouth and his arms wrapped around Erik. No father looked more loving. If Erik behaved well while getting his hair cut, Julio rewarded him by creating a water-soluble tattoo using a colored pencil. For Erik's fourth birthday, Julio covered the dining room walls with paper and painted cowboys on it. On occasion, he sent Erik painted notes depicting his own activities during the day. For Erik's sixth birthday party, Julio performed magic tricks. Erik proudly used the surname De Diego when he began to attend school even though De Diego had not adopted him.[11]

Gypsy redecorated her house on Sixty-third Street for her new husband. Trading her Victorian furniture, except in her bedroom, for a more modern style, she took down her cupids and other decorations. Julio objected to the large painting of a nude called *La Toilette*, so out it went. His dislike may have stemmed from the painting's realism, which was anathema to his beloved surrealism—but he may have also found the painting offensive because Mike Todd had given it to Gypsy. Together, Julio and Gypsy entertained in the terra-cotta kitchen decorated with garlands of garlic, dried herbs, and hanging copper pots. Julio restored the big kitchen stove in the basement. When they cooked together, Gypsy was second in command, chopping ingredients while Julio created their lavish meals. Guests sat at a wooden table in the middle of the room. Art on the walls complemented shelves filled with Mexican pottery and figurines.[12]

During the day Julio worked in his own studio on Fifty-sixth Street. Gypsy rarely posed for him. Once Julio teased that Gypsy lacked the aplomb of a good model. "She's nervous," he contended; "she always wants to put her clothes back on." Regardless of the veracity of the story, the press ran it several times. The columnists enjoyed the irony of a stripper who wished to stay dressed. They never fathomed that a stripper in other contexts could act modest.[13] Julio and Gypsy created other art together. They enjoyed craft projects and made bizarre lamps. One Christmas season, Gypsy threw clay ashtrays that Julio painted. In an interview, Gypsy exclaimed, "What more could a bride want?"[14]

The "more" this particular bride wanted was money. Julio's art did not bring in sufficient income to support Gypsy's lavish lifestyle. Gypsy's occasional writings provided little revenue, and her movie career had stalled after Erik's birth and her return to New York. Stripping continued to be her main source of income, but New York

City had banned stripteasing. Periodically, Gypsy toured. She commanded five thousand dollars a week gross but had to pay all the expenses, including salaries for the younger women in the act and the cost of costumes. "It's the same old thing," Gypsy acknowledged. "It may be corny and it sure isn't art, but it pays. I'm no dramatic actress—I'm an entertainer."[15] One opportunity in that vein unexpectedly arose.

Gypsy and Julio's marriage became a literal carnival in 1949 as they joined the Royal American Shows, a touring company known as the "World's Largest Midway." Unconventional and unpretentious, Julio eagerly participated in the new experience. At first, Gypsy expressed reservations. Her limited outdoor show business experiences did not imbue her with enthusiasm. When she did a three-day stint in Syracuse, New York, at an agricultural exhibition, rain fell on the outdoor stage the entire time. Gypsy declared that was her last state fair: "They can have their mud operas; from now on I'll take my jobs in a nice warm saloon."[16] Gypsy, however, changed her mind. The carnival enticed Gypsy with its four Ferris wheels and her troupe's own private car, one of seventy Pullman cars on the tour. She fell in love with her dressing room wagon, with its emerald silk draperies, large closets, and full-length mirrors.[17]

Most important, the salary impressed Gypsy. Royal American paid her ten thousand dollars a week plus a fifty-fifty split of the gross, including concessions and programs. The carnival expected a total of seventeen million people to attend as it traveled across the continent all the way to Saskatoon, Saskatchewan. Of course, H. William Fitelson reviewed all the contracts. "I'm probably the highest paid outdoor entertainer since Cleopatra," Gypsy proclaimed, "and I don't have to stand for some of the stuff she had to." Even so, Gypsy held few illusions. She commented bluntly, "For $10,000 a week I can afford to climb the slave block once in a while." The carnival expected her to perform twelve to fourteen shows a day in a tent holding fourteen thousand people who paid one dollar each for the privilege of seeing Gypsy strip.[18]

For *Flair* magazine, Gypsy wrote a long article, "I Was with It," about her carnival experience. "There is something magical in the word carnival," she began. "It means ferris wheels, merry-go-rounds, candied apples on a stick, music, lights and gaiety." Carnival life appealed to her because the business did not tolerate weakness any more than she did. She lauded the ads for carnival hands: "If you can't put it up and take it down, don't apply." Besides the work ethic, carnival employees were privately modest about women's dress, a trait Gypsy respected. She always wore a jacket over her halter tops on the carnival lots because her coworkers "would frown" on "bare shoulders."[19]

To prepare for the tour, Gypsy bought casual clothing, high boots, oil lamps, pails, small appliances, and a heating element for bathwater. She already owned her own trailer. She and Julio decorated it with their distinctive touches. Julio fashioned the lampshades from lard tins. Gypsy's new Cadillac convertible pulled the trailer. For Gypsy, the carnival reminded her of her youth, traveling and camping with her mother and sister. "What were fourteen shows a day to me?" she asked rhetorically. "A new town every week? So what? I didn't get the name Gypsy for nothing." Gypsy's motorcar and trailer rode on a flatcar between the wild animals and Ferris wheels. The start of the ride shook the trailer sufficiently to rattle dishes and to make groceries fly around the place. Over time, Gypsy secured things. She carved a groove to hold her bed and placed a piece of Masonite between the mattress and box spring to keep the mattress from bouncing. She even learned the appropriate time to dump her garbage from the moving train. As always, Gypsy traveled with a couple of dogs.[20]

Staying in the trailer with Gypsy and Erik, Julio, who loved to cook, creatively prepared meals over a small stove. His circle of art friends considered his famous paella simmered over an open fire a special treat. Gypsy was relegated to cooking the vegetables. During the tour, Julio occasionally left to arrange shows of his artwork. "I don't mind being on the road as long as he is with me. But when he's not here, I get lonesome. It makes a lot of difference to me," declared Gypsy in a rare admission of vulnerability.[21]

Gypsy struggled to write the article for *Flair* through constant interruptions. "Every time I put a piece of paper in the typewriter, one of the girls breaks a shoulder strap or a garter...I'm called on for help," she complained in exasperation. "To anyone else it's just an accident, but here it takes on all the aspects of a national emergency." *Flair* published the piece as an insert to the regular magazine. Julio drew marvelous illustrations. Gypsy even added a glossary of carnival idioms in the back, including "gilly" for "small, cheap carnival" and "gazonny" for a "worthless character." Gypsy's tour also garnered publicity from more popular media outlets.[22]

"Gypsy Joins the 'Carney,'" *Life* magazine proclaimed, in the introduction to an article on Gypsy's opening in Memphis. The first page displayed a photograph of Gypsy in a corset, her arms outstretched to the crowd. The item featured her even more scantily clad troupe in their costumes. South Africa banned this issue of *Life* because of the risqué pictures, but in the United States the article helped business for the carnival.

The *Life* article, like others about Gypsy in the carnival, mentioned Erik. Since four-year-old Erik had already trouped with his mother for years, Gypsy never questioned his ability to cope with the trip. She brought along a nursemaid for him. Gypsy teased Julio that she hoped her son had talent—or maybe, like his mother, he would have no talent but get along without it. A preschooler, Erik completely accepted his mother's stage performance. When one man in the audience yelled, "Take it off," Erik rushed to reassure him, "Don't worry mister, she'll take it off. She always does." *Life* magazine showed a photograph of Erik sitting next to the censor at a show in Memphis. A proud Erik piped up: "That's my mommy! Can your mommy do that?" The picture drew outrage from a reader who condemned Gypsy for letting her son see her strip. Gypsy defended herself using an argument tailored to fit postwar norms. "Where else should a child be but with its mother?" she responded pointedly. The censor approved the show for Memphis audiences.[23]

After her opening in Memphis, Gypsy performed nine shows in five hours. The rain began that night, and the audience stood on benches to keep their feet from getting wet. The rain caused a myriad of problems. Gypsy lost her voice and failed to cue the orchestra on time. The rain loosened the supports for the stage and some of the sections separated, catching Gypsy's heel. The zipper key (for the carnival she used standard zippers as opposed to her usual pins) on her dress failed and one show closed with her still in her gown. A few of the patrons demanded refunds, but most loved it. At one point, one of the workers suggested the women perform in bathing suits to keep the rain from ruining their costumes. After three days and thirty-eight performances, the sun returned. The show grossed more than thirty-three thousand dollars in its first weeks.[24]

Gypsy refined her recent innovation of stripping while dressing others in her act. Bringing out barely dressed women, Gypsy swathed them in long, flowing silks. The performance parodied the fairy godmother in Cinderella. Gypsy began in a tight-fitting strapless evening gown as she started her reverse strip. Nothing held up the dress, contended Gypsy, "except me and some of the best engineering in the country." She stripped to a black corset, and the women left the stage clothed. Gypsy hired tall women; two were over six feet, and the smallest was five feet eight and a half inches. "I'm big and I like them my size," she explained. Besides, it had a practical advantage: "Ten big ones fill the stage better than ten little ones, and they all cost the same."[25]

Each show was only half an hour long. "That doesn't give us much time to warm up the audience," Gypsy noted. Usually she liked to amuse the audience for the first ten or fifteen minutes before getting down to what they had come to see, but for the carnival she speeded up the act. "It's fun," she declared, "even when you have to go on before a crowd and look glamorous with dirt in your finger nails and sand between your toes."[26]

Even though "carnival crowds don't go for satire," Gypsy preferred the working-class carnival-goers to nightclub audiences. The crowds were raucous, she remarked, "but it's a good healthy boisterous noise," unlike the drunken laughter in a nightclub. Gypsy also preferred performing before the mixed-gender carnival audience. She enthused, "As a matter of fact, I love working to women."[27]

The audience was treated to a provocative but never lewd program when they attended Gypsy's show. Julio and Gypsy designed the printed program for her act. On the cover, only Gypsy's head and her legs in black net stockings showed. A lacy front flap covered her body, allowing the holder of the program to fantasize nudity within. The viewer had to unfold the program to discover Gypsy in her celebrated black corset. The schedule for the performances was printed inside.

Gypsy paid the musicians, two vaudeville acts, and twelve women, providing costumes for everyone. On the road, Gypsy managed the show with her usual grit. "Sometimes I suppose I'm not a pleasant person," she conceded. Although she enjoyed being with the women in her act, she never forgot that they were her employees. She yelled at them when they wore their expensive costumes while eating hot dogs or other greasy foods. When men in the crowd brawled, Gypsy worried more about blood splattering on the performers' costumes than about the hicks getting their noses broken. Adapting the attitude that became standard for the rest of her career, she stated, "I'm a heel—so what." A perfectionist, Gypsy was possessed by a passion for detail. She demanded competence from anyone who worked for her. She kept a careful eye on the mechanics doing maintenance on her trailer, explaining that "a breakdown would mean the loss of a show."[28]

Gypsy became part of the carnival's self-contained community. There was a water truck in case of fire, a cook tent to feed everyone, a neon shop, a welding shop, and a carpenter shop. One night, the carnival survived a tornado while Erik slept. On another occasion, the carnies put out a fire without help from the local fire department. The community coped with other seemingly impossible conditions. The fairgrounds at St. Louis sat in two feet of mud. That night, Gypsy's trailer got stuck twice as she drove it to its proper position. By the time she awoke the workers had laid shavings on the mud and set up games of chance. The merry-go-round music played, and various shows started their performances.

Gypsy introduced herself to the other performers, visiting with Purcilla the Monkey Girl and her husband, Emmett the Crocodile Man. She admired how they decorated their wagon with lace curtains, potted plants, rugs, and a canary, pronouncing it homelike and cheerful.[29] Besides her occasional socializing and her numerous performances each day, Gypsy chatted with the local press at every stop. She also took time for charity appearances, visiting Shriners' hospitals along the tour. As she often did when she was trouping, Gypsy entertained the cast, crew, and press with a spaghetti dinner right before closing in each town.

With her excellent local and national publicity, Gypsy ran into few problems with local censors on the tour. In Tulsa, where schools often gave children the day off to attend fairs and carnivals, the PTA opposed the idea because of Gypsy's act. The press correctly pointed out that the PTA's condemnation would probably increase rather than discourage attendance. The fair manager gamely asserted that Gypsy's act was "clean."

About halfway through the tour, De Diego opened a sophisticated "girlie show" for the carnival based on an earlier concept by Salvador Dali. "Dream Show" gave Julio work as he traveled with Gypsy for part of the tour. He painted the entrance of the show in his remarkable surrealist style, portraying nude women with cow-, horse-, or dragon-shaped heads and bodies in a dreamlike sequence on the front. Inside, as part of the act, he set up distorted mirror reflections that created surreal images based, according to De Diego, on Freudian interpretations. On the stage a woman pretended to be asleep, dreaming of being naked in public, while another woman representing the dream appeared in front of the mirror. She wore strategically placed furs and little else. Meanwhile, the dreamer acted embarrassed, as if she were living through the experience. The sexual effect both disconcerted and aroused the audiences.[30]

In Minneapolis, Julio's "Dream Show" did not pass the state fair censors. They allowed the show but opposed the murals in front because everyone coming to the carnival saw the paintings of the nudes. Declaring his murals to be art, Julio refused to remove them or paint over them. Local Artists Equity, an advocacy group devoted to enhancing artists' economic interests and their right to freedom of expression, protested against the censors. "What do these people know about art?" Julio complained. "What do they know about surrealism? And for that matter what do they know about Freud?" Equity even dispatched two psychiatrists to evaluate the correctness of Julio's interpretation of Freud. While Gypsy sympathized with Julio's convictions, she worried about the lost revenue. When the show did not open, she bought drinks for newspaper reporters to try to soften them up. As a compromise, Julio created a new temporary front for the entrance panel with maroon and yellow stripes.[31]

Despite the carnival's occasionally pleasant diversions such as "Farmer's Day," when customers arrived in carriages, surreys, and vehicles reminiscent of the musical *Oklahoma!*, Gypsy felt exhausted by the end of the tour.[32] She asked Julio to hit her if she ever gushed that traveling in a carnival would be exciting. Gypsy's calendar for 1949 demonstrates how exhausting the work with the constant traveling was despite the glowing accounts she provided for the media. In mid-August Gypsy checked into the hospital. Although her ailment was not disclosed, she probably suffered from heat exhaustion. When Julio suggested staying in hotels, she opposed the idea because of the cost. The carnival spent October traveling from one small city to another across the South. Only in December did she return to New York.

Performing on the carnival circuit was the mirror opposite of the postwar family ideal. The star had acquired a husband and child, but in reverse order. Only for Gypsy did this tour represent a return to normalcy. Their trailer, a far cry from a suburban bungalow, took the notion of commuting to work to extremes. The impulsive foreign-born painter hardly fulfilled the stable male breadwinner ideal. And Gypsy herself was a living parody of prevailing notions of feminine domesticity and sexual restraint. For the present, Gypsy knew she needed the revenue, which is why she decided to tour with the carnival. After expenses, she made more than $200,000. "Me quit? Don't be silly," she responded to a question about her leaving stripping. "Show business is my life. It's the air I breathe. Quit, that's a laugh."[33]

Two years before she went on the carnival circuit, a men's magazine interviewed her. Determined to investigate "How Long Can a Body Last," the author sought out burlesque queens. The question irritated most of those interviewed. First Gypsy was asked if she wore falsies in her act. She used engineering principles to demonstrate the limitations of falsies. Leaning back, she explained the "law of torque and tension at work." Then the writer asked the leading question. "You know in my business you have to make it when you're young," Gypsy answered. She queried the author, "See anything run-down and busted about me?" When he replied in the negative, she lectured him about the reality of stripping. "When I'm old and gray I'm going to settle down and write books. Nobody wants to see a grandmother take her clothes off." Gypsy had already changed her act to emphasize younger bodies.[34]

Gypsy's art at this time revealed her ambivalence about stripping. As a gift for Julio, Gypsy painted a picture of a bowl of what at first looked like pieces of fruit but were actually breasts. On the table were four knives. Strippers were pieces of female anatomy, never real people, regardless of how hard they tried to escape being turned into objects of others' lust.

In 1950, Gypsy finally had it all: a husband, a child, and success. The years solidified her reputation, and she was convinced that she would be able to parlay it into other careers. TV and radio beckoned her, and she had not deserted writing completely. The future looked promising. She never suspected that her past political activities and her strongly held convictions would come back to haunt her.

15

Nothing to Conceal

D uring the 1940s, understanding that her aging body necessitated a new profession, Gypsy gravitated to radio and television. The media returned the compliment. Although putting a stripper on radio or squeaky-clean television did not seem so smart, Gypsy's popularity steadily rose. On the radio, her slightly affected but clear and well-paced speech pattern worked well. Although she quipped double-entendres to keep the audience amused, as a guest star, Gypsy was careful to remain appropriate for a family audience.

Gypsy insisted that working in the new communications media represented "a good investment. I feel that I'm building toward something now." Burlesque comics such as Phil Silvers had made successful transitions to TV, so why not a burlesque queen? Radio and television promised a great future for Gypsy and guaranteed her a very large audience. Fear of obscurity haunted Gypsy constantly. For her, as for all celebrities, fame was a significant part of the commodity she sold, as well as central to her identity.

In 1950, Gypsy emceed two quiz programs for ABC TV and radio, *Think Fast* and *What Makes You Tick?* In *Think Fast*, five panelists competed by discussing various subjects. The moderator would decide which contestant knew the most on a range of topics. *What Makes You Tick?* was broadcast in front of a live audience in New York City. Gypsy was thrilled to participate in "a program designed for listeners who enjoy a battle of wits and a genuine chance to investigate the psychological significance of their own behavior," she explained. As emcee, Gypsy interviewed guests from the studio audience about how they felt about a selected topic, such as romance. Then trained psychologists rated the contestant's responses on how closely they corresponded to the psychologists' knowledge of human behavior. The winner whose self-appraisal best matched the psychologists' judgments won. Gypsy teased about appearing with experts—"entertainment is my racket, and they're muscling in on it." She generously conceded that scholars were "notoriously underpaid, and if they can make a few extra bucks by going on TV, I'm all for it."[1]

The show's appeal to fantasy reminded Gypsy of her burlesque act. "As an illusion kid, I went through plenty of years of show business—name it, I played it," Gypsy insisted. In *What Makes You Tick?* Gypsy emphasized the psychological element of the program. She knew that when she asked a male contestant how romantic he was with his wife, every husband listening daydreamed about his own response. Men envisioned themselves to be as desirable as actor Clark Gable. The studio guest "has it a lot tougher than the man in his parlor, because Gable No. 2 can answer any way his heart and ego desire," Gypsy argued. "That's illusion at its fanciest and fulsomest and *I'm all for it.*"[2]

Gypsy adored the show. The live audience, who reminded her of the well-behaved spectators of vaudeville, responded enthusiastically. Loyal fans attended the program show after show. "If anything happens to me, half the audience could understudy me," she noted wryly. Gypsy was delighted to read such comments as "Gypsy Rose Lee...is making a stir with her quick wit and ad lib ability in radio," from the Associated Press. The *Los Angeles Mirror* summed up her performance: "In new role, she still wows 'em."[3]

Just as everything was "coming up roses," as the song from the musical *Gypsy* proclaimed, the second Red Scare destroyed her new career. The first Red Scare had occurred immediately after World War I, when the U.S. government arrested people suspected of subversive activities even if they had never committed a crime. Immigrants and naturalized citizens were harassed and deported. The second, popularly known as McCarthyism after its leading proponent in the U.S. Senate, followed World War II.

Although the Soviet Union had been a U.S. ally during the conflict, anti-Communist, anti-Soviet feeling grew after the war. Russia's control of Eastern Europe as well as the successful Communist revolution on mainland China enhanced Americans' nervousness. Powerful officials in government, such as J. Edgar Hoover, the head of the Federal Bureau of Investigation, and Senator Joseph McCarthy, believed that a domestic Communist conspiracy existed. Even though membership in the Communist Party remained lawful in the United States, Hoover and McCarthy wanted Communism expunged from American society. Unfortunately, rather than concentrating on actual security threats, the government hounded innocent people out of their jobs. Labor organizers, civil rights activists, and homosexuals all were targeted—as were entertainers, whose pervasive influence over public opinion was especially feared by vehement anti-Communists.

During this time, government agencies at every level, businesses, and nonprofit organizations searched for alleged subversives. Even if they had withdrawn from the Communist Party decades before, had never joined the party, or had merely associated with alleged Communists, government employees were vulnerable to losing their jobs because of these actual or alleged affiliations. Colleges, labor unions, and television stations purged their employees if they were suspected of being former Communists or sympathetic to Communism.

America's second Red Scare swept up Gypsy in its broad net. In 1947, three former FBI employees established an independent company called American Business Consultants to combat alleged subversion. American Business Consultants published the weekly *Counterattack: The Newsletter of Facts to Combat Communism*, and it sold well. *Counterattack* assailed a swath of Americans from union leaders to Eleanor Roosevelt for their ties to Communist organizations. It also condemned a few major corporations and numerous newspapers and magazines.[4]

At one point the publication criticized the Blatz Beer Company for sponsoring a show with an actress its editors considered disloyal. The authors of *Counterattack* suggested other advertisers avoid Blatz's horrible mistake of supporting shows that hired the wrong people. Since entertainers might use their charm and personality to spread Communist propaganda and brainwash the population, *Counterattack* considered performers especially dangerous. Like the House Committee on Un-American Activities chaired by Martin Dies in 1938, the American Business Consultants finally discovered Gypsy.[5]

In June 1950, *Counterattack* published a slim volume titled *Red Channels: The Report of Communist Influence in Radio and Television*. It cited 151 entertainers, writers, and directors who worked in TV and radio. Alongside each name, the book listed each person's alleged subversive activities. In the back of the book, the authors added a handy guide to subversive organizations so sponsors and watchful groups could easily check out people's past activities for themselves. The broadcast industry had previously kept an informal blacklist, but *Red Channels* provided more direct targets.

The book was criticized as well as praised, but the controversy only increased its publicity. In Newark, the superintendent of schools distributed *Red Channels* as a "reference book" for principals and teachers. Since the book disregarded the civil rights of those listed, the National Association for the Advancement of Colored People condemned the Newark superintendent's actions, but the NAACP's objection had little impact on the effectiveness of *Red Channels*.[6]

The publishers of *Red Channels* selected their audience expertly. Businesses sponsored radio and television entertainment in order to sell their products. To protect their economic interest, the sponsors began to interfere in programming, seeking to safeguard themselves against any problems that might hurt sales. In the chilly climate of the Cold War, they were desperate to avoid looking un-American by showcasing alleged Communist sympathizers. To avert any hint of controversy and to ensure they would not inadvertently fund shows with any leftist actors, advertisers consulted *Red Channels*. When prodded by the American Legion or other groups, the networks protected their revenue base by blacklisting anyone targeted in *Red Channels*. In fact, neither *Red Channels* nor any other publication proved that a Communist conspiracy existed in the broadcast industry.

Gypsy was listed along with many other entertainers such as Lena Horne, respected journalists such as Howard K. Smith, actors such as Edward G. Robinson and Lee J. Cobb, composers such as Leonard Bernstein and Aaron Copland, and playwrights such as Arthur Miller. *Red Channels* contained five allegations about her: It accused her of speaking at a meeting of the Hollywood Anti-Nazi League and of sending "greetings" to Dr. Edward K. Barsky, who was being honored at the Joint Anti-Fascist Refugee Committee. Even worse, she had entertained at the New York Council of the Arts, Sciences and Professions and acted as an auctioneer for the League of American Writers and for International Labor Defense. *Red Channels* labeled all five organizations "Communist fronts"—groups that were secretly controlled by Communists and, like Trojan horses, threatened to subvert American society.[7]

Gypsy denied all the charges. In a statement dated September 10, 1950, for the press, Gypsy responded with a ringing denial when confronted with the accusation that she was a Communist or a Communist sympathizer. She proclaimed, "My sympathies are completely and entirely opposed to everything the Communist party and their ilk stand for." Then she continued assertively: "As an officer of a large trade union, the American Guild of Variety Artists [AGVA], I made a loyalty affidavit which is a matter of public record. There are no qualifications to the statement I made under oath." To the press, Gypsy called the allegation that she was a Communist sympathizer "the most outrageous assertion I've ever heard." She stood by her union activity and denied that her friends were Communists. For example, she refused to name Fanny Brice, who according to the FBI had joined the Communist Party in 1936.[8]

Refuting the specific allegations made against her in *Red Channels*, she stated that she had never spoken at the Hollywood Anti-Nazi League; she did not know Dr. Barsky and never signed a message sending him "greetings." She had joined the New York Council of the Arts, Sciences and Professions in 1944 when the organization supported the reelection of President Roosevelt but had been a member only for a short time. As a guest, rather than as an entertainer, she had attended a banquet sponsored by the council featuring playwright Moss Hart and composer Oscar Hammerstein. Gypsy had refused to entertain at another of the council's functions, so when the council used her name in its publicity she was so incensed that she consulted her lawyer. She refuted the claim that in the late 1930s she had acted as an auctioneer at a function for the League of American Writers, which had a reputation for its ties with the U.S. Communist Party.[9]

Other entertainers also protested the absurd inaccuracy of their identifications in *Red Channels*. The malicious nonsense bemused actress Marcia Hunt years later. "They had listed several affiliations under my name—some I'd never heard about, complete lies," she complained. "One, I think, had me attending a peace conference in Stockholm. I had never been to Stockholm, nor to a peace conference."[10]

Although no one accused Gypsy of actual membership in the Communist Party or of disloyalty to the United States, charges against her grew and flourished. For example, she had to defend herself against allegations that by selling *The G-String Murders* to United Artists she had allied herself with a subversive group. Gypsy protested that she had negotiated directly with Hunt Stromberg and the movie was independently produced. At the same time, she defended United Artists, whose founders included Charlie Chaplin and Mary Pickford, against allegations that it was run by subversives. She thought it unfair that the studio was charged with distributing politically suspect films when its major box office successes of the late 1930s included *Gone with the Wind*.

Repeatedly, Gypsy denied contributing to subversive groups or political parties, but past associations proved troublesome both at the time and afterward. In 1941, Gypsy had attempted to convince the International Longshoremen's and Warehousemen's Union, based in the San Francisco waterfront, to contribute to the USO. In response to her appeal, the union voted to give the organization five hundred dollars. After her talk, Gypsy impulsively kissed the union's leader, Harry Bridges, as a thank-you for the generous donation. Immediately, while still at the event, she regretted her display of affection. Bridges urged the union to delay the contribution, since the USO was suspected of financial corruption. A union committee was formed to conduct an investigation of the USO's fund drive and given two weeks to file its report. Gypsy expressed outrage: "Our servicemen need the money now." Bridges outmaneuvered Gypsy when the union voted to delay giving the money, and Gypsy excoriated him after the decision. The mainline press found Gypsy's spontaneous kiss and subsequent quarrel with the rough-hewn Bridges amusing. The militant, Australia-born labor organizer was suspected of being a Communist, and the government had been trying to deport him since he led a successful general strike on the Northern California waterfront in 1934. In 1941, misled by the photographed kiss, the *San Francisco Chronicle* described Bridges as a friend of Gypsy's. The inaccuracy haunted her in the 1950s.[11]

Years later, while touring Europe, Gypsy confessed that some of the benefits in which she performed "turned into Communist demonstrations." However, she never knowingly participated in pro-Communist events. "Entertainers are always being asked to help causes and they all sound innocuous," she explained. "Should we wire our Congressmen to investigate before we do a benefit performance? I'm not a Red and never have been."[12]

From the floor of the Illinois American Legion convention in September 1950, Edward Clamage, a former Legion commander, called Gypsy "a dear and close associate of the traitors of our country." He cited evidence from *Red Channels*. The chairman of the Illinois Legion's Anti-Subversive Committee sent a telegram to the American Broadcasting Company asking if Gypsy, about to perform in an ABC program, would appear "as a true American or if she is going to be serving her Communist friends." He smeared Gypsy, hoping that ABC would ban her from the airways.

Clamage claimed that all his information about Gypsy came from *Red Channels* and that the authors alone were responsible for what they had written. Clamage's reliance on *Red Channels* infuriated Gypsy, because its authors refused to provide any proof for their charges other than an occasional article in the *Daily Worker*, the Communist Party newspaper. The *Worker* reported on organizational activities with which the paper agreed and mentioned Gypsy only when she attended such events. Gypsy insisted that she had been the victim of vicious lies in *Red Channels* and now "everyone is trying to pass the buck." She contended, "No one uses a newspaper as documentary proof and certainly not a Communist newspaper." To the valid point that newspaper reports cannot be taken at face value, she added an anti-Communist twist: A paper openly committed to advancing the Communist Party's cause through subversive means was by definition untrustworthy. To counter the allegations, Gypsy offered to provide "absolute proof that I had nothing to do with those groups" listed in *Red Channels*.[13]

After spending considerable time entertaining the troops and raising money for the Allies during World War II, Gypsy deeply resented being labeled un-American. In her statement refuting the charges made in *Red Channels* and repeated by the Legion, Gypsy pointed out her support of the U.S. war effort: She had played hundreds of benefits under the auspices of the army, the Red Cross, War Bond drives, salvage drives, the YMCA, the Community Chest, and similar organizations. Gypsy pointed particularly to her work on behalf of Bundles for Britain to remind her attackers that, unlike the Communist Party, she had supported Britain after the Hitler–Stalin nonaggression agreement. The party had shifted from antifascism to neutrality and reversed course only when Hitler invaded Russia.

The year after the publication of *Red Channels*, Gypsy speculated that the publishers really opposed her union activism with AGVA and simply used her antifascist activities as a cover. Her theory has great merit. During the Cold War, unionists were often attacked as subversives. Articles about Gypsy's union activities had appeared just a month before *Counterattack* published *Red Channels* and three months before the American Legion blasted Gypsy. In 1950, the membership of AGVA elected Gypsy vice president by a landslide of 893 votes to 401 and appointed her editor of its newsletter.

With Gypsy on the board, AGVA raised its dues to strengthen the welfare fund for actors. She was concerned with the part-time status of actors that made them ineligible for unemployment benefits when they were out of work. Since entertainers often traveled for their work, they also needed extra insurance. The newly elected AGVA board advocated establishing a national basic agreement for wages for stage shows and announced a plan to fight bias against "Negro performers." Concerned with the rapidly expanding new medium, AGVA decided to explore the possibility of producing its own shows for television.[14]

AGVA's new quarterly newsletter had more than thirty pages in the first issue. Gypsy's loyalty to vaudeville entertainers motivated her to work hard as editor. In 1950, former vaudevillians were still one of the largest groups of show business performers. Improving their working conditions was her primary concern. The newsletter would speak to their needs. "Their lot has been pitiful. They're cheated and shoved around," Gypsy explained to her publicist. "I'm going to work and make others work," declared the committed editor, who planned to recruit advertisements and articles aggressively. She emphasized the exploitation of workers who had no union to protect them. Aware of working conditions before and after the formation of her union, she told other members, "For your $120 a year in dues you're a lucky S.O.B."[15]

During Gypsy's term as editor, the theater unions decided to organize a Television Authority to investigate actors' treatment by the burgeoning new industry. Violations of child labor laws especially concerned the union, an issue near to Gypsy's heart given the exploitation she and her sister suffered as children. The group aimed to unionize all actors performing on television. AGVA selected Gypsy to represent the union on the central board of this new organization. Although *Red Channels* and the American Legion never mentioned any of Gypsy's union activism, television executives knew about it when they blacklisted her. Although Gypsy's advocacy of labor unionism and her work to address working conditions in the television industry hurt her economically, Gypsy refused to repudiate her union activism.

Cleverly, Gypsy ended her September statement that she was not sympathetic to Communism with an indictment of the attacks on her. She compared the tactics of private and government groups during this second Red Scare to those of a dictatorship: "I abhor totalitarianism—whether red, brown or black—and their treacherous methods of guilt by smear and without trial. This may be all right for Russia, but I hope not for us." Sadly, Americans frequently used "treacherous methods" against people such as Gypsy during the 1950s.[16]

Following her statement of denial, Gypsy listed all her memberships in various organizations, including her various unions. She included the Ziegfeld Girls Club (a "benevolent organization composed of former members of the cast of Ziegfeld shows") and the Parent Teacher Association. Loving animals, Gypsy mentioned her support of the Bronx Zoo, the American Society for the Prevention of Cruelty to Animals, and the Greenwich Village Humane Society. Gypsy worked tirelessly for the Greenwich Village Humane Society, becoming vice president. She enjoyed visiting animal hospitals where she felt the animals were receiving good care, and her trips also lifted the morale of the staff. She was worried that her problems with the American Legion might hurt the Humane Society.

Gypsy's denial that she was ever a Communist is borne out by the available historical evidence, and its truthfulness should have been apparent at the time. None of her attackers ever proved her loyal to the Communist Party. *Red Channels* did not offer any proof that she had joined it. Trying to distance herself from charges of being a Communist sympathizer, Gypsy emphasized that Communist Party publications had occasionally attacked her, just as they did burlesque in general. Criticizing Gypsy's writings, art, and performances, the *Daily Worker* had assailed striptease as a "capitalist cancer." The party's embrace of American popular culture in the 1930s during the popular front period, when the party was interested in becoming more mainstream by building coalitions, had not extended to burlesque. Not surprisingly, the Communist Party line on stripteasing failed to prevent the Young Communist League from occasionally inviting a stripper to entertain at a function.[17]

Gypsy created various ploys to make the charge of being a Communist sympathizer vanish. Along with her statement of denial, she released a picture of herself looking like an all-American mom with Erik in a cowboy hat riding on her back. On all fours as the horse, Gypsy managed to look very pretty and show a little cleavage. The photograph implied that her domesticity kept her too busy as a mother to be a Communist. Such a gimmick showed her desperation. But none of her tactics worked.

In the 1930s and early 1940s, Gypsy's political views had fit her friendships, her marriages, and her professional life. Often her social circles were progressive. But aside from her victorious encounter with the Dies Committee in 1938, she faced little criticism for her political activism. In 1950, her professional work and her politics collided. Suddenly, commitment to one interfered with the other.

In contrast to her response in 1938, Gypsy did not joke with the press about the attacks. By 1950, the public was more sympathetic to accusations of subversion than it had been during the Depression. The country seemed poised for a nuclear war with the Soviet Union, and concerns about stability at home were elevated by Cold War anxieties. The U.S. foreign policy strategy to contain the spread of Communism abroad had a domestic counterpart in the containment of women and sexuality within nuclear families.[18] In the sexual politics of the 1950s, "loose" women and homosexuals, who were regarded as deviant, were particularly vulnerable to suspicions of subversion. Gypsy knew that she had always skirted the edges of respectability, and in the postwar period open expressions of sexuality and of political liberalism had become more dangerous. Smear campaigns ruined careers, and Gypsy tried to be prudent. Now she had a child to provide for, and she was growing older. She knew that her stripping career, always her financial mainstay, would end. Respectability was an essential prerequisite for a new career in the entertainment business.

After advertisers read Gypsy's listing in *Red Channels*, they refused to buy time during *What Makes You Tick?*[19] Luckily for Gypsy, at least in the short run, the liberal Robert Kintner headed ABC. Kintner informed the American Legion that he required concrete evidence against Gypsy other than the citations in *Red Channels* before he would cancel the program. He sent the Legion a copy of the loyalty oath that Gypsy signed as a union official and demanded that the authors of *Red Channels* prove their statements about her. The authors demurred, saying that the evidence from the book sufficed. Keeping Gypsy on the air was one of the earliest attempts by a network station to stand up to the blacklist. Kintner decided not to cave in to the American Legion and its supporters. He kept the show running for thirteen weeks without advertising, and in October 1950, Gypsy emceed her last show. In 1953, Kintner won a Peabody Award for his "courageous stand in resisting organized pressure." When Martin Agronsky presented the award, he quipped that Kintner had "the good sense to recognize the absurdity of various ill-founded allegations that that well-known figure—Gypsy Rose Lee—had something she wished to conceal."[20]

Several columnists joked about Gypsy's situation and defended her patriotism. For the *New York Post*, Leonard Lyons wrote a light but pointed piece about watching Gypsy perform to raise money at the Aid to Britain Ball in New York. Communists, he reminded his readers, opposed Great Britain during the early part of the war. Lyons's wife helped organize the event and had asked him for Gypsy's private telephone number so she could invite her to perform. Lyons noted that his wife acknowledged that she would be furious if he had actually known it.[21]

Liberal journalists employed the case against Gypsy to attack the blacklist. With Gypsy, the charges were so absurd that the incident made the anti-Communist zealots look ridiculous. "It certainly counts to Gypsy's credit that she was criticized by the political witch hunters of Washington," one columnist insisted. "They considered her undressing in public an act of virtue compared with the fact that she had once appeared to help the unemployed."[22]

The *Milwaukee Journal*, in an article titled "No, No, Not Our Gypsy," concluded: "But chances are that any investigations will show that if Gypsy approached any Red groups it was like her performance— she stopped and always just in time." An article in the *New York Post*, "Gypsy's Past Bared," began: "The guardians of political morality have now exposed Gypsy Rose Lee, heretofore renowned for her ability to expose herself." The article recounted the Legion's charges, making them sound slightly sexual. For example, the Illinois Legion "says she is a dangerous woman who has freely associated with menacing men." Suggesting that *Red Channels* might in some cases "be appropriately subtitled 'muddy waters,'" the journalist ended with the major point about the blacklist: "We can't picture her as a threat to the American way of life and we doubt that many Americans will be persuaded that she is." Gypsy's blacklisting made the United States "look silly."[23]

Support for Gypsy came from various sources. To convey a message after the American Legion incident, a friend sent Gypsy a postcard rather than a more private letter "so that everyone may read it. I think the entire report is a malicious rumor and completely untrue. I will never believe one iota of it." An attorney who belonged to the American Legion in Illinois expressed concern about his own organization's tactics. He declared that the Legion's procedures contradicted its own belief in "fair play," arguing emphatically, "The possibility of a career being harmed or ruined, without some sort of hearing whereby the accused can bring out pertinent facts by way of defense, is repugnant to the basic tenets of Americanism." Suggesting Gypsy speak before the Legion, he offered to help arrange the open forum. While the letter cheered both Gypsy and her lawyers by its common decency, Gypsy equivocated about appearing before the Legion on this issue. She preferred to defuse the situation. A public event would allow the other side to restate its charges and publicize them yet again.[24]

Julio De Diego fought the blacklist by helping establish a journal, *Improvisations*, to help the Artists Equity Association, to which Gypsy also belonged. The journal insisted that advertisers had to allow artists to express themselves with no outside interference—which in 1950 represented a courageous concept for both the artists and the advertisers, since artistic freedom of expression underwritten by advertisers was under fire. Cloak and Dagger Jamaica Rum bravely allowed Julio to create an ad for the brand. Julio rewarded the company with a clever lithograph of two masked spies holding knives and a sign urging the consumer to try Cloak and Dagger rum. In 1954, the membership elected him president of the national Artists Equity Association.

Gypsy's sister, June, also publicly opposed the blacklist. Agitated by the HUAC activities, she signed a petition to the U.S. House of Representatives that began, "The investigative function of the Committee on Un-American Activities has been perverted from fair and impartial procedures to un-fair, partial and prejudiced methods." The petition was a response to the treatment of the Hollywood Ten: screenwriters, directors, and an organizer for the Screen Actors Guild who in the fall of 1947 refused to testify as to whether they were members of the Communist Party. Congress declared them in contempt, and their court appeals failed. After the sentences were handed down, the Hollywood Ten were blacklisted from studios in Hollywood unless they recanted and served as friendly witnesses. The majority did not.[25]

The Actors' Equity Association forcefully condemned the blacklist and the "irresponsible manner of vigilantes smearing the reputations of actors to an extent which is becoming alarmingly dangerous." Similarly, Henry Dunn, president of AGVA, announced furiously, "We won't take it lying down. Red Channels is a violator of civil liberties." Dunn promised that when a private organization attacked his members and "takes away their bread and butter, we'll be in there battling."[26]

Other organizations' reactions were more ambiguous. Although the ACLU would purge Communists from its own board, the organization decided to conduct an inquiry into blacklisting from television and radio. Author Merle Miller directed the project and was to write a report, which he later turned into a book. A month after the incident with the American Legion in Illinois, the executive director of the American Civil Liberties Union wrote Gypsy. The ACLU wanted to ascertain the truth of the charges made against her in Red Channels and find out whether anyone writing for Red Channels had tried to verify the information with her. The ACLU, however, did not intend to take any legal action based on information received, the letter said.

Eventually, in 1952, the ACLU contacted the Federal Communications Commission about unfair practices in relation with the blacklist, but to little effect.[27]

Always strongly anti-Communist, the Americans for Democratic Action was even more vague in its help during the blacklist. Its National Arts Division planned to hold a panel discussion so that people could learn more about the problem. While the director of the National Arts Division expressed her regrets about the situation in which Gypsy found herself, she offered little advice. She invited Gypsy and Julio to her Christmas party and suggested that Gypsy try to forget the issue and leave everything to the ADA, although the organization had no concrete plans.[28]

The 151 people listed in *Red Channels* began to organize to consider their options. At one meeting, fifteen lawyers explained the legal procedures that could be used against *Counterattack* and *Red Channels*. After the first meeting, some of the victims of *Red Channels* began to refer to themselves as the "Committee of 151" and stated, "At last, for the first time since we were placed in the same boat, we began to row together." Some decided on a safer course: They went before HUAC as friendly witnesses and divulged names of former Communists.[29]

In keeping with his tough temperament, H. William Fitelson, Gypsy's lawyer, advocated that Gypsy sue the group that published *Red Channels*. The authors were unlawfully preventing her from earning a livelihood, he argued. At one point an article in the City College of New York *Mercury* reported that Gypsy was then suing *Red Channels*, but her personal papers contain no reference to a suit, and there is no other evidence that she actually took legal action.[30]

Fitelson's political persuasion could not be categorized in the simplistic terms that prevailed in the early 1950s. Fitelson had always classified Stalin with Hitler as a brutal dictator. He sent director Elia Kazan a subscription to a magazine that ran an article stating, "No one can call himself a liberal who is not anti-Communist." According to Kazan, Fitelson was a Trotskyite, among the many radicals who followed the Russian Bolshevik leader when he broke with Stalin and quit the U.S. Communist Party. Many American intellectuals and artists supported Leon Trotsky's views. Fitelson was visible enough among New York City's anti-Stalinist leftists that the FBI referred to him as the "Red Angel of Trotskyites."

By 1954, the FBI described Fitelson as anti-Communist and observed that he aided people in their defection from the Communist Party. The file also indicated that he would be willing to cooperate with the FBI in its hunt for Communists, but it contained no evidence that Fitelson had actually identified former Communist Party members to the government. The FBI agents probably did not comprehend the intricacies and passion of disputes on the left. Fitelson's rejection of Stalin did not make him sympathetic to the blacklist. He was not cowed by the fear-mongering tactics of the anti-Communists.[31]

While Fitelson was fearless about going after the *Red Channels* authors, Gypsy may have felt intimidated about bringing suit. Given the climate of the Cold War, few people chanced taking on the former FBI men who authored *Red Channels*. The tract began with several pages on the threat Communists posed to popular culture. Following this tirade, the authors added a short paragraph stating that real liberals who were also anti-Communist needed to be protected from false allegations during any screening process. Contrary to their written statement, the authors had not contacted anyone listed in *Red Channels* in advance of publication to discuss the allegations. In complaints against *Red Channels*, anti-Communist judges allowed the weak disclaimer as proof that the book did not libel anyone whom it listed. In one of the best-known cases, Joseph Julian, an actor on CBS, lost his case because the defense claimed that *Red Channels* specifically urged the protection of the innocent. The judge also suppressed testimony on the impact of the blacklist. The political climate swayed judges around the country.[32]

Given her blacklisting, Gypsy was particularly concerned with protecting her income. She decided to get tough with pesky female impersonators who appropriated her name and sullied her reputation for their own profit. At the same time she struggled with the American Legion, H. William Fitelson threatened legal action against the improper use of Gypsy's name in an advertisement. Billed as the "Brazilian Gypsy Rose Lee," a talented impersonator named Billy Herrero earned $325 a week. Gypsy was incensed. In November 1950, she expressed concern that her impersonator played in cities where she needed to maintain a unique presence. She protested that he even used her poses in photographs. Gypsy needed the uniqueness of her act to carry her through these dark times. A cheaper version of her threatened her livelihood. Gypsy's law firm settled the problem by getting the impersonator to give up the act without Gypsy having to testify in court.[33]

Gypsy also worried about her reputation to a much greater extent than in the past. When *Cabaret* magazine in July 1955 published a potentially damaging article entitled "Strip Tease Intellectual," she protested. The author based his article in large part on already published material, particularly a 1941 *American Mercury* article. *Cabaret* neglected to consider the reaction of Gypsy's pit bull lawyer, H. William Fitelson. Fitelson refused to allow his client to receive unfavorable publicity without protesting since it might injure her professionally. A month after the article appeared in *Cabaret*, the law firm of Fitelson and Mayers wrote *Cabaret* enumerating the ways it libeled Gypsy, including descriptions of drug use and of a pornography collection, which was said to be an extensive collection of smutty black-and-white movies. The *American Mercury* had mentioned both points, but the alleged vices had been indulged in during the 1930s. Two decades later, the charges were no longer relevant. They were, however, potentially damaging.

Gypsy's lawyers argued emphatically that such statements were untrue and hurt her professional status, particularly as she was attempting to reestablish her reputation due to the blacklist. The publication agreed to retract the statements through a formal apology if Gypsy dropped the threat of a potential lawsuit.[34]

Morton Minsky's book about burlesque, published in 1986, mentioned Gypsy's minor use of marijuana, her major brandy drinking, and her pornographic film collection, which her mother and the gangster Waxy Gordon's henchmen enjoyed. Indeed, in the 1930s, Gypsy was an occasional social drug user and a serious drinker. By 1950, her drug use had ended and her drinking was moderate. She wanted as clean an image as she could manage.

Gypsy never mentioned the blacklist in interviews in the United States but explained that she worked less in order to stay close to Erik. Onstage for only ten to fifteen weeks a year, she used the rest of the time to "take it easy." Even with all the benefits she customarily enjoyed, she managed to get "much more rest than in my burlesque days."[35] Occasionally, she appeared at charity fundraisers. At a March of Dimes Fashion Show, she collected more than three hundred dollars by allowing the audience to place their dollar bills down her bodice. The master of ceremony teased the audience, "Come up with a big bill, you can make your change."[36] A significant exception was her support of racial equity in the early 1950s. The cause of racial integration was controversial because it was deemed subversive by many groups and because many white Americans in the North as well as the South still believed in the inferiority of other races. Once blacklisted, Gypsy demonstrated courage to support the cause. Immediately after the American Legion attacked her at its convention in Chicago in 1950, Gypsy accepted an invitation to appear at a benefit for the Negro Actors' Guild of America produced by Ed Sullivan. The next year Gypsy contributed to the guild.[37]

On January 21, 1951, Gypsy performed on *The Big Show*, one of the rare radio appearances she made after the publication of *Red Channels*. She acted in a skit with Judy Holliday, who was also listed in that publication, and Tallulah Bankhead, who flouted convention on a regular basis. As usual, Gypsy managed to get the last laugh. When Holliday offered to get Bankhead an audition for television, Bankhead glowered, "Don't you *dare* mention that medium on this program!" Then, when Bankhead introduced Gypsy to Holliday, Holliday responded, "Pleased to meet ya. Hey, I remember you. You're the one who did the dance with the fans." At this allusion to the well-known fan dancer Sally Rand, Gypsy fumed, "Don't you *dare* mention that name on this program!"[38] Since *The Big Show* featured a variety of guests, the show's producers may have courageously decided to use the blacklisted women at Bankhead's urging, hoping they could get away with it because Gypsy and Holliday were such good comedians. At least three other guests during the two seasons of *The Big Show* were cited in *Red Channels*.

Gypsy attempted to rescue her career in radio and television by denouncing Moscow. Since she never had much sympathy for the Soviet regime, anti-Russian remarks came easily to her. The Korean War, in which another Communist state was clearly the enemy of the United States, gave her the perfect opportunity. At that time, most Americans failed to distinguish between Russian Communists and Chinese Communists. In October 1950, an anti-Communist organization, the New York Crusade for Freedom, invited Gypsy to speak briefly at the Majestic Theater on Broadway and renounce Communism. Since the organization believed that Communism tainted the entertainment industry, they expected performers to declare their loyalty. According to Victor Reisel, in his anti-Communist syndicated column "Inside Labor," Gypsy spoke passionately of the need to protect American troops: "Those are Russian bombs and Russian guns killing our boys. We're at war with Russians. Let's say so. The hell with them. Let's not be polite. Let's get together and fight." Delivering an extremely clever speech, Gypsy repudiated Communist regimes abroad without betraying her own liberal views.[39]

A *New York Post* article analyzed the fundamental problem with all the attention and energy directed toward Gypsy's dubious ties to alleged Communist sympathizers: Attacking hundreds of entertainers, writers, and artists took time and effort away from investigating real threats to the government's national security. As the *Post* suggested, "If we were Joseph Stalin, we would want to hear that Americans were fixing their minds on Gypsy Rose Lee, concentrating hard and forgetting every thing else."[40] Such articles may have lifted Gypsy's spirits, but they had no real impact on her situation.

Without much paying work, Gypsy responded to the blacklisting with her feet. Less than a year after the American Legion episode and still unable to appear on radio and television, she announced to Fitelson that she would tour in Europe. Tired of fighting against false charges, Gypsy left the criticism behind her. On July 10, 1951, she sailed to Europe with Erik. At forty, Gypsy's physical condition was enviable. "A woman over thirty should keep on her clothes," she declared. "I was asked why I took mine off and I replied, 'just to prove my point.'"[41]

16

Strip Around the World

Sweden's nude bathing surprised Gypsy. "I guess I'm more easily shocked than the average person," she told a local interviewer, who thought she was joking. Ten-year-old Erik surpassed his mother's punch line by adding, "The YMCA or the YWCA is the only place you can do that in America." Aspects of the European trip challenged Gypsy, but most audiences reacted favorably to the old routines. Throughout Europe, Gypsy created a variation of her carnival show. Four women, usually recruited from the host country, in fishnet stockings and strategically placed sequins sauntered onstage with a well-dressed Gypsy. Slowly, Gypsy stripped her clothing: a pink ermine coat; a dress laden with rhinestones, furs, and jewels. "Thus loaded," she joked, "it would certainly be difficult to run for a bus." She placed her extensive wardrobe on the other women. By the end of the act, Gypsy wore only a few leaves that, as one reporter pointed out, "had the autumnal tendency to fall." After a few changings of the seasons in London, the County Council intervened, causing Gypsy to be "more painstaking in applying the spirit gum which keeps the leaves from slipping."[1]

Gypsy traveled with Erik to fourteen countries in Europe and in North Africa, but Julio for the most part stayed in the United States, involved with showing his work. She found Europe sometimes puzzling but often wonderful. Gypsy got caught between the liberal nudity of Sweden and France and the postwar conservatism of Great Britain and

Spain. In Copenhagen, she learned that the Danes routinely enjoyed attending the theater, and they gave Gypsy a warm reception. The Swedish tour, however, ran into obstacles. Often Gypsy relied on local talent to appeal to the home crowd, but she found it difficult to communicate with women who spoke only Swedish. Above all, Gypsy joked, "it's tough for a girl there to sell what everyone is giving away."

Cultural differences, of course, affected the performance's reception, especially since Gypsy's act depended as much on understanding a turn of phrase as on the perfectly timed stripped garment. In Sweden, people flocked to the show and enjoyed looking at beautiful Swedish women, but reviewers commented that the audience failed to understand "the combination of nudity and comedy." The performances failed to inspire lust or even much sexual curiosity. Given mixed nude bathing on beaches in Sweden, Gypsy's show seemed tame and anachronistic. Meanwhile, terrible accommodations, especially the intermittent running water, vexed Gypsy. High expenses and taxes curtailed profits. Even the museums disappointed her because they contained few familiar art works.[2]

Just next door in Oslo, audiences loved the act. Gypsy returned the compliment by adoring Norway. She planned picnics by the fjords and visited the Viking museum. Gypsy performed with a multicultural, multiracial cast from Britain, Norway, Italy, and Nigeria. Enjoying the experience, she remarked about the humor that ensued as the women communicated in multiple languages and translated for one another.[3]

In more straitlaced London, where she played the Palladium in August 1951, Gypsy ran afoul of local officials. Audiences cheered her, but the authorities greeted her act with skepticism. Gypsy teased that the British attended her show because a newspaper photographer snapped her from behind, literally. As she explained, "Everything in front is pasted on. In the rear, nothing." She speculated that the audience kept expecting her to turn around.

During Gypsy's tour, the London County Council forbade the removal of garments onstage. The regulation would go into effect the following year. Pragmatic public officials decided not to interrupt Gypsy's show or infuriate crowds expecting to see her. Exploiting the impending prohibition to garner publicity, she protested the absurdity of the decision to the press. Every reporter who interviewed her asked her to comment. Gypsy pointed out that although the council barred men and women from taking off their hats and coats, the order allowed completely nude women onstage if they performed in tableaux or behind fans. Many people in the United States and Great

Britain considered such a presentation more artistic and tasteful than a striptease routine. Gypsy used the occasion to distinguish between herself and a woman "who puts on an exotic sexual spectacle." Her act was "straight comedy and boy, they love it."

Comparing the prudish British to the uninhibited Scandinavians, Gypsy noted that the latter "have a healthy, wholesome respect for the human body. That is why their moral standards are so high." Moreover, she argued, psychologists analyzing stripteasing found that "people who watch nude shows are unconsciously protecting themselves from becoming sexual offenders.... They are satisfying a sexual activity that has its place in the normal needs of some individuals." Gypsy understood that prohibitions "always increase the demand."[4]

The British capital seemed more provincial and less broad-minded than the provinces, Gypsy remarked. In Bristol, she broke all house records for the previous fifteen years. Success also greeted her in Edinburgh and Belfast; she loved the people, and they reciprocated. "The Scotch aren't interested in sex, but they like the comedy," Gypsy discovered. In Belfast, she noted, the Irish liked both. Audiences in Glasgow noisily showed their appreciation: "The galleries made so much noise and shook so hard I thought I was back in Minsky's."

In contrast to the London County Council's ban on future striptease performances, the *Birmingham Gazette* found Gypsy's act tame and complained that it included "too much of Miss Lee's mind." The men in the audience were disappointed that she stayed semiclothed. The reporter commented that Gypsy's act was "quite witty, a little naughty, and the whole act could quite easily be put on by a broad-minded vicar to open the parish bazaar." In Liverpool, where she expected the sailors to love her, the men apparently did not respond with much enthusiasm and the performance was a disaster. Gypsy had wired her manager, "I want Liverpool. Seaports *love* me," but acting in Liverpool's three-thousand-seat theater seemed like performing in a barn: "Even if you have a good crowd they rattle around like they were lost." Gypsy did not blame herself, though; she concluded that people from Liverpool enjoyed being difficult.[5]

Fearing condemnation by local officials, Gypsy refused to take her show to strictly Catholic locations, such as Dublin or Spain. In "those places," she speculated, "if I took off a pair of gloves they'd say I was doing it suggestively." At the same time, she decided not to compete with the strippers in Paris, who displayed much more flesh than her act.[6] The French led the way in Western Europe for sensual shows with naked women, who sashayed and twirled across the stage. The

Folies Bergère, a music hall that produced shows with lavish sets and costumes even though the women often wore very little, was a French institution. In 1926, Josephine Baker had performed there wearing a skimpy skirt made out of bananas; in the years since, the Folies had become even more suggestive.

Gypsy disparaged the French strippers' technique, which emphasized nudity: "The French ignore the subtle way of revealing charms, instead they splash them all over the scene."[7] As she critically watched French adult entertainment, Gypsy acknowledged that the Parisian women were more beautiful than strippers in the United States. Flawlessly executed shows featured women who were "better coached by professional choreographers" than American performers. Gypsy found the lighting enchanting. Although bare-breasted, the women were "never vulgar" because they refrained from bumps and grinds. Still Gypsy lamented that in Paris "it's all so clinical," with well-behaved audiences: "No one ever shouted 'take it off.'"[8]

Gypsy's biggest disappointment in Europe came when the U.S. Army vetoed her plans to visit American armed forces stationed in Germany. Soldiers had written letters begging her to come. Gypsy hated not fulfilling their wish that she perform for them. The official rationale stated that mothers of the soldiers might object to her act. Gypsy countered that her act had been appreciated by the military during World War II and she was unconvinced that her striptease would hurt any of the soldiers in Germany. She raged: "If I ever do go to play before the European Armed Forces I've got a great new idea for a G-string. Red tape."

Army officials never mentioned the blacklist, but they probably supported the attempt. In typical style, she joked about her failure to gain permission for her act. "What hurts," she contended, "is I expected trouble from the army so I had bigger bows made and extra ruffles on my skirts and things like that in case they did object." When she was informed that her act was not essential for the soldiers, she disagreed: "They're wrong of course—that's just what the boys need."[9]

Despite her foiled plans to go to Germany to entertain the troops, Gypsy enjoyed many other aspects of her European tour. She purchased a Rolls-Royce with her earnings from the Palladium. "I'm sure some girls have gotten 'em quicker," Gypsy remarked suggestively to a reporter, "but I paid for mine myself." Always the businesswomen, Gypsy did not pay the full sticker price of twenty-eight thousand dollars for the car, in part because it was previously owned. In exchange for a further reduction, she posed for photographs that Rolls-Royce could use for publicity. Sounding like Fanny Brice, who believed in spending money on quality items, Gypsy rationalized her choice: "If you're getting value for your money, it's okay to go ahead and spend it. If you're being overcharged, scream like hell." Built in 1949, the car was designed to be driven by the owner since it did not possess a chauffeur partition. Instead of the traditional black, the Rolls company had painted it maroon and gray. Gypsy added her initials in gold on a crystal vase that came with the car.[10]

Always interested in improving herself intellectually, Gypsy educated herself and Erik as they went sightseeing in Europe. A serious tourist, she planned outings at least once a week. She was as appreciative of local cultures as audiences were of her. In Oslo, Erik and Gypsy saw the original *Kon-Tiki*, the balsa log raft that Norwegian explorer Thor Heyerdahl built and sailed across the Pacific in 1947 to demonstrate that people in South America and Polynesia could have come into contact long before Columbus reached the American hemisphere from Europe. In Great Britain, Erik played with other children and learned about cricket, describing it as "baseball with a funny squashed out bat." Gypsy managed to visit Sherwood Forest and Byron's home.

She read Gibbon's *History of the Decline and Fall of the Roman Empire*, in order to answer Erik's historical questions about Pompeii and other places in Italy. Gypsy explained that she had come to prefer the *Decline and Fall* to historical fiction; fiction distorted "the facts to improve the love interest so I have turned to reading the proper history books."[11]

In Europe, as in the United States, Gypsy included charity visits on her tour. In 1952, she and Erik visited the Gracie Fields Home and Orphanage in England. They brought toys with them, and the war orphans responded by singing for them and writing touching letters. One eleven-year-old girl thanked them for the tennis and rounders sets; she loved bouncing her new ball in the garden. While the younger girls adored nursing their dolls, the boys gazed at ships and planes with their new telescopes.[12]

During her trip, Gypsy expanded her interests to include North African culture and toured less frequented destinations, including Algeria and Tunisia. In North Africa, Gypsy simply played tourist. Her scrapbook is full of photographs, postcards, and menus, mainly from hotels. She did not add any commentary.

In one of her longest stopovers, Gypsy stayed in Spain for five months in 1952 to costar in the movie *Babes in Baghdad* with Paulette Goddard. Julio joined her and Erik in his native country and remained with them there longer than at any other time. The family expanded.

While in Spain, Gypsy adopted her first Siamese cat, Gaudi, named for a famous Catalonian architect. In Italy, she acquired her second Siamese, Teena. The cats, Gypsy confessed, were "an international ménage." Later the couple had kittens. Gypsy quickly pointed out to the press that although she gave the kittens pretty Siamese names, they were "solid sound substantial American citizens." Even the kittens had to be politically above reproach.[13]

While parts of the trip to Spain were pleasant, Gypsy found the movie's plot silly. In the film, the Caliph of Baghdad has twelve wives but fawns over one, Zohara, played by Gypsy. When the caliph forces Kyra (Paulette Goddard) to join his harem, she argues that women have the same rights as men. To the caliph's consternation, his godson, Ezar, agrees with her. The caliph and Ezar make a bet that Ezar will start his own harem in ten days unless Zohara outwits the caliph within the same period. The three plotters, Zohara, Ezar, and Kyra, drug the caliph. Dressing him in beggar's clothes, they leave him in the square. Ten days later, they rescue a humbled caliph, who permits Ezar to marry just one woman, Kyra. Ezar and Kyra achieve the ultimate victory for the 1950s: monogamous, heterosexual marriage.

Unimpressed with the unsophisticated plot, Gypsy never bothered to see the movie. Back in New York, she dismissed it as "made strictly for Muncie, Indiana." Muncie stood for socially conservative Middle America, much as Peoria did. The reviews described the film as "fluffy" fare. Columnist Ed Sullivan, who previously criticized Gypsy's performance in *Stage Door Canteen*, was offended: "Gypsy Rose Lee is the perfect indication of the trend of the motion picture industry." Because of poor box office returns, he said, "the mental has yielded to the physical" throughout the industry, and Gypsy was a prime example. Sullivan's indignation may have stemmed, in part, from political differences with Gypsy; he vehemently and vocally opposed suspected Communists, although he maintained liberal views on race relations.[14]

Babes in Baghdad was perfectly attuned to 1950s culture. The promotional materials commercialized women far more creatively than burlesque had done. The movie's press book regaled theater owners with ways they could make money off women's bodies and, even better, from women taking their bodies shopping. "Show 'em the 'Milk and Lotus' Bath of the Harem Queens! For lobby or department store window. Rig a real bath as shown with milk (a little will do) and lots of bubbles and flowers," the press book advised. "Two bathing suit beauties reveling in the bath will complete the picture. Add a display saying: 'SEE THE SPECTACULAR MILK-AND-LOTUS BATH OF THE HAREM QUEENS in *BABES IN BAGHDAD*!' You might also make the display the setting for a Beauty Clinic, with a local beauty expert on hand to dispense advice on beauty hints."

The promoters offered other creative ideas for small local retailers. Under the heading "Baghdad Leads Off Your Citywide Merchant CO-OP Campaign," they suggested that a pretty young woman dressed like Paulette Goddard in the picture register at a hotel under the name "Ba-Be from Baghdad." Merchants were encouraged to arrange with the local hotel for publicity declaring that "Ba-Be from Baghdad" had come to town to enjoy a shopping spree. The local newspaper, in full compliance with the stunt, could follow her into local stores and photographs of the "Ba-Be" purchasing clothes and other items could accompany a "Woman's Page story comparing American stores and shopping ideas with Baghdad or oriental bazaars." This approach to selling the film epitomized Western attitudes toward the exotic Orient, located in the imagination anywhere from the Middle East to North Africa and Asia. The open expression of sexuality was made safe by being situated elsewhere, while its commercial potential was shamelessly exploited in America.[15]

The relentless heterosexuality and consumerism portrayed in the movie's ad campaign were codified during the 1950s. Using women's bodies to sell products and turning women's bodies into commodities were hardly new developments, but during the 1950s American culture was saturated with powerful images of heterosexual marriage as consumer bliss. This cultural emphasis on marital fulfillment was not confined to celluloid or the airwaves. The average age of women at first marriage was lower during the fifties than during any other decade of the twentieth century. The Great Depression and World War II were followed by what was labeled a return to "normalcy." In magazines and on television, this middle-class ideal took the form of a nuclear family with a stay-at-home mother and homemaker living in a single-family, detached suburban house filled with gadgets, and an automobile in the driveway. Exhorted to take jobs outside the home during the war, women were pressured after the peace to give them up to returning soldiers. Gender-segregated help-wanted advertisements and gender discrimination in the workplace forced middle-class women to learn their proper place in society. With varying degrees of success, people tried to fit the image. Ironically, for many families women's earnings from part-time or full-time jobs outside the home were necessary to cover the mortgage and car payments, as well as to buy consumer goods now defined as necessities.

The plot of *Babes in Baghdad* epitomized the tension between women's sexuality and the subordinate role wives and mothers played in the family. The film also exemplified real problems in Gypsy's own marriage. She attempted unsuccessfully to negotiate her relationship to her third husband while in Europe, as well as to figure out how to combine motherhood with her unconventional work. Julio's near invisibility during Gypsy's European trip emphasized the rockiness of their marriage. Once Julio left Gypsy in Spain in 1952, the marriage was close to ended.

While her personal life was disrupted by her trip to Europe, Gypsy fell in love with traveling. Less than two years after returning to the United States, Gypsy embarked on an extensive world tour. In the fall of 1954, she traveled to Australia and South Asia, as well as returning to Europe. In South Asia, she was strictly a tourist. In Australia, she selected large and lovely women for the show. Gypsy's act sold out for the entire engagement. Australians rarely encountered stripteasing, and some viewed it as immoral. The entertainment form had never gained popularity because of strict regulation against it. Before Gypsy's first performance, some clergy and women's groups in Australia unwittingly assisted her publicity campaign. The Women's Christian Temperance Union opposed the "degrading effect" of her act. The Housewives Association worried that young girls were losing their modesty and that Gypsy corrupted their moral standards. Gypsy countered that her act was "chic and sophisticated and I have to play to a sophisticated audience." The teenage girls about whom the Housewives Association professed concern would not have been interested in Gypsy's act, with its references to art and books.

When several churchmen asked to preview her act, Gypsy refused. She contended that they would be a very hostile audience and teased that if they really wanted to see it, they should pay for it like everyone else. Advising the clergymen to join the audience on opening night, Gypsy dismissed their objections. She never worried about preshow criticism in which people imagined the licentiousness of her act. Rather she responded to real concerns after the audiences saw the show. Erik willingly reassured anyone nervous about the act. As he watched the routine, the ten-year-old commented in a blasé manner to a reporter, "It's the usual."

Gypsy never allowed her act to veer close to obscenity. "I have to think of my reputation," she joked. She also pointed out that she and the clergy shared common values. "I'm all for do-gooders," she contended. "I'm rather a do-gooder myself." The controversy meant that two policemen stood less than twelve feet away from her while she performed to ensure the act did not break any of the laws about public nudity, which, in fact, it did not. Their unnecessary presence annoyed Gypsy.[16]

After Gypsy left Australia, she avenged herself on her Australian critics. She told reporters in Bangkok that the Australian women in the chorus shocked her: "They wear much less than we do." In the United States, she pointed out, the strippers in burlesque wore neck-to-ankle net bodysuits. In comparing the scantily clad Australian women with U.S. stripteasers, Gypsy emphasized the point that her relatively modest performance did less to defile Australian virtue than Australian chorus girls did.[17]

Gypsy vacationed as hard as she worked, and she traveled to southern Asia and northern Africa. For a time June joined Gypsy in Europe, and the sisters decided to drive to Morocco. June's husband objected to the two women traveling by car without a male escort, but they ignored his concerns. After touring all over the United States in their youth, they remained adventurous. They teased that men did not pester them on the trip, although they both swore not to tell June's husband that men had left them alone. Gypsy found time for all the tourist attractions including shopping in bazaars. In Asia, she adored visiting Buddhist temples, mosques, botanical gardens, and floating markets. In one of the mosques in Calcutta, the Koran in Muhammad's grandson's writing awed her.

All along the trip, she derived pleasure from looking at the exotic animals. In Australia, she fell in love with marsupials, noting in her journal "one with a baby in her pouch—not her baby incidentally but just a friend who was chilly."[18] In India, although she enjoyed seeing the cows in the street, she found Calcutta overwhelming with its masses of people. Visiting the Taj Mahal, she also enjoyed watching monkeys, dancing bears, and trained birds. In Cairo, she rose at five in the morning for a camel ride to the Pyramids.

Some of the photographs that Gypsy took during this tour were published in a book entitled *Shooting Stars: Favorite Photos Taken by Classic Celebrities*. Unable to explain just why she took pictures, she quipped, "I shoot pictures for the same reason some women buy diamonds and furs." In India, Gypsy photographed a barely clothed holy man. She joked that he had "nothing to do with my business." His quest for penance impressed her; although she wore a coat on the chilly day, he did not seem bothered by the cold.[19]

Gypsy renewed her love affair with traveling a few years later, vacationing in Europe with Erik and Boyd Bennett. A young baritone, Bennett had toured with Gypsy during the carnival tour in 1949 and later moved into her house as a paying tenant. Serving as both friend and unpaid worker, he cleared snow, kept the ancient furnace functioning, and performed other odd jobs.[20]

Erik described the trip with Bennett and Gypsy in great detail. At her departure on the ship *Flanders*, one reporter asked if she had given up stripping because of her age. She responded, "I have everything I had twenty years ago. It's just a little lower, that's all." On the voyage, Gypsy raised more than eight thousand dollars for the Seamen's Relief Fund and proved that her age still did not hinder her charity work.[21]

She practiced frugality while on the trip—except for her shopping. Gypsy always traveled to Europe in the off-season because the fare was lower. Usually she bought a ticket for an inexpensive stateroom and the ship lines upgraded her for free. She enjoyed her status as the only celebrity: "In my experience the only other notable aboard is someone like Thomas Mann who couldn't shake a bead."[22]

To avoid scandal, Boyd left Europe earlier than Gypsy and Erik did. Gypsy made the trip unbearable by criticizing him over small matters after syndicated gossip columnist Dorothy Kilgallen hinted that they were having an affair while traveling. Even if Bennett's homosexuality had been known, magazines and newspapers would have presented him as heterosexual, as they did with most gay actors during the 1950s. Since the blacklist, Gypsy protected her reputation at any cost.[23]

Gypsy enjoyed visiting with her friend Janet Flanner, who had settled in Paris and wrote as a foreign correspondent in France for the *New Yorker*. Flanner characterized Gypsy as "always a burden, bless her heart." When she traveled, Gypsy expected her friends to wait on her and help her run errands. Even so, her friends enjoyed her. Flanner affectionately described Gypsy as, "the funniest, drollest, woman on earth, a wonderful friend, and I adore her." According to Flanner, Gypsy told hilarious "stories, which she acts out, half-dressed in her room, with son Eric [*sic*] and some albino actor." For her costumes, Gypsy had used a special French corsetiere; she had ordered new corsets while on her trip, but her unique French complicated such situations. Flanner sometimes intervened on the telephone to help clarify Gypsy's orders.

During her stay in Paris, Gypsy told Flanner about a nightmare she had at the hotel. She dreamed that fire destroyed her homes, pets, and son. She woke up at one in the morning, phoned the hotel desk, and demanded to know the location of the fire escape. The staff misunderstood and panicked, believing a fire had broken out in Gypsy's room. After an hour, the hotel employee finally comprehended. Dreaming about fire, he explained, was very lucky. Gypsy took a sleeping pill, putting an end to that night's drama. Flanner was concerned because she had pressured the hotel staff to let Gypsy stay, and she was sure they would not permit Gypsy to lodge there again. Only half joking, Flanner concluded: "Next time she comes, I am going to hire an office staff, a hypnotizer, somebody from the Folies-Bergère to give corseting advice and a large French fireman with a bucket outside her door."[24]

Europe gave Gypsy solace from her political woes, a broader education, and enjoyable tourist experiences. She needed to return home periodically to consider new directions for her life, especially in light of the imperative to reinvent herself politically given the accusations that she was a Communist sympathizer. She also wanted another livelihood; eager to find a new source of income, Gypsy became involved in posing for Springmaid sheets, but it all started because of Erik's love of his model train.

17

Back Home

On Christmas Eve 1952, Gypsy happily returned to New York City. She gushed that New York was "so alive and in the center of things." Culturally, she preferred New York to Hollywood, which in her summation "TV and movies—that seems to be about the end of it." She enjoyed New York's theater and art galleries, and she met friends at its fine restaurants. Domestic life resumed; Gypsy visited her hairdresser, sent Erik to school, and dealt with her relatives.[1]

When Gypsy and Erik arrived home, Julio was not with them for long. Gypsy's stay in Europe weakened her marriage. As early as 1950, when Gypsy lived in New York, Julio had traveled to mount exhibitions of his work and to paint. Artists recalled Julio spending large amounts of time in an artists' community in Woodstock, New York, sans Gypsy. In her journal, Gypsy tersely noted the number of days he stayed away. During her tour of Europe, their separations lengthened. Although he joined Gypsy and Erik in Spain, he returned to the United States months before they arrived in New York. In February 1952, June asked Gypsy about the truth of William Fitelson's hints about the breakup of her marriage. Not unsurprisingly, Gypsy had confided her troubles to her lawyer before telling her sister. Gypsy and Julio obtained a divorce in Reno in 1955 on the grounds of separation for more than three years.

"I was not cut out be a prince consort," De Diego remarked to the press when asked about the demise of his marriage. "What is a man that he should have to follow his wife around?" De Diego continued his successful career as an artist. After he moved to California in 1958, the Pasadena Museum gave him a retrospective exhibition. Paramount Pictures hired him as a color consultant, a technical adviser to cinematographers, and he even played a small role in the movie *The Buccaneers*. He refused other movie roles in order to paint. In 1962, *Time* magazine published his series of paintings on the Spanish Armada. He and Gypsy remained friends; one magazine insinuated that they occasionally still slept together.[2]

June Havoc teased that Julio was "one of our removed husbands. He's very talented. We couldn't handle him. He was a bit much for us." After Gypsy's divorce, June grew concerned about her sister's emotional state; she found Gypsy "man-timid, man-frightened and man-shy." June boosted Gypsy's spirits by emphasizing her successes and arguing with Gypsy when she claimed she had "made a failure of her life."[3]

Gypsy's success as an entertainer apparently doomed her to marital failure. She resisted throwing away fame and fortune for a conventional 1950s marriage. "Any woman who makes more money than her husband and is a more outstanding personality can't hope for a happy marriage," she declared firmly. She also conceded that her three husbands "were all brave men for having married me." Insisting that the institution of marriage did not work for her, Gypsy never reconciled her independence and ambition with being the subordinate partner in a marriage. She never desired the role of helpmate. "If I could truthfully say my husbands were all stinkers, it would be okay. But they were all very nice men, and I must assume it's been my fault. I was always too independent—that's what you get when you start working as a baby." When the shingles came off her house, Gypsy climbed a ladder, inspected the damage, and ordered new shingles. Her first husband was furious. "A man doesn't want that kind of efficiency and that's the story of my life. I am used to buying my own shingles."[4]

Advice literature, especially women's magazines, and popular culture, as epitomized in *Babes in Baghdad*, reinforced Gypsy's assessment of what men wanted. Even one of the most progressive sex education books for married couples, *Sex Without Fear*, told women that "feminine daintiness is one of woman's greatest attractions."[5] Gypsy never described herself as soft or dainty. Personally and professionally, Gypsy accurately saw herself as hard and tough.

In 1957 in a newspaper interview in the *New York Post*, the confrontational interviewer Mike Wallace asked Gypsy about the "surplus" of almost two million single women in the United States, a figure that included divorcées like Gypsy. The interview demonstrated Gypsy's high level of literacy, knowledge, and wit. By feeding her straight lines, Wallace provided Gypsy with one of her most intellectual interviews and allowed her to express her feelings about becoming a single mother. When he asked Gypsy what she thought was the worst tragedy for an unmarried woman, she responded, "Living out her entire life without having a child." She favored more liberal laws to allow single women to adopt children. Gypsy's conversation with Wallace mixed 1930s liberalism, especially the belief in social supports provided by the federal government, with a 1950s view of the sanctity of motherhood. She recommended that the government provide "a new type of annuity" for single women with adopted children, "an insurance of some kind to substitute for a husband's paycheck." Although she preferred a tax deduction, Gypsy offered to pay higher taxes to fund such a government program. All parents, she thought, needed a larger deduction than six hundred dollars per child; she proposed three thousand dollars. She also believed that the government should allow women to deduct childcare expenses. Gypsy used patriotism as a rationale for her plan: Healthy, well-educated "children are an investment not just for parents but for the country."

When Wallace facetiously mentioned polygamy as one solution to the problem of excess women, Gypsy cited anthropologist Margaret Mead's theory that conflict pervaded such families. Gypsy acknowledged that women involved in the arrangement often argued about power within the family. An early proponent of the "men are for dessert" theory, Gypsy admitted that women needed men as escorts to theater or to dinner but argued that the men could be friends rather than husbands. At the close of the interview, Gypsy criticized Wallace's use of the word "spinster." Her friends who were "unmarried are attractive women in their thirties and are having a pretty nice time, it never occurs to me to call them 'spinsters.' I don't think they think of themselves as 'spinsters.'" She referred to these friends as "single." When Wallace queried her as to why she opposed the word "spinsters," Gypsy scoffed, "Oh Mike…nobody spins anymore. We might whirl a bit, but we don't spin."[6]

As a single mother by choice when her son was born, Gypsy made all the decisions regarding his upbringing. Upon returning to New York City in 1952, Gypsy enrolled eight-year-old Erik in the third grade of the Professional Children's School. The school was not just for children who worked as entertainers or trained seriously in music and attended classes part-time or irregularly; it also served the children of performers. Tolerating parents who removed their children from school at odd times to go on the road, it specialized in educating children like Erik. "If he went to an ordinary school," Gypsy explained, "he'd get into the 'civilian' atmosphere and it would be too hard for him to adjust to the theatre atmosphere on holidays." When Gypsy and Erik traveled, the school sent lessons by correspondence.

While on tour in Europe, Gypsy had taught Erik history and English, subjects she knew well, and he learned much of his history and geography from traveling. She gave him math problems but felt inadequate to teach him long division and struggled through fractions. Her only other experience with that math function, she said, was the "agent's 10 percent." In Spain, she hired a tutor for Erik, and he quickly learned Spanish, his stepfather Julio's native language. But now she decided the Professional Children's School best suited her requirements. Erik was not so eager. "I hate school. I would like to travel all the time," he once commented.[7]

Gypsy's main concern was making a living. Her reentry into her career as a performer came from an unexpected direction: advertising. Gypsy posed for advertisements for bed linens, and it proved as suggestive and controversial as her stripping. Courageously or selfishly ignoring the blacklist, Colonel Elliot White Springs, the owner of Springmaid Cotton Mills, hired Gypsy to promote the company's fabrics and linens. Colonel Springs, a U.S. Air Force pilot in World War II who had written popular stories about his exploits, contacted Gypsy after he discovered, through a newspaper article, that Gypsy and Erik played with a two-hundred-foot O-gauge model train set in her basement. A train enthusiast, Colonel Springs owned the Lancaster and Chester Railway, twenty-nine miles of track that fed into the Southern Railway System. In May 1951, he invited Gypsy to dedicate a new depot in Lancaster, South Carolina. Displaying his characteristic wit, he promised to appoint her "Vice-President in Charge of Unveiling." Short of paying work, Gypsy cheerfully accepted his invitation. By wearing a harem-style dress made out of Springmaid fabric, she configured herself into a walking advertisement for the company.

Fifteen hundred people attended the dedication in hundred-degree heat. The press loved it. One editor wrote, "Stripteaser Gypsy Rose Lee unveiled a railroad station and nothing more here today." Gypsy flirted with Colonel Springs. "Take the throttle of the train for a little trip," Springs suggested. "What's a throttle?" asked Gypsy. "That's something that when you pull it something happens," answered the colonel. "Oh," she responded, "like a zipper." Before she took the throttle, she asked coyly, "You don't mind if I take off my gloves?" and added sweetly, "I can assure you that will be all."[8]

At least "J.H. from North Carolina" objected to the colonel's use of Gypsy to advertise this product; it was, he wrote, the equivalent of "telling all of the young women who work in your mills: 'Girls, go strip and tease. That is the way to a big textile man's heart, to his respect, to his pocketbook!'" The unhappy letter writer argued that endorsing a striptease performer encouraged a deteriorating moral attitude in the United States. Worse, "when womanhood is unholy, God is forgotten."[9]

The controversy probably pleased Colonel Springs. He enjoyed challenging the staid advertising establishment. Teasingly, he wrote Gypsy's friend Fay Emerson, "This organization already has three sheets in the wind" over Gypsy's recent visit. Gypsy's verbal antics and comely form led the colonel to invite her to star in his Springmaid advertisements. The company's magazine ads, filled with sexual double entendres, were already notorious—and profitable.[10]

Gypsy had appeared in both sexy and serious ads for products such as deodorant and shampoo since leaving Minsky's. In the mid-1930s, she did a sexy advertisement for the Flameless Lektrolite lighter. Wearing a very tight, low-cut velvet dress from the show, Gypsy sat backstage at the *Ziegfeld Follies*. She leaned slightly forward, showing maximum cleavage and casting a knowing glance at the camera, to light her cigarette.

Gypsy was perfectly suited to star in Colonel Springs's provocative and funny promotional campaign for Springmaid. One ad appeared, among other places, on the back cover of *Esquire* in June 1954. Lying on her own frilly bed in her pink negligee, Gypsy looked sufficiently inviting. The text began, "My favorite nite spot is a Springmaid sheet." Identifying Gypsy as a "prominent hostess of New York and Paris," the ad commented, "Like so many aristocrats, Miss Lee finds Springmaids a 'must' for her guests. Those favored leaders of fashion who share her hospitality are treated to the very finest of bedroom appointments." In case anyone missed the point about the "bedroom appointments," the advertisement ended: "Living in the grand manner, Miss Lee has never felt it necessary to mingle with cafe society. Her favorite nite spot is in her own home, a Springmaid sheet."

A more controversial ad showed Gypsy pouring tea for several young women. The caption began, since Gypsy was not yet legally divorced,

"Mrs. Julio De Diego, charming collector of modern art, and one of the ten best dressed women in New York," and emphasized Gypsy's role as an art collector. The joke was that although Gypsy dressed elegantly in public in couture clothes, few people connected her with fashion. The women were planning a grand ball to be held at Madison Square Garden to raise money to restore George Washington's Distillery. The ad stressed Mrs. De Diego's passion for taking Springmaid sheets with her on trips. The sheets proved "American superiority," an important virtue during the Cold War. The ad prompted adverse reactions because it mocked both the first president and society women who organized benefits.

"'I couldn't give top performances,' says Gypsy Rose Lee famous author, actress and ecdysiast, 'for fear a wriggle would turn into a wrinkle,'" asserted a Springmaid advertisement touting DAZZLE, a new wrinkle-resistant fabric. "Now I can confidently put my liabilities on the skids and my assets on DAZZLE." Everyone familiar with Gypsy's assets understood the allusion. In the Springmaid advertisements, Gypsy parodied her own attempts at respectability as well as her stripping. Gypsy enjoyed making them.

Gypsy and Colonel Springs visited each other several times after her initial turn at the throttle. Once she arrived with several other stripteasers and Erik. On that occasion, Frances Springs, the colonel's wife, stormed out of the house. In 1958, on Gypsy's fourth visit as Vice-President of Unveiling, she smashed a huge champagne bottle to christen a new freight car. She wore a coat and matching strapless dress made of a Springmaid print. Meanwhile, the colonel wrote to the divorcée that he looked forward to seeing her weekly in New York City. Burke Davis, Colonel Springs's biographer, implies that Colonel Springs enjoyed intimate relationships with women other than his wife, who occupied herself with charitable work in the textile mill villages. Certainly he enjoyed bragging about attractive women, but Gypsy's papers give no indication of an affair.[11]

After her return from Europe, Gypsy resumed her charity work, almost always for uncontroversial and apolitical charities that the public could not perceive as subversive. She led tours of her house for the Arthritis Rheumatism Foundation and the Wellesley Club and auctioned art for the United Jewish Appeal. In the 1930s, Gypsy began her support of the March of Dimes fund-raising campaign to eradicate polio. In the mid-1940s, she was a starring guest at a fashion show and luncheon for the organization. On *Helping Hand* the quiz show, in early 1950, Gypsy won five hundred dollars that was donated to a sixteen-year-old boy living on a farm in Iowa so he could travel to Hot Springs, Arkansas, like President Roosevelt, for therapy. After her blacklisting, Gypsy eagerly renewed her association with the March of Dimes, and in 1955, she modeled in a fashion show in a brown chiffon gown designed by Charles James. Disabled children were politically safe.

Gypsy even ingratiated herself with the American Legion. In response to a request from a Legion post, she sent two autographed copies of *The G-String Murders* for an auction. In 1954, she performed at a Legion event in Washington, D.C. Capturing the high bidders at a Christmas fund-raiser at another Legion post, she promised cocktails at her home for those who donated the largest amount. She also acted as auctioneer at the event. "We love that gal! Too bad she isn't a war veteran, so we could elect her commander of Ad Men's Post," an official wrote in a newsletter article. All had been forgiven, if not entirely forgotten.[12]

Reporters happily ignored her previous politics and discovered silly reasons to write columns about her. They helped her gain a nonthreatening, nonsubversive reputation. Earl Wilson devoted a column to Gypsy's failure to pay a fine for not having her garbage covered. Defending herself, Gypsy insisted that she had bought ten covers but they never stayed on the garbage can. Besides, she noted, her neighbors shared the same problem and the city did not fine them. Gypsy resolved the situation by spending $8.95 on a garbage can with a cover chained to it. Gypsy gave Wilson a quote to end his column: "It seems a little ironic that Gypsy Rose Lee should have the only garbage can in the block that's covered up. After all my years of not being covered." A picture of Gypsy in a corset or showing her magnificent legs always accompanied such copy.[13] Fluff like this helped Gypsy seem like the next-door neighbor.

Although Gypsy was silenced and silent on political issues after the blacklisting, she did comment on social issues. In 1953, she discussed the Kinsey Report on the sexual behavior of women, which had just appeared in print. Gypsy believed that morals had not really changed. Women were just more honest. "I doubt whether I will read the book. Statistics on sex bore me," she admitted She voiced her liberal views on sex education even though the topic was controversial: "If the book leads to a better understanding of sex problems, it will serve a useful purpose. I think sex discussion has been suppressed too much in the case of children."[14]

Unable to find employment on television or in the movies because of the blacklist, Gypsy took to the road at home and abroad as a stripteaser.

As always, the shows were lucrative. Her fans readily forgave her politics after her European tour—many of them had never taken the charges of her being a Communist sympathizer as seriously as the radio and TV producers in the first place—and greeted her with enthusiasm and teased her about her profession. In Boston, police recognized her Rolls-Royce and saluted her. At a market, a man admired her car and asked her teasingly whether the fenders came off.[15]

June set out to help Gypsy reestablish herself professionally. She hated Gypsy's reliance on stripteasing and wanted her to perform in more serious venues. Unfortunately, the blacklist negated any other career options. In 1953, June had been a gifted movie star appearing in such films as *Gentlemen's Agreement*. A slim, beautiful blonde, she played both serious roles and comedy, and she also was interested in directing. June decided to cast Gypsy as one of the leads in a road show production of Clare Boothe Luce's play *The Women*. Gypsy teased June about her new role. When they lunched together at the Algonquin, Gypsy picked up the check because she was the elder sister, even though, as she explained to columnist Leonard Lyons, the director really should have paid.

The Women is a biting, unromantic play about how upper-class women battle for and keep their men. Although male directors always suggested that Gypsy play the sexy character Crystal, who lounges in a bubble bath onstage, June wisely cast her sister in the role of acerbic Sylvia Fowler. Asked why she did not play Crystal, she shrugged: "Now look honey, what would I want to play that for? I've been taking bubble baths all my life. I don't want to take them in the legitimate theater. That wouldn't be progress." In one of the scenes in the play, Sylvia Fowler cat-fights with her former husband's second wife; using their long fingernails, they scratch and gouge. For Gypsy, Sylvia was the only good part.

Gypsy's performance pleased June. Unable to keep to the script, Gypsy mentioned to the author that the cast had criticized her for playing the show for laughs. Luce looked bewildered and remarked, "That's what I wrote the play for," so Gypsy felt vindicated for her portrayal. Excellent reviews for both sisters followed: "Sister, Daughters, Sock Syracuse *Women* Over; Havoc's Sure Direction," asserted a headline in *Variety*. One reviewer reported honestly that Gypsy "actually...doesn't play the role but rather horses around in it and the result is not Sylvia but still a raucously amusing performance."[16]

June also directed Gypsy in a 1954 production of Gypsy's own play, *Naked Genius*. Their friends encouraged the production. One wished good luck to the "Naked Genius in the *Naked Genius* and to June Legs Director." The reviewers were less kind. Gypsy had written an "aimless, silly script," snarled reviewer Louise Mae. She added, "Miss Havoc's staging is no better than the play. There is no play." Gypsy's acting "is charming, utterly competent, heaven to look at, but she has been stabbed in the back by Miss Lee the playwright." One reporter understood *Naked Genius* better. Pointing out that "if one does not take it seriously, and certainly Miss Lee does not, the show adds up to frothy entertainment, a few chuckles, an occasional belly laugh."[17]

June cheered Gypsy whenever she performed in legitimate theater. She wrote Gypsy very encouraging notes about her acting. Effusive in her praise, June wanted Gypsy to be self-assured on the stage rather than critiquing her own performance. Gypsy needed to feel confident of her instincts about the part. June exhorted Gypsy to believe in herself and to be happy.[18] Although they were both busy with their own careers, sometimes on opposite coasts, they came together in a crisis to support each other.

In August 1954, Gypsy played in Anita Loos's *Darling, Darling* in Westport, Connecticut. Her character, a manipulative fashion designer, forces her spouse to be a househusband and runs her friends' lives as well. The reviewers condemned the play as badly written, but one newspaper declared that Gypsy was its saving grace, "a comedienne of a high order who can turn ridiculous nonsense into something bordering on high comic art." Gypsy herself recognized it was "no critics' play," but she enjoyed the part.[19]

Such comedic roles demonstrated Gypsy's talent onstage and contributed to her growing reputation as an actress. After *The Women*, Gypsy performed in various plays. "Everything About Her Is Delightful," touted a 1956 review of Gypsy's role in George Kaufman's *Fancy Meeting You Again*. It added that she was as "exciting in clothes as the other way." While on tour with the play, Gypsy started a fashion craze by creating a dress out of Indian bedspreads. So many women copied her that the store where she bought the bedspreads sold out.[20]

The critics also liked Gypsy's performance in the witty play by Charles MacArthur and Ben Hecht *Twentieth Century*, in which she played Lily Garland, a movie queen who argues with her theater producer over a part while they are riding a train. The *Palm Beach Post* declared, "Miss Lee throws all her exuberant talent for humor into the role from the moment she moves on stage." Gypsy's stage career assured her reputation as a comic actress, but it never paid as well as stripteasing.[21]

In 1956, a television network finally offered Gypsy a spot in a drama, *Sauce for the Goose* on the United States Steel Hour. Although she made no public comment on the fact, she was returning after the blacklist to television with a major corporation sponsoring the show. At least for occasional roles, her blacklisting on radio and television had ended. She gushed about performing on TV as a featured actress. The publicity shots thrilled her even more. Many of them were head shots, and as Gypsy pointed out, "Nobody's ever paid attention to my face before." She confessed, "Really—my head has never been considered my best part."

In *Sauce for the Goose*, Gypsy played an author who wrote a marital advice book, *Marriage—Trick or Treat*. "I'm playing a lady novelist. Now spell that correctly—it's novelist, not navelist," Gypsy teased. After reading her book, an advertising writer who composes a blurb for it decides his happy marriage is turning dull and stale. By following the book's advice, he almost destroys his marriage. Gypsy commented that her character thought that she was "terribly chic. Actually, she's just a little overdressed." She added wryly, "And I should know about that."

The blacklist had made getting legitimate acting jobs more difficult, but slowly, with the help of her sister and friends, Gypsy was building a fine career playing comedic parts.[22] But her life was not simply work; she also had to contend with her family. Relations returned to normal once Gypsy returned to New York City. Gypsy sent money to her grandmother and Aunt Belle. Belle complained that she rarely heard from her sister Rose and when she did the letters teemed with self-pity. Obviously Belle rarely read her own letters, which were full of complaints about her own life. Belle experimented with various business ventures that Gypsy supported, but they invariably failed. If she worked outside the home, Belle faced the real problem of finding and paying for nursing care for her ailing mother, Big Lady.[23] Meanwhile, Gypsy's own mother reentered her life.

During the late 1930s, Gypsy had been estranged from the stage mother who encouraged her to become a stripteaser. Gradually, as Gypsy and June matured, Rose became more of a bit player making walk-on appearances in her role as the evil mother. With the support of their husbands, their lovers, and, most important, their lawyers, Gypsy and June learned how to control the damage Rose could inflict. Privately, Gypsy paid off her mother often and well.

In 1951, doctors diagnosed Gypsy's mother with terminal colon cancer. In her dying, as in the rest of her life, Rose combined tenacity with courage and viciousness. When Gypsy learned about Rose's terminal cancer, she and Erik visited her at the hospital. Gypsy thought the visit with her mother had gone well, but she deluded herself about her mother's emotional balance. Immediately after Gypsy's visit, Rose wired Gypsy to express her gratitude for the money and all the hospital arrangements. While still hospitalized, Rose switched tone and wrote Gypsy accusing her of neglect and stinginess. She condemned her daughter as "absolutely heartless, unnatural, incapable of a feeling God gives." After careful reflection, Rose considered herself in no way responsible for her daughters' antagonism toward her. In a moment of great irony and psychological transference tinged with some truth, she told Gypsy, "You made money your god and goal and that is all you ever cared about." Once again, Rose threatened to tell the press the truth about both her daughters. Desiring to salvage her own reputation, she planned to show how her daughters had consumed her energy and resources and then flung her away when they no longer needed her. This familiar emotional seesaw of denunciations followed by pronouncements of love succeeded by venomous attacks would end only with Rose's death.[24]

Gypsy made a final attempt to respond to her mother's complaints. Rose's last letter repeated all the other "cruel letters and threats" sent throughout the years. Noting in a written response that she had kept her mother's letters and carefully filed them away, Gypsy expressed shock that her mother had written her such a vicious letter. To refute Rose's charge that she had ignored her financially, Gypsy estimated her mother's wealth as considerable, given the payments that Gypsy made to her. After twenty years, her mother's attempts at blackmail disgusted her. In a moment of bravado, Gypsy wrote her mother that everything in Gypsy's life could be made public.[25]

Gypsy knew that their mother's terminal illness meant she could no longer deal with Rose only through lawyers. "Impossible to keep her out of our lives now," Gypsy regretfully commented to June. Nothing about Rose's dying came easily. In 1953, as Rose's disease progressed, Gypsy located a reputable, expensive, and elegant nursing home where Rose finally agreed to go. Although the transition to the nursing home was an ordeal, Gypsy felt relieved. But less than a week later, Gypsy wrote privately in her journal that her mother had gone on a rampage, and the nursing home demanded that she be removed. Gypsy's next journal entry described it as an "Awful day!...No place will take her." So June and Gypsy decided to move Rose back to her own home. Rose quickly went through a series of nurses, including one whom she struck with sufficient force to loosen the woman's teeth. Gypsy paid the dental bills.[26]

Rose felt angry about dying and jealous of her daughters' success. Pain and medication intensified her abusiveness. Accusing Gypsy of being greedy and selfish and wanting her to die, Rose told her that she wished "with all my heart I could take you all the way with me—all the way down." Rose wheezed out her final threat to her oldest daughter, the "no-talent" child she had attempted to cast off. In her autobiography, June wrote that Rose threatened her eldest daughter, "So go on. Louise, tell all your classy friends how funny I was, how much smarter you were than me. When you get your own private kick in the ass, just remember; it's a present from me to you."[27]

By the mid-1950s, Gypsy's life was poised for a new direction once again. Divorced for the third time, she never remarried. Her mother had died, and her son was nearly a teenager. Emotionally freer than she had been in years, she began work on a book that ultimately guaranteed her legendary status for decades after her death. Ultimately Gypsy avenged herself by writing about her departed mother in such a compelling way that they both won immortality.

18

Immortality in Book and Song

I t's here, Papa, it's here! Girls, the letter is here!' Mother closed the
front door and stood with her back pressed against it. She let the
other letters fall to the floor, holding the important one to her chest.
'Oh, please,' she murmured, 'please, God, make it good news.'" Had
the girls been accepted as a vaudeville act? So begins Act I, chapter 3 of
Gypsy's autobiography, *Gypsy: A Memoir*, which Gypsy wrote in three
acts as if it were a stage play. It was published in 1957. Gypsy told such
a compelling story about her childhood that her book ends with Gypsy
still in her twenties.[1]

Before Gypsy decided to write mysteries, she had attempted and failed
at a memoir. She worried that her witticisms about her experiences might
not be funny. In the 1940s, she composed shorter articles about her childhood for the *New Yorker* and *Harper's*. Ten years later she protested, "It's
not the time for it. Not yet." Autobiographies "always seem so final," she
reflected. Besides, "I've been too busy living it to be writing it."[2]

In the mid-1940s, Gypsy wrote a fictitious article about discussing
a potential autobiography with a book editor. In the piece, in order to
prepare, she collected her scrapbooks and a signed release from her
mother in which Rose promised not to sue her. According to Gypsy,
the release was notarized, but below the seal her mother had added in
her own hand, "I was a sick woman and not in my right mind when I
was forced to sign this."[3] The fictional account portrayed a very real
threat to the possibility of Gypsy writing about Rose.

Gypsy's mother proved to be a perfect protagonist. Earlier Gypsy had joked about wanting to write a book about her: "If you had a mother like mine you wouldn't go around handing her out to everyone." She commented, "She's one of the wonders of the world, like the Hanging Gardens of Babylon or the Colossus of Rhodes."[4]

Around the time of her mother's death, Gypsy wrote a play entitled *The World on a String*. She based the play, like *Naked Genius*, on episodes in her life. As in her mystery novels, the major characters were Gypsy and Biff. The play's loose plot revolved around Gypsy's conversion from a "no-talent" girl playing bit parts while her sister starred in vaudeville to a famous burlesque queen. The play moved briefly through her failed Hollywood career and on to her triumph on Broadway in *Star and Garter* and as a writer. At the end she reconciled with her career as a stripper.

The chaotic play jumped from scenes of her childhood to those of her as an adult. It laid out the same themes as Gypsy's autobiography, discussing her interfering stage mother and her own aspirations to culture. As she should have done with *Naked Genius*, Gypsy wisely turned the play into her autobiography with fleshed-out characters and vivid background.[5]

Gypsy incorporated into *Gypsy: A Memoir* earlier articles she had written, as well as many scenes from *World on a String*. While writing, Gypsy admitted to keeping a strange schedule of getting up at four o'clock in the morning and working on the manuscript throughout the day until she prepared dinner. She had graduated to an electric typewriter from the manual on which she had written her novels. When she composed seven pages a day, she felt particularly productive and proud. Gypsy thought her writing was improving. Approaching the task with her usual intensity, she noted, "I love to write. I like to work anyway. I love the feeling of accomplishment."[6]

The day after Christmas 1956, Gypsy completed her manuscript. She ignored the word limit placed on her by the publisher, Harper and Brothers; by the end of the first section (of three) she had already exceeded the hundred-thousand-word maximum. "These technical details probably will iron themselves out," she declared airily. By and large, the publisher accepted the longer text. "That's what comes of being a primitive—they don't want to spoil what they refer to as 'that wonderful freshness,'" she teased. She dedicated her autobiography to twelve-year-old Erik, "so he'll stop asking so many questions."[7]

In the first and longest act in the book, Rose charms her father into giving her money to help further June's career. The section focuses on

Gordon, a lover of Rose's, who acts as June's agent. Rose and Gordon fight over June's future and over money, since Rose cheats the other children in June's act. Gordon finally leaves. Act II, like Act I, starts in Seattle with Gypsy's grandfather helping revitalize the family. The action moves through Gypsy's start in burlesque. In Act III, a fistfight in a bar with another stripper who ridicules her pretentiousness helps her decide to forsake burlesque for the *Follies*. The book ends with her leaving the *Follies* for Hollywood.

As with all her writing, the book contains marvelous individual anecdotes and great dialogue, but it lacks a coherent plotline. It proceeds episodically in chronological order, but that does not hold the book together; Act III seems completely unrelated to Acts I and II, and Act II clings tenuously to Act I. Gypsy's remanufactured childhood, with a quirky but not emotionally abusive mother, provides an interesting tale. Gypsy explained ironically, "As mother said, everything nice that could happen to a girl on her way up had happened to me. And that is putting it mildly."[8]

In May 1957, the book hit the *New York Times* best-seller list. Gypsy promoted the book incessantly, making a grueling three-month tour of the country. She found book tours nerve-wracking and exhausting, but she was ever the trouper, aware that they were crucial to her financial success. She thought about wearing a beaded dress so people would not know whether she or the beads were "quivering" when she was discussing the book. She may have found talking seriously about her book more difficult than her usual stage routines or chats with the press.

Describing the difference between burlesque audiences and book luncheon attendees, usually predominately women, Gypsy wondered aloud why no bald men came to hear her; after all, she had built a career by teasing them in the audience during her striptease routine.[9] Such a line always generated laughter until one poignant moment during a talk at a writers' conference. After she made the joke about bald men not attending her lectures, she pointed to a man in the audience with "the dearest bald head I ever knew." Jack Hovick had come to hear his eldest daughter. Gypsy started to cry and had to sit down.[10] Throughout the years, she had spent little time visiting her father and stepmother on the West Coast.

During her tour, Gypsy—always savvy with the press—controlled her interviews. Along with her standard one-liners, she gave some of the most reflective interviews of her career when asked about the memoir. Gypsy offered insights into being an author. "You don't have to be a top notch writer," she advised, "and don't try to imitate others—but if you want to write something, sit down and write it. There's no other way." For Gypsy, creativity took courage: "Don't be too critical of your own writing; you're not the one best able to judge it. Let the public be the judge." Although the readers ultimately had to decide on the worthiness of a text, the author should not write for the fickle reader. "I think you've got to write what pleases you and take your chances," she insisted. Her gamble with her memoir paid off well.[11]

Newspapers and magazines serialized chapters. Gypsy was completely vindicated after the failure of *Naked Genius*. "This Stripper Can Write" summed up the vast majority of the reviews that appeared across the country. "Just about the biggest thing since *David Copperfield*," gushed one enthusiastic reviewer. "The Jane Austen of the striptease set," another columnist proclaimed.[12]

For its time, the book was slightly racy. Gypsy detailed how strippers cared for their breasts, an important asset to them. She candidly discussed her married lover Eddy. Even though Gypsy feared that people would expect a more gossipy book exposing famous entertainers, she kept the focus on her childhood and early adulthood.[13]

With *Gypsy*, as with her first two books, she vehemently denied insinuations that she had employed a ghostwriter, and she had to fight for credit for own work. "I write my own books, catch my own fish and Erik here isn't an adopted child," she insisted. In a society that considered women ornamental or smart but rarely both, the press underestimated Gypsy's talent as a writer. No one accused her of hiring a ghostwriter for the flopped play *Naked Genius*. Gypsy mocked her accusers at one book-and-author luncheon as she slowly removed her hat, gloves, and jacket in front of the audience and purred, "I don't want you to think that all I can do is write books."[14]

Wisely, the paperback version opened with a blurb from John Steinbeck: "I found it irresistible. It's quite a performance. I bet some of it is even true, and even if it wasn't, it is now."[15] Perceptive reviewers noticed that the memoir lacked introspection. Once again, Gypsy kept her audience distant from her inner thoughts. Like her act onstage, the highly entertaining book revealed little. She contended, "I have told all up to a certain point because up to that point I had nothing to conceal." The worst part of writing, she felt, was exposing oneself. As in show business, "you're setting yourself up as a clay pigeon." But "staying within a framework of truth" was Gypsy's biggest challenge, even in conversation. After telling so many different versions of stories, she had trouble remembering events accurately. Gypsy claimed that she tried very hard to keep the story true. But, in truth, she lied.[16]

Throughout her memoir, Gypsy downplayed Rose's mental illness and rationalized her mother's character defects. "Maybe she had a peculiar set of values but she stuck with them," Gypsy wrote. As an adult, Gypsy resented her childhood, but she curbed her bitterness in her autobiography. When asked if she ever became embarrassed about her career as a stripper, she responded sarcastically, "This would be a great time for me to start being embarrassed, after I've capitalized on it so long." Besides, she added disingenuously, she had entered it unintentionally; her mother had booked her into a theater and they did not realize it was a burlesque house. The statement contradicted other claims she made in various interviews over the years about a broken shoulder strap leading to her first striptease act.[17]

Keeping the book noncontroversial, Gypsy never mentioned her mother's lesbianism in print or to reporters. Once June and Gypsy grew more successful, they probably feared the unfavorable publicity that would have resulted. Similarly throughout her life, people gossiped about Gypsy's sexual preference. As Arthur Laurents recalled, "There had always been speculation that Gypsy was a lesbian." Gypsy openly mentioned such rumors in her autobiography, recalling that they started while she was performing in the *Follies* in 1936–37. Characteristically, she made a joke of it.[18]

In the 1950s, families rarely discussed sexuality that was then perceived as deviant. Given discrimination in hiring and other reprisals, gay and lesbian actors and writers usually hid their sexual preferences. *Life* magazine, like most publications of the day, kept people in the closet by presenting everyone as heterosexual, including male celebrities whose homosexual inclinations and relationships were an open secret. During the Cold War, oppression joined repression. The FBI obsessed about people's sexual orientation; an agent labeled Fanny Brice a lesbian because a known lesbian went to her house. Homosexuality was a taboo topic in public, even though it was acknowledged in private.[19]

Gypsy's reinterpretation of her mother's behavior toward her and June was also consonant with the way mothers were viewed in books and the media after World War II. Gypsy wrote in the 1950s, when American society both revered and feared the power of motherhood. Philip Wylie's popular and influential 1942 book *Generation of Vipers* condemned "Momism" in American culture, which defeminized women and emasculated men. In this context, Rose represented everyone's controlling but lovable mother.

Although Gypsy's book had a dark undertone, particularly in its treatment of Rose, it attempted to appear lighthearted. Gypsy's friends thought the book seemed sad, but Gypsy disagreed. "Many people think a life is sad if it's different," she protested. "Really my life has been gay and fruitful." Indeed, she characterized her life as a comedy. If she ever felt depressed about her mother, Mike Todd, her divorces, or her career, Gypsy never conveyed it openly, so the press and public never knew.[20]

Through her autobiographical narrative, Gypsy reinvented herself politically. She left out her leftist politics entirely. She never discussed her commitment to antifascist causes, the NAACP, or labor unions. She distanced herself from the Communist Party and joked about it sufficiently to prove her anti-Communism. Above all, she never mentioned being accused of left-wing sympathies or being blacklisted.

In interviews, Gypsy was mellow about Hollywood and minimized her political commitment, perhaps because she hoped to return there someday. "I've loved it every time I've been out there," she purred. Defending a place that made her miserable in the 1930s, she argued that "Hollywood is called brittle and oversexed, but I can't believe it can be bothered by anything but all this genius packed so tightly in one place." She also repudiated early stories of her working-class solidarity, terming stories that she insisted on being different by eating with the stagehands "just nonsense." In the postwar era, it was not a good idea to insist on being different.[21]

Tabloids and magazines enjoyed telling readers about what Gypsy left out of her book, especially about her marriages. In March 1958, *Hush-Hush* magazine ran an article entitled "Hey Gypsy! Why Are You Keeping So Mum About Those Men in Your Life?" In a never-ending search for truth or a scoop, the magazine followed up with "Why Did Gypsy Rose Lee Keep Mum About Her Three Mystery Men?" in November 1959. The magazines blamed her for all three divorces because "she is driven by an insatiable urge to achieve for the sake of achievement, succeed for the sake of success." Gypsy was too ambitious to be a "real woman," a theme commonly used in the postwar era to explain—or predict—the downfall of career women.[22]

A few movie magazines vindicated Rose. In an article in *On the Q.T.* magazine, "How Gypsy Rose Lee Ratted on Her Mother," the writer protested that in her autobiography Gypsy vilified the mother to whom she owed her career, "shamelessly degrading her mother" in order to make money from the book. *On the Q.T.* never knew the extent to which Gypsy underrepresented Rose's vicious abuse.[23]

All the publicity, whether favorable or unfavorable, promoted the book and created new markets for the work. MGM and Warner

Brothers each offered $200,000 for the movie rights. Both David Merrick and the team of Lerner and Loewe wanted to convert the book into a musical. Although Merrick had graduated from St. Louis University Law School in the 1950s, he hired H. William Fitelson as his lawyer. Fitelson approached Gypsy about a deal. Gypsy decided to sell the rights to Merrick for only four thousand dollars and a percentage of the gross box office sales. Erik asked her why, and Gypsy explained her calculated decision: she gambled on the royalties from a potential future hit over an immediate payment. The risk would ultimately pay her well.

The youthful David Merrick organized an impressively talented group for the musical *Gypsy*. He asked Leland Hayward to coproduce, and Hayward brought in Jerome Robbins as director and choreographer. Everyone thought that the lyrics would be difficult to write because of the complex and sophisticated plot; Robbins suggested the young Stephen Sondheim, who had worked with him and Arthur Laurents on *West Side Story*. Merrick agreed, but the star, Ethel Merman, thought he was too young and inexperienced to write music for her voice. So Merrick recruited Jule Styne to compose the music. Styne and Sondheim had never collaborated and barely knew each other. Although only twenty-eight, Sondheim refused to let the fifty-three-year-old Styne use any recycled music, insisting on new songs for the show. He also believed in working closely with the librettist, and he waited until several scenes were written before he composed lyrics. Sondheim created musical numbers that perfectly fit the script rather than interrupting it as earlier musicals had often done.[24]

Merrick wanted Laurents, who wrote plays and the book for *West Side Story*, to write the libretto. Laurents declined at first, since he saw little drama in the story of a stripteaser. Soon after, at a party in his beach house, Laurents met by coincidence one of Rose's former lovers. She described Rose as "very sweet and an absolute killer." He heard that Rose had killed a hotel manager she was fighting with by shoving him out of a window and had shot a woman on her farm.[25]

Regardless of the truthfulness of these tales, Rose intrigued Laurents, and he took on the assignment—but he decided to leave out Rose's lesbian relationships. Laurents found his theme elsewhere: "What we've got here is a mother who has to learn that if you try to live your children's lives, you'll end up by destroying yourself." Jerome Robbins also found Rose compelling. Both Robbins and Laurents thought the musical centered on "recognition." As Robbins put it, the term encompassed "all kinds of recognition. Not merely the kind that comes with fame, but people recognizing each other and themselves—what they really are." Moreover, "it's about family life—how a mother comes to recognize her daughter, and a daughter learns to know her mother." Similarly, Laurents believed that Rose needed recognition in lights, while Louise needed it from her mother.[26]

Thus Rose became the main character in the musical based on Gypsy's autobiography. The musical version of Rose presents her as a con artist, eccentric and lovable rather than evil. She sinned by living through her children. She sacrificed the love of a good man to promote her daughter's career. Since marriage represented the ultimate happy ending, Rose's choice deviated from that of most 1950s heroines. At the same time daring and conservative, *Gypsy* depicts Rose as she saw herself rather than as she was. The musical shows Rose as an overly ambitious woman capable of love, and the audience mourns when her lover Herbie walks out on her.

Merrick wanted the brassy Ethel Merman for the part of Rose. He had an easy sell. Sounding much like Rose herself, Merman had previously told Gypsy, "I've read your book. I love it. I want to do it. I'm going to do it. And I'll shoot anyone else who gets the part." The script offered Merman an opportunity for dramatic acting, not just singing. "In most musicals," she later wrote, "there is a hairline story, a thin plot and thinner characterizations. *Gypsy* was a full-fledged play. It could have dispensed with the music." Gypsy agreed with the choice of Merman and informed the press, "I told Ethel to drink lots of milk and stay healthy. She's going to be my annuity."[27]

The role of Gypsy was formidable to play. It required an innocent, vulnerable young woman in Act I and a sexy stripper in Act II. Although fetching as the young Gypsy, the actress Sandra Church executed her strip routines poorly because Robbins refused to choreograph these numbers. Although the behind-the-scenes drama was relativity tame in comparison with other musical productions, *Gypsy* had its occasional flare-ups between Robbins and both Styne and Laurents over Robbins's desire for top billing. Robbins took his revenge by not attending to Church's striptease numbers. During a rehearsal, Gypsy turned to Merman and murmured, "It isn't right. No zip, no zing." Merman responded, "My God, nobody knows how to do it better than you. Why don't you show 'em?" Gypsy uncharacteristically demurred because she did not want to interfere with the musical that had such promise. Thinking of the fight between the director and various others, Merman replied, "You're the only gentleman here!" Privately, Gypsy spent hours with Church demonstrating her old routine. She even gave Church a pair of her pants for good luck.[28]

Gypsy commented favorably on Church's strip to the press, saying, "This is Broadway, not burlesque"—an imitation of striptease, not the real thing. In fact, no one acting her part in the musical has successfully imitated Gypsy's unique technique onstage: part strip, part theater, and all tease.[29]

The musical *Gypsy* romanticized June and Gypsy's childhood even more than Gypsy's book did. June thought the musical distorted her life because it minimized Rose's destruction of June's childhood and her exploitation of her younger daughter. The mythical characterizations of the family infuriated June more deeply than Gypsy suspected. June refused to sign a release when Laurents and Hayward presented her with one. She insisted on major changes. Laurents, committed to the story he created, refused to accede to all of June's demands.[30]

June stated her many objections to the musical to her sister. Among them, she argued that it minimized Gypsy's strength and pictured her only as a victim, ignoring how Gypsy had taken control of her own life. Gypsy understood that the musical took license with the story of her life as presented in her autobiography, but she did not care. She wanted *Gypsy* to be "a smash." For Gypsy the musical represented "my monument."[31]

June finally took legal action. She called Gypsy to say she had hired the New York attorney Louis Nizer to represent her. Nizer often represented entertainers. When broadcaster John Henry Faulk sued the organization that incorrectly identified him as a communist, Nizer won the case for him; the suit represented a major victory against the blacklist. June informed Gypsy that her lawyer forbade them to have any direct contact until the case was settled. Gypsy did not sleep that night. Her ulcer troubled her, and she was haunted by nightmares. Over the years, June and Gypsy had established a loving relationship. They had worked together, lived together, traveled together, and worried about each other's personal lives and careers. They attended each other's dinner parties. Together they searched for antiques. Just a few days after June hired Nizer, Gypsy crossed out a date in her calendar she had reserved to attend a play with June.

A few weeks later, June and Gypsy worked out a settlement. The subtitle of the musical would clearly state the fictitious nature of the story by calling it a fable—and June would receive part of the profits. Later Gypsy joked about her disagreement with June: "We just have two different memories of mother—like when two people try to recall the scene of an accident." Candid about her interest in the production, June told gossip columnist Louella Parsons, "I'm so happy it's so good, because I have a percentage."[32]

When the show opened in Philadelphia, the reviews were mostly favorable. Merman insisted on a sympathetic portrayal of Rose, believing that "Mama Rose sacrificed her whole life, gave up the love of her life for Louise and June. That's why when I played her, I got sympathy. People cried." On opening night in Philadelphia, Gypsy shed tears. After Gypsy thanked the cast, Merman responded warmly, "I'm glad you liked it."[33]

Almost a decade later, Merman and Gypsy publicly discussed the role on Gypsy's talk show. They agreed that Rose thought only about her daughters. Gypsy admitted receiving letters saying that she must have hated her mother to write such a book. Gypsy denied it, saying she loved her mother deeply. Gypsy compared Merman to her mother—both possessed resourcefulness, energy, and, most important, a sense of humor. In reality, Gypsy had a much clearer sense of her mother's mental illness, cruelty, and utter self-centeredness.

On May 21, 1959, Gypsy opened in New York at the Winter Garden. Gypsy was a vision of understated elegance, wearing a black taffeta skirt and white silk blouse with a sable jacket. Along with the flowers that Gypsy sent Merman, she wrote on a card, "How Mother would have loved seeing you tonight." Rose would probably have demanded exorbitant compensation, but she would undoubtedly have been pleased that she had the starring role.

The musical received excellent notices from the most influential critics. Walter Kerr loved the finale but noted that the musical "doesn't even need it. Its generous authors have already provided it with a great beginning, a great middle, and a great future." Brooks Atkinson declared it "a good show in the old tradition of musicals." Kerr was even more enthusiastic, although less precise: "I'm not sure whether Gypsy is new-fashioned, or old-fashioned, or integrated, or non-integrated. The only thing I'm sure of is that it's the best damn musical I've seen in years."[34]

Best of all for Gypsy, once again she was praised for her writing ability. Variety noted, "Gypsy is an emphatic credit to original authoress Gypsy Rose Lee, to librettist Laurents, composer Styne and lyricist Sondheim." Having damned Naked Genius, John Chapman admitted: "I envy Arthur Laurents for the skill with which he wrote the libretto...And you've got to admire Gypsy Rose Lee for writing her fascinating book."[35]

Although based on the stage show, the movie Gypsy, released in 1962, disappointed many. Merman regarded the part as her personal property, but Rosalind Russell was cast as Rose, while Natalie Wood played Gypsy. One Canadian newspaper sneered, "Natalie Wood couldn't play Gypsy Rose Lee on the Bryn Mawr daisy chain." But after Wood's death, the movie attracted a cult following among her fans.[36]

Her mother's death freed Gypsy to reconcile herself to her own life and to write about it. Gypsy's memoir allowed her to reinterpret her life and her politics. She needed a mother figure for public consumption, and she carefully created one, just as she molded her own personal persona. Ironically, the autobiography and the musical loosely based on the book permanently fixed her association with stripping in the public's mind. Rather than completely changing her public identity, she merely shifted the emphasis, telling one interviewer, "You may refer to me as an authoress who sometimes strips."[37]

Despite minor disappointments, the success of the musical *Gypsy* delighted its namesake. She had created her own legend. Asked if her earlier professional career embarrassed her, she responded, "Not at all. Being an author-stripteaser assures me that I'll be remembered for SOMETHING."[38]

19

The Most Famous Former
Stripper in the World

As she moved into her forties, Gypsy began to perform her classic routine "Psychology of a Strip-Tease Dancer" behind a
screen so her audience saw her in silhouette and was forced to
use its imagination. She constructed a shadow box out of aluminum
beams and scrim with discreet pink satin on the sides that prevented
unwanted peeking. But as always, Gypsy worked hard mugging and
coaxing laughter. By the finale, perspiration covered her entire body.
Amazingly, she still performed at least ten to twelve weeks a year.[1]

With great fatigue, she explained to her son that she felt "too old to
be taking my clothes off in front of strangers." Longing to end her stripping career, she conceded wearily, "There's nothing left for me to show."[2]
Although Gypsy still thrilled the crowds, the cultural milieu had changed
by the 1950s. Gypsy's satirical routines became more difficult for audiences to appreciate. In the postwar political climate, people took what
Gypsy referred to as "nudity and the sanctity of American womanhood"
seriously. Popular culture constructed the roles of women quite rigidly.
Equally important, Gypsy's routines were parodies of burlesque. Audiences
too young to remember the original acts did not comprehend the cleverness of Gypsy's satire. In 1951 at age forty, she told an interviewer, "Don't
ask me what's new in burlesque—I'm what's old in burlesque." But Gypsy
kept the act current. In 1955, one of the strippers displayed a G-string

similar to the popular Davy Crockett coonskin cap. "He's everywhere," Gypsy declared to the biggest laugh of the evening.[3]

Gypsy speculated on the audience's reaction to her aging. When she appeared onstage, she was convinced that patrons commented to each other, "My, but she's well preserved—I remember seeing her in burlesque 40 years ago." She heard customers speculate that she must be at least fifty. Women her own age tried to figure out how she managed to look so wonderful. She encouraged their hopes for graceful aging. Women often came to see her with groups of friends, to give themselves courage and companionship in their slightly naughty but pleasurable lark. More often, men entered clubs alone to play out their sexual fantasies. But Gypsy had always appreciated women in the audience. In the company of women, men relaxed and laughed harder, she thought.

Over the decades, the striptease industry had steadily grown sleazier. No longer was it a place for women seeking lasting "fame and fortune" such as Gypsy had achieved. Stripteasers found it increasingly hard to switch venues. Legal restrictions and high expenses made luxurious burlesque theaters impossible to operate. Gypsy stripped in clubs that she hated. Fans stole her clothes, so she paid busboys to keep an eye on the outfits she shed. "I like working in small smoky, noisy rooms. It challenges my ability to win over an audience," she commented sarcastically. She preferred Las Vegas, with its superior facilities, which reminded her of her good old days in vaudeville.[4]

The hazards of stripping troubled Gypsy, and she pointed them out more frequently. Strippers endured colds and respiratory illnesses; Gypsy suffered four bouts of pneumonia. Strippers were injured by falling off runways lighted only by a few blue spotlights or pitched into complete darkness at the end of the act. "Exotic dancers" performed in bare feet; one woman who got a splinter contracted blood poisoning. Male audiences teased strippers maliciously, popping dancers' balloons with pins or lit cigarettes.

Even the language used to describe striptease artists bothered her because it indicated a lack of respect for the profession. She resentfully remarked that the word "stripper" made it sound as if she worked in a tobacco factory; she preferred the unions' term, exotic dancers. Gypsy grew weary of the stale jokes about her stripping; although she joked about herself, she resented humor at her expense. Men who demeaned Gypsy as a stripper but refused to acknowledge their own participation as members of her audience risked public ridicule. When a retiring president of a service club introduced her at a ceremony with the line "I didn't recognize you with your clothes on," she retaliated by announcing, "I've heard everybody praise Mr. X and how he gave himself unstintingly to every worthy cause and project. Well, I know him from my days at the Troc [a burlesque theater]. Mr. X was one of our regulars. He frequently sat through both the matinee and evening shows. I want to tell you he gave unstintingly of himself in those days."[5]

Over the years, Gypsy's frugality on the road took an increasingly heavy toll. She lived cheaply when she traveled, and this lifestyle became more arduous. At this stage of her life, she preferred to sleep in her own bed and eat in her own home. Gypsy yearned for her former solo role. "I don't like the responsibility of the whole troupe," she admitted. In 1955 at age forty-four, she took her company and Erik to Las Vegas. She packed her Rolls with her sewing kit and a record player for Erik's French lessons. Gypsy decided to teach the women in her company French as well. "It can't do any harm," she reasoned, "and they might learn to say 'non.'" In many ways she lived on the road as she had when she toured with her mother, but she added staying in a hotel. She worked out a daily schedule. At approximately four o'clock, they stopped at a motel, bathed, washed out stockings and other intimate apparel, and mixed cocktails. Gypsy fixed dinner and packed lunches for the next day. She took pride in her meals: "Eat in those roadside joints and die on the highway. I'd rather cook for the mob than risk ptomaine and hold heads. I can get more out of that electric frying pan than Philippe of the Waldorf gets out of a six burner stove."[6] Cooking with one pan, however, had long ago lost its attraction, and she began to think about options.

In that same year, one magazine ran an article titled "Burlesque in the 1955 Manner: The Old Favorites Are Still on Top." The article pointed out that Gypsy's act depended on her witty repartee and had changed very little in more than twenty years. "Mother used to say, 'When you get a good pose, stick to it,'" she recalled. Moreover, the men in the audience, often repeaters, refused to allow her to alter the act. At one point, she decided to keep her stockings on rather than slowly rolling them down, but the male fans made such a fuss she had to restore the technique.[7]

Once she completed her autobiography, Gypsy willingly gave up her primary occupation. She retired at the height of her fame. In 1955, her agent bragged that Gypsy was the "most publicized woman in the world," interviewed, painted, and photographed more often than any other. During her final year in striptease, she was better paid than at any time before and had no problems getting bookings. Gypsy grew philosophical. "Sure, things have backfired in certain respects," she admitted, but the money and the "prestige" made it worthwhile. "I couldn't have gone around the world twice like I have playing Ibsen's Hedda Gabler," she insisted. For Gypsy, stripteasing inspired and supported a long and productive professional career as a writer, artist, and activist.[8]

At the beginning of this new phase of her life, Gypsy assessed her financial situation carefully. Over the years, she had developed into a shrewd businesswoman. She paid a flat 10 percent to agents when they obtained employment for her rather than exclusively use one agent. Often, she negotiated her own contracts with the help of her lawyer, whose fee was smaller than an agent's commission. She kept a very small staff: a cleaning woman and a once-a-week secretary.

Where money was concerned, Gypsy compromised honesty. When Edward R. Murrow came to interview her in her recently redecorated New York City home, Gypsy accidentally dropped a hammer on her new marble floor. She later billed CBS for the damage, claiming that a camera caused the cracks.[9] Again and again, people doing business with her ultimately felt deceived. She seemed generous by giving them gifts, but she always wrung a hard deal. Gypsy's interaction with her designer, Charles James, was typical. James gave her a discount on clothes because she convinced him that she provided free publicity for him when she wore his creations. James frequently felt used and underpaid, and they fought when she received a bill and refused to pay because she felt it was too high.

Gypsy's anxiety about making a living led her to try many different endeavors. Her first major business venture after retiring from performing as a stripteaser was a one-woman show combining her home movies with a live narration that she entitled *A Curious Evening with Gypsy Rose Lee*. After a brief but well-received appearance using that format on Arlene Francis's *The Home Show*, an NBC talk show, in April 1957, Gypsy decided to put together a feature film on her life by distilling twenty-four hours into ninety minutes of home movies she had shot since the early 1930s. Bill Kirkland, her former husband, offered his gallery in Palm Beach for the premiere, which gave her a hospitable venue for her first showing. The generally complimentary reviews pointed out the movie's choppiness and repetition. "Gypsy Finds That Video Has Its Bumpy Moments," *Washington Post and Times Herald* declared. Gypsy's humorous and clever narration helped the viewers understand the chaotically edited film, and audiences responded more enthusiastically to her in-person dialogue than to the ninety-minute movie.[10]

In October 1960, Gypsy narrated five Monday performances of *A Curious Evening* at the off-Broadway Cherry Lane Theatre in New York City. Along with her chain-smoking and numerous cups of strong tea, the stress and anxiety of appearing led to a recurrence of ulcers, a problem that had plagued her since the early 1930s. *Curious Evening* helped neither her ulcer nor her bankbook. In addition to other problems, the film itself broke. She jotted sarcastically in her journal that if she had listened to her mother she could have been a successful accordion player. Increasingly she expressed her doubts about the project.[11] More bravely than wisely, Gypsy decided to produce *Curious Evening* on Broadway. It opened on May 9, 1961, with Gypsy herself backing it financially. Although the reviews complimented the production, the audiences failed to come. She closed the show at a loss of almost seven thousand dollars, in addition to all the time she had put into creating the film.

Her home movies were not her financial answer. Nor did Hollywood furnish Gypsy with enough work to make a movie career; she played only secondary roles in a few minor films in the later 1950s. And before doing so, she had cosmetic surgery on her face, fearing that, as she aged, her wrinkles would show on film. Portraying a lesbian nightclub owner in the movie *Screaming Mimi* displeased her. "Even the title's ridiculous," she told her son. Released in 1958, the movie was a late-noir psychological thriller. A murder that she may or may not have committed after being raped in a shower haunted the protagonist, played by Anita Ekberg. Gypsy relied on one of her old acts, rubbing a bald man's head; her club was called El Madhouse.[12]

After appearing in the movie, Gypsy received publicity and short-term employment in other venues. "I am pricing myself into clothes," Gypsy teased. A humorous ad for the radio station WPAI parodied Gypsy's reputation as an intellectual. Gypsy stood in front of a podium with two kindly older women in hats looking up at her intently. The caption read, "Miss Gypsy Rose Lee, author, lecturer, actress, artiste and co-star of Columbia Pictures' *Screaming Mimi* speaks often on such wide ranging topics as art, the creative life, and her favorite station...."[13]

During the filming of *Screaming Mimi*, Gypsy was offered the role of a madam in another movie, *Wind Across the Everglades*. The studio paid Gypsy $2,500 a week for three weeks' work. *Wind* was about a man tracking down poachers of rare migratory birds in South Florida.

Despite its conservationist theme, the film relied on violence to keep the strange plot moving. The protagonist, played by Christopher Plummer, spent his time either fighting villains in swamps or drinking heavily in a Miami bordello where Gypsy's character worked.

According to Erik, who accompanied his mother on location in the Everglades, the shooting was a mess. After a venomous snake bit one cameraman, the production company hired hunters to rid the set of reptiles. One morning between five and eight o'clock, the men killed nine snakes. Gypsy commented dryly that she worried about the hunters' effectiveness since they had both lost fingers to snakebites. Adding to the challenge, the costumes never arrived from New York. Gypsy helped sew new outfits for the extras and was horrified when the costumes got wet in the rain. She was relieved when filming ended.[14]

In order to increase her income and keep herself before the public, Gypsy endured the rigors of summer stock theater. Though she was successful in regional theater, she found it physically more taxing and less lucrative than stripping. In June 1958, Gypsy appeared in *Happy Hunting* on the circuit, including Atlanta, Georgia, and the Valley Forge Music Fair in Pennsylvania. She played a multimillionaire's widow who felt snubbed because she was not invited to Grace Kelly's wedding to Prince Rainier. During the play, Gypsy suffered from an abscessed tooth, an intermittent problem since the 1930s, and oppressive heat caused her voice to fizzle periodically. At one performance, she fainted ten minutes before the final curtain. When the director suggested sending in her understudy, Gypsy protested, "When I'm dead you can send in my understudy."[15]

During each of the two nightly performances, she had to run up and down the aisles thirty-seven times. Gypsy told one reporter that because of her mediocre singing voice she made sure she sang "good and loud," concentrating on "voice presence." With two thousand people in a tent, she knew that she needed to work hard to be heard. She concluded, "I say the hell with pear-shaped tones." Favorable reviews followed: a "tour de force for Miss Lee, who dominated the show throughout." Gypsy ad-libbed the best lines all through the show, and audiences responded to her wit. In Atlanta, when rain fell, she reassured them, "Don't worry about my clothes... I can always take them off."[16]

In 1959, Gypsy toured with *Auntie Mame*, Jerome Lawrence and Robert E. Lee's stage adaptation of Patrick Dennis's novel about his loving but madcap aunt. Mame represented the perfect role for her. With gusto, she portrayed the lovable, freethinking woman raising an orphaned nephew. In Detroit, *Auntie Mame* attracted the biggest Thursday crowd in the theater's history. Mame required many costume changes, and to save money Erik acted as her dresser. When not onstage, Gypsy styled her wigs and fixed broken zippers. Despite the show's success, Gypsy expressed dissatisfaction with the cast, particularly the young actor playing her nephew, whose acting she described as awful. Although audiences greeted her enthusiastically, Gypsy faced mixed reviews. She was exhausted.[17]

During the summer of 1960, Gypsy again played Auntie Mame, this time at Coconut Grove Playhouse in Miami, Florida. The audiences adored her, and the management added extra matinees. Gypsy was totally focused while onstage: "It's like you're suspended in a transparent ball. You can see out, but you can't hear so well because you're closed off. How dare anyone talk to you when you're in your vacuum!" When a fan screamed at her during the show, "Hey Gypsy, baby! Way to go, Gypsy," she had him removed. At the curtain call, she addressed her audiences with her new standard line, "This is the most applause I've ever received with all my clothes on." After shows, she socialized with her fans in the bar connected with the playhouse. At the end of the run she invited the cast of sixty to a catered Chinese dinner, keeping up a tradition she maintained throughout her stage career.[18]

The blacklist finally forgotten, Gypsy guest-starred on a variety of television programs, particularly game shows such as *I've Got a Secret*. As the mystery guest on *What's My Line?* she placed marbles in her mouth to keep her distinctive voice from being recognized. Being interviewed on the *Today* show, she asked host Dave Garroway, "May I take off my gloves, just to keep in practice?" When a cautious television producer worried that she might not behave herself on a show, Gypsy squelched his fears. "I shan't embarrass you by even the faintest suggestions of a strip tease," she reassured him, "at least not at the prices you're paying."[19]

With an amazing run of professional problems, however, Gypsy never completed other projects. In 1959, she hosted a short-lived syndicated television talk show, *The Gypsy Rose Lee Show*. The program was planned for syndication opposite NBC's popular *Jack Paar Show*, so its time slot doomed it. One of her own harshest critics, Gypsy realized that she hogged the conversation and kept the guests from talking. Complaining about sloppy camera work, she worried about the lack of definite rehearsal times or a guaranteed studio for the ninety-minute show. The poor organization bothered her; Gypsy always demanded a tightly run show. She unsuccessfully fought for a more scripted show while the station wanted the program to be more spontaneous. One review by Jack Gould in the *New York Times*, of the premiere in April 1959, declared that with the exception of one burlesque-style sketch about a traveling salesman and Gypsy's clever interview of actress Paulette Goddard, the program was choppy. Gypsy seemed unsure of what to do between the scheduled segments. After only a few shows, the network quickly canceled the program.

Gypsy also aborted her plans for a novelty cookbook based on her life. Perhaps she felt it might reveal too much. The recipes from her childhood were simple because "that's how we lived" on the road, she explained. She wrote a chapter on cooking in a trailer. "Then the years became better. The recipes progress in the book too." The obliging Bill Kirkland ate many experimental meals while married to Gypsy. "He had absolutely no palate and would eat anything. I could really let my imagination run wild." The book also included ethnic recipes. Norwegian recipes came from Gypsy's own background. Her first mother-in-law, Ruth Mizzy, gave her Jewish recipes. The Spanish recipes were from her "last, and I do mean, last husband," emphasized Gypsy. She always sampled her recipes: "How else could I know just how something will taste?"[20] The book was never published and probably was never completed. Occasionally, however, she contributed to celebrity cookbooks in which famous people shared their favorite recipes.

Gypsy's money problems might have ended with impresario Billy Rose. Gypsy and Rose both appeared on the *Jack Paar Show* in 1959. Talking to each other about old times, they forgot the audience and enjoyed a riotous time getting reacquainted on camera. Rose invited Gypsy on a date. To the gossip columnists, Gypsy and Billy downplayed their relationship as merely a friendship. Both loved to talk and to eat. Rose enjoyed having a handsome woman like Gypsy on his arm. Like Mike Todd, he charmed women and knew how to ensure that they enjoyed themselves in his company. Gypsy prepared dinner for Rose at her house and visited his spectacular home. She kept his photograph by her bed and even gave him veto power over her wardrobe, returning items to the store if he did not approve.[21]

Billy Rose had great success as a songwriter, with such hits as "It's Only a Paper Moon" and "Me and My Shadow." He invested his money wisely and became exceptionally wealthy. Like Gypsy, he spent carefully. "Billy Rose is no check dodger," teased columnist Earl Wilson. "He merely has a slight impediment of reach." At the same time, Rose was a philanthropist who once raised more than a million dollars for the

United Jewish Appeal; that year, he contributed twenty thousand dollars himself. Gypsy shared his passion for art. Over the years he acquired a choice collection. Rose confided to Gypsy, before anyone else, his plans to make a large art donation to the Israel Museum in Jerusalem.[22]

Gypsy retained her independence within the relationship, and Rose found her difficult to handle. Nevertheless, according to Erik, Rose proposed to Gypsy—but Gypsy refused. Marriage would relegate her to number two within the relationship with a very limited role as a hostess and date. At one of his dinner parties, Gypsy recalled, he had interrupted her continually. He finally told her that, since she was wrong, she need not bother finishing her sentence. Gypsy stormed out. Rose called the next day to apologize, but Gypsy's perception of his lack of respect upset her.[23] Also, as Gypsy explained to Erik, there was a basic lack of chemistry between them; she did not even want to contemplate having sexual relations with him.

Rose had a different explanation of why they ceased dating: "She's a doll, but she's a boss-lady." In his version Rose dropped her for the same reason her marriages failed: Gypsy never played a supporting role to a man for long.[24] Equal in intelligence and ambition to all her lovers and husbands, she saw no reason to be submissive to them. Billy Rose attracted Gypsy, but not enough for her to concede her independence.

Always attracted to strong men, Gypsy rebelled against being dominated by them. In 1957, she wrote an ironic review of a book of essays entitled *Man Against Woman*. Men worried about their masculinity, she said, so they constantly proved it by reminding society of their superiority over women. Tongue firmly in her cheek, Gypsy agreed that "they're bigger, stronger and smarter, and I know this to be true because a man told me so."[25]

Adding to her personal and professional woes, Gypsy's relationship with her teenage son deteriorated. Continually pleading poverty, Gypsy economized in ways that greatly irritated Erik. She even convinced a friend, the Broadway producer Leonard Sillman, who was cleaning out his closet, to give his old suits to Erik. Her son refused to wear the outdated clothes for fear of being laughed at when at school. Erik saw how much his mother spent on herself, not fully accepting that she considered these business expenses. Not only did she believe that her fans expected a certain lifestyle of her, but she so closely tied her ritzy image to her own identity that economizing would have destroyed her sense of self. She no longer made a distinction between her image and her identity.[26]

Gypsy used Erik as an unpaid servant on many occasions. During an interview, she handed him an empty plate and ordered in an authoritative, though soothing, tone, "Erik darling, go out and get us some more of these cheese puffs, darling." As Erik trudged off with the plate, she cooed, "That's an angel, sweetheart." Erik's other chores included delivering flowers and wigs and gardening, tasks for which his mother occasionally paid him.[27]

Because of her schedule in summer stock, Gypsy failed to attend Erik's eighth-grade commencement from the Professional Children's School. After graduation, Erik joined her on tour. To help him make money and to promote herself, Gypsy urged him to sell copies of her autobiography outside her shows; he would keep the net profits. To the press, however, Gypsy duplicitously depicted the scheme as Eric's idea; she did not want to look as if she exploited her son. So few books sold that the plan actually lost money. Erik hated the chore because he found it embarrassing. Few adolescents wish to call attention to themselves, especially in connection with their mother. Easily ignored by potential customers, Erik stood mute behind the book display.

Erik's boyish poise and amazingly good manners charmed reporters. In 1959, one interviewer described him as "a most sophisticated teen-ager." When asked at fourteen if he missed a normal childhood, his answer was both wise and matter-of-fact: "For me, this is normal."[28]

A sensitive adolescent keenly aware of Gypsy's moods, Erik hated tension but nonetheless rebelled against his controlling mother. He particularly resented the one area where she spent money on him, his schooling. Over his protests, she refused to allow him to remain at the Professional Children's School for high school. Instead, she enrolled him in the elite Riverdale Country School for Boys in the Bronx to prepare him for college; Erik boarded there during the week and joined Gypsy on the weekends. The rigid and formal atmosphere at Riverdale Country School smothered and discomfited Erik in contrast to the freer atmosphere at his former school.

As personal problems with her son escalated, so did professional difficulties. In 1961, Gypsy spent New Year's Day traveling alone to San Juan to play the lead in *Auntie Mame*. At first she loved the renovated theater and seemed relatively satisfied with the cast, but things quickly deteriorated. Working in a theater without air-conditioning bothered her. Even worse, she had not known that the cast and crew were nonunion, and unionized actors picketed the performances, hollering "Yankee Go Home." Gypsy quipped that she felt like President Lincoln and Marie Antoinette. After one performance, police had to escort her from the theater. A fire damaged the stage, scenery, and Gypsy's dressing room. Although officials blamed a short circuit, most believed that union sympathizers set the fire as an act of sabotage. Gypsy met with striking actors over coffee, but they felt she patronized them. Soon after, the show was canceled to ensure the safety of the cast. Following the closing, the theater acceded to the actors' union's demands and agreed to hire union actors. The producer told Gypsy he could not afford to pay her for the full extent of her contract. They agreed on one-third of her promised salary, the hotel expenses, and a boat ticket home.

A family catastrophe immediately followed this professional one. An argument with Erik on the phone caused Gypsy to fly back to New York instead of taking her planned cruise. Without Gypsy's permission, Erik had informed his headmaster at Riverdale that he would be living at home during the holidays as opposed to boarding. Erik wanted to stay home with his new girlfriend, who was allowed to visit him without a chaperone. Gypsy tried and failed to break up the relationship, even suggesting Erik visit a prostitute. She succeeded only in alienating Erik and making him more mendacious. Gypsy felt betrayed by her son's rebellion and need for independence. The son who had sent her valentines as a child now forgot her birthday. She felt used, "like a dollar sign and not a person at all."[29]

Gypsy's strong will and her desire to make people bend to her wishes collided with her teenage son's desire to distance himself from his mother. Her attempts to manipulate him made the relationship hellish until they both simply walked away. As her problems with her son escalated, Gypsy asked advice from her lawyer. Wisely, H. William Fitelson suggested therapy for Erik. Although she had reservations, she consented. She probably resented a stranger discussing intimate details with her son, as well as the cost. But the psychiatric analysis probably helped save Erik's sanity.

Gypsy rose above her mother's treatment of those closest to her. Although manipulative, she almost never became ruthless, her own description of her mother. Rose did not seem to have any capacity to love anyone—not her own mother, her sisters, or her daughters. Her emotional illness completely crippled her capacity to give to anyone. Gypsy showed some of the same traits. She certainly used people, including her son, throughout her life. She also expressed great tenderness toward the same people in time of crisis. While her warmth sometimes seemed artificial, she loved her sister and son with a depth of which her mother was incapable.

Because of her deprivation as a child, Gypsy obsessed about money. Trying different forms of entertainment such as movies and theater, she felt that nothing clicked and she grew frustrated. Periodically she went on binge shopping sprees for herself and her exquisitely furnished house. Such uncontrolled spending was predictably followed by belt-tightening. Although her autobiography sold well and the musical *Gypsy* was widely performed, even by high school students, the royalties did not sustain her lifestyle. She also struggled with a sullen teenage son who rebelled against her attempts to economize at his expense.

The late 1950s seemed like lost time as Gypsy struggled to find a new career. Actually, those years prepared her for the fruitful final decade of her life. From summer stock she learned to ad lib in front of an audience while staying fully clothed. She made good use of those improvisational techniques in her next job, and kept her old fans while reaching new, younger ones as well. Her failed television show led to her new role as a successful talk show host. Not long after the curtain fell on her striptease act, it rose again in a new venue and with a new setting.

Upset by the changes in the urban landscape, Gypsy left New York City. New York had ceased to be the center of the entertainment universe. As the economic situation in the city worsened, even Gypsy's posh neighborhood deteriorated until she described it as "rather dismal." Her increasingly precarious financial situation and lack of steady work made her future in New York City bleak. She lost hope of pursuing a successful career if she stayed. So, to maintain her lifestyle, she sold her house and moved west.[30]

20

Aging Gracefully in Public

In 1961, Gypsy bought a seventeen-room mansion situated on two acres at 1240 Cerrocrest Drive in Beverly Hills. She paid $63,500 for it and was convinced that she had made a good buy. Built in the 1920s on one of the highest sites in the city, the house was some seventy-five feet above the street and was reached by steep steps. Gypsy wisely built a retaining wall and placed tall cypresses in front. She chose the house in California because she adored its breathtaking view at night and the spaciousness inside. She teasingly referred to it as "early *Sunset Boulevard*"—a self-conscious parody of the movie about a reclusive former silent film actress's inability to cope with her aging.[1]

But the house required a great deal of remodeling to make it livable. She knew she had her work cut out for her to transform the place into her home. She hired ironworkers, plumbers, and gardeners and an interior designer, Jane Ashley. Even as she labored to give it her own style, she found the setting relaxing. Outside, Gypsy puttered relentlessly and with great satisfaction in her garden, which contained a small moat stocked with fish. Inside, she cleaned to the point of bleeding knuckles and broken fingernails.[2]

The California house, like Witchwood Manor and the house in New York City, signified Gypsy's rise from humble beginnings into a life of luxury. Gypsy believed that "a house is the things that are in it, the things that you know and love." Off the drawing room, as in her New York house, stood an atrium with five arched windows and a glass-domed roof. The atrium teemed with tropical plants. The drawing room's dark green, gold, and brown décor complemented the plants' lush coloring. The chairs were Regency. Gypsy also kept a Regency harp; years before, when the management could not afford to pay her for a performance in the *Threepenny Opera*, she took the harp as payment. She displayed much of her art collection along a circular staircase.

Gypsy treasured the dining room because it gave the impression of "eating outdoors indoors." The walls were pale blue, with silver and gold clouds on the ceiling. The green dining table stood on the legs of an antique sewing machine and was surrounded by matching wrought-iron and wicker chairs. Large picture windows flooded the room with light.

The guest bedroom, in dark green and mauve, boasted several floor-length windows, Victorian-style chairs, and a sofa. Huge windows with rose-patterned drapes dominated Gypsy's own bedroom. She wallpapered the ceiling with a floral design. A silk and lace canopy topped a wrought-iron bed with elaborate scrollwork. As in her New York home, the bathroom was a wonder. Wicker swans decorated the toilet. The carpet and drapes were purple, the walls and ceiling gold, the fixtures green. Unique touches accented Gypsy's brick kitchen: Julio, who remained a friend over the years and visited her occasionally, created a mobile on which Gypsy hung pots and pans, and he designed an embossed copper ventilator over the stove as well as metal shades for the light fixtures. Gypsy's house received acclaim as a trendsetter in *The Hollywood Style*, a book of photographs by her friend and former escort Eliot Elisofon. Such books emphasized the taste of entertainers, setting a standard to which everyone was supposed to aspire.[3]

As always, animals played a central role in Gypsy's household. When Gypsy witnessed a priest blessing the animals, she wrote a touching article about the experience. Gypsy recalled that once she and June had taken their guinea pig to Sunday school in Omaha, but the church officials removed it. Listening to the priest, Gypsy felt comforted when she "heard the words that would have reassured me on that day in Omaha." The priest chanted, "So God formed every kind of living creature and He blessed them." The young boy standing near Gypsy told his "pink eyed white rat, 'See Pinkie, what did I tell you.'"[4]

The California household included seven dogs and four tropical goldfish. Gypsy created aviaries on the property stocked with cockatoos and a toucan. Later she added finches, which bred with gusto. Gypsy laughed as she watched the hen's pride in her egg, and she wrote June that the bird thought she was "raising a dynasty." Later she added a peacock and peahen. "When they strut they spread their 4 tail feathers and their topknot quivers just like a showgirl's headdress when she's walking down the ramp," Gypsy observed.[5]

In California, Gypsy continued to mate her hairless toy Chinese Crested dogs, also known as Chinese Powder Puffs, hoping to gain acceptance for them as a breed. June had first presented the dogs to Gypsy, and both sisters bred them. "You have no idea what a difficult thing it is to breed little dogs," she told a reporter. "Fortunately it's much easier with people," she noted suggestively.[6]

Content to live alone with her pets in California, she announced, "I've nothing against men." Yet she understood why she had not remained married for long: Since her career always came first, her husbands had never felt "needed or dominant." Instead of relying financially on a husband, she counted on "annuities" that "will last as long I do." Gypsy treasured the independence and the solitude of her new house on a hill. She insisted, "I love my life just exactly the way it is."[7]

Erik did not reside with Gypsy in California. When Gypsy left New York in 1961, she effectively abandoned the sixteen-year-old Erik. At first she insisted that he join her, but he refused. He stayed in New York City, in an apartment on the top floor of her house, to finish his senior year of high school. Their relationship quickly spun downward.

Just after his mother moved to California, Erik asked her for money to buy a car. Gypsy, who had become obsessed about her financial state when the musical *Gypsy* closed, told Erik that if she gave him the money for the car, she would have to give up paying for his psychiatrist. Erik refused his mother's deal.

Erik turned to the man he knew as his father, Gypsy's second husband, Bill Kirkland, for help in buying the car. Kirkland contacted Erik's psychiatrist because he was being married for the third time and did not want to be burdened any longer with a demanding, fictitious son. The psychiatrist then told Erik that Kirkland had informed him that he was not Erik's father and Erik should not ask him for any further financial help. Erik was deeply shocked. Not long afterward, during a horrible argument with his mother over the telephone, Erik referred to himself as a bastard and told Gypsy he knew Kirkland was not his father. At that point, Gypsy refused to continue the conversation, insisting on talking to him in person. She hung up without any words of comfort.

Gypsy's refusal to tell Erik about his father seems deeply callous. Rarely introspective, she probably gave little thought to Erik's feelings about the situation. She believed that she fulfilled her son emotionally, so he did not need any father. Gypsy lacked empathy toward other people, even those she loved most—another gift from her own mother. Gypsy waited until she had arranged for the *Jack Paar Show* to pay her airfare to New York before she came to see her son.

Erik described the scene in his autobiography. First, Gypsy defended her actions in keeping Erik ignorant of his birth father's identity and lying about Kirkland. She had hoped that he would be older before she told him. Gypsy refused to tell Erik the name of his father, but she finally relented on one condition: She made him promise not to get in touch with him. Erik was surprised, since he had inferred that his father was the late Mike Todd. His mother had never mentioned Preminger or any other lovers she had had around the time Erik was conceived. Gypsy insisted that Erik must let his father make the first move to contact him. Since she had extracted the same promise from Preminger, Gypsy had set up the situation so that the two might never get together.[8]

After assuring him that it made no difference to her, Gypsy urged Erik to be discreet about his parentage. The statement bordered on disingenuousness. A relationship between Preminger and Erik made Gypsy nervous because she did not want her extramarital affair to become known. She had just begun her new talk show, and she worried about the repercussions if stations airing her program discovered the secret. Her fear of scandal was probably reasonable, since the show was aimed at married, middle-aged women. (These days, the story would boost the ratings.) Gypsy was also concerned about Erik's reputation. She warned him about people who might be prejudiced against him because of his unwed parents. Last, she asked Erik to write more often to limit the expense of long-distance calls. She was not consciously attempting a parody of total insensitivity; her obtuseness seemed unfeigned. After her heartless talk with her son, Gypsy appeared on Paar's show and immediately left New York.[9]

Despite other arguments with Gypsy over money over the next year and a half, Erik decided to reconcile with her. In California in 1963, he learned to accept her and to cope with her attempts to control him. After spending a pleasant and peaceful summer with Gypsy, he enlisted in the army in September. The military stationed him in Germany, where he enrolled in the University of Maryland's overseas program. Gypsy visited him there and spent time with his company.

She even narrated *A Curious Evening with Gypsy Rose Lee* in service clubs in Munich and Augsburg, thereby managing to write off the trip as a business expense.

Gypsy was not the only parent to visit Erik in Germany. While Erik was serving in the army, Otto Preminger discovered from a colleague who knew from the Kirkland family that Erik knew his true parentage. Erik had confided the secret to Kirkland's daughter, Erik's supposed half sister. Preminger immediately begged Gypsy to allow him to communicate with his son. Gypsy relented, but she asked that Preminger keep his true relationship with Erik private. Erik agreed to see his father on his next leave, and the sixty-year-old Preminger flew to Europe to get acquainted with his son. After a bit of awkwardness, the two began to forge a close relationship.

Meanwhile, Gypsy's carefully calculated gamble about California and her career proved correct. Although in the press Gypsy referred to the California house as her "retirement" home, she continued to work. At the Sombrero Playhouse in Phoenix in 1962, she played in a revival of *Auntie Mame*.[10] As always, she charmed reporters and stayed very visible. Also in 1962, Gypsy went to Toronto to promote a "Gypsy" rose. She looked sexy in an off-the-shoulder blanket of roses. When asked how many roses she had worn in her act, Gypsy replied coyly, "Three, dear—one for decency and two for the cops." When presented with a plastic bag containing the root of the rosebush, she shouted to the reporters, "Give me three bars of 'A Pretty Girl Is Like a Melody' and I'll take the cellophane off!"[11]

Soon after she arrived in California, Gypsy landed a small part in the movie *The Stripper*, starring Joanne Woodward. In the film, Lila Green, a former beauty queen and dancer, reluctantly becomes a stripper in order to earn a living. Gypsy played Madame Olga, the manager of the stage show in which Woodward's character performed. Gyspy helped Woodward learn stripping.

Television offers continued to arrive. In the mid-1960s she was a guest on *The Celebrity Game*, hosted by Carl Reiner. Reiner questioned the stars, and the contestants had to guess the answers. In response to "Do romantic screen heroes tend to make their wives dissatisfied at home?" Gypsy jabbed, "I think women aren't really stupid, you know. We know all about these swashbuckling heroes. What swashes on the screen sometimes buckles at home!" Later, on the *Johnny Carson Show*, she told the same joke she had used with Mayor La Guardia more than twenty years earlier. Before she came onstage Carson said, "Gypsy Rose Lee said she was going to take all her clothes off." When Gypsy came out, she contradicted him, saying, "Johnny, you know I'd never end a sentence with a preposition." The audience still adored it.[12]

In September 1964, she appeared on a detective show, *Burke's Law*, which always featured stars in cameo roles. In an episode called "Who Killed Vaudeville?" Gypsy portrayed the owner of a school for aspiring strippers. Both the star of the successful series, Gene Barry, and the producer, Aaron Spelling, decided to watch the taping of the segment of Gypsy teaching stripping to (incongruously) a minuet. Gypsy teased Spelling by asking, "Who's watching the front gate?"[13]

Gypsy had a small part in the movie *The Trouble with Angels*, released by Columbia Pictures in 1966. The plot involved two mischievous adolescent girls at a convent school. In a marvelous appearance, Gypsy portrayed a progressive interpretive dance teacher, Mrs. Mabel Dowling Phibbs. In the strict convent school, Gypsy urged her students to be "fluid" like "young willows."

Starting the same year the picture was released, Gypsy appeared with comedienne Phyllis Diller in a situation comedy on ABC-TV, *The Pruitts of Southampton*. A rich widow, played by Diller, discovered that she owed her entire fortune in back taxes. She kept her mansion but had to learn to cook and do other mundane chores. Gypsy played a snooty neighbor. According to Diller, Gypsy "could talk endlessly on her own on any subject, but couldn't stay within the confines of a script." As a result of this experience, Gypsy was adamant she did not want to do a TV series. Before appearing in this sitcom, she had said "it seems like slow death to me. I can't imagine a worse way to earn a living." By January, ABC changed the program's name, but it lasted only thirteen weeks. Gypsy was actually happy that it had ended, since she was already involved in a TV program that she loved.[14]

Simultaneously to acting with Phyllis Diller on television, Gypsy finally succeeded with her own talk show, *Gypsy*, a perfect avenue for her at this stage of her life.[15] KGO-TV in San Francisco produced the morning talk show, and Seven Arts television syndicated it around the country. Gypsy always pushed to expand the show's viewing audience. When one guest casually mentioned that English convicts were the first white settlers in Australia, Gypsy responded with mock outrage, "How dare you! Next you'll be attacking the Mayflower." Afterward she explained, "We can't offend Australia. We might sell the show there."[16]

In the 1960s, talk shows aimed at women proliferated on the airwaves. Gossip columnist Virginia Graham hosted a very successful program, *Girl Talk*. Graham's and Gypsy's programs followed a similar format. As opposed to Jack Paar's and Merv Griffin's shows, which were usually interviews with individual guests in succession, on Gypsy's shows, as on *Girl Talk*, the guests often interacted with each other. Gypsy preferred to perform in front of a studio audience, but there was no audience participation. The programs tended to showcase the more humorous sides of celebrities, and the conversation sometimes related to a particular theme. Gypsy developed into one of the best talk show hosts for the female viewing audience. She commented airily yet perceptively, "We yak about this and that, and people seem to like it."[17]

Gypsy appreciated the discipline that the television show demanded. Taping five shows in two days, she expected as much from the staff as she did from herself. She hated sloppiness and expected perfection. As with her striptease troupe, she remained a tough and exacting boss: "There's no time for hurt feelings. After all, we're not going out dancing."[18]

At the beginning, Gypsy exhibited the same faults as she had in her earlier stint hosting a TV talk show. The director and executive producer, Marty Pasetta, recalled, "She was so used to being a guest that she'd rattle away for the whole show instead of drawing her guests into the conversation." Interaction proved difficult for her. Gypsy recognized that she had spent more of her life answering questions; now she was asking them, and "you can't shed a skin that easily." Gypsy explained that when she first started to host the show, she felt "really naked" when responding to others' comments. Offering a perceptive analysis of the situation, she explained: "Remarks are thrown at you out of the blue. You don't have time to pretend, or even to think, and your opinion, for what's it worth, shoots out of your mouth to be heard and judged. It's more revealing of yourself than acting any role."[19]

Even her guests teased Gypsy about her loquaciousness. On one program, actor Jimmy Stewart suddenly fell out of his chair and landed sideways on the floor. "What happened?" Gypsy asked. "Sorry," Stewart responded, "I was just trying to get a word in edgewise." Gypsy learned to be quieter. According to Pasetta, she became "fantastic at getting the best out of the celebrities who visit her."[20]

The show succeeded because it emphasized what Gypsy always did best: talk. On-screen, Gypsy looked wonderful, with her slim figure and the posture of a dancer. She talked about herself. When one viewer advised her to stop "being so cute and act your age," Gypsy snapped back on the air, "What—and be wheeled in?"[21]

Gypsy alluded to her past with occasional remarks such as "I'm stripping away all the barriers on conventional kaffeeklatsch conversation and letting the audience in on the bare facts." Commenting on her childhood, she told her guests, "I always wanted to be a bareback rider. You must admit I got halfway there." Occasionally, if she saw a bald-headed man, she gleefully pointed out, "I built a career on heads like that." She used her former profession to good effect, with such quips as "With my clothes off, I'm a better dancer" and "In my earlier line of business, I developed muscles in all the wrong places."[22]

The show emphasized crafts and cooking and often involved the guests' hobbies rather than what had made them famous. When fan dancer Sally Rand appeared, she and Gypsy discussed needlepoint. One show featured a British actress and Gypsy sampling a recipe from a new cookbook. Richard Blackwell, the fashion critic, appeared many times to talk about current trends in women's clothing. Pianist Liberace discussed antiques and interior decorating, including a barbershop he had designed with a turn-of-the-century San Francisco theme, which he called the Barbary Coast. Liberace played his favorite song, "The Impossible Dream," and then, just for Gypsy, "Let Me Entertain You." Wearing several diamond rings, he teased Gypsy that he did not have to do anything to get his diamonds. Earlier in her career, Gypsy would have been offended—but on her own show, she went along with the gag.

Gypsy chose a diverse array of celebrity guests, from singer Judy Garland to pop artist Andy Warhol. Many revealed—or pretended to reveal—little-known aspects of their private lives. The show relied on informality and sexual humor, which suited Gypsy perfectly. Phyllis Diller chatted about losing her contact lenses down the plumbing, but she also talked seriously about her daughter, whom she adored. Actor Bob Crane talked about his decision to leave a very successful radio career for a risky television show, *Hogan's Heroes*. At fourteen, he had played drums for strippers, so Gypsy and Crane discussed burlesque. Ethel Merman talked about her son, who planned a career as a producer, and her mother, who had wanted Ethel to become a schoolteacher.

Celebrities often participated in activities that were amusing and a bit incongruous. Actress Gale Storm and actor/singer Robert Goulet helped with a leapfrog contest, and actresses Pat Carroll and Nanette Fabray joined Gypsy in making apple snowballs. Author and comedian Fannie Flagg discussed ant farms, and Gypsy proudly displayed her own. On a memorable show, professional misfit writer/director Woody Allen and actor Richard Deacon dryly commented on the sexy men's clothes that Gypsy bought for Erik, who was then serving in the military. Finally, Allen held up see-though men's briefs and asked if Erik served "in special services."

In one of the funniest episodes, Allen and character actress Selma Diamond refused to share Gypsy's enthusiasm for camping out of doors, the theme for that particular show. Allen explained that he hated to go outside, stayed indoors for twelve to fourteen months at a time, and disliked taking off his shoes. He watched while Gypsy and Diamond assembled a tent. Allen crawled into the completed tent and refused to come out because the audience laughed at him. He asked Diamond to join him. When Gypsy reminded Woody that he would get hot in the tent, Diamond—who was never noted for her sex appeal—snapped, "That's why he called for me."[23]

Gypsy sought to please her audience of stay-at-home women by showing new ways to do household chores. She discovered a beauty adviser who made facials out of tomatoes. Actor Edward G. Robinson appeared with his invention, a rubber band that stretched four ways. Gypsy did not approve of every gadget. Frustrated by a needle threader, she remarked, "Now that I can do it, I won't do it again." Gypsy loved to swap recipes on the show and demonstrated cooking techniques regardless of how messy it made the set.[24]

Her show attracted a loyal audience. Even actor John Wayne enjoyed it; he said it was "like eavesdropping on a ladies' powder room." The male secretary of a local chapter of the Hell's Angels commented, "You kind of hate her at first because she talks too much, but after a few times you really get hooked." A teenager wrote, "We like you, Gypsy, except when you're knitting."[25]

Most of Gypsy's fan mail expressed stay-at-home women's yearning for more intelligent programming than soap operas and game shows. Her show crossed class barriers. Middle-class suburban women wrote her; so did fans living in trailer parks. Their letters expressed the concerns of women caring for their families. Women used her show as a break in their day. After getting their husbands off to work and their children off to school, they poured themselves a second cup of coffee and watched *Gypsy* before starting the rest of their daily chores. One viewer ironed her family's laundry in front of the television.[26]

Many of these women found the program entertaining and educational; they particularly appreciated the domestic tips. One woman wrote that Gypsy had solved one of the world's biggest problems by having a designer of men's pants explain how to alter trousers properly. With a tone of amusement, she related that she had improperly sewed pants for her four sons and her "crotchety old" husband. If the Communist leaders Fidel Castro and Nikita Khrushchev had better-fitting crotches, she teased, they might be less warlike. She found Gypsy's show better than the doctor she had visited recently for her tension headaches.[27] Another viewer, who had been married for nine years, confessed that her relationship with her husband had become a "little rutty." But programs in which Gypsy and her guests gave suggestions on how to please a man had brought "real spicy changes in our routine."[28]

Loyal viewers sent her small gifts. One fan crocheted jackets for Gypsy's puppies; another made her apricot jam; yet another made her a tea cozy. One woman sent Gypsy an old *Follies* program with her name in it. A nine-year-old drew her a picture. Amazingly, Gypsy wrote back to these women without using a standardized answer. Some of the women corresponded with her more than once and revealed stories about their families.[29]

Reciprocally, Gypsy shared her private moments with her audience. In March 1967, while serving in the army, Erik married an American flight attendant, Barbara Ann Van Noten. Gypsy attended the wedding in Germany and brought back film of the event for airing on the show. She explained that she had brought pearls for the bride. She teased that the only old pearls she owned were from G-strings, so for " 'something old,' I brought a sock that I had knit for Eric when he was one year old."[30] When fans saw her cry at the wedding, they wrote to reassure her that such behavior was perfectly appropriate. For many women, their children's weddings, one woman confided in a letter, "are the only outward expression of love, great job and many memories."[31]

Although Gypsy had a loyal audience, her swearing and her choice of themes challenged the station's standards. The network always taped the show because it did not trust Gypsy live. A crew member could then delete forbidden words and replace them with blips. The director knew that blips often made Gypsy sound more risqué than her actual dialogue. Gypsy complained, "They even 'blipped' me one day when I purposely mentioned damming a river."[32]

Censorship seriously annoyed her, just as it had during her work in burlesque and her first short career in Hollywood and on Broadway. "There seems to be a double standard of censorship for me," she complained. The censors blipped her over "anything anatomical.... Is there another word for pelvis?" She claimed that the censors allowed other talk show hosts to use racier language, but actually other talk shows were expurgated. In 1960, Jack Paar stormed off his show when NBC censors cut a joke about a water closet, and *Girl Talk* was occasionally edited if the guest's comments were considered too off-color.

Gypsy fought with the producers over topics and guests for the show. She thought that her female audience members were curious about other women's views on children, clothes, and cooking. The producers, all men, were convinced that only men fascinated women, even though Virginia Graham succeeded with women guests. "My only disastrous shows have been with men guests," Gypsy said, "like show-business types who moan about their budgets."[33]

When the producers wanted Gypsy to invite a former madam and the owner of a topless restaurant to appear on her show, Gypsy refused. "I spent a lifetime kidding nudity," she said indignantly. "But there's no humor here for me." She would have preferred to invite one of the prostitutes or one of the waitresses, but the producers were scandalized at the idea. "I can't relate to people who profit from human misery," she said, and elaborated: "I deplore a man who exploits nude waitresses, even though he is usually considered a respectable citizen." Gypsy knew that the topless waitress who made far less than the owner was the one who was criticized. The old debate on definitions of respectability rankled her as much in the 1960s as it had in the 1930s.[34]

Gypsy explained that she was actually a bit straitlaced—"I'm not as broad minded as I sound, with my boisterous way of talking." She "took a prudish point of view on certain films, books and trends. Then, I pull myself up short and ask myself how Gypsy Rose Lee could possibly be this way."[35]

Gypsy's critique of sex work was more than sheer prudishness; it resembled nascent feminist understandings of the exploitation of women. The double standard trapped women in their sexuality rather than liberating them. Gypsy extended her pro-labor point of view by arguing that the commercial use of women's bodies enriched their employers far more than themselves. For Gypsy, such sexualized situations oppressed women workers. By the 1960s, Gypsy's use of her own body as a commodity had made her a wealthy woman. The majority of topless waitresses and prostitutes did not achieve such economic security, and Gypsy understood the distinction.

The producers objected when Gypsy hinted to her viewers that her own body required help. She bluntly described her face-lift. To the horror of the producers, she even talked about her first operation for cancer in 1966. She felt she could help her fans if she spoke about it publicly. "If I could force just one person to have a check-up on account of me," she insisted, "then I'd feel more than justified in having made my cancer public." The press and fans respected her candor. "It isn't because I feel that honesty is *always* the best policy," Gypsy admitted; "I just happen to feel it's my personal battle against the phonies in the business. I've fought them all my life and it hasn't hurt me yet."[36]

At the beginning of 1968, Gypsy was upset by contractual problems with KGO. After weeks of negotiations, Gypsy could not come to terms with the station and claimed that she was relieved at the show's demise. It had entirely absorbed her. Neglecting her friends, she had forgotten her pleasant private life and "what a bore" her public life had become. Her tenuous relationship with her father, who was also living in California, underlined the point. Once he wrote reminding her that he and her stepmother loved her; although she rarely visited them, they watched her on her television show, which he conceded was "better than nothing, you know." Even though the show had consumed her, she told June realistically that she would probably long for it in two weeks.[37]

When the network canceled the show, Gypsy's fans wrote her about their disappointment. One woman rhetorically asked, "Where else can we housewives learn to cook flowers one day, make a beautiful skirt the next, and third, listen to a nightclub performer do part of his act?"[38] But Gypsy soon received other television offers, including several guest appearances on *Hollywood Squares*. Gypsy did not socialize with the other celebrities, mostly TV actors and comedians, who appeared on the program, refusing to join them when they went out after a taping. While she went to parties given by her old friends, she did not mingle with many entertainers in Hollywood. Little had changed from her 1930s movie career, when she had kept primarily to herself. Hollywood did not offer the rich intellectual life of New York City. She had fewer chances to meet brilliant writers and artists.

She was able to see Erik and his wife, Barbara, more frequently, but the tug-of-war between Gypsy and her son resumed as soon as the army discharged Erik. Gypsy had offered him employment on her television show, but he chose instead to work with his father. Preminger offered Erik a job as his assistant when he left the army. While he was directing for a short period of time in Los Angeles, he offered Erik the option of starting with him there or learning the operation in New York. Unsubtle about her preference, Gypsy lobbied hard for Erik and his wife to move to Los Angeles. Erik decided to move there temporarily and, wisely, showed his independence immediately. He gave up the allowance he had taken from his mother during his army years and even returned some of it. He also declined Gypsy's invitation to live with her.

Unlike many other women in the entertainment industry in California, Gypsy grew older quite gracefully and publicly; she looked wonderful. Her occasional appearances on *Hollywood Squares* were uproariously funny. One of Gypsy's final appearances was a made-for-TV movie called *The Over-the-Hill Gang*, which was released in 1969. A former Texas Ranger calls his best three men out of retirement to help his crusading newspaperman son-in-law clean up a corrupt town. The plucky saloon owner, Cassie, rekindles their sense of mission. Cassie, played by Gypsy, wants to help elect the town's honest newspaper owner as mayor. The former rangers convert Cassie's place into their headquarters, and she becomes a love interest of sorts. The men flirt with her, and she promises to do her famous spider dance for them. With blond hair, Gypsy wore impossibly tight dresses reminiscent of *Belle of the Yukon*; this time, though, her acting was more relaxed.

Other opportunities did not pan out so well. In 1965, Prentice-Hall asked Gypsy to write a book entitled *How to Enjoy Being a Woman*. But when the publisher hired a man to ghostwrite it, Gypsy disassociated herself from the project. Later Gypsy proposed a different kind of book: a guide to a healthy and more natural way of living. After her surgery for cancer, she finally quit smoking, but she gained more than ten pounds. She went on a diet that included eating less processed food to lower her weight and to increase her energy. She became an advocate of organic foods. In keeping with the theme of using fewer manufactured goods, she anticipated including knitting and embroidery patterns in the book, as well as recipes for homemade cosmetics.[39]

Gypsy's book would probably have appealed to a younger generation of women. Her ideas about a healthier lifestyle, including a lighter diet, were welcome not only in Southern California, where fruits and vegetables were plentiful, but in other parts of the country, where people were also adopting new views about food with less frying, less red meat, and more fresh produce. Young women favored a more natural beauty, relying less on heavy makeup. Women of all ages were growing more concerned about the artificial chemicals in their cosmetics, so they would likely have been receptive to homemade beauty potions. As younger women espoused anticommercial views, particularly as part of a counterculture, knitting and sewing became more popular. The book might have given some mothers and daughters common ground as both groups sought new ways to stay thin and trendy. The men who ran Prentice-Hall, however, did not understand the marketability of such a book and ultimately declined to publish it.

Gypsy took up new charities in the 1960s. While she kept working for hospitals, the March of Dimes, and animal welfare, she also showed her concern for environmental issues. She spoke in a public service tape for a Clean Waters Contest sponsored by the Water and Wastewater Equipment Manufacturers and the National Water Institute, which was comprised of sports enthusiasts interested in clean water for their recreational activities. Gypsy supported folk singer Pete Seeger's effort to clean up the Hudson River. Seeger sailed his sloop, the *Clearwater*, up and down the river to remind people of its past beauty, facilitate grassroots participation in environmental protection, and prevent or mitigate pollution. The *Clearwater* sloop was involved in a legal battle to clean up toxic PCBs (polychlorinated biphenyls) dumped into the river and opposed a nuclear reactor that poured environmentally harmful warm water into the Hudson. Gypsy kept an itinerary of the *Clearwater*'s travels on the river.[40]

During the war in Vietnam, Gypsy traveled to Southeast Asia for the USO. As in her journey through the southern United States in 1943, she visited places that big tours missed, wowing another generation of GIs. At one stop, Gypsy emerged from a helicopter and, spotting a shirtless soldier, called out: "All right, young man, go put your shirt on. We don't have any undressed people in my performance." In hospitals, she flirted with injured soldiers and posed on their beds for photographs that she autographed. "When I go into a hospital ward I'm going to ask one of the boys if I can join him in bed," she explained. "I always ask that when I visit the boys in the hospitals. The first one's jaw drops about a foot. And when he says OK, I jump up on the bed with him and we talk. Of course by the time I get to the end of the ward, the guys figure out what is going on. Then I have to explain I meant on the bed and not in it." She perceived herself as "sort of like a sexy grandmother." Gypsy felt the soldiers deserved entertainment, and she willingly provided as much as she could without actually performing her old routine. She wrote that going to Vietnam was one of the most satisfying things she had ever done. In 1968, USO gave her its Woman of the Year award.[41]

The move to California helped her professionally, enabling her to work in movies and television after she left stripping. The 1960s offered her personal peace, as she managed to play on her career as a stripper without the old pain of not getting respect. Gypsy achieved new fame as a chatty but scintillating talk show host. The audience appreciated her delightfully uninhibited and relaxed public personality. She brought to the show the same skills she had honed as a stripper, wit, poise, intelligent conversation, and a lively sense of fun. Even in her fifties, Gypsy still knew how to captivate an audience. "My talk was always better than my strip anyhow," Gypsy correctly contended. "I like to keep things light. I don't mind working awfully hard but I work hard to keep it light."[42]

But even with her full life in California, when Eric and his wife left Los Angeles to live permanently in New York, Gypsy missed them and felt lonely. This was especially true after Barbara had a child. Gypsy was delighted; she believed that being a grandmother was one of the great joys of being a mother. She was very proud of her grandson and constantly showed off pictures of him. After Thanksgiving 1967, even though she spent the holiday with Julio, she sank into a depression. To June, she admitted that Julio was "warm and funny and dear," but his presence did not keep her from yearning for her son. Family would become increasingly important as she aged.[43]

Since the 1966 surgery, which the doctors assured her had been successful, Gypsy's health had seemed fine, though she continued to be concerned about it. Then, in 1969, she was diagnosed with metastatic lung cancer; surgery was attempted, but the cancer had spread too widely. In one of the most poignant passages of his autobiography, Erik described visiting his mother's house after she was hospitalized for the surgery. He observed her projects: pictures from her Vietnam tours, quilting, breeding dogs, gardening, and taking care of her aviaries. "All this life," he wrote. "How could death intrude into such aliveness?"[44] While Gypsy had sometimes quarreled with both Erik and June, her personal life had been transformed by reconciliation with them. According to her son, Gypsy never accepted her impending death but vowed continuously, "I'm going to beat this thing, Erik, I'm going to beat it."[45]

Gypsy died at the UCLA Medical Center five months after her diagnosis, on April 26, 1970, at the age of fifty-nine. Fulfilling Rose's curse, she died at roughly the same age as her mother. Even within months of the end, she explained to her son how lucky she had been to have such a full and interesting life.

Throughout that life, one of Gypsy's favorite pastimes had been fishing. As a child, she went salmon fishing with her dad in Seattle, and she often took a rod and reel with her when she traveled. One of her fondest memories of being on the carnival circuit was being able to fish. Fishing best expressed Gypsy's philosophy of life: It required hard work, intelligence, independence, a competitive spirit, and common sense, and it offered a strong feeling of accomplishment from a job well done. Musky fishing, a difficult challenge, inspired some of Gypsy's best prose and emphasized her interest in besting men at their own sport. A magazine on fishing published a long article by Gypsy on "How to Catch a Musky," and her passion for writing shines. With lyrical language, she described her love of fishing for musky in "cool green-blue lakes." She enjoyed the "crisp air" and "the deep, deep silence" while fishing. She wrote about how she bonded with the fish by lifting it up to stare into its eyes. Musky fishing involved Gypsy's two other leisure passions: writing and cooking. With Gypsy, though, "leisure" is probably the wrong word. Gypsy made everything work: vacationing, home improvement, cooking. "Labor unrelated to stripping" expresses the idea more accurately.[46]

Gypsy advised women to display their independence when fishing. After she was named "Fisherman of the Year," a female reporter interviewed her. She summed up her personal outlook: "Light your own cigarette. Bait your own hook. Clean your own fish before you leave the boat." Those three lines sum up Gypsy's philosophy. She always "baited her own hook" as an entertainer and writer, bringing her unique style to her act and her books. Much like a fish, Gypsy Rose Lee lived as a determined swimmer, sometimes with the current and sometimes against, but always tenacious: "I think it's important to rise above whatever surroundings you're thrown into, to make the best of whatever you do, to be a success in whatever spot you're in."[47]

Acknowledgments

I want to thank my wonderful family and friends who read various drafts or parts of the manuscript over the past ten years and who never wavered in their support: James Green, Cecile Klayton, John McClymer, Chuck Mosberger, Gayle Mowry, Donald Ritchie, Elissa Scheinberg, Peter N. Stearns, Jason Wozniak, and Rosemary Wozniak. Rachel Rutter and Jennie Grant helped me conduct image and photographic research. Other friends who gave me good advice include Robert Strom, Marilyn Young, and Judith Zinsser.

The staffs at the National Archives, the Library of Congress, and the Gelman Library at George Washington University were very helpful. Ann Y. Evans, White Homestead, Fort Mill, South Carolina, and Reagan Fletcher, Shubert Archives, were wonderful. Lisa R. Marine from the Wisconsin Historical Society was prompt and efficient. Sarah Serafimidis from North Atlantic Books was very gracious. Most important, the staff at the New York Public Library, Billy Rose Collection, was exceptional. It was a pleasure to work with them both at the Annex and at the remodeled facility at Lincoln Center. May they live long and prosper.

Danianne Mizzy and Jeanne LaMarche Mizzy shared information with me. I also want to thank the people who sent me copies of the programs and articles they purchased on eBay, including R. Kent Allen, Dave Bach, James Barenie, David Burd, James Camner, Terri Griffin, Dave Shallowsky, Rosaria Sinisi, and Rick and Sandy Traylors.

I want to thank Grey Osterud, the best editor on the planet. The professionals at Oxford University Press gave me a beautiful cover. Nancy Toff committed herself to the project. Brigit Dermott also contributed to the editing process, and Leora Bersohn took the time to explain the mysteries of publishing to me. Joellyn Ausanka kept the project on track, and India Cooper, a talented copyeditor, even added a few puns of her own.

Bill Kost was my enthusiastic eBay researcher and indexer. We now have an interesting collection of men's magazines. I want to thank him and my daughter, Elizabeth, for their good humor and patience during the research, writing, and publishing process.

Notes

1. "Gypsy Rose Lee," Filmstrip #1306, TRU VUE, photography by MV Wray.

2. Arthur Laurents, *Original Story By: A Memoir of Broadway and Hollywood* (New York: Knopf, 2000), 378–79.

3. *Gypsy*, written by Arthur Laurents and Stephen Sondheim with music composed by Jule Styne (New York: Theatre Communications Group, 1959), 34, 107.

4. Morton Minsky and Milt Machlin, *Minsky's Burlesque* (New York: Arbor House, 1986), 140.

5. Richard Gehman, "A Visit with Gypsy: Meet the Best Undressed Woman of Our Time," *Star Weekly*, October 22, 1960, 11.

6. Series I, Subseries 1, Personal, Box 3, Folder 2, From George Davis, Saturday night, GRL Papers, NYPL.

7. Roll 6, Elizabeth Ford, "How She Got Her Name, 'Gypsy Rose Lee'—It's Not Official,'" no header, GRL Papers, NYPL; Gypsy Rose Lee, *Gypsy: A Memoir* (New York: Harper & Brothers, 1957), 227.

8. Lee, *Gypsy*, 227.

Chapter 1

1. Richard E. Lauterbach, "Gypsy Rose Lee: She Combines a Public Body with a Private Mind," *Life*, December 14, 1942, 96; Florabel Muir and Robert Sullivan, "Gypsy and June—Mother's Girls: Hovick Sisters, in Chips Now, Can Grin at Frantic Youth," *New York Sunday News*, June 22, 1941, 8.

2. June Havoc, *Early Havoc* (New York: Simon & Schuster, 1959), 22.

3. Gypsy Rose Lee, *Gypsy: A Memoir* (New York: Harper & Brothers, 1957), 11.

4. *Seattle City Directory* (Seattle: R. L. Polk, 1913), 1557; Muir and Sullivan, "Gypsy and June," 8.

5. Seattle School District No. 1 enumeration record for J. O. Hovick, May 15, 1916, Seattle Public Schools.

6. Lauterbach, "Gypsy Rose Lee: She Combines," 96.

7. Havoc, *Early Havoc*, 15.

8. Ibid., 24.

9. Series I, Subseries 1, Personal, Box 1, Folder 6, Mrs. John H. Hovick, 2516 Cliff Drive, Newport Beach, California, May 31, 1966, GRL Papers, NYPL.

10. Series I, Subseries 1, Personal, Box 2, Folder 9, From June [used Julia] to Gypsy, April 25, 1949, GRL Papers, NYPL.

11. Kathryn Murray, *Family Laugh Lines* (Englewood Cliffs, N.J.: Prentice-Hall, 1966), n.p.

12. Lauterbach, "Gypsy Rose Lee: She Combines," 97.

13. Roll 3, Elizabeth B. Peterson, "Education for a Home Girl—Surprising Slant on Gypsy Rose Lee," no header, GRL Papers, NYPL.

14. Havoc, *Early Havoc*, 16, 122.

15. June Havoc, *More Havoc* (New York: Harper & Row, 1980), 174.

16. Lee, *Gypsy*, 76; Fannie Brice, "I Knew Gypsy Rose Lee When," *Cosmopolitan*, July 1948, 8.

17. Brice, "I Knew Gypsy Rose Lee When," 8.

18. Havoc, *Early Havoc*, 204.

19. Michiko Kakutani, "June Havoc Breaks Her Silence About Gypsy and Their Mama," *New York Times*, August 12, 1980, C7.

20. Roll 1, *Pittsburgh Press*, October 12, 1930, GRL Papers, NYPL. The chronology found in Roll 1 contradicts the chronology in *Gypsy*, 164, as to when Gypsy performed with Rose Louise and Her Hollywood Blondes. The 1930 chronology suggests that the Blondes did not start until after Saugerties, while the autobiography suggests that the new act developed before the trips to El Paso and Mexico.

21. Lee, *Gypsy*, 194.

22. Kyle Crichton, "Strip for Fame: Miss Gypsy Rose Lee, in Person," *Collier's*, December 19, 1936, 47.

Chapter 2

1. Gypsy Rose Lee, *Gypsy: A Memoir* (New York: Harper & Brothers, 1957), 228, 229–30. There is no record in Gypsy Rose Lee's scrapbook that her first strip was done in Toledo.

2. Gypsy Rose Lee, *The G-String Murders* (New York: Pocket Books, 1947), 2.

3. "Burlesque," *Fortune*, February 1935, 73.

4. Morton Minsky and Milt Machlin, *Minsky's Burlesque* (New York: Arbor House, 1986), 49.

5. June Havoc, *Early Havoc* (New York: Simon & Schuster, 1959), 258–59; Morton Cooper, "Profile of a Character: Gypsy Rose Lee," *Modern Man*, September 1959, 38.

6. Roll 2, *New York Mirror*, August 24, 1940, GRL Papers, NYPL.

7. "Gypsy Rose Take Off Those Clothes," *For Laughing Out Loud!* January–March 1963, 32.

8. Polly Rose Gottlieb, *The Nine Lives of Billy Rose: An Intimate Biography* (New York: Crown, 1968), 230.

9. Richard E. Lauterbach, "Gypsy Rose Lee: She Combines a Public Body with a Private Mind," *Life*, December 14, 1942, 99; Roll 6, "Gypsy Rose Lee on Life, Strife—And Women 'Around Forty,'" no header, GRL Papers, NYPL; "By and About Gypsy," *Life*, May 27, 1957, 104.

10. Roll 1, "Stripper Queen Struts Her Stuff," *National Police Gazette*, October 1936, GRL Papers, NYPL; Louis Nizer, *Reflections Without Mirrors: An Autobiography of the Mind* (New York: Doubleday, 1978), 115.

11. Erik Lee Preminger, *Gypsy & Me* (Boston: Little, Brown, 1984), 9; Cartoon, "Backstage Chivalry at 'Ziegfeld Follies,'" by Ken Chamberlain, rpt. from *New York Herald Tribune*, in Lee, *Gypsy*, between 298 and 299.

12. "Gypsy Rose Lee: Her Start Working in Burlesque," in *Sketches of Naughty Ladies* (Detroit: Johnson Smith, n.d.), 1.

13. F. C. Palmer, "Is There Too Much Gypsy in Gypsy Rose Lee's Love Life?" *Tip-Off*, April 1956, 49.

14. Jennifer Blessing, "The Art(ifice) of Striptease: Gypsy Rose Lee and the Masquerade of Nudity," in *Modernism, Gender, and Culture: A Cultural Studies Approach*, ed. Lisa Redo (New York: Garland, 1997); L. Sprague de Camp, *Time and Change: An Autobiography* (Hampton Falls, N.H.: Donald M. Grant, 1996), 119; June Havoc, *More Havoc* (New York: Harper & Row, 1980), 96. For a present-day analysis of stripteasing that is similar to Gypsy's experiences, see Bernadette Barton, *Stripped: Inside the Lives of Exotic Dancers* (New York: New York University Press, 2006). For background on the striptease, see Rachel Shteir, *Striptease: The Untold History of the Girlie Show* (New York: Oxford University Press, 2004).

15. Minsky and Machlin, *Minsky's Burlesque*, 150.

16. Roll 1, "Some New Faces at Jimmy Lakes," *Washington Post*, June 14, 1931; "Republic Has Good Show," *Zit's Theatrical Newspaper*, December 12, 1931, GRL Papers, NYPL.

17. Havoc, *More Havoc*, 217.

18. Roll 6, "Lyons Den," New York, April 21, 1953; Roll 1, "Follies Strip Dancer Sees Doom for Art," no header, GRL Papers, NYPL.

19. Lee, *Gypsy*, 263, 268.

20. Background on Waxy Gordon includes: Alan A. Block, *East Side–West Side: Organizing Crime in New York, 1930–1950* (Cardiff: University College

Cardiff Press, 1980); Rich Cohen, *Tough Jews: Fathers, Sons, and Gangster Dreams* (New York: Vintage Books, 1999); Albert Fried, *The Rise and Fall of the Jewish Gangster in America* (New York: Columbia University Press, 1993); Paul Sann, *Kill the Dutchman! The Story of Dutch Schultz* (New York: Da Capo Paperback, 1971); Craig Thompson and Allen Raymond, *Gang Rule in New York: The Story of a Lawless Era* (New York: Dial Press, 1940); Jenna Weissman Joselit, *Our Gang: Jewish Crime and the New York Jewish Community, 1900–1940* (Bloomington: Indiana University Press, 1983).

21. Havoc, *More Havoc*, 66.

22. Lee, *Gypsy*, 263.

23. Ibid., 272.

24. Roll 1, Gypsy Rose Lee, "The Men I Love"; "Walter Winchell on Broadway," n.d. August, GRL Papers, NYPL.

25. Edythe Farrell, "An Unusual Strip-Tease: Gypsy Rose Lee Is First to Do a 'Talking' Strip," *National Police Gazette*, August–September 1940, 3.

26. Gottlieb, *Nine Lives of Billy Rose*, 229–30; Roll 1, Gypsy Rose Lee, "The Men I Love"; "Walter Winchell on Broadway," n.d. August, GRL Papers, NYPL.

27. Farrell, "An Unusual Strip-Tease," 3.

28. "Intimate Secrets of a Strip Dancer: Gypsy Rose Lee Tells of Her Love and Life," *Romantic Stories*, April 1937, 33, 88.

Chapter 3

1. Morton Minsky and Milt Machlin, *Minsky's Burlesque* (New York: Arbor House, 1986), 143.

2. J. P. McEvoy, "More Tease than Strip," *Reader's Digest*, July 1941, 73; Roll 6, Red Ritson, *New Jersey Press* (Atlantic City), April 8, 1957, GRL Papers, NYPL.

3. Roll 3, *Newsweek*, April 29, 1957; Roll 4, Louella Parsons, "Gypsy Rose Lee Happy to Abandon Strip Tease for Western Film Role," no header, GRL Papers, NYPL.

4. Gretta Palmer, "She Undressed Her Way to Fame," *New York Woman*, October 7, 1936, 18.

5. Roll 3, John K. Hutchen, *New York Herald Tribune*, April 29, 1957, GRL Papers, NYPL; Kyle Crichton, "Strip for Fame: Miss Gypsy Rose Lee, in Person," *Collier's*, December 19, 1936, 47; "Intimate Secrets of a Strip Dancer: Gypsy Rose Lee Tells of Her Love and Life," *Romantic Stories*, April 1937, 90.

6. Gypsy Rose Lee, *Gypsy: A Memoir* (New York: Harper & Brothers, 1957), 296.

7. Gypsy Rose Lee, "Stripping the Strip Tease: From Minsky's to Ziegfeld to Hollywood in Ten Teasy Lessons," *Ad Lib: Show Book of the Show World*, June 1937, 9; Roll 2, William S. Cunningham, *Columbus Citizen*, n.d., GRL Papers, NYPL.

8. "Intimate Secrets of a Strip Dancer," 90.

9. June Havoc, *More Havoc* (New York: Harper & Row, 1980), 157.

10. Palmer, "She Undressed Her Way to Fame," 18; Laura Jacobs, "Taking It *All* Off," *Vanity Fair*, March 2003, 207 (this article mistakenly gives Eddy's surname as Braun).

11. Havoc, *More Havoc*, 106–7.

12. Lee, *Gypsy*, 297–98.

13. Havoc, *More Havoc*, 62.

14. Morton Cooper, "Profile of a Character: Gypsy Rose Lee," *Modern Man*, September 1959, 56; Neal Gabler, *Winchell: Gossip, Power and the Culture of Celebrity* (New York: Vintage Books, 1994), 184.

15. Bernard Sobel, *Broadway Heartbeat: Memoirs of a Press Agent* (New York: Hermitage House, 1953), 128–29.

16. Palmer, "She Undressed Her Way to Fame," 17.

17. Roll 1, *Princeton Tiger*, "The 'Bare Facts': An Interview" n.d.; *Princeton Tiger*, no title, November 5, 1935, GRL Papers, NYPL.

18. Lee, "Stripping the Strip Tease: From Minsky's to Ziegfeld to Hollywood in Ten Teasy Lessons," 9.

19. Roll 1, Florabel Muir and Robert Sullivan, "Gypsy and June—Mother's Girls: Hovick Sisters in Chips Now, Can Grin at Frantic Youth," *New York Sunday News*, June 22, 1941, 12, GRL Papers, NYPL.

20. Havoc, *More Havoc*, 160; Lee, "Stripping the Strip Tease," 35.

21. Roll 1, "Gypsy Rose Lee Stripped by Burglars," *New York Post*, November 28, 1936; "Six Strip Gypsy Rose Lee and They're Not Teasing," *New York World*, November 28, 1936; George Dixon, "Gems Gone, Gypsy Rose Is So Cold," no header, GRL Papers, NYPL.

22. Wesley Sheldon, "Gypsy Rose Lee Tangles with the Murder Mob," *Complete Detective Cases*, June 1943, 4–9, 41–44; Michael Stern, "Gypsy Rose Lee's Favorite Mystery: The Murder of the Artist's Model," *Master Detective*, September 1942, 76.

23. Letter from Gypsy to Annie, n.d., private collection of Chuck Mosberger.

24. Havoc, *More Havoc*, 146, 218.

25. Roll 3, Hanner Swaffer, "They Think Dollars Can Be Wasted on Strip-tease," *The People*, July 8, 1951, GRL Papers, NYPL. For a fuller discussion of the closing of burlesque theaters, see Rachel Shteir, *Striptease: The Untold History of the Girlie Show* (New York: Oxford University Press, 2004), 156–76, 157–58.

26. Palmer, "She Undressed Her Way to Fame," 16, 17; Roll 4, no header, January 1943, GRL Papers, NYPL; Minsky and Machlin, *Minsky's Burlesque*, 103, 144.

27. Roll 1, Norma Adams, "Ada Onion Is No Rose to Summer," no header, April 11, 1931, GRL Papers, NYPL; Palmer, "She Undressed Her Way to Fame," 16.

28. Dick Humer, "Burlesque: Our First Line of Defense?" *Spark*, June 1942, 6; W. J. Cash, "The Censor's Lewd Eye Scans Gypsy Rose Lee," *Charlotte News*, May 23, 1937, available at www.wjcash.org/Elkcash/Charlotte.News.Articles/Gypsy.htm.

29. Roll 5, *New York World Telegram and Sun*, April 21, 1951; Roll 3, "Gypsy Rose in Favor of Reviving Burlesque in New York," *Chicago American*, December 26, 1956, GRL Papers, NYPL.

30. Roll 3, James T. Kaull Jr., "Take It Off Mommy—And Gypsy's Son Comes Through," *Newport* (R.I.) *News*, August 1, 1956, GRL Papers, NYPL.

31. Roll 3, *Newsweek*, April 29, 1957, GRL Papers, NYPL.

32. Roll 2, William S. Cunningham, *Columbus Citizen*, n.d., GRL Papers, NYPL; Leonard Pereira, "From Burlesque to Movie Fame: Gypsy Rose Lee Made Good 'Strip-Teasing,'" *Picture Review: America's Variety Digest*, July 1937, 9.

33. Roll 1, "Stripper Queen Struts Her Stuff," *National Police Gazette*, October 1936, GRL Papers, NYPL; Sobel, *Broadway Heartbeat*, 127–28.

34. Gladys Hall, "The Things I Want: As Revealed by Gypsy Rose Lee," *Personal Romances*, November 1944, 58.

Chapter 4

1. Gypsy Rose Lee, *Gypsy: A Memoir* (New York: Harper & Brothers, 1957), 323.

2. Eugene Pawley, "Strip Tease Intellectual," *Cabaret*, July 1955, 38; Gretta Palmer, "She Undressed Her Way to Fame," *New York Woman*, October 7, 1936, 16; Earl Wilson, *Hot Times: True Tales or Hollywood and Broadway* (Chicago: Contemporary Books, 1984), 17; Lawrence Lee and Barry Gifford, *Saroyan: A Biography* (New York: Harper & Row, 1984), 92.

3. Gypsy Rose Lee, *The G-String Murders* (New York: Pocket Books, 1947), 176.

4. Georgia Sothern, *Georgia: My Life in Burlesque* (New York: New American Library, 1972), 131, 166, 208.

5. Norman Katkov, *The Fabulous Fanny: The Story of Fanny Brice* (New York: Knopf, 1953), 59.

6. Ibid., 74.

7. Ibid., 201, 231.

8. FBI file for Fanny Brice, FOIPA no. 441151.

9. Gypsy Rose Lee, "Fanny Brice and I," *Town & Country*, April 1957, 75, 122; *Gypsy*, 321, 322, 323; "The Fabulous Gypsy," *Pageant*, October 1957, 160.

10. Pawley, "Strip Tease Intellectual," 40.

11. FBI file for Fanny Brice, FOIPA no. 441151.

12. Lee, *Gypsy*, 310.

13. Gladys Hall, "The Things I Want: As Revealed by Gypsy Rose Lee," *Personal Romances*, November 1944, 58.

14. Fannie Brice, "I Knew Gypsy Rose Lee When," *Cosmopolitan*, July 1948, 156.

15. Palmer, "She Undressed Her Way to Fame," 16.

16. Lee, *Gypsy*, 314.

17. Ibid., 247–48.

18. June Havoc, *More Havoc* (New York: Harper & Row, 1980), 126, 175; Series I, Subseries 1, Personal, Box 1, Folder 14, To Louise (n.d. from Rose), GRL Papers, NYPL.

19. Havoc, *More Havoc*, 145.

20. Lee, *Gypsy*, 319.

21. Ibid., 318.

22. Ibid., 319.

23. Series II, Subseries 6, Red Ties, 1950–1951, Box 19, Folder 1, Gypsy's statement denying membership in Communist Party, September 1950, GRL Papers, NYPL.

24. Kyle Crichton, "Strip for Fame: Miss Gypsy Rose Lee, in Person," *Collier's*, December 19, 1936, 13, 47.

25. Lowell Thomas, *Good Evening Everybody: From Cripple Creek to Samarkand* (New York: William Morrow, 1976), 329.

26. Roll 2, Jack Turcott, "Gypsy Rose Lee Talks 3 Agents into Price of One," by *Daily News*, April 16, 1937; "Gypsy Rose Strips Her Three Agents," no header, GRL Papers, NYPL.

27. Roll 1, Letter to Lee Wright from Gypsy Rose Lee, Hotel Ambassador, Chicago, February 19, 1941, GRL Papers, NYPL.

28. Roll 2, Clarke Wales, "From Hollywood to Burlesque to Hollywood," *Screen & Radio Weekly*, May 30, 1937, GRL Papers, NYPL.

Chapter 5

1. For an excellent description of the development of movies during this period, see Tino Balio, *Grand Design: Hollywood as a Modern Business Enterprise, 1930–1939* (History of the American Cinema, vol. 5; Berkeley: University of California Press, 1996), particularly the introduction, 1–12, and chapter 6, "Selling Stars."

2. "How Movies Are Censored: The Amazing Story of Will Hays, Czar of the Movie Industry," *Look*, August 2, 1938, 12–19.

3. Ibid.; Roll 2, *Boston Post*, May 31, 1937; "Is Sex Coming Back to Hollywood?" *Screen and Radio*, n.d., GRL Papers, NYPL.

4. Roll 2, Letter from Twentieth Century–Fox, *Los Angeles Times*, June 1, 1937, GRL Papers, NYPL.

5. J. P. McEvoy, "More Tease than Strip," *Reader's Digest*, July 1941, 73; Roll 2, "Gypsy Rose Lee Stripped—But Only of Name," no header, GRL Papers, NYPL.

6. Roll 2, "Gypsy Rose Lee Refuses to Remove Fur Coat," *Los Angeles Examiner*, April 10, 1937, GRL Papers, NYPL.

7. Roll 2, Ann Marsters, "The Rise of Gypsy Rose Lee from Burlesque to the Follies to the Films," *Boston Sunday Advertiser*, n.d., GRL Papers, NYPL.

8. Roll 2, Frank Sullivan, "Revolt of the Celebrities," *New Yorker*, n.d., GRL Papers, NYPL.

9. Roll 2, "Welcome Wasted—Gypsy Dressed," *Los Angeles Daily News*, April 19, 1937; *New York Herald*, August 4, 1937; Ed Sullivan, "Broadway," *New York Daily News*, June 30, 1937, GRL Papers, NYPL.

10. Roll 2, *New York World Telegram*, October 20, 1937, GRL Papers, NYPL.

11. Roll 2, "Gypsy Rose Lee Refuses to Remove Fur Coat," *Los Angeles Examiner*, April 10, 1937, GRL Papers, NYPL; "Gypsy Changes Name," *Norfolk Ledger Dispatch*, May 26, 1937.

12. Richard E. Lauterbach, "Gypsy Rose Lee: She Combines a Public Body with a Private Mind," *Life*, vol. 13, no. 24, December 14, 1942, 93; Eugene Pawley, "Strip Tease Intellectual," *Cabaret*, July 1955, 41.

13. Roll 2, "She Strips in New York but Dresses in Hollywood," *Hollywood Citizen*, April 19, 1937, GRL Papers, NYPL.

14. Andrew Bergman, *We're in the Money: Depression America and Its Film* (New York: New York University Press, 1971), 132; Jeanine Basinger, *A Woman's View: How Hollywood Spoke to Women, 1930–1960* (New York: Knopf, 1973), 20.

15. Roll 1, Frank Nugent, *Screen*, n.d.; Roll 2, *Variety*, July 24, 1937; Roll 2, James Francis Crow, *Hollywood Citizen News*, n.d.; Roll 1, *Hollywood Spectator*, July 31, 1937, GRL Papers, NYPL; Morton Cooper, "Profile of a Character: Gypsy Rose Lee," *Modern Man*, September 1959, 56.

16. Roll 2, *New York World Telegram*, October 20, 1937, GRL Papers, NYPL.

17. Roll 2, Jimmy Star, "Preview," no header, GRL Papers, NYPL.

18. Roll 2, Louella Parsons, *Sunday Mirror*, April 7, 1938; Elizabeth Yeaman, *Hollywood Citizen News*, April 7, 1938, GRL Papers, NYPL.

19. Roll 2, "Strip Queen Detests It," *Indianapolis Times*, n.d., GRL Papers, NYPL.

20. Lauterbach, "Gypsy Rose Lee: She Combines," 95; Roll 2, Clarke Wales, "The Philosophy of Undressing," *Screen & Radio Weekly*, May 30, 1937, GRL Papers, NYPL.

21. Edythe Farrell, "An Unusual Strip-Tease: Gypsy Rose Lee Is First to Do a 'Talking' Strip," *National Police Gazette*, August–September 1940, 3.

22. Ibid.

23. Roll 2, *Norfolk Ledger Dispatch*, May 17, 1937, GRL Papers, NYPL.

24. Farrell, "An Unusual Strip-Tease," 3.

25. June Havoc, *More Havoc* (New York: Harper & Row, 1980), 251.

26. Roll 3, Elizabeth Wilson, "Gypsy's Back in Hollywood," *Movie Show Magazine*, n.d., GRL Papers, NYPL.

27. "Gypsy Rose Lee: Knows All About It," *It*, November 1941, 7.

28. Roll 2, "Gypsy Rose Lee Changes Names," *Norfolk Ledger Dispatch*, May 26, 1937, GRL Papers, NYPL.

29. Lauterbach, "Gypsy Rose Lee: She Combines," 93; Cooper, "Profile of a Character," 56.

30. Joseph Jennel, "Interview With: Gypsy Rose Lee," *Jem*, February 1960, 64; McEvoy, "More Tease than Strip," 72.

31. Roll 2, "Walter Winchell on Broadway," no header, July 29, 1937, GRL Papers, NYPL.

32. Havoc, *More Havoc*, 194, 226.

33. Roll 2, Clarke Wales, "The Philosophy of Undressing," *Screen & Radio Weekly*, May 30, 1937, GRL Papers, NYPL.

Chapter 6

1. Morton Minsky and Milt Machlin, *Minsky's Burlesque* (New York: Arbor House, 1986), 237–38. Minsky's aunt was married to Professor Morris Raefield Cohen, an important Jewish leftist intellectual who influenced activists in the Socialist Party.

2. Series I, Subseries 1, Personal, Box 2, Folder 8, From Ruth Mizzy to Louise, December 20, 1938, GRL Papers, NPYL; telephone interview with Robert Mizzy's fourth wife, Jeanne Lucille LaMarche Mizzy, June 23, 2005.

3. E-mail message from Robert Mizzy's daughter, Danianne Mizzy, May 2005; Roll 1, *National Police Gazette*, October 1936, GRL Papers, NYPL.

4. Roll 2, "Lyons Den," *New York Post*, May 18, 1937, GRL Papers, NYPL.

5. David Niven, *Bring on the Empty Horses* (New York: G. P. Putnam's Sons, 1975), 28.

6. Florabel Muir and Robert Sullivan, "Gypsy and June—Mother's Girls: Hovick Sisters in Chips Now, Can Grin at Frantic Youth," *New York Sunday News*, June 22, 1941, 9; Richard E. Lauterbach, "Gypsy Rose Lee: She Combines a Public Body with a Private Mind," *Life*, December 14, 1942, 96; Minsky and Machlin, *Minsky's Burlesque*, 238–39.

7. "Private Lives," *Life*, August 30, 1937, 84.

8. Series I, Subseries 3, General, Box 7, Folder 3, Carl Anderson to Jack Mulcahy, Twentieth Century–Fox Studio, Pico St. Losa, August 26, 1937; Telegram to Robert Mizzy from Frank L. McNeny, Director General, Greater Texas and Pan American Exposition, August 1937, GRL Papers, NYPL.

9. Muir and Sullivan, "Gypsy and June"; Minsky and Machlin, *Minsky's Burlesque*, 239.

10. Lauterbach, "Gypsy Rose Lee: She Combines," 99; June Havoc, *More Havoc* (New York: Harper & Row, 1980), 207.

11. Edythe Farrell, "An Unusual Strip-Tease: Gypsy Rose Lee Is First to Do a 'Talking' Strip," *National Police Gazette*, August–September 1940, 3; Gladys Hall, "The Things I Want: As Revealed by Gypsy Rose Lee," *Personal*

Romances, November 1944, 58–59; Roll 2, unidentified newspaper article, Dallas, Texas, September 2, 1937, GRL Papers, NYPL; copy of letter from Gypsy to Bob, n.d., private papers of Jeanne Lucille LaMarche Mizzy.

12. Havoc, *More Havoc*, 63–64.

13. Minsky and Machlin, *Minsky's Burlesque*, 240.

14. Roll 2, unidentified newspaper article, Dallas, Texas, September 2, 1937; telephone interview with Mizzy's fourth wife, Jeanne Lucille LaMarche Mizzy, June 23, 2005.

15. Havoc, *More Havoc*, 190; "Gypsy Rose Lee at Home at Witchwood Manor," *Pic*, August 6, 1940, 38, 40–41.

16. Copy of letter from Gypsy to Bob, n.d., private papers of Jeanne Lucille LaMarche Mizzy.

17. Ruth Mizzy's FBI file, no. 0951324-000.

18. Series 1, Subseries 1, Personal, Box 2, Folder 8, From Ruth Mizzy to Bob, n.d., GRL Papers, NYPL.

19. Series 1, Subseries 1, Personal, Box 2, Folder 8, From Ruth Mizzy to Louise, December 20, 1938, GRL Papers, NYPL.

20. Series III, Legal, Box 23, Folder 3, Decree for Divorce, State of Illinois, Cook Co., March 17, 1941, Rose L. Mizzy vs. Arnold R. Mizzy; Roll 2, *New York City News*, January 28, 1941; Roll 2, "She Moves to Shed her Husband," *Herald American*, January 21,1941; Roll 1, "She's Going to Shed a Husband," *Wisconsin Journal* (Milwaukee), March 11, 1941; Roll 1, unidentified newspaper article, Huntington, West Virginia, January 28, 1941, GRL Papers, NYPL; Thomas Blair, "What Gypsy Rose Didn't Tell in "*Gypsy*," *Uncensored Magazine*, January 1960, 33.

21. Farrell, "An Unusual Strip-Tease," 3; Roll 2, *Milwaukee Sentinel*, March 18, 1941, GRL Papers, NYPL; Minsky and Machlin, *Minsky's Burlesque*, 238.

22. Morton Cooper, "Profile of a Character: Gypsy Rose Lee," *Modern Man*, September 1959, 38; Roll 3, "Inquiring Report," no header, November 15, 1946, GRL Papers, NYPL.

23. Havoc, *More Havoc*, 195.

24. Farrell, "An Unusual Strip-Tease," 3; copy of letter from Gypsy to Bob, n.d., private papers of Jeanne Lucille LaMarche Mizzy.

Chapter 7

1. "Woman Art Student a Suicide," *New York Times*, June 3, 1937; "Jury Visits Home of Strip Teaser," *Los Angeles Times*, November 27, 1937; "Indictment Refused in Death at Home of Gypsy Rose Lee," *Los Angeles Times*, November 30, 1937; June Havoc, *More Havoc* (New York: Harper & Row, 1980), 175; Laura Jacobs, "Taking It *All* Off," *Vanity Fair*, March 2003, 212. Series I, Subseries 1, Personal, Box 1, Folder 9, From Rose E. Hovick, Witchwood Manor, Highland Mills, New York, May 10, 1938; Louise and Bob from Mother, n.d.; From Gypsy (to mother), n.d., GRL Papers, NYPL.

2. Florabel Muir and Robert Sullivan, "Gypsy and June—Mother's Girls: Hovick Sisters, in Chips Now, Can Grin at Frantic Youth," *New York Sunday News*, June 22, 1941, 12; Havoc, *More Havoc*, 210. Roll 3, Elizabeth B. Peterson, "Education for a Home Girl—Surprising Slant on Gypsy Rose Lee," no header; Series I, Subseries 1, Personal, Box 1, Folder 9, From Rose E. Hovick, Witchwood Manor, Highland Mills, New York, n.d.; From Mother, May 5 and 26, 1938; From Gypsy (to mother), n.d.; From Rose E. Hovick, Witchwood Manor, Highland Mills, New York, May 10, 1938, GRL Papers, NYPL.

3. Series I, Subseries 1, Personal, Box 1, Folder 1, From Gypsy to Mr. Smith (caretaker), Highland Mills, May 4, 1938; From Lester Smith, October 17, 1938; Folder 8, To Mother, May 4, 1938; Mother, Wire, May 5, 1938; Mother to Louise, May 6, 1938; Folder 9, Telegram to Mrs. Rose E. Hovick from Louise Hovick, n.d.; Letter to Louise and Bob from Mother, n.d.; From Gypsy, 1938, GRL Papers, NYPL.

4. Havoc, *More Havoc*, 209, 211.

5. Ibid., 274.

6. Roll 1, Douglas Gilbert, "Strip Tease Goes in for the Dough, so She's Deserting Burlesque for Broadway Plunge," no header, GRL Papers, NYPL.

7. Series I, Subseries 1, Personal, Box 1, Folder 1, Big Lady, Telegram to Gypsy, September 5, 1938; From Welfare Department, 718 County-City Building, Seattle, Washington, November 14, 1938; Belle to Louise Dear, May 20, 1941, GRL Papers, NYPL.

8. Series I, Subseries 1, Personal, Box 1, Folder 1, From Big Lady to Gypsy, August 26, 1938; Folder 2, From Big Lady to Louise Darling, May 13, 1943; Folder 1, From Big Lady to Louise Dear and Family, June 9, 1940; Folder 2, From Big Lady to Gypsy, July 7, 1945; Folder 7, Mama to Rose, October 4, [1938], GRL Papers, NYPL.

9. J. P. McEvoy, "More Tease than Strip," *Reader's Digest*, July 1941, 73.

10. Eugene Pawley, "Strip Tease Intellectual," *Cabaret*, July 1955, 41.

11. Roll 1, "Red Prober Gets Publicity by Phoning Gypsy Rose Lee," n.p., November 25, 1938; Roll 2, "Strip Queen Detests It," *Indianapolis Times*, n.d., GRL Papers, NYPL.

12. Roll 1, "'Too Busy' Says Gypsy," *Columbus* [*Chronicle?*—name illegible], November 26, 1938; "Red Prober Gets Publicity by Phoning Gypsy Rose Lee," n.p., November 25, 1938; Ben Hayes, "Ready to Bare All Strip-Teaser Says," no header, GRL Papers, NYPL; Richard E. Lauterbach, "Gypsy Rose Lee: She Combines a Public Body with a Private Mind," *Life*, December 14, 1942, 95; Pawley, "Strip Tease Intellectual," July 1955, 41.

13. Roger Kahn, "Strip Teaser: The Ups and Downs of Gypsy Rose Lee," *Real: The Exciting Magazine for Men*, November 1956, 65; Roll 1, John Richmond, "Gypsy Rose Lee: Striptease Intellectual," *American Mercury*, January 1941, GRL Papers, NYPL.

14. Roll 1, John Richmond, "Gypsy Rose Lee: Striptease Intellectual," *American Mercury*, January 1941, GRL Papers, NYPL.

15. Roll 1, *Washington Herald*, n.d., GRL Papers, NYPL.

Chapter 8

1. Gypsy Rose Lee, *The G-String Murders* (New York: Pocket Books, 1947), 1. For a detailed plot analysis, see Rachel Shteir, "Gypsy Rose Lee: Striptease Intellectual," the afterword to the edition published by the Feminist Press at the City University of New York, 2005.

2. George McGrath, "A Gangster Helped Her to Fame: Gypsy Rose Lee's True Story," *National Police Gazette*, September 1957, 3, 24.

3. Roll 4, Kasper Monahan, "Show Shops," *Pittsburgh Press*, October 14, 1943, GRL Papers, NYPL.

4. Roll 1, Gypsy Rose Lee, "The Men I Love," for "Walter Winchell on Broadway," no header, August 1940, GRL Papers, NYPL.

5. Gerald Clark, *Capote: A Biography* (New York: Simon & Schuster, 1988), 81. The most authoritative source on 7 Middagh Street is Sherill Tippins, *February House* (New York: Houghton Mifflin, 2005), 37.

6. Rachel Shteir, "Everybody Slept Here," *New York Times Book Review*, November 10, 1996; Jon Stallworthy, *Louis MacNeice: A Biography* (New York: W. W. Norton, 1995), 284; Humphrey Carpenter, *Benjamin Britten: A Biography* (New York: Charles Scribner's Sons, 1993), 144; Millicent Dillon, *A Little Original Sin: The Life and Work of Jane Bowles* (New York: Holt, Rinehart & Winston, 1981); Gunther Stuhlmann, ed., *The Diary of Anaïs Nin*, vol. 5, *1947–1955* (New York: Harcourt Brace Jovanovich, 1974), 206; Tippins, *February House*, 136.

7. Tippins, *February House*, 86; Charles Osborne, *W. H. Auden: The Life of a Poet* (New York: Harcourt Brace Jovanovich, 1979), 196, 199.

8. Virginia Spencer Carr, *The Lonely Hunter: A Biography of Carson McCullers* (New York: Anchor Press, 1976); Tippins, *February House,* 108–9.

9. Tippins, *February House*, 100–101; Carpenter, *Benjamin Britten*, 144; Series I, Subseries 1, Personal, Box 3, Folder 2, Valentine from George, n.d., GRL Papers, NYPL.

10. Series I, Subseries 3, General, Box 7, Folder 4, From Carmel Snow, Editor, *Harper's Bazaar*, 572 Madison Avenue, New York City, to Gypsy Rose Lee, 206 East 57th Street, New York City, October 7, 1940, GRL Papers, NYPL.

11. Series I, Subseries 1, Personal, Box 3, Folder 2, From George to Gypsy, December 26, 1940, GRL Papers, NYPL.

12. Series I, Subseries 1, Personal, Box 3, Folder 2, From [George] to Gypsy, Saturday night (n.d.), GRL Papers, NYPL.

13. Series I, Subseries 1, Personal, Box 3, Folder 2, From George Davis, *Mademoiselle*, 122 East 42nd Street, New York City, January 5, 1945; From George Davis, 7 Middagh Street, Thursday (n.d.), GRL Papers, NYPL.

14. "A Note About the Author" in Lee, *G-String Murders*; Series 1, Subseries 3, General, Box 7, Folder 7, From Alexander Woollcott, Bomoseen, Vermont, to Dear Authoress (Gypsy), August 20, 1941; Subseries 1, Personal, Box 3, Folder 2, From George to Gypsy, January 15, 1941, GRL Papers, NYPL.

15. Lee, *G-String Murders*, 187.

16. Series I, Subseries 3, General, Box 7, Folder 2, Kiddiegram from Rags Ragland, New York City, to Gypsy (n.d.); From Rags Ragland, The Emerson, Baltimore, Maryland, to Punkin (Gypsy), May 27, 1935, GRL Papers, NYPL.

17. Roll 2, "Gypsy Rose Proves That Talk About Book Is Strip Tease," no header, GRL Papers, NYPL.

18. Roll 1, To Lee Wright from Gypsy Rose Lee, Hotel Ambassador, Chicago, Illinois, January 20, 1941, GRL Papers, NYPL.

19. Roll 1, "Gypsy Rose Lee: An Intellectual Strip Teaser Arrives in Dayton," *Dayton Herald*, October 10, 1941, GRL Papers, NYPL.

20. Roll 4, Robbin Coons, "Clues Tease Gypsy Rose Lee," *Rushville Indiana Telegram*, May 11, 1944; Roll 1, John Mason Brown, "Gypsy Rose's Novel Is a Teasing Mystery," *New York World Telegram*, October 16, 1941; P. Richard Smith, "Gypsy's Murder Mystery Has a Bare Plot but It's Authentic if It Ain't Literary," unidentified newspaper, El Paso, Texas, July 7, 1941; "Gypsy Rose Lee: An Intellectual Strip Teaser Arrives in Dayton," *Dayton Herald*, October 10, 1941, GRL Papers, NYPL.

21. Roll 1, "New Fiction," *Greensburg Press* (New York), November 7, 1971; "It's Good Entertainment, G String or No," *Richmond Times-Dispatch*, October 19, 1941; Will Cuppy, "Mystery and Adventure," *New York Herald Tribune*, October 5, 1941, GRL Papers, NYPL.

22. Roll 3, Frank Beaven, cartoon, *Saturday Evening Post*, n.d., GRL Papers, NYPL; "The G-String Murders: Gypsy Rose Lee Turns Mystery Author," *Life*, October 6, 1941, 110–17.

23. Roll 4, "Burlesque Will Soon Be Making Its Bow in Film," no header, GRL Papers, NYPL. For the way Stanwyck was viewed, see June Sochen, *From Mae to Madonna: Women Entertainers in Twentieth-Century America* (Lexington: University Press of Kentucky, 1999), 8.

24. Advertisement for *Lady of Burlesque*, *Life*, April 26, 1943, 8.

25. Roll 3, "In Movie Censured by Legion," no header, GRL Papers, NYPL; Frank Walsh, *Sin and Censorship: The Catholic Church and the Motion Picture Industry* (New Haven: Yale University Press, 1996), 185–86.

26. Roll 4, "Gypsy Rose Lee Happy to Abandon Strip Tease for Western Film Role," interview with Louella Parsons, no header, GRL Papers, NYPL; Ella Smith, *Starring Miss Barbara Stanwyck* (New York: Crown, 1974).

27. Gypsy Rose Lee, *Mother Finds a Body* (New York: Simon & Schuster, A Popular Library Mystery Wartime Book, 1942).

28. Ibid., 70.

29. Ibid., 22, 60.

30. Ibid., 64, 94.

31. Ibid., 19, 161.

32. Ibid., 93–94.

33. Ibid., 32, 140–41.

34. Ibid., 35.

35. June Havoc, *More Havoc* (New York: Harper & Row, 1980), 208.

36. Florabel Muir and Robert Sullivan, "Gypsy and June—Mother's Girls: Hovick Sisters, in Chips Now, Can Grin at Frantic Youth," *New York Sunday News*, June 22, 1941, 8–9, 12.

37. Richard E. Lauterbach, "Gypsy Rose Lee: She Combines a Public Body with a Private Mind," *Life*, December 14, 1942, 101; Series I, Subseries 1, Personal, Box 2, Folder 16, To Eric Kirkland from Floria Lasky, c/o Sigma Productions, 71 Fifth Avenue, New York, New York 10022, September 25, 1970, GRL Papers, NYPL.

38. Roll 3, Will Cuppy, "Mystery and Adventure," *New York Herald Tribune*, October 11, 1942; Richard McLaughlin, "Gypsy Rose Scores Again," no header; Jay Lewis, "Books and Authors," no header, GRL Papers, NYPL.

39. Roll 3, "Expectant Publisher," n.p., n.d.; Roll 1, Robert Marks, "Trill on the G-String," *Esquire*, December 1941; Roll 4, "Miss Lee Continues Job as Author," *Columbus* (Ohio) *Citizen*, August 16, 1942, GRL Papers, NYPL.

40. Roll 3, Letter to Lee Wright from Gypsy Rose Lee, Backstage Music Box Theatre, August 26, 1942; "Expectant Publisher," no header; Roll 4, "Gypsy Rose Lee Discloses Passion for Precise Word," n.p., Baltimore, October 4, 1943, GRL Papers, NYPL.

41. Lauterbach, "Gypsy Rose Lee: She Combines," 101; Roll 2, "Gypsy Rose Lee Is in Town, Hints Age Withers Glamour," no header, GRL Papers, NYPL.

42. Roll 3, "If You Weren't Yourself Who Would You Like to Be," no header, GRL Papers, NYPL.

43. Series I, Subseries 3, General, Box 7, Folder 4, Western Union Telegram from Craig Rice, Somerset Hotel, New York City, to Gypsy, October 3, 1941, GRL Papers, NYPL.

44. Series I, Subseries 3, General, Box 7, Folder 10, To Gypsy Rose Lee from Craig Rice, January 24, 1946; Folder 5, From Lawrence Lipton to Gypsy Rose Lee, May 29, 1942, GRL Papers, NYPL.

45. Roger Kahn, "Strip Teaser: The Ups and Downs of Gypsy Rose Lee," *Real: The Exciting Magazine for Men*, November 1956, 65. Tippins, *February House*, 84–86, 99–101, describes the process by which Gypsy composed the first two chapters.

46. Tippins, *February House*, 85–86; Series III, Legal, Box 23, Folder 5, To Gypsy from Fitelson and Mayers, June 16, 1944, GRL Papers, NYPL.

47. Richard Gehman, "A Visit with Gypsy: Meet the Best Undressed Woman of Our Time," *Star Weekly*, October 22, 1960, 25; Roll 4, "Miss Lee

Continues Job as Author," *Columbus* (Ohio) *Citizen*, August 16, 1942, GRL Papers, NYPL.

48. "G-String Murders: Gypsy Rose Lee Turns Mystery Author," 110.

49. Roll 1, Letter to Lee Wright, Fairmont Hotel, Nob Hill, San Francisco, June 16, 1941, GRL Papers, NYPL.

50. John Richmond, "Gypsy Rose Lee: Striptease Intellectual," *American Mercury*, January 1941; Roll 4, Elizabeth Wilson, "Gypsy's Back in Hollywood," no header; crossword puzzle, *New York World Telegram*, February 18, 1943, GRL Papers, NYPL.

Chapter 9

1. Roll 1, Otis Chatfield-Taylor, "Strips to Conquer," *Town & Country*, n.d., GRL Papers, NYPL.

2. Roll 3, Elizabeth B. Peterson, "Education for a Home Girl—Surprising Slant on Gypsy Rose Lee," no header, GRL Papers, NYPL.

3. Series I, Subseries 3, General, Box 7, Folder 4, From Mrs. Carl Van Doren (Jean), 41 Central Park, West, New York City, to Gypsy, November 17,1941 to Gypsy, 206 E. 57th, GRL Papers, NYPL; Georgia Sothern, *Georgia: My Life in Burlesque* (New York: New American Library, 1972), 178–79,

4. Gladys Hall, "The Things I Want: As Revealed by Gypsy Rose Lee," *Personal Romances*, November 1944, 59.

5. Gypsy Rose Lee, "Stripping the Strip Tease: From Minsky's to Ziegfeld to Hollywood in Ten Teasy Lessons," *Ad Lib: Show Book of the Show World*, June 1937, 9; Roll 1, clipping, no header, GRL Papers, NYPL.

6. Roll 2, "Sidney Skolsky Presents," *Hollywood Citizen*, February 11, 1938, GRL Papers, NYPL.

7. Don Manning, "Gypsy Rose Lee Talks About Music and Musicians," *Music and Rhythm*, February 1941, 6–8.

8. "Gypsy Rose Lee: A General Collector," *Hobbies*, October 1942, 6–7.

9. Series I, Subseries 3, General, Box 7, Folder 12, September 7, 1950, Letter from Museum of the City of New York to Gypsy, GRL Papers, NYPL.

10. Roll 5, "Stripper Scoffs at Gibson Girl," *Boston Traveler*, November 21, 1950, GRL Papers, NYPL.

11. Roll 1, Letter to Lee Wright from Riverside Theatre, Milwaukee, February 26, 1941, GRL Papers, NYPL.

12. Roger Kahn, "Strip Teaser: The Ups and Downs of Gypsy Rose Lee," *Real: The Exciting Magazine for Men*, November 1956, 64; "The Fabulous Gypsy," *Pageant*, October 1957, 160.

13. "The Eyes of Arnold Newman: At the Portrait Gallery, the Photographer's Famous Faces," *Washington Post*, April 15, 1992.

14. Jacqueline Bograd Weld, *Peggy: The Wayward Guggenheim* (New York: Dutton, 1986), 254.

15. Ibid., 254.

16. "The Fabulous Gypsy," 160, 159.

17. Weld, *Peggy*, 356.

Chapter 10

1. J. P. McEvoy, "More Tease than Strip," *Reader's Digest*, July 1941, 73; Roll 2, *Norfolk Ledger Dispatch*, May 17, 1937, GRL Papers, NYPL.

2. Roll 2, William S. Cunningham, *Columbus* (Ohio) *Citizen*, n.d., GRL Papers, NYPL.

3. Roll 1, "Gypsy Rose Lee Will Play Role with Clothes On," no header, GRL Papers, NYPL.

4. One of the best sources is David Gelernter, *1939: The Lost World of the Fair* (New York: Free Press, 1995).

5. June Havoc, *More Havoc* (New York: Harper & Row, 1980), 198.

6. Joel Sayre, "Mike Todd and His Big Bug-Eye," *Life*, March 7, 1955, 146; "In or Out of the Chips, Todd Always Audacious, Up & At 'Em Showman with 'World' as His Final Oyster," *Variety*, March 26, 1958, rpt. in *Variety Obituaries* (New York: Garland, 1988), n.p.

7. Michael Todd Jr. and Susan McCarthy Todd, *A Valuable Property: The Life Story of Michael Todd* (New York: Arbor House, 1983), 33.

8. Edward Linn, "Mike Todd: The Man Who Can't Go Broke," *Saga: True Adventures for Men*, August 1955, 62; Todd and Todd, *A Valuable Property*, 64.

9. Richard Blackwell with Vernon Patterson, *From Rags to Bitches: An Autobiography* (Los Angeles: General Publishing Group, 1995), 47, Linn, "Mike Todd," 62.

10. Rachel Shteir, *Striptease: The Untold History of the Girlie Show* (New York: Oxford University Press, 2004), 186, 386; Edythe Farrell, "An Unusual Strip-Tease: Gypsy Rose Lee Is First to Do a 'Talking' Strip," *National Police Gazette*, August–September 1940, 3; "News of the Fair," *PM New York Daily*, July 18, 1940, 20; Erik Lee Preminger, *Gypsy & Me* (Boston: Little, Brown, 1984),16–18; George McGrath, "A Gangster Helped Her to Fame: Gypsy Rose Lee's True Story," *National Police Gazette*, September 1957, 3. The version of "A Stripteaser's Education" presented here is a composite.

11. McGrath, "A Gangster Helped Her to Fame," 3.

12. "She Strips to Conquer," Michael's Todd's Hall of Music presents *Streets of Paris*, New York World's Fair of 1940 program, author's private collection.

13. Roll 1, Brooks Atkinson, "Abbott and Costello and Gypsy Rose Lee in *Streets of Paris* at the World's Fair," *New York Times*, May 21, 1940, GRL Papers, NYPL.

14. H. Allen Smith, *Low Man on a Totem Pole* (Garden City, N.Y.: Doubleday, Doran, 1943), 92–93; Eugene Pawley, "Strip Tease Intellectual," *Cabaret*, July 1955, 39.

15. McEvoy, "More Tease than Strip," 71.

16. Roll 1, *Life*, September 9, 1940, GRL Papers, NYPL; Eliot Elisofon, *Food Is a Four Letter Word* (New York: Rinehart, 1948), vi.

17. *Stage* (playbill), November 1940, Royale Theater, 10; Roll 1, *New York City News*, October 4, 1940.

18. Gelernter, *1939*, 11; Todd and Todd, *A Valuable Property*, 70.

19. Roll 2, Lloyd Lewis, "Mike Todd, The General Boniface," *New York Times*, January 19, 1941, GRL Papers, NYPL; Todd and Todd, *A Valuable Property*, 70.

20. Todd and Todd, *A Valuable Property*, 70; Roll 1, Charlie Dawn, "Mike Todd's Theatre-Café; His Brilliant Premier," *Chicago Herald-American*, n.d.; Ward March, "Gypsy Rose Lee Steals Theater," no header, GRL Papers, NYPL.

21. Roll 1, Prepublication Letter to Publishers, Letter to Lee Wright, Oriental Theatre, Chicago, March 5, 1941; Fairmont Hotel, Nob Hill, San Francisco, May 15, 1941; Fairmont Hotel, Nob Hill, San Francisco, June 16, 1941; Hotel Onondaga, Syracuse, New York, August 28, 1941, GRL Papers, NYPL.

22. Roll 1, Prepublication Letter to Publishers, Letter to Lee Wright, Fairmont Hotel, Nob Hill, San Francisco, May 15, 1941, GRL Papers, NYPL.

23. Todd and Todd, *A Valuable Property*, 76.

24. Georgia Sothern, *Georgia: My Life in Burlesque* (New York: New American Library, 1972), 344–48.

25. Erik Lee Preminger, *Gypsy & Me* (Boston: Little, Brown, 1984), 60; Todd and Todd, *A Valuable Property*, 78–79; Art Cohn, *The Nine Lives of Michael Todd* (New York: Random House, 1958), 143; Sothern, *Georgia*, 350.

26. Todd and Todd, *A Valuable Property*, 79.

27. Linn, "Mike Todd," 63.

28. "I Can't Strip to Brahms" (Cabot, Lee), on *Gypsy Rose Lee: That's Me All Over*, phonograph record, Westminster Stereo Corp., WST 15040, n.d.

29. Roll 4, Gilbert Seldes, "Those Star and Garter Blues," no header, GRL Papers, NYPL.

30. Roll 3, "Expectant Publisher," no header, GRL Papers, NYPL.

31. Roll 4, "New York Stages in Throes," *Sunday News*, November 15, 1942, GRL Papers, NYPL.

32. Roll 3, cartoon by Daniel "Alain" Brustlein, GRL Papers, NYPL.

33. "Star and Garter: Rowdy Fun and Well-Fed Beauties Make a Rich Man's Burlesque Show," *Life*, July 27, 1942, 63.

34. Louis Hochman, "The Mechanix of Gypsy Rose Lee," *Mechanix Illustrated*, June 1943, 46–50, 145.

35. Todd and Todd, *A Valuable Property*, 79, 143; Roll 4, Louis Sobel, *Cavalcade*, February 20, 1943, GRL Papers, NYPL.

36. Richard E. Lauterbach, "Gypsy Rose Lee: She Combines a Public Body with a Private Mind," *Life*, December 14, 1942, 101; Morton Cooper, "Profile of a Character: Gypsy Rose Lee," *Modern Man*, September 1959, 56; Roll 4, Elizabeth Wilson, "Gypsy's Back in Hollywood," no header, GRL Papers, NYPL.

37. Havoc, *More Havoc*, 228.

Chapter 11

1. Art Cohn, *The Nine Lives of Michael Todd* (New York: Random House, 1958), 113; Erik Lee Preminger, *Gypsy & Me* (Boston: Little, Brown, 1984), 57.

2. C. David Heymann, *Liz: An Intimate Biography of Elizabeth Taylor* (New York: Birch Lane Press, 1995), 152.

3. Excerpts from Todd's FBI file, 149-12170-1, from Cohn, *Nine Lives of Michael Todd*, 150, rpt. in *New York Herald Tribune*, November 25, 1958.

4. Series I, Subseries 3, General, Box 7, Folder 7, From Gypsy to Dick Williams, August 9, 1942; Subseries 1, Personal, Box 3, Folder 8, Telegrams from Mike Todd, GRL Papers, NYPL.

5. Cohn, *The Nine Lives of Michael Todd*, 356–57.

6. Roll 6, "Eyes Are Piercing," no header, GRL Papers, NYPL.

7. Todd's FBI file, 149-12170-1.

8. "Hovick-Kirkland: Miss Gypsy Rose Lee, Author, Weds Broadway Actor," *Life*, September 14, 1942, 41–44; "The Wedding of Gypsy Rose Lee," *Spot*, November 1942, 11; Roll 3, Elizabeth Wilson, "Triumph with Torso and Typewriter," *This Week's Liberty*, March 24, 1945, GRL Papers, NYPL; Letter to Annie from Gypsy Rose Lee, n.d., private collection of Charles Mosberger.

9. Series I, Subseries 1, Personal, Box 3, Folder 8, Mike Todd, ca. 1930–46, Telegram, January 24, 1943, GRL Papers, NYPL.

10. Gladys Hall, "The Things I Want: As Revealed by Gypsy Rose Lee," *Personal Romances*, November 1944, 58; Roll 3, "Gypsy Rose and Muse," *Cue*, July 17, 1943, GRL Papers, NYPL.

11. Series I, Subseries 1, Personal, Box 2, Folder 9, From June Havoc (Julia) to Gyp, December 1942, GRL Papers, NYPL.

12. Series VI, Writings, Boxes 3 and 4, *The Ghost in the Woodpile*, GRL Papers, NYPL.

13. June Havoc, *More Havoc* (New York: Harper & Row, 1980), 252; Roll 4, Earl Wilson, "Not So Mad Mike," GRL Papers, NYPL.

14. Roll 4, Marion Leslie, "Gypsy Rose Lee Sighs over Her 'Naked Genius,'" *New York Evening Sun*, October 5, 1943, GRL Papers, NYPL.

15. Series VI, Writings, Box 44, *Naked Genius*, Folders 1, 2, draft of *The Ghost in the Woodpile*, GRL Papers, NYPL.

16. Roll 4, Elliot Worton, "Gypsy Rose Lee's 'The Naked Genius' Could be Better," no header, GRL Papers, NYPL.

17. Roll 4, Elinor Hughes, "Lee Comedy Misses, 'Kiss and Tell' Good as Ever," no header, GRL Papers, NYPL.

18. Series VI, Writings, Box 44, Folder 8, Correspondence, *Naked Genius*, From Gypsy to George S. Kaufman; Folder 9, From Gypsy to Todd, n.d., GRL Papers, NYPL.

19. Preminger, *Gypsy & Me*, 64; Richard Gehman, "A Visit with Gypsy: Meet the Best Undressed Woman of Our Time," *Star Weekly*, October 22, 1960, 10.

20. Cohn, *The Nine Lives of Michael Todd* 172; Preminger, *Gypsy & Me*, 63.

21. Todd and Todd, *A Valuable Property*, 108; Roll 4, Review from *New Yorker*, n.d., GRL Papers, NYPL.

22. Todd and Todd, *A Valuable Property*, 107.

23. Roll 3, "The Theater: Todd's in His Heaven," *Time*, November 8, 1943, GRL Papers, NYPL; "Naked Genius," *Life*, November 15, 1943, 49–50, 52; Todd and Todd, *A Valuable Property*, 107–8.

24. Havoc, *More Havoc*, 270; Gehman, "A Visit with Gypsy," 25; Todd and Todd, A Valuable Property, 108.

25. Todd and Todd, *A Valuable Property*, 107–8; Roll 4, Robert Garland, *New York Journal American*, October 22, GRL Papers, NYPL; Cohn, *The Nine Lives of Michael Todd*, 175.

26. Scott Meredith, *George S. Kaufman and His Friends* (New York: Doubleday, 1974), 582; Cohn, *The Nine Lives of Michael Todd*, 175.

27. Cohn, *The Nine Lives of Michael Todd*, 356.

28. Series I, Subseries 3, General, Box 7, Folder 7, From Gypsy to Richard Haydn, May 18, 1942; Roll 3, Hyman Goldman, "Keeping Up with Gypsy Rose Lee...New Address Secret to Foil Jerks," *PM*, n.d.; Roll 4, clipping, no header, November 10, 1943; Roll 3, Elizabeth B. Peterson, "Education for a Home Girl—Surprising Slant on Gypsy Rose Lee," no header, GRL Papers, NYPL; Preminger, *Gypsy & Me*, 23, 63, 65; Havoc, *More Havoc*, 270; "Gypsy Rose Lee House," *House & Garden*, December 1943, 66–70, 106–7.

29. Roll 4, Mel Heimer, "Sisters, and Now So Polite: How Gypsy and June Became Reconciled to Living in Same 24-Room Bungalow," no header, GRL Papers, NYPL.

30. Roll 4, "Mama Stripped of Aid? Never, Says Gypsy Rose," *New York World Telegram*, May 12, 1943, GRL Papers, NYPL.

31. Roll 4, Walter Winchell, "In New York," no header; "Mama Stripped of Aid? Never, Says Gypsy," *New York World Telegram*, May 12, 1943, GRL Papers, NYPL.

32. The correspondence is in Series I, Subseries 1, Personal, Box 1, GRL Papers, NYPL.

33. Series I, Subseries 1, Personal, Box 1, Folder 11, From Gypsy, Belvedere, Baltimore, Maryland, to Mother, October 6, 1943, GRL Papers, NYPL.

34. Roll 3, Hyman Goldman, "Keeping Up with Gypsy Rose Lee...New Address Secret to Foil Jerks," *PM*, n.d., GRL Papers, NYPL.

35. Elia Kazan, *Elia Kazan: A Life* (New York: Knopf, 1988), 457, 331.

36. H. William Fitelson, ed., *Theatre Guild on the Air* (New York: Rinehart, 1947), xi.

Chapter 12

1. Roll 3, Derek Barat, "$3000 a Week for Taking Her Clothes Off," *Tid Bit*, September 8, 1951, GRL Papers, NYPL.

2. Linda Patterson, *Letters from the Lost Generation: Gerald and Sara Murphy and Friends* (New Brunswick: Rutgers University Press, 1991), 228.

3. Carl Rollyson, *Lillian Hellman: Her Legend and Her Legacy* (New York: St. Martin's Press, 1988), 163.

4. Series 1, Subseries 3, General, Box 7, Folder 6, From Arthur Pollack, *Brooklyn Eagle*, Brooklyn, New York, to Gypsy, November 20, 1942; Series II, Subseries 6, Red Ties, Box 19, Folder 1, GRL Papers, NYPL.

5. Rachel Shteir, *Striptease: The Untold History of the Girlie Show* (New York: Oxford University Press, 2004), 159; Gypsy Rose Lee, *The G-String Murders* (New York: Pocket Books, 1947), 43, 91.

6. Letter to Selectee from Gypsy, Amusement Headquarters, New York, July 10, 1941, *Jest: The Zest of Life*, September 1941, 15.

7. Gypsy Rose Lee, "They Need It for Bullets!" *Mademoiselle*, May 1943, rpt. in R. M. Barrows, comp., *Home Was Never Like This! An Anthology* (Chicago: Consolidated Book Publishers, 1944).

8. Series II, Subseries 6, Red Ties, Box 19, Folder 1, *Kansas City Star*, September 5, 1938, GRL Papers, NYPL.

9. Series V, Subseries 1, Benefits & Contribution, Box 28, Folder 7, Treasury Department, Washington, D.C., March 20, 1945, From Julian Street Jr., Consultant, Office of the Secretary, Treasury Department, to Gypsy, GRL Papers, NYPL.

10. Morton Cooper, "Profile of a Character: Gypsy Rose Lee," *Modern Man*, September 1959, 56.

11. "Gypsy Rose Lee: She Takes It Off for Charity," *Sir*! August 1942, 12–13.

12. "U.S. Balls, Brawls, Pageants, Parades Turn War Relief into Show Business," *Life*, January 6, 1941, 15, 19; *Life*, Letters to the Editor, January 27, 1941, 2.

13. Series 1, Subseries 3, General, Box 7, Folder 7, From Gypsy to Harry Braun, June 23, 1943, GRL Papers, NYPL; Letter to Annie Doll [Winslow] from Gypsy Rose Lee, n.d., private collection; Gypsy Rose Lee, "What's New in War-Wolves," *Mademoiselle*, March 1943, 110–11, 161–63.

14. Roll 4, Sgt. Roper, "Gypsy Rose Lee Strips in Style as GI Cast Shares Applause," *Del Valle News*, Bergstrom Field, Austin, Texas, February 7, 1944, GRL Papers, NYPL.

15. Series II, Subseries 6, Red Ties, Box 19, Folder 1, Camp Tour, December 1943; Roll 4, Jane Fuller, "One Woman Show," no header, GRL Papers, NYPL.

16. Roll 4, Sgt. Roper, "Gypsy Rose Lee Strips in Style as GI Cast Shares Applause," *Del Valle News*, Bergstrom Field, Austin, Texas, February 7, 1944, GRL Papers, NYPL.

17. Letter to Annie Doll [Winslow] from Gypsy Rose Lee, n.d., private collection; Series V, Subseries 1, Benefits & Contributions, Box 28, Folder 6, To Jack, December 1943, GRL Papers, NYPL.

18. Series I, Subseries 3, General, Box 7, Folder 10, Program for Gypsy Rose Lee in Person, Friday night, January 28, 1944, Gunter Field, Alabama, GRL Papers, NYPL.

19. Series V, Subseries 1, Benefits & Contributions, Box 28, Folder 3, GRL Papers, NYPL.

20. Roll 6, "Gypsy Rose Lee on Life, Strife—And Women 'Around Forty,'" no header; Roll 4, Robbin Coons, "Clues Tease Gypsy Rose Lee," *Rushville Indiana Telegram*, May 11, 1944; Roll 3, Jane Fuller, "One Woman Show," *Fort Bragg Post*, Fort Bragg, North Carolina, January 19, 1944; Roll 4, Sgt. Roper, "Gypsy Rose Lee, Strips in Style as GI Cast Shares Applause," *Del Valle News*, Bergstrom Field, Austin, Texas, February 7, 1944, GRL Papers, NYPL.

21. James M. Gavin, *On to Berlin: Battles of an Airborne Commander, 1943–1946* (New York: Viking Press, 1978), 5.

Chapter 13

1. Leslie Halliwell, *Halliwell's Film Guide* (New York: Charles Scribner's Sons, 1983), 769.

2. *Stage Door Canteen*, directed by Frank Borzage, produced by Sol Lessor, 1943; Letter from Gypperola to Annie Winslow, n.d., private collection of Chuck Mosberger.

3. Roll 3, *New Republic*, July 26, 1943; Roll 4, Ed Sullivan, "New York," no header, GRL Papers, NYPL.

4. Roll 4, Earl Wilson, "It Happened One Night," *New York Post*, June 16, 1944, GRL Papers, NYPL.

5. Series 1, Subseries 3, General, Box 7, Folder 9, From H. William Fitelson to Gypsy, March 30, 1944, GRL Papers, NYPL.

6. "Belle of the Yukon," *Movie Story Magazine*, January 1945, 50–53, 89–90.

7. Gladys Hall, "The Things I Want: As Revealed by Gypsy Rose Lee," *Personal Romances*, November 1944, 5; Roll 4, *Hollywood Reporter*, November 29, 1944; "Belle of the Yukon," no header, GRL Papers, NYPL.

8. Roll 4, Gypsy Rose Lee, "A 'Belle' Peels," by Gypsy Rose Lee, June 3, 1945, GRL Papers, NYPL.

9. Roll 4, Louise Hovick, "G String Forgot," *Los Angeles Times*, May 7, 1944, GRL Papers, NYPL; Hall, "The Things I Want," 59.

10. Series 1, Subseries 3, General, Box 7, Folder 2, Rags Ragland, The Emerson, Baltimore, May 27, 1936, GRL Papers, NYPL; June Havoc, *More Havoc* (New York: Harper & Row, 1980), 103–4.

11. Malcolm Forbes with Jeff Bloch, *What Happened to Their Kids: Children of the Rich and Famous* (New York: Simon & Schuster, 1990), 153.

12. Willi Frischauer, *Behind the Scenes of Otto Preminger: An Unauthorized Biography* (New York: William Morrow, 1974), 91, 95.

13. Letter to Anne Winslow, April 6, 1944, private collection of Chuck Mosberger.

14. Erik Lee Preminger, *Gypsy & Me* (Boston: Little, Brown, 1984), 258, 95–96. Forbes, *What Happened to Their Kids*, 153.

15. Series I, Subseries 3, General, Box 7, Folder 9, Letter in response to Gwen, Tom Firzdale, Inc., Pubic Relations, 485 Madison Avenue, June 1944, New York, GRL Papers, NYPL.

16. Series 1, Subseries 1, Personal, Box 1, Folder 4, From Bill Kirkland, 1355 Miller Drive, Hollywood, to Dear Gypsy, November 6, 1944; Preminger, *Gypsy & Me*, 48.

17. Roll 4, "Gypsy Rose Lee Discusses Maternity," no header, GRL Papers, NYPL.

18. Ibid.

19. Thomas Blair, "What Gypsy Rose Didn't Tell in 'Gypsy,' " *Uncensored*, January 1960, 54, 56; Roll 4, "Gypsy Rose Lee Discusses Maternity," no header, GRL Papers, NYPL.

20. Shana Alexander, *Happy Days: My Mother, My Father, My Sister and Me* (New York: Doubleday, 1995), 198.

21. Roll 3, Elizabeth Wilson, "Triumph with Torso and Typewriter," *This Week's Liberty*, March 24, 1945, GRL Papers, NYPL.

22. Roll 4, "Gypsy Rose Lee Discusses Maternity," no header, GRL Papers, NYPL.

23. Roll 4, "Nothing Stopping Good Old Gypola," *Milwaukee Journal*, March 4, 1945, GRL Papers, NYPL.

24. Roll 3, "Gypsy's Ex Wed as Son Is Born," *New York Daily News*, n.d., GRL Papers, NYPL.

25. Preminger, *Gypsy & Me*, 258.

26. Forbes with Bloch, *What Happened to Their Kids*, 153; Frischauer, *Behind the Scenes*, 93.

27. Letters from Rose: Series I, Subseries 1, Personal, Box 1, Folder 11, Hotel Plymouth, New York, 49th Street, to Louise, November 4, 1944; Hotel Plymouth, to both June and Louise, November 21, 1944, GRL Papers, NYPL.

28. Letters from Rose: Series I, Subseries 1, Personal, Box 1, Folder 11, Hotel Plymouth, to Louise, December 19, 1944; Plymouth Hotel, n.d. [probably December 16, 1944]; Folder 12, To Louise, August 18, 1945; To Louise, September 23, 1945; To Louise, September 27, 1945, GRL Papers, NYPL.

29. Roll 3, Elizabeth Wilson, "Triumph with Torso and Typewriter," *This Week's Liberty*, March 24, 1945, GRL Papers, NYPL.

30. Roll 4, Fred D. Moon, "Gypsy Vociferous but Beautiful," *Atlanta Journal*, March 30, 1945; Roll 3, Elizabeth Wilson, "Triumph with Torso and Typewriter," *This Week's Liberty*, March 24, 1945, GRL Papers, NYPL.

31. "A Newly Maternal Gypsy Rose Lee Pins Up Her Son Eric," photograph, *Life*, February 19, 1945, 28–29. *Life*, Letters to Editor, March 12, 1945, 8.

32. John J. McAleer, *Rex Stout: A Biography* (Boston: Little, Brown, 1977), 335.

33. Roll 4, Inez Robb, "Gypsy Rose Back—Will Peel Off Her Own to Keep Baby in Clothing," no header; "Gypsy Rose Just 'Takes Off' Burley-Que in Act at Fox," *Atlanta Constitution*, March 20, 1945; "Gypsy Rose Lee Discusses Maternity," no header, GRL Papers, NYPL.

34. "Scrapbook Views of a Smart Stripper," *Life*, May 27, 1957, 106; Roll 4, Hedda Hopper, "Looking at Hollywood," no header, May 27, 1946, GRL Papers, NYPL.

35. Roll 4, Inez Robb, "Gypsy Rose Back—Will Peel Off Her Own to Keep Baby in Clothing," no header; Roll 5, "Gypsy Rose Corset Talk," *Tide*, May 5, 1950, GRL Papers, NYPL.

36. Roll 4, *Buffalo Courier Express*, February 15, 1946; "Gypsy Rose Here," no header, GRL Papers, NYPL.

37. Roll 5, Earl Wilson, "It Happened One Night," *New York Post*, January 22, 1948; Roll 4, "Night Life Note Book," *Sunday Times*, April 21, 1946, GRL Papers, NYPL.

38. Roll 4, "She's Wedged in Small Strip," *Milwaukee Journal*, July 17, 1946; "'Stripping and Literature Don't Mix,' Gypsy Finds," *Baltimore Evening Sun*, April 16, 1946, GRL Papers, NYPL.

39. "Julio De Diego: He Paints Weird War and Peace," *Life*, March 11, 1946, 80–82.

Chapter 14

1. Roll 3, Alonzo Landsford, "Gypsy Rose by Another Name," *Kirkeby Hotel Magazine*, November 1948, GRL Papers, NYPL.

2. Roll 5, Sarah Worth, "Gypsy Rose, Her Appetite Comes to Tampa for the Fair," *Tampa Daily Times*, February 8, 1949, GRL Papers, NYPL; Erik Lee Preminger, *Gypsy & Me* (Boston: Little, Brown, 1984), 206–7; "From Woolworth Tower," *Time*, February 1, 1954.

3. "The New Gypsy Rose Lee: She Is a Dynamo Without Direction," *Look*, September 28, 1948, 46; Roger Kahn, "Strip Teaser: The Ups and Downs of Gypsy Rose Lee," *Real: The Exciting Magazine for Men*, November 1956, 64.

4. Roll 5, Myles Standish, "Know What It Takes to Be Stripteaser? Brains, That's What It Takes, Says the One and Only Gypsy Rose Lee, Pointing to Her Forehead," no header, May 20, 1949, GRL Papers, NYPL.

5. Jerome Klein et al., eds., *Artists Against War and Fascism: Papers of the First American Artists' Congress*, introduction by Matthew Baigell and Julia Williams (New Brunswick, N.J.: Rutgers University Press, 1986; orig. pub. 1936), 48.

6. Roll 5, "Wedding Bells to 'Peel' for Gypsy and No. 3," *Daily Mirror*, March 12, 1948; GRL Papers, NYPL.

7. Ibid.; "Gypsy Rose Lee's New Role," *American Weekly*, May 23, 1948, 4.

8. Preminger, *Gypsy & Me*, 206.

9. Gladys Hall, "The Things I Want: As Revealed by Gypsy Rose Lee," *Personal Romances*, November 1944, 28–29, 58–59.

10. "Gypsy Rose Lee's New Role," 4.

11. "Gypsy Joins the 'Carny,'" *Life*, June 6, 1949, 145; Preminger, *Gypsy & Me*, 48, 206.

12. Roll 3, Patricia Coffin, "When Is a Kitchen Not a Kitchen," *Waldorf-Astoria [Magazine] on New York*, January 1950, GRL Papers, NYPL; "Gypsy Rose Lee's New Role," 4.

13. "People vs. People," *People Today*, July 15, 1953, 42.

14. "Gypsy Rose Lee's New Role," 4.

15. Ibid.

16. Gypsy Rose Lee, "I Was with It," *Flair*, June 1950, 72.

17. Ibid.

18. "Gypsy Joins the 'Carny,'" 141.

19. Lee, "I Was with It," 72; Roll 5, Myles Standish, "Know What It Takes to Be Stripteaser? Brains, That's What It Takes, Says the One and Only Gypsy Rose Lee, Pointing to Her Forehead," no header, May 20, 1949, GRL Papers, NYPL.

20. Lee, "I Was with It," 72–73.

21. Ibid., 85; Roll 3, Jack Kytle, "All About Meeting with Gypsy Rose Lee," *Byways of Birmingham*, GRL Papers, NYPL.

22. Roll 3, Bruce Peacock, "Strip Tease in Reverse," no header, GRL Papers, NYPL; Lee, "I Was with It," glossary.

23. Series I, Subseries 1, Personal, Box 2, Folder 13, From Gypsy, Edmonton, to Honey [probably Julio, n.d.], GRL Papers, NYPL; "Gypsy Joins the 'Carny,'" 143; Letters to Editor, *Life*, June 27, 1949.

24. Lee, "I Was with It," 74.

25. Roll 5, Ron C. Day, *Mirror of the Davenport Agency*, June 20, 1949; Roll 3, "Gypsy Grinds Out Merry Midway Modes," *Pittsburgh Post-Gazette*, May 9, 1949, GRL Papers, NYPL.

26. Roll 3, "Gypsy Grinds Out Merry Midway Modes," *Pittsburgh Post-Gazette*, May 9, 1949, GRL Papers, NYPL.

27. Roll 5, Myles Standish, "Know What It Takes to Be Stripteaser? Brains, That's What It Takes, Says the One and Only Gypsy Rose Lee, Pointing to Her Forehead," no header, May 20, 1949; Ron Pouton, "Burlesque Net Gypsy $1000 a Week," no header, GRL Papers, NYPL.

28. Roll 5, Myles Standish, "Know What It Takes to Be Stripteaser? Brains, That's What It Takes, Says the One and Only Gypsy Rose Lee, Pointing to Her Forehead," no header, May 20, 1949, GRL Papers, NYPL.

29. Lee, "I Was with It," 75.

30. Roll 3, "Censors Clear Gypsy Rose Lee," *Minneapolis Morning Tribune*, August 27, 1949, GRL Papers, NYPL.

31. Ibid.; "State Fair Okays Gypola but Censors Artist Mate for Exhibit," *Variety*, August 31, 1949, GRL Papers, NYPL.

32. Series I, Subseries 1, Personal, Box 2, Folder 13, From Gypsy, Winnipeg, to Julio, n.d, GRL Papers, NYPL.

33. Series I, Subseries 1, Personal, Box 2, Folder 13, Gypsy's Letters on Carnival Trip; Roll 3, "Gypsy Takes Off…A Few Minutes to Tell How She Envies Fisherman," no header, August 29, 1949, GRL Papers, NYPL.

34. Howard Byrne, "How Long Can a Body Last?" *Salute*, April 1947, 36–37.

Chapter 15

1. Roll 5, "Gypsy Rose Lee, MC," *New York Times*, December 24. 1950; "Gypsy Rose Lee Is Preparing to Embrace Video," *Chicago Daily Tribune*, August 29, 1950; PoMo, "TV Guest Star," no header, GRL Papers, NYPL.

2. Roll 5, "It's a Big Illusion, Whether Done on Strip or on the Mike," *Variety*, September 6, 1950, GRL Papers, NYPL.

3. Roll 5, "Gypsy Rose Lee, MC," *New York Times*, December 24, 1950; Roll 3, Associated Press, *Cincinnati Enquirer, Los Angeles Mirror*, no headers, GRL Papers, NYPL.

4. Ellen Schrecker, *Many Are the Crimes: McCarthyism in America* (Boston: Little, Brown, 1998), 44, 75, 126, 214, 218.

5. Ibid., 44, 218.

6. Roll 5, Ted Poston, "Equity Blasts 'Smear' Firing of Jean Muir," *New York Post*, September 13, 1950, GRL Papers, NYPL.

7. American Business Consultants, *Red Channels: The Report of Communist Influence in Radio and Television* (New York: *Counterattack*, 1950), 98–99.

8. Roll 5, "State Legion Assails Gypsy Lee as Pro Red," no header; "Gypsy Rose Denies She's Pal of Traitors," *Chicago Herald American*, n.d.; Series II, Subseries 6, Red Ties, Box 19, Folder 1, Gypsy's statement denying membership in Communist Party, September 1950, GRL Papers, NYPL.

9. Series II, Subseries 6, Red Ties, Box 19, Folder 2, From Gypsy Rose Lee to Att. Mr. Robert Kintner, President, American Broadcasting Company, Inc., 30 Rockefeller Plaza, New York, September 15, 1950; Roll 5, Ted Poston, "Equity Blasts 'Smear' Firing of Jean Muir," *New York Post*, September 13, 1950, GRL Papers, NYPL.

10. Patrick McGilligan and Paul Buhle, *Tender Comrades: A Backstory of the Hollywood Blacklist* (New York: St. Martin's Griffin, 1997), 319.

11. Series II, Subseries 6, Red Ties, Box 19, Folder 1, *San Francisco Chronicle*, June 25, 1941; Roll 2: *Davenport Times*, June 24, 1941, GRL Papers, NYPL.

12. Roll 3, Terence Robertson, "Queen of the Striptease," *Reynolds News*, n.d.; Roll 5, "The Accused," *Time*, September 17, 1950, GRL Papers, NYPL

13. "Artists Blast 'Red' Charges," *Daily Compass*, September 12, 1950; Roll 3, unidentified clipping; Roll 5, Jack Gould, "Legion Won't Back Lee Case Charges," no header; "Vigilantes of the Air," *Washington Post*, GRL Papers, NYPL.

14. Roll 5, Irving Hirsch, "When Gypsy Rose Lee Goes into Action, Her Union Takes Notice," *Union Courier*, May 7, 1951; "AGVA Raised Dues Taxes Employers," *Trade Union Courier*, June 19, 1950; Series II, Subseries 6, Red Ties, Box 19, Folder 1, Gypsy's statement denying membership in Communist Party, September 1950, GRL Papers, NYPL.

15. Bernard Sobel, *Broadway Heartbeat: Memoirs of a Press Agent* (New York: Hermitage House, 1953), 133; Roll 3, *Extra*, n.d. May, GRL Papers, NYPL.

16. Series II, Subseries 6, Red Ties, Box 19, Folder 1, Gypsy's statement denying membership in Communist Party, September 1950, GRL Papers, NYPL.

17. Series II, Subseries 6, Red Ties, Box 19, Folder 1, *Daily Worker*, April 30, 1937, GRL Papers, NYPL.

18. Elaine Tyler May, *Homeward Bound: American Families in the Cold War Era* (New York: Basic Books, 1988).

19. Jeff Kisseloff, *The Box: An Oral History of Television, 1920–1961* (New York: Viking, 1995), 417; Karen Sue Foley, *The Political Blacklist in the Broadcast Industry: The Decade of the 1950's* (New York: Arno Press, 1979), 167–68.

20. Roll 6, Oliver Pilat, "Blacklist: The Panic in TV-Radio," *New York Post*, January 26, 1953; "A Reporter's Service," *Variety*, April 29, 1953, GRL Papers, NYPL.

21. Roll 5, Leonard Lyons, "The Lyons Den," *New York Post*, n.d., GRL Papers, NYPL.

22. Roll 3, Hanner Swaffre, "They Think Dollars Can Be Wasted on Strip-tease," *The People*, July 8, 1951, GRL Papers, NYPL.

23. Roll 5, "No, No, Not Our Gypsy," *Milwaukee Journal*, September 13, 1950; "Gypsy's Past Bared," *New York Post*, September 13, 1950, GRL Papers, NYPL.

24. Series II, Subseries 6, Red Ties, Box 19, Folder 2, Jack T. Edwards, 120 Boylston St., Boston, September 13, 1950; Rudolph A. Vasalle, Attorney at Law, Suite 1308–1310, 134 North Lasalle Street, Chicago, to Gypsy Rose Lee, American Broadcasting Plaza, RCA Building Plaza, New York, September 12, 1950, GRL Papers, NYPL.

25. John Cogley, *Report on Blacklisting: I—Movies* (New York Fund for the Republic, Inc., 1956), 4–5.

26. Roll 5, Ted Poston, "Equity Blasts 'Smear' Firing of Jean Muir," *New York Post*, September 13, 1950; "GF (General Foods), Red Book Take Beatings from Unions," no header, GRL Papers, NYPL.

27. Series II, Subseries 6, Red Ties, Box 19, Folder 2, Letter from Patrick Murphy Main, Executive Director, American Civil Liberties Union, 170 Fifth Avenue, New York, to Miss Gypsy Rose Lee, 153 E. 63rd St., New York, October 9, 1950; H. William Fitelson, Law Offices Fitelson and Mayers, 673 Fifth Avenue, New York, to Gypsy Rose Lee, 153 E. 63rd St., New York, October 19, 1950, GRL Papers, NYPL; Foley, *The Political Blacklist in the Broadcast Industry*, 282.

28. Series II, Subseries 6, Box 19, Red Ties, Folder 2, Mrs. Louis H. Harris, Director, Americans for Democratic Action, National Arts Division, 9 East 46th Street, New York, to Gypsy Rose Lee, 153 East 63rd St., New York, October 30, 1950, GRL Papers, NYPL.

29. Series II, Subseries 6, Red Ties, Box 19, Folder 2, Memo, "Dear Friend," Working Committee, GRL Papers, NYPL.

30. Series III, Legal, Box 23, Series 3, Folder 4, H. William Fitelson to Gypsy, October 9, 1950; Roll 6, "Gypsy Rose Lee," CCNY *Mercury*, n.d., GRL Papers, NYPL.

31. Elia Kazan, *Elia Kazan: A Life* (New York: Knopf, 1988), 457–58: H. William Fitelson, FBI file, 0965009–000.

32. William L. Shirer, *A Native's Return, 1945–1988* (Boston: Little, Brown, 1990), 165; Foley, *The Political Blacklist in the Broadcast Industry*, 282–94.

33. Series III, Legal, Box 23, Folder 4, Letters on Brazilian Gypsy Rose Lee, GRL Papers, NYPL.

34. Eugene Pawley, "Strip Tease Intellectual," *Cabaret*, July 1955. Series III, Legal, Box 23, Folder 6, Fitelson's letters on *Cabaret* article; Roll 1, John Richmond, "Gypsy Rose Lee, Striptease Intellectual," *American Mercury*, January 1941, GRL Papers, NYPL.

35. Roll 5, Marie Torre, *New York World Telegram and Sun*, April 21, 1951, GRL Papers, NYPL.

36. Roll 5, *Look*, April 21, 1951, GRL Papers, NYPL.

37. Roll 5, "Salute to Josephine Baker," no header, GRL Papers, NYPL.

38. Excerpt from *The Big Show*, January 21, 1951, available at: www.wtv zone.com/lumina/radio/judytallu1.html.

39. Roll 5, Victor Reisel, "Inside Labor," *Daily Mirror,* October 19, 1950, GRL Papers, NYPL.

40. Roll 5, *New York Post*, September 13, 1950, GRL Papers, NYPL.

41. Roll 5, "Gypsy Rose Lee Rehearsal About to Go to Europe," *Carasol*, Pittsburgh, June 25, 1951; Roll 6, Frank O'Neill, "Gypsy Rose Pulls a Veil over Her Strip-Tease Act," *Sunday Telegraph*, September 26, 1954, GRL Papers, NYPL.

Chapter 16

1. Roll 6, Frank O'Neill, "Gypsy Rose Pulls a Veil over Her Strip-Tease Act," *Sunday Telegraph*, September 26, 1954; Roll 3, Nancy Baume, "Gypsy

Rose, Authoress and Angler," *The Western Mail*, August 1951, GRL Papers, NYPL; "Gypsy's New Leaf," *People Today*, September 24, 1952, 16.

2. Roll 6 and Roll 3, "Gypsy Tea," no header, New York, March 1953, GRL Papers, NYPL; Hotel Malmen, Stockholm, Sweden, From Gypsy to Anna Della Winslow, 206 E. 57th Street, New York, U.S.A., private collection of Charles Mosberger.

3. To Annie Doll from Gypola, Grand Hotel, Satsjobaden, private collection of Charles Mosberger.

4. Roll 6, "Gypsy Tea," no header, New York, March 1953; Roll 5, "Gypsy Rose Told to Dress by January," *Daily News*, July 31, 1952; *Evening Citizen*, Glasgow, September 4, 1951; John Harvey, "Stripteaser," *Reynolds News*, August 3, 1952, GRL Papers, NYPL.

5. Roll 5, "Too Much of Miss Lee's Mind," *Birmingham Gazette*, n.d.; Roll 6 and Roll 3, "Gypsy Tea," no header, New York, March 1953; Roll 5, Art Buchwald, "Banned in Germany," *New York Herald Tribune*, Paris, September 27, 1951, GRL Papers, NYPL.

6. Roll 6 and Roll 3, "Gypsy Tea," no header, New York, March 1953, Roll 5, Robert Ahier, "'I Could Teach Them a Lot,' Gypsy Yawns at French Shows," no header, GRL Papers, NYPL.

7. Ibid.

8. Roll 3, "Paris: Gypsy Rose Lee Learns Naked Truth," no header, October 20, 1957, GRL Papers, NYPL.

9. Roll 5, Art Buchwald, "Banned in Germany," *New York Herald Tribune*, Paris, September 27, 1951; Robert Ahier, "'I Could Teach Them a Lot,' Gypsy Yawns at French Shows," no header; Roll 3, "Gypsy Banned from Performing for American Armed Forces in Europe," *New York Post*, September 14, 1951, GRL Papers, NYPL.

10. Roll 6, Margaret Wynn, "Gal Has to Give Up Clothes for Rolls Royce, Gypsy Says," Buffalo, March 2, [1953], GRL Papers, NYPL; Erik Lee Preminger, *Gypsy & Me* (Boston: Little, Brown, 1984), 44.

11. Postcard to Anna Della Winslow, 206 E. 57th Street, New York, from Gypsy, Versailles Seine-et Olae, Le Chateau et l'Orangerie, The Palace and the Orangery, Northern Window, private collection of Charles Mosberger; Roll 5, unidentified clipping, probably late July or early August 1951; "From Strip-tease to History," *Nottingham Evening Post*, August 5, 1952, GRL Papers, NYPL.

12. Series V, Subseries 1, Professional Work/Engagement, Benefits & Contribution, Box 28, Folder 13, Variety Artists Ladies' Guild & Orphanage, 18 Charing Cross Road, July 29, 1952, GRL Papers, NYPL.

13. Roll 3, "Gypsy Discusses Cats, Books, Wardrobe," *Fall River* (Mass.) *Herald News*, August 5, 1956, GRL Papers, NYPL.

14. Roll 6, George Jackson, "'Babes in Baghdad' Is Fluffy Screen Item," no header; Ed Sullivan, "Little Old New York," no header, February 8, 1953, GRL Papers, NYPL.

15. United Artists Press Book for *Babes in Baghdad*, author's collection, 9.

16. Roll 6, "Stripper's Visit Harmful," no header; "A Coy 'Stripsy Gypsy' Won't Drop Even a Hint," no header; Frank O'Neill, "Gypsy Rose Pulls a Veil over Her Strip-Tease Act," *Sunday Telegraph*, September 26, 1954; "Gypsy's Nudes Hit by Prudes," no header; "Gypsy Claims She's a Real Goodie, Goodie," no header; "Gypsy Rose Lee Talks on Life, Strife—And Women 'Around Forty,'" no header; Roll 3, "Gypsy Rose Lee Gives Nothing Away," *Sidney* (Australia) *Sun*, September 25, 1954, GRL Papers, NYPL.

17. Roll 6, "Aussie Show Girls' Attire Shocks US Strip Teaser," *Bangkok Post*, October 20, 1954.

18. Series II, Subseries 1, Appointment Calendar, Box 10, Folder 5, September 26, 1954.

19. David I. Zeitlin and Harriet Zeitlin, *Shooting Stars: Favorite Photos Taken by Classic Celebrities* (Los Angeles: General Publishing Group, 1998), 176–181.

20. Roger Kahn, "Strip Teaser: The Ups and Downs of Gypsy Rose Lee," *Real: The Exciting Magazine for Men*, November 1956, 64; Roll 6, "Gypsy Rose Lee, Fined $50 in Housing Case," *New York Herald Tribune*, December 21, 1957, GRL Papers, NYPL.

21. Preminger, *Gypsy & Me*, 101, chapter 7.

22. Roll 3, Leonard Lyons, no header, GRL Papers, NYPL.

23. Preminger, *Gypsy & Me*, 134–35.

24. Janet Flanner, *Darlinghissima: Letters to a Friend*, ed. Natalia Danesi Murray (New York: Random House, 1985), 248, letter dated June 28, 1959.

Chapter 17

1. Roll 6, Muriel Maclaren, "It's Hard to See Gypsy with Her Clothes On," *Australian Magazine AM*, October 12, 1954, GRL Papers, NYPL.

2. Roll 6, "Art," *Time*, February 1, 1954, GRL Papers, NYPL; Erik Lee Preminger, *Gypsy & Me* (Boston: Little, Brown, 1984), 208.

3. Roll 6, Earl Wilson, "June Havoc Tells How She and Sister Gypsy Rose Lee Handle Their Hubbies," *Los Angeles Mirror News*, June 11, 1957, GRL Papers, NYPL.

4. Roll 3 and Roll 6, Helen Wells, "Queen of Strippers Looks Like an Average Housewife," *Miami Herald*, March 21, 1956; Roll 3, Interview with Morris Goldberg, no header; Roll 6, Phyllis Battelle, "Gypsy Bares All—In a Book," *New York Journal American*, date illegible, GRL Papers, NYPL.

5. S. A. Lewin and John Gilmore, *Sex Without Fear* (New York: Medical Research Press, 1951), 26.

6. Roll 6, "Mike Wallace Asks Gypsy—What will we do with 2,000,000 single women?" *New York Post*, September 3, 1957, GRL Papers, NYPL.

7. Roll 6, Dorothy Dram, "Gypsy Rose Does Catch Her Own Fish," *Australian Women's Weekly*, October 6, 1954; Roll 5, Art Buchwald, "Banned

in Germany," *New York Herald Tribune*, Paris, September 27, 1951, GRL Papers, NYPL.

8. Elliot White Springs, *Clothes Make the Man; or, How to Put the Broad in Broadcloth* (New York: Empyrean Press, 1954), 241–44.

9. Ibid., 248.

10. Ibid., 259.

11. Burke Davis, *War Bird: The Life and Times of Elliott White Springs* (Chapel Hill: University of North Carolina Press, 1987), 256, 204.

12. Roll 6, "...And the Take Was $6930!" *Ad Poster—Advertising Men's Post of American Legion No. 209*, New York, January 1956, GRL Papers, NYPL.

13. Roll 6, Earl Wilson, "Litterbug Gypsy Rose Lee Fined over a Garbage Can," *New York Post*, January 21, 1955, GRL Papers, NYPL.

14. Roll 6, Herman Appelman, "Kinsey Interpretation Is the Rub; Grandma'd Slap His Face, Statistics on Sex a Bore," *New York Journal American*, August 21, 1953, GRL Papers, NYPL.

15. Roll 6, George Clark, "Around Boston: In Her Rolls," no header, GRL Papers, NYPL.

16. Roll 6, "Lyons Den: Gypsy Rose Back in New York," no header; "Gypsy Rose Lee Scores as Catty Star of 'Women,'" *Syracuse Post Standard*, n.d.; Evans Clincy, "Gypsy Rose Lee in *Women*," *Hartford Times*, July 29, 1954; "Sister, Daughters, Sock Syracuse *Women* Over; Havoc's Sure Direction," *Variety*, November 4, 1953; Tom Donnelly, "Why Would Gypsy Take a Legitimate Bubble Bath?" no header, GRL Papers, NYPL; "Offstage," *Theatre Arts*, October 1954, 14.

17. Roll 6, Evans Clincy, "No Genius," no header, April 6, 1954; Louise May, "The Naked Genius' Most Curious Stage Affair," *Springfield* (Mass.) *Union*, March 20, 1954; "Have You Seen...The Naked Genius," no header; Series I, Subseries 1, General, Box 7, Folder 15, From Ethel Britton, Springfield, Mass., to Gypsy, backstage, Court Square Theatre, n.d., GRL Papers, NYPL.

18. Series I, Subseries 3, General, Box 7, Folder 15, Telegram, Western Union, 1954, from Havoc to Gypsy Rose Lee, Court Square Theatre, Springfield, Mass.; From Julia to Dip [pet name], Hotel Onondaga, Jefferson & Warren, Syracuse, N.Y., GRL Papers, NYPL.

19. Roll 6, Rita Hassan, "Darling, Darling," *Show Business*, August 23, 1954; Leonard Randolph, "Gypsy Rose Lee's Fine Performance Saves Almost Plotless 'Darling' from Failure," *East Stroudsburg* (Pa.) *Daily Record*, August 25, 1954; Tom Donnelly, "Why Would Gypsy Take a Legitimate Bubble Bath?" no header, GRL Papers, NYPL.

20. Roll 6, "Gypsy in George Kaufman's *Fancy Meeting You Again*," no header, August 1956, GRL Papers, NYPL.

21. Roll 6, Leon King, "Laughs Bursting Out All Over as Gypsy Stars at Playhouse," *Palm Beach Post*, February 14, 1956, GRL Papers, NYPL.

22. Roll 3, George Montgomery, "Gypsy Rose Wraps Herself in Drama," no header; Marie Torre, "The Stripper Yearns for Drama," *New York Tribune*, September 26, 1956; *Newsday* (Garden City, N.Y.), October 9, 1956; Charles Mercer, "Novelist Role on TV Fits Gypsy Rose Lee," *Sunday Bulletin*, October 7, 1956; Roll 6, Walter Kempley, "A Reaction to Television from Gypsy Rose Lee," *Dallas Times Herald*, October 7, 1956, GRL Papers, NYPL.

23. Series I, Subseries 1, Personal, Box 1, Folder 5, From Belle to Gypsy, GRL Papers, NYPL.

24. Series I, Subseries 1, Personal, Box 1, Folder 13, From Mother, Suffern, N.Y., to Gypsy, April 30, 1950, GRL Papers, NYPL.

25. Series I, Subseries 1, Personal, Box 1, Folder 13, From Gypsy, Toronto, Ontario, to Rose Hovick, n.d., GRL Papers, NYPL.

26. June Havoc, *More Havoc* (New York: Harper & Row, 1980), 1, 115; Series II, Personal, Subseries 1, Appointment Calendars, Box 10, Folder 3, November 21, 22, 24, 1953, GRL Papers, NYPL.

27. Havoc, *More Havoc*, 275–76.

Chapter 18

1. Gypsy Rose Lee, *Gypsy: A Memoir* (New York: Harper & Brothers, 1957), 17.

2. Roll 6, Tom Donnelly, "Why Would Gypsy Take a Legitimate Bubble Bath?" no header, GRL Papers, NYPL.

3. Roll 3, "The Bare Facts," no header, November 1945, GRL Papers, NYPL.

4. Florabel Muir and Robert Sullivan, "Gypsy and June—Mother's Girls: Hovick Sisters, in Chips Now, Can Grin at Frantic Youth," *New York Sunday News*, June 22, 1941, 12; June Havoc, *More Havoc* (New York: Harper & Row, 1980), 210; Gretta Palmer, "She Undressed Her Way to Fame," *New York Woman*, October 7, 1936, 16.

5. Series VI, Writings, Box 44, Folder 10-18, "World on a String," no header, GRL Papers, NYPL.

6. Roll 6, Martha MacGregor, "A Visit with Gypsy," *New York Post*, April 28, 1957, GRL Papers, NYPL; Roger Kahn, "Strip Teaser: The Ups and Downs of Gypsy Rose Lee," *Real: The Exciting Magazine for Men*, November 1956, 20, 63–64.

7. Roll 3, unidentified clipping; Ben Kubasik, "Gypsy Rose Lee Views Career, She Would Not Change Anything," *Newsday* (Garden City, N.Y.), October 9, 1956; Roll 6, Mary Ellin and Marvin Barrett, *Good Housekeeping*, May 1957, GRL Papers, NYPL; Lee, *Gypsy*, dedication.

8. Roll 6, Red Ritson, *New Jersey Press* (Atlantic City), April 8, 1957, GRL Papers, NYPL.

9. Roll 6, Elizabeth Ford, "How She Got Her Name, Gypsy Rose Lee—It's Not Official," no header, GRL Papers, NYPL.

10. Roll 6, D.B.B., "Gypsy Blows Lines," *Washington Times*, July 26, 1957, GRL Papers, NYPL.

11. Roll 3, E. P. Chalcraft, "Gypsy Rose Lee Comes Home Flying," *Seattle Intelligencer*, July 25, 1957; *Newsweek*, April 29, 1957, GRL Papers, NYPL.

12. Roll 3, Tom Donnelly, "Gypsy Takes Off a Strip of Life," *New York World, Telegram and Sun*, April 30, 1957; Roll 6, Luther Nichols, "This Stripper Can Write," *San Francisco Examiner*, May 2, 1957; Roll 3, EJD, "Gypsy Rose Lee Pens Lively Autobiography," *New Bedford Standard Times*, May 12, 1957, GRL Papers, NYPL.

13. Roll 3, Peter Rahn, "Gypsy Rose Lee Will Star in Comedy on 'Steel Hour' Program," *St. Louis Globe Democrat*, October 7, 1956, GRL Papers, NYPL.

14. Roll 3, John J. Redden, "Gypsy Rose Lee Comes Home," *Seattle Times*, July 26, 1957; George Montgomery, "Gypsy Rose Wraps Herself in Drama," no header; *Big Time*, TV, no header; "Book and Author Luncheon," *Chicago Sun Times*, n.d., GRL Papers, NYPL.

15. Thomas Blair, "What Gypsy Rose Didn't Tell in 'Gypsy.'" *Uncensored*, January 1960, 32.

16. Roll 3, "Book and Author Luncheon," *Chicago Sun Times*, n.d.; Roll 6, Phyllis Battelle, "Gypsy Bares All—In a Book," *New York Journal American*, n.d.; Roll 6, Lee Segal, "Under Cover," *Louisville Courier-Journal*, August 4, 1957, GRL Papers, NYPL.

17. Roll 6, Mary Ellin and Marvin Barrett, *Good Housekeeping*, New York, May 1957; Roll 6, Phyllis Battelle, "Gypsy Bares All—In a Book," *New York Journal American*, n.d., GRL Papers, NYPL.

18. Series 1, Subseries 3, General, Box 7, Folder 7, From Alexander Woollcott, Bomoseen, Vermont, to Dear Authoress (Gypsy), August 20, 1941, GRL Papers, NYPL; Arthur Laurents, *Original Story By: A Memoir of Broadway and Hollywood* (New York: Knopf, 2000), 376; Lee, *Gypsy*, 310.

19. FBI file for Fanny Brice, FOIPA no. 441151.

20. Roll 3, Winsola McLendon, "After All Those Bumps, Gypsy Still Loves the Grind," no header; Roll 6, Phyllis Battelle, "Gypsy Bares All—In a Book," *New York Journal American*, n.d., GRL Papers, NYPL.

21. Roger Kahn, "Strip Teaser: The Ups and Downs of Gypsy Rose Lee," *Real: The Exciting Magazine for Men*, November 1956, 64.

22. "Hey Gypsy! Why Are You Keeping So Mum About Those Men in Your Life?" *Hush-Hush*, n.d.; Thomas Blair, "What Gypsy Rose Didn't Tell in 'Gypsy,'" *Uncensored*, January 1960, 33; F. C. Palmer, "Is There Too Much Gypsy in Gypsy Rose Lee's Love Life?" *Tip-Off*, April 1956, 10–11, 48.

23. Robert Shirley, "When Gypsy Rose Lee Ratted on Her Mother," *On the Q.T.*, February 1960, 47.

24. Keith Garebian, *The Making of Gypsy* (Toronto: ECW Press, 1994), 65, 79.

25. Ibid., 35; see chapter 4 in *More Havoc* for June Havoc's version.

26. Garebian, *The Making of Gypsy*, 40; Laurents, *Original Story By*, 382; Greg Lawrence, *Dance with Demons: The Life of Jerome Robbins* (New York: G. P. Putnam's Sons, 2001), 267.

27. Garebian, *The Making of Gypsy*, 35–36, 38, 84, 113.

28. Bob Thomas, *I Got Rhythm: The Ethel Merman Story* (New York: G. P. Putnam's Sons, 1985), 149.

29. Roll 6, George Allen, "Gypsy Rose Lee Take Off Wins Raves for Sandra," no header, GRL Papers, NYPL

30. Garebian, *The Making of Gypsy*, 39.

31. Havoc, *More Havoc*, 184; Garebian, *The Making of Gypsy*, 39; Laurents, *Original Story By*, 379.

32. Roll 6, Terrence O'Flaherty, "Let Me Entertain You," no header; Louella Parsons, "Hollywood Highlights," *New York Journal American*, April 28, 1959, GRL Papers, NYPL.

33. Roll 6, "Culled from a Stripper's Fabulous Past," *New York Times*, May 17, 1957, GRL Papers, NYPL; Garebian, *The Making of Gypsy*, 103.

34. Garebian, *The Making of Gypsy*, 104, 113; Roll 6, Walter Kerr, *New York Herald Tribune*, May 22, 1958, GRL Papers, NYPL; Laurents, *Original Story By*, 399; Greg Lawrence, *Dance with Demons*, 277.

35. Roll 6, *Variety*, May 27, 1959; "Merman's Perfect in Musical 'Gypsy,'" John Chapman, *Chicago Sunday Tribune*, GRL Papers, NYPL.

36. "Two Flourishing Gypsy Roses," *Canadian Weekly*, October 6–12, 1962, 6.

37. "The Fabulous Gypsy," no author, *Pageant*, October 1957, 160.

38. Roll 3, Winsola McLenson, "After All Those Bumps, Gypsy Still Loves the Grind," no header, GRL Papers, NYPL.

Chapter 19

1. Erik Lee Preminger, *Gypsy & Me* (Boston: Little, Brown, 1984), 11.

2. Ibid., 15; Roll 6, *Variety*, June 20, 1955, GRL Papers, NYPL.

3. Preminger, *Gypsy & Me*, 18; Roger Kahn, "Strip Teaser: The Ups and Downs of Gypsy Rose Lee," *Real: The Exciting Magazine for Men*, November 1956, 63; "What's Happened to Burlesque?" *Quick*, July 2, 1951, 59; Roll 6, *Variety*, June 20, 1955, GRL Papers, NYPL.

4. Roll 3, John J. Redden, "Gypsy Rose Lee Comes Home," *Seattle Times*, July 26, 1957; *Newsweek*, April 29, 1957; unidentified fragment, probably August 1956; Roll 6, "Gypsy Rose Lee Talks on Life, Strife—And Women 'Around Forty,'" no header; Eleanor Darton, "If I Were 20 Again I Would...," no header, GRL Papers, NYPL.

5. Roll 6, "Tanfield Diary, 'Gypsy' Flies In," *Daily Mail*, September 27, 1957; Roll 3, Jerry Gaghan, "Gypsy Isn't Pear-Shaped," *Philadelphia Daily News*, n.d. [July 1958], GRL Papers, NYPL.

6. Roll 6, Inez Robb, "Gypsy Royce to Roll," no header; Eleanor Darton, "If I Were 20 Again I Would…," no header, GRL Papers, NYPL.

7. Petey Williams, "Burlesque in the 1955 Manner: The Old Favorites Are Still on Top," *Suppressed*, January 1955, 15, 56; Roll 6, "Gypsy Rose Lee Talks on Life, Strife—And Women 'Around Forty,'" no header, GRL Papers, NYPL.

8. *Cabaret*, July 1955, 48; Roll 3, Ben Kubasik, "Gypsy Rose Lee Views Career, She Wouldn't Change Anything," *Newsday* (Garden City, N.Y.), October 9, 1956, GRL Papers, NYPL.

9. Roll 6, Hy Gardner, "Coast to Coast," *New York Herald Tribune*, January 26, 1957, GRL Papers, NYPL; Preminger, *Gypsy & Me*, 32.

10. Roll 6, Lawrence Laurent, "Gypsy Finds That Video Has Its Bumpy Moments," *Washington Post and Times Herald*, GRL Papers, NYPL.

11. Series II, Subseries 1, Appointment Calendar, Box 12, Folder 3, November 14, 1961, GRL Papers, NYPL; Preminger, *Gypsy & Me*, 210.

12. Preminger, *Gypsy & Me*, 39.

13. Roll 6, "Bare Facts by Gypsy Rose Lee," *Time Star*, September 30, 1957; Roll 3, Ad for radio station, *New York Journal American*, May 8, 1958, GRL Papers, NYPL.

14. Roll 3, Betty Carrollton, "Now They Call Gypsy Rose a Real Sewing Machine Girl," *Atlanta Constitution*, August 1, 1958, GRL Papers, NYPL; Preminger, *Gypsy & Me*, 42.

15. Preminger, *Gypsy & Me*, 83.

16. Roll 3, Jerry Gaghan, "Gypsy Isn't Pear-Shaped," *Philadelphia Daily News*, July 1958, "Gypsy's 'Happy Hunting' a Good-Natured Romp," *Atlanta Constitution*, n.d.; "Gypsy Rose in Rain; Crowds All Remain," *Atlanta Constitution*, August 3, 1958, GRL Papers, NYPL.

17. Series II, Subseries 1, Appointment Calendar, Box 12, Folder 1, Journal entry, July 13, 1959, GRL Papers, NYPL.

18. Carol Cohan, *Broadway by the Bay: Thirty Years at the Coconut Grove Playhouse* (Miami: Pickering Press, 1987), 25, 26.

19. Roll 6, unidentified clipping; Roll 3, John Fuller, no header, GRL Papers, NYPL.

20. Roll 3, Nancy Taylor, "Gypsy Collected Recipes with Husbands," *Miami News*, August 19, 1958; Betty Jo Ramsey, "Gypsy Rose Lee at Smith's for Tea," *Herald Tribune*, Paris, October 17, 1957; E. P. Chalcraft, "Gypsy Rose Lee Comes Home Flying," *Seattle Intelligencer*, July 25, 1957, GRL Papers, NYPL

21. Preminger, *Gypsy & Me*, 144.

22. Joey Adams, *From Gags to Riches* (New York: Frederick Fell, 1946), 150.

23. Preminger, *Gypsy & Me*, 147.

24. Ibid.; Polly Rose Gottlieb, *The Nine Lives of Billy Rose: An Intimate Biography* (New York: Crown, 1968), 230.

25. Roll 3, *Man Against Woman*, review, *Herald Tribune*, January 27, 1957, GRL Papers, NYPL.

26. Preminger, *Gypsy & Me*, 192.

27. Richard Gehman, "A Visit with Gypsy: Meet the Best Undressed Woman of Our Time," *Star Weekly*, October 22, 1960, 11.

28. Ibid., 10–11; Preminger, *Gypsy & Me*, 102.

29. Series II, Subseries 1, Appointment Calendar, Box 12, Folder 3, January 9, 1961, GRL Papers, NYPL; Preminger, *Gypsy & Me*, 202, 205.

30. From Gypsy Rose Lee, 1240 Cerrocrest Drive, Beverly Hills, California, to Mr. and Mrs. Edward L. Bernays, 7 Lowell Street, Cambridge 38, Massachusetts, June 2, 1963, Performing Arts Division, Manuscript Division, Library of Congress.

Chapter 20

1. Series II, Subseries 1, Appointment Calendar, Box 12, Folder 3, July 25, 1961, GRL Papers, NYPL; Erik Lee Preminger, *Gypsy & Me* (Boston: Little, Brown, 1984), 221.

2. Series II, Subseries 1, Appointment Calendar, Box 12, Folder 3, July 26, 1961, GRL Papers, NYPL; Preminger, *Gypsy & Me*, 221; Series I, Subseries 1, Personal, Box 2, Letter to Erik and Barbara, April 3, 1967, GRL Papers, NYPL.

3. Arthur Knight and Eliot Elisofon, *The Hollywood Style* (Toronto: Macmillan, 1969),136–37.

4. Roll 3, Gypsy Rose Lee, "One Day in Omaha," *Parade*, July 8, 1956, GRL Papers, NYPL.

5. Series I, Subseries 1, Personal, Box 2, Folder 11, From Gypsy to June, June 7, 1967; Roll 6, Terrence O'Flaherty, "Let Me Entertain You," no header, GRL Papers, NYPL.

6. Roll 6, "The Roving Eye: Rudolf Elis," no header, GRL Papers, NYPL.

7. Helen Vallis, "Gypsy Rose Lee: The Girl They Couldn't Keep Under Wraps," *TV/Radio Show*, March 1968, 78; "Here She Is—The One and Only Gypsy," *TV/Radio Mirror*, October 1965, 69.

8. Series II, Subseries 1, Appointment Calendar, Box 12, Folder 3, September 21, 1961, GRL Papers, NYPL; Preminger, *Gypsy & Me*, 233, 235–38.

9. Preminger, *Gypsy & Me*, 237, 240.

10. Vallis, "Gypsy Rose Lee," 76.

11. "Two Flourishing Gypsy Roses," *Canadian Weekly*, October 6–12, 1962, 6.

12. For the exchange with Reiner, see www.classicsquares.com/celebrity game.html.

13. "How to Undress Gracefully—In Front of Millions," *TV Guide*, September 12, 1964, 13.

14. Bart Andrews with Brad Dunning, *The Worst TV Shows Ever: Those TV Turkeys We Will Never Forget... (No Matter How Hard We Try)* (New York:

Dutton, 1980), 136; Roll 6, Barry Learned, "Gypsy Rose Lee, Now a Writer, Looks at Paris," *American Weekend*, October 26, 1957, GRL Papers, NYPL.

15. Charles E. Alverson, "Take It Off to Keep Them Talking," *TV Guide*, December 11, 1965, 15.

16. "Gypsy Rose Lee: Dowager Stripper," *Look*, February 22, 1966, 64.

17. "Stripper Turns Yakker: Gypsy Rose Lee Has Daily TV Show," *Chicago Tribune TV Week*, August 14–20, 1965, 2.

18. Alverson, "Take It Off to Keep Them Talking," 15; "Gypsy Rose Lee: Dowager Stripper," 64.

19. Alverson, "Take It Off to Keep Them Talking," 15; Vallis, "Gypsy Rose Lee," 80; "Gypsy Rose Lee: Dowager Stripper," 64.

20. Alverson, "Take It Off to Keep Them Talking," 15–16.

21. "Gypsy Rose Lee: Dowager Stripper," 56, 64.

22. "Here She Is—The One and Only Gypsy," 69; "Gypsy Rose Lee: Dowager Stripper," 62; Alverson, "Take It Off to Keep Them Talking," 16.

23. *Gypsy Rose Lee Show*, various episodes moderated by Erik Lee Preminger, author's collection.

24. "Gypsy Rose Lee: Dowager Stripper," 61, 62.

25. Alverson, "Take It Off to Keep Them Talking," 16; "Gypsy Rose Lee: Dowager Stripper," 64.

26. Series V, Subseries 2, Box 30, Fan Mail, Folders 1–5, GRL Papers, NYPL.

27. Series V, Subseries 2, Box 30, Fan Mail, Folder 1, February 9, 1967, GRL Papers, NYPL.

28. Series V, Subseries 2, Box 30, Fan Mail, Folder 2, GRL Papers, NYPL.

29. Series V, Subseries 2, Box 30, Fan Mail, Folder 1, Folder 3, March 1968, GRL Papers, NYPL.

30. Vallis, "Gypsy Rose Lee," 16; "Here She Is—The One and Only Gypsy," 69.

31. Series V, Subseries 2, Box 30, Fan Mail, Folder 1, GRL Papers, NYPL.

32. Alverson, "Take It Off to Keep Them Talking," 16.

33. "Gypsy Rose Lee: Dowager Stripper," 62.

34. Ibid., 64; Vallis, "Gypsy Rose Lee," 80.

35. "Gypsy Rose Lee: Dowager Stripper," 64.

36. Vallis, "Gypsy Rose Lee," 80; Joseph Jennel, "Interview With: Gypsy Rose Lee," *Jem*, February 1960, 37.

37. Series I, Subseries 1, Personal, Box 2, Folder 11, From Gypsy to June, January 8, February 27, 1968; Box 1, Folder 6, 1966, From Dad, GRL Papers, NYPL.

38. Series V, Subseries 2, Box 30, Fan Mail, Folder 2, GRL Papers, NYPL.

39. Series VI, Writings, Files on *How to Enjoy Being a Woman*, Box 43, Folder 11, Correspondence, 1966, Prentice Hall, Inc., Englewood Cliffs, NJ 07632, GRL Papers, NYPL.

40. Series V, Subseries 1, Benefits & Contributions, Box 28, Folder 16, Information about the *Clearwater*.

41. Series V, Subseries 1, Benefits & Contributions, Box 28, Folder 17, December 5, 1968, To Mrs. Blitzblan from Gypsy Rose Lee, GRL Papers, NYPL; Preminger, *Gypsy & Me*, 261. For her USO appearances, see "Gypsy Rose Lee Visits LZ Cork," *Trident*, January 24, 1969, available at www.zyworld.com/lobo6869/DAN_1/DOCS_Trident.htm; and James Linn, "Gypsy Rose Lee Adds an Exotic Touch to the Orient," *Stars and Stripes*, Pacific edition, January 24, 1969, available at www.stripes.com/article.asp?section=104&article=19612&archive=true.

42. Roll 6, Eleanor Darton, "If I Were 20 Again I Would…," GRL Papers, NYPL; Vallis, "Gypsy Rose Lee," 82.

43. Series I, Subseries 1, Personal, Box 2, Folder 10, From Gypsy to June, November 25, 1967, GRL Papers, NYPL.

44. Preminger, *Gypsy & Me*, 263.

45. Ibid., 264.

46. Gypsy Rose Lee, "How to Catch a Musky," *Sports Afield*, July 1957, 20, 21, 75.

47. Roll 6: "Bait Your Own Hook to Land Fishermen," by Betty Scheibl, *Times Record*, Fort Smith, Arkansas, March 5, 1957; Roll 6: "If I Were 20 Again I Would…." by Eleanor Darton, GRL Papers, NYPL.

Bibliography

Primary Sources

The Gypsy Rose Lee Papers are housed in the Billy Rose Theater Collection, New York Public Library, Lincoln Center. The collection includes personal, business, and legal papers. The NYPL also microfilmed Gypsy Rose Lee's scrapbooks; many of the clippings contain only partial information about their source (author, name of publication, date, etc.). Cites in the notes beginning, e.g., "Roll 1" are to the scrapbooks; cites beginning, e.g., "Series I, Subseries 1" are to the boxed papers.

Books

Adams, Joey. *From Gags to Riches*. New York: Frederick Fell, 1946.

Alexander, Shana. *Happy Days: My Mother, My Father, My Sister and Me*. New York: Doubleday, 1995.

American Business Consultants. *Red Channels, The Report of Communist Influence in Radio and Television*. New York: *Counterattack*, 1950.

Andrews, Bart, with Brad Dunning. *The Worst TV Shows Ever: Those TV Turkeys We Will Never Forget... (No Matter How Hard We Try)*. New York: E. P. Dutton, 1980.

Balio, Tino. *Grand Design: Hollywood as a Modern Business Enterprise, 1930–1939*. Berkeley: University of California Press, 1996.

Barton, Bernadette. *Stripped: Inside the Lives of Exotic Dancers*. New York: New York University Press, 2006.

Basinger, Jeanine. *A Woman's View: How Hollywood Spoke to Women, 1930–1960*. New York: Knopf, 1973.

Bentley, Toni. *Costumes by Karinska*. New York: Harry N. Abrams, 1995.

Bergman, Andrew. *We're in the Money: Depression America and Its Film*. New York: New York University Press, 1971.

Blackwell, Richard, with Vernon Patterson. *From Rags to Bitches: An Autobiography*. Los Angeles: General Publishing Group, 1995.

Block, Alan A. *East Side–West Side: Organizing Crime in New York, 1930–1950*. Cardiff: University College Cardiff Press, 1980.

Carpenter, Humphrey. *Benjamin Britten: A Biography*. New York: Charles Scribner's Sons, 1993.

Carr, Virginia Spencer. *The Lonely Hunter: A Biography of Carson McCullers*. New York: Anchor, 1976.

Clarke, Gerald. *Capote: A Biography*. New York: Simon & Schuster, 1988.

Cogley, John. *Report on Blacklisting: I—Movies*. New York: Fund for the Republic, 1956.

Cohen, Rich. *Tough Jews: Fathers, Sons, and Gangster Dreams*. New York: Vintage, 1999.

Cohn, Art. *The Nine Lives of Michael Todd*. New York: Random House, 1958.

Davis, Burke. *War Bird: The Life and Times of Elliott White Springs*. Chapel Hill: University of North Carolina Press, 1987.

Elder, Jane Lenz. *Alice Faye: A Life Beyond the Silver Screen*. Jackson: University Press of Mississippi, 2002.

Elisofon, Eliot. *Food Is a Four Letter Word*. New York: Rinehart, 1948.

Fariello, Griffin. *Red Scare: Memories of the American Inquisition—An Oral History*. New York: W.W. Norton, 1995.

Farnsworth, Marjorie. *The Ziegfeld Follies*. New York: G. P. Putnam's Sons, 1956.

Fitelson, H. William, ed. *Theatre Guild on the Air*. New York: Rinehart, 1947.

Flanner, Janet. *Darlinghissima: Letters to a Friend*. Ed. Natalia Danesi Murray. New York: Random House, 1985.

Foley, Karen Sue. *The Political Blacklist in the Broadcast Industry: The Decade of the 1950's*. New York: Arno Press, 1979.

Forbes, Malcolm, with Jeff Bloch. *What Happened to Their Kids: Children of the Rich and Famous*. New York: Simon & Schuster, 1990.

Fried, Albert. *The Rise and Fall of the Jewish Gangster in America*. New York: Columbia University Press, 1993.

Frischauer, Willi. *Behind the Scenes of Otto Preminger: An Unauthorized Biography*. New York: William Morrow, 1974.

Gardner, Gerald. *The Censorship Papers: Movie Censorship Letters from the Hays Office, 1934 to 1968*. New York: Dodd, Mead, 1987.

Garebian, Keith. *The Making of "Gypsy."* Toronto, Ontario: ECW Press, 1994.

Gelernter, David. *1939: The Lost World of the Fair*. New York: Free Press, 1995.

Goldman, Herbert G. *Fanny Brice: The Original Funny Girl*. New York: Oxford University Press, 1992.

Gottlieb, Polly Rose. *The Nine Lives of Billy Rose: An Intimate Biography*. New York: Crown, 1968.

Grossman, Barbara W. *Funny Woman: The Life and Times of Fanny Brice*. Bloomington: Indiana University Press, 1991.

Havoc, June. *Early Havoc*. New York: Simon & Schuster, 1959.

——. *More Havoc*. New York: Harper & Row, 1980.

Hendrick, George, ed. *To Reach Eternity: The Letters of James Jones*. New York: Random House, 1989.

Heymann, C. David. *Liz: An Intimate Biography of Elizabeth Taylor*. New York: Birch Lane Press, 1995.

Joselit, Jenna Weissman. *Our Gang: Jewish Crime and the New York Jewish Community, 1900–1940*. Bloomington: Indiana University Press, 1983.

Katkov, Norman. *The Fabulous Fanny: The Story of Fanny Brice*. New York: Knopf, 1953.

Kazan, Elia. *Elia Kazan: A Life*. New York: Knopf, 1988.

Kisseloff, Jeff. *The Box: An Oral History of Television, 1920–1961*. New York: Viking, 1995.

Klein, Jerome, et al., eds. *Artists Against War and Fascism: Papers of the First American Artists' Congress*. Introduction by Matthew Baigell and Julia Williams. New Brunswick, N.J.: Rutgers University Press, 1986; orig. pub. 1936.

Knight, Arthur, and Eliot Elisofon. *The Hollywood Style*. Toronto: Macmillan, 1969.

Laurents, Arthur. *Original Story By: A Memoir of Broadway and Hollywood*. New York: Knopf, 2000.

Laurents, Arthur, Stephen Sondheim, and Jule Styne. *Gypsy*. New York: Theatre Communications Group, 1998.

Lee, Gypsy Rose. *The G-String Murders*. New York: Pocket Books, 1947.

——. *Gypsy: A Memoir*. New York: Harper, 1957.

——. *Mother Finds a Body*. New York: Simon & Schuster, A Popular Library Mystery Wartime Book, 1942.

Lee, Lawrence, and Barry Gifford. *Saroyan: A Biography*. New York: Harper & Row, 1984.

Lewin, S. A., and John Gilmore. *Sex Without Fear*. New York: Medical Research Press, 1951.

Lisle, Laurie. *Louise Nevelson: A Passionate Life*. New York: Summit Books, 1990.

Madsen, Axel. *Chanel: A Woman of Her Own*. New York: Henry Holt, 1990.

McAleer, John J. *Rex Stout: A Biography*. Boston: Little, Brown, 1977.

McAuliffe, Mary Sperling. *Crisis on the Left: Cold War Politics and American Liberals, 1947–1954*. Amherst: University of Massachusetts Press, 1978.

McGilligan, Patrick, and Paul Buhle. *Tender Comrades: A Backstory of the Hollywood Blacklist*. New York: St. Martin's Griffin, 1997.

McNeil, Alex. *Total Television: A Comprehensive Guide to Programming from 1948 to 1980*. New York: Penguin, 1980.

Meredith, Scott. *George S. Kaufman and His Friends*. New York: Doubleday, 1974.

Miller, Linda Patterson. *Letters from the Lost Generation: Gerald and Sara Murphy and Friends*. New Brunswick, N.J.: Rutgers University Press, 1991.

Minsky, Morton, and Milt Machlin. *Minsky's Burlesque*. New York: Arbor House, 1986.

Murray, Kathryn. *Family Laugh Lines*. Englewood Cliffs, N.J.: Prentice-Hall, 1966.

Nin, Anaïs. *The Diary of Anaïs Nin*, vol. 5, *1947–1955*. Ed. Gunther Stuhlmann. New York: Harcourt Brace Jovanovich, 1974.

Niven, David. *Bring on the Empty Horses*. New York: G. P. Putnam's Sons, 1975.

Nizer, Louis. *Reflections Without Mirrors: An Autobiography of the Mind*. New York: Doubleday, 1978.

Nolan, Frederick. *Lorenz Hart: A Poet on Broadway*. New York: Oxford University Press, 1994.

Osborne, Charles. *W. H. Auden: The Life of a Poet*. New York: Harcourt Brace Jovanovich, 1979.

Preminger, Erik Lee. *Gypsy & Me*. Boston: Little, Brown, 1984.

Rollyson, Carl. *Lillian Hellman: Her Legend and Her Legacy*. New York: St. Martin's, 1988.

Sann, Paul. *Kill the Dutchman! The Story of Dutch Schultz*. New York: Da Capo, 1971.

Schrecker, Ellen. *Many Are the Crimes: McCarthyism in America*. Boston: Little, Brown, 1998.

Scott, David A. *Behind the G-String: An Exploration of the Stripper's Image, Her Person and Her Meaning*. Jefferson, N.C.: McFarland, 1996.

Shirer, William L. *A Native's Return, 1945–1988*. Boston: Little, Brown, 1990.

Shteir, Rachel. *Striptease: The Untold History of the Girlie Show*. New York: Oxford University Press, 2004.

Sillman, Leonard. *Here Lies Leonard Sillman, Straightened Out at Last: An Autobiography*. New York: Citadel Press, 1959.

Smith, H. Allen. *Low Man on a Totem Pole*. Garden City, N.Y.: Doubleday, Doran, 1943.

Sobel, Bernard. *Broadway Heartbeat: Memoirs of a Press Agent*. New York: Hermitage House, 1953.

——. *A Pictorial History of Burlesque*. New York: Bonanza Books, 1956.

Sochen, June. *From Mae to Madonna: Women Entertainers in Twentieth-Century America*. Lexington: University Press of Kentucky, 1999.

Sothern, Georgia. *Georgia: My Life in Burlesque*. New York: New American Library, 1972.

Springs, Elliott White. *Clothes Make the Man; or, How to Put the Broad in Broadcloth*. New York: Empyrean Press, 1954.

Stallworthy, Jon. *Louis MacNeice: A Biography*. New York: W.W. Norton, 1995.

Thomas, Bob. *I Got Rhythm! The Ethel Merman Story*. New York: G. P. Putnam's Sons, 1985.

Thomas, Lowell. *Good Evening Everybody: From Cripple Creek to Samarkand*. New York: William Morrow, 1976.

Thompson, Craig, and Allen Raymond. *Gang Rule in New York: The Story of a Lawless Era*. New York: Dial Press, 1940.

Tippins, Sherill. *February House*. New York: Houghton Mifflin, 2005.

Todd, Michael, Jr., and Susan McCarthy Todd. *A Valuable Property: The Life Story of Michael Todd*. New York: Arbor House, 1983.

Vaughn, Robert. *Only Victims: A Study of Show Business Blacklisting*. New York: Putnam, 1972.

Walsh, Frank. *Sin and Censorship: The Catholic Church and the Motion Picture Industry*. New Haven: Yale University Press, 1996.

Weld, Jacqueline Bograd. *Peggy: The Wayward Guggenheim*. New York: Dutton, 1986.

Whitfield, Stephen J. *The Culture of the Cold War*. Baltimore: Johns Hopkins University Press, 1996.

Wilson, Earl. *Hot Times: True Tales of Hollywood and Broadway*. Chicago: Contemporary Books, 1984.

Zeitlin, David I., and Harriet Zeitlin. *Shooting Stars: Favorite Photos Taken by Classic Celebrities*. Los Angeles: General Publishing Group, 1998.

Articles

Alverson, Charles E. "Take It Off to Keep Them Talking." *TV Guide*, December 11, 1965, 14–16.

"Belle of the Yukon." *Movie Story*, January 1945, 50–53, 89–90.

Bennington, Ralph. "GI Son Greets Gypsy Rose Lee." *Stars and Stripes*, European edition, September 19, 1965, available at http://www.stripes.com/article.asp?section=104&article=17315&archive=true.

Blair, Thomas. "What Gypsy Rose Didn't Tell in 'Gypsy.'" *Uncensored*, January 1960, 32–33, 54, 57.

Blessing, Jennifer. "The Art(ifice) of Striptease: Gypsy Rose Lee and the Masquerade of Nudity." In *Modernism, Gender, and Culture: A Cultural Studies Approach*. Ed. Lisa Redo. New York: Garland, 1997.

Brice, Fannie. "I Knew Gypsy Rose Lee When." *Cosmopolitan*, July 1948, 8, 156.

"Burlesque." *Fortune*, February 1935, 66–73, 140–44, 147–50.

"But Is It Art?" *Hit*, May 1950, 36–37.

Byrne, Howard. "How Long Can a Body Last?" *Salute*, April 1947, 36–38.

Cash, W. J. "The Censor's Lewd Eye Scans Gypsy Rose Lee." *Charlotte News*, May 23, 1937, available at http://www.wjcash.org/Elkcash/Charlotte .News.Articles/Gypsy.htm.

Conney, Terry A. "Cosmopolitan Values and the Identification of Reaction: *Partisan Review* in the 1930s." *Journal of American History* 68, no. 3 (December 1981): 580–98.

Cooper, Morton. "Profile of a Character: Gypsy Rose Lee." *Modern Man*, September 1959, 36–38, 56.

Crichton, Kyle. "Strip for Fame: Miss Gypsy Rose Lee, in Person." *Collier's*, December 19, 1936, 13, 47.

"The Fabulous Gypsy." *Pageant*, October 1957, 158–61 (includes Fanny Brice's study of Gypsy, after Degas).

Farrell, Edythe. "An Unusual Strip-Tease: Gypsy Rose Lee Is First to Do a 'Talking' Strip." *National Police Gazette*, August–September 1940, 3.

Gehman, Richard. "A Visit with Gypsy: Meet the Best Undressed Woman of Our Time." *Star Weekly*, October 22, 1960, 10–11, 25.

"*The G-String Murders*: Gypsy Rose Lee Turns Mystery Author." *Life*, October 6, 1941, 110–17.

"Gypsy Joins the 'Carny.'" *Life*, June 6, 1949, 141–45.

"Gypsy Rose Lee: A General Collector." *Hobbies*, October 1942, 6–7.

"Gypsy Rose Lee and Her Golden G-String." *Uncensored*, August 1954, 44–46.

"Gypsy Rose Lee at Home at Witchwood Manor." *Pic*, August 6, 1940, 38–41.

"Gypsy Rose Lee: Dowager Stripper." *Look*, February 22, 1966, 56–64.

"Gypsy Rose Lee: Her Start Working in Burlesque." In *Sketches of Naughty Ladies*. Detroit: Johnson Smith, n.d.

"Gypsy Rose Lee: Knows All About It," *It*, November 1941, 6–7.

"Gypsy Rose Lee: She Takes It Off for Charity." *Sir!* August 1942, 12–13.

"Gypsy Rose Lee's New Role." *American Weekly*, May 23, 1948, 4.

"Gypsy Rose Lee Visits LZ Cork." *Trident*, January 24, 1969, available at http://www.zyworld.com/lobo6869/DAN_1/DOCS_Trident.htm.

"Gypsy Rose Take Off Those Clothes." *For Laughing Out Loud!* January–March 1963.

"Gypsy's New Leaf." *People Today*, September 24, 1952, 13–16.

Hall, Gladys. "The Things I Want: As Revealed by Gypsy Rose Lee." *Personal Romances*, November 1944, 28–29, 58–59.

"Here She Is—The One and Only Gypsy." *TV/Radio Mirror*, October 1965, 68–69.

Hochman, Louis. "The Mechanix of Gypsy Rose Lee." *Mechanix Illustrated*, June 1943, 46–50, 145.

"Hovick-Kirkland: Miss Gypsy Rose Lee, Author, Weds Broadway Actor."
   Life, September 14, 1942, 41–44.

"How Movies Are Censored: The Amazing Story of Will Hays, Czar of the
   Movie Industry." *Look*, August 2, 1938, 12–19.

"How to Undress Gracefully—In Front of Millions." *TV Guide*, September
   12, 1964, 12–13.

Humer, Dick. "Burlesque: Our First Line of Defense?" *Spark*, June 1942,
   6–7.

"Intimate Secrets of a Strip Dancer: Gypsy Rose Lee Tells of Her Love and
   Life." *Romantic Stories*, April 1937, 30–33, 89–90.

Jacobs, Laura. "Taking It *All* Off." *Vanity Fair*, March 2003, 198–220.

Jennel, Joseph. "Interview With: Gypsy Rose Lee." *Jem*, February 1960, 37,
   63–65.

Jest: The Zest of Life, September 1941, 15–16.

"Julio De Diego: He Paints Weird War and Peace." *Life*, March 11, 1946,
   80–82.

Kahn, Roger. "Strip Teaser: The Ups and Downs of Gypsy Rose Lee." *Real:
   The Exciting Magazine for Men*, November 1956, 18–20, 63–65.

Keating, Jack. "Gypsy II." *Nugget: The Man's World*, August 1959, 15–16.

Lauterbach, Richard. "Gypsy Rose Lee: She Combines a Public Body with a
   Private Mind." *Life*, December 14, 1942, 92–101.

Lee, Gypsy Rose. "Fanny Brice and I." *Town & Country*, April 1957, 74–77,
   120–22.

———. "Gypsy Rose Lee House." *House and Garden*, December 1943, 66–70.

———."How to Catch a Musky." *Sports Afield*, July 1957, 19–23, 74–75.

———. "I Was with It." *Flair*, June 1950, 71–86.

———. "Kathleen Dear Kathleen." *Swank: A Modern Magazine for Men*,
   September 1945, 10–11, 38.

———. "On the Road to Burlesque." *Toronto Sunday Telegram*, July 28, 1957,
   6–9, 24–25.

———. "Stranded in Kansas City." *Harper's*, April 1957, 44–50.

———. "Stripping the Strip Tease: From Minsky's to Ziegfeld to Hollywood in
   Ten Teasy Lessons." *Ad Lib: Show Book of the Show World*, June 1937, 9, 35.

———. "They Need It for Bullets!" In *Home Was Never Like This! An Anthology*,
   comp. R. M. Barrows. Chicago: Consolidated Book Publishers, 1944. "

———. "Tips by an Improbable Pro." *Life*, June 29, 1959, 108–13.

———. "What's New in War-Wolves." *Mademoiselle*, March 1943, 110–11,
   161–63.

Linn, Edward. "Mike Todd: The Man Who Can't Go Broke." *Saga*, August
   1955, 18–21, 60–63.

Linn, James. "Gypsy Rose Lee Adds an Exotic Touch to the Orient." *Stars and
   Stripes*, Pacific edition, January 24, 1969, available at http://www.stripes
   .com/article.asp?section=104&article=19612&archive=true.

Manning, Don. "Gypsy Rose Lee Talks About Music and Musicians." *Music and Rhythm*, February 1941, 8.

McEvoy, J. P. "More Tease than Strip." *Reader's Digest* (condensed from *Variety*), July 1941, 71–73.

McGrath, George. "A Gangster Helped Her to Fame: Gypsy Rose Lee's True Story." *National Police Gazette*, September 1957, 3, 24.

McLain, Louis. "The Lady Behind the Gypsy." *American Weekly: The Sunday Bulletin*, January 17, 1960, 14–15.

Muir, Florabel, and Robert Sullivan. "Gypsy and June—Mother's Girls: Hovick Sisters, in Chips Now, Can Grin at Frantic Youth." *New York Sunday News*, June 22, 1941, 8–9, 12.

"The New Gypsy Rose Lee: She Is a Dynamo Without Direction." *Look*, September 28, 1948, 42, 45, 46.

"A Newly Maternal Gypsy Rose Lee Pins Up Her Son Eric." *Life*, February 19, 1945, 28–29.

"Offstage." *Theatre Arts*, October 1954, 14.

Palmer, F. C. "Is There Too Much Gypsy in Gypsy Rose Lee's Love Life?" *Tip-Off*, April 1956, 10–11, 48–49.

Palmer, Gretta. "She Undressed Her Way to Fame." *New York Woman*, October 7, 1936, 16–18.

Pawley, Eugene. "Strip Tease Intellectual." *Cabaret*, July 1955, 37–41, 48.

"People vs. People." *People Today*, July 15, 1953, 42.

Pereira, Leonard. "From Burlesque to Movie Fame." *Picture Revue*, July 1937, 8–9.

"Private Lives." *Life*, August 30, 1937, 84.

Sayre, Joel. "Mike Todd and His Big Bug-Eye." *Life*, March 7, 1955, 140–42, 144, 146, 148, 151, 152, 154, 157.

"Scrapbook Views of a Smart Stripper." *Life*, May 27, 1957, 103–6, 109.

Sheldon, Wesley. "Gypsy Rose Lee Tangles with the Murder Mob." *Complete Detective Cases*, June 1943, 4–9, 41–44.

Shirley, Robert. "When Gypsy Rose Lee Ratted on Her Mother." *On the Q.T.*, February 1960, 34–35, 47–48.

Sobel, Bernard. "Strip Cycle." *Mid-Week Pictorial*, November 18, 1936, 16–17.

"'Star and Garter' Is a Sizzling Burlesque Hit at $4.40." *Spot*, September 1942, 20–23.

"'Star and Garter': Rowdy Fun and Well-Fed Beauties Make a Rich Man's Burlesque Show." *Life*, July 27, 1942, 60–63.

Stone, Hal. "Why Did Gypsy Rose Lee Keep Mum About Her Three Mystery Men?" *Hush-Hush*, November 1959, 32–34, 64.

"Stripper Turns Yakker: Gypsy Rose Lee Has Daily TV Show." *Chicago Tribune TV Week*, August 14–20, 1965, 2.

Turner, Hal. "Hey, Gypsy! Why Are You Keeping So Mum About Those Men in Your Life?" *Hush-Hush*, March 1958, 22–25, 46–47.

"Two Flourishing Gypsy Roses." *Canadian Weekly*, October 6–12, 1962, 6.

"U.S. Balls, Brawls, Pageants, Parades Turn War Relief into Show Business." *Life*, January 6, 1941, 15–19.

Vallis, Helen. "Gypsy Rose Lee: The Girl They Couldn't Keep Under Wraps." *TV/Radio Show*, March 1968, 16, 76, 78, 80, 82.

"The Wedding of Gypsy Rose Lee." *Spot*, November 1942, 10–13.

"What's Happened to Burlesque?" *Quick*, July 2, 1951, 58–61.

Williams, Petey. "Burlesque in the 1955 Manner: The Old Favorites Are Still on Top." *Suppressed*, January 1955, 13–15, 56.

Index